Roger G. Kennedy

GREEK REVIVAL
AMERICA

 A NATIONAL TRUST FOR HISTORIC PRESERVATION BOOK

Photographs by

John M. Hall   Jack Kotz   Robert Lautman   Mark Zeek

STEWART   TABORI   &   CHANG · NEW YORK

Front jacket and title page: An Ionic capital in the North Carolina Capitol (1833–40) in Raleigh (see also pages 354–55)

Page i: New York City's Lafayette Terrace (detail), which may have been designed by Charles F. Reichardt in 1831–32

Page ii: A view of the interior of John Francis Rague's Old State Capitol (1837) in Springfield, Illinois (see also pages 357 and 358)

Page v: Barton Hall (1847–49), in Cherokee, Alabama, is also known as the Cunningham Plantation

Page vi: Washington City Hall (1817–25)—now the U.S. District Court Building in Washington, DC—was created by George Hadfield.

Back jacket: Inside the Samuel Russell House (1843), in Middletown, Connecticut (designed by the firm of Town and Davis; see also pages 153 and 304)

Text © 1989 Roger G. Kennedy
Picture credits are found on page 455.

Acknowledgements begin on page 453.

Published in 1989 by Stewart, Tabori & Chang, Inc.
740 Broadway, New York, New York 10003

Distributed in the United States by Workman Publishing
708 Broadway, New York, New York 10003

Distributed in Canada by the Canadian Manda Group
P.O. Box 920 Station U, Toronto, Ontario M8Z 5P9

Printed in Japan
89 90 91 92 93 9 8 7 6 5 4 3 2 1

Library of Congress Cataloging-in-Publication Data

Kennedy, Roger G.
  Greek revival America / Roger G. Kennedy ; photographs by John M. Hall...[et al.].
     p.   cm.
  Bibliography: p.
  Includes index.
  ISBN 1-55670-094-6 : $85.00
  1. United States—Social life and customs—1783-1865. 2. Greek revival (Architecture)—United States—History—19th century. 3. Architecture and society—United States—History—19th century.
  I. Hall, John M.   II. Title
E165.K46   1989
973.5—dc20   89-4449
                                                  CIP

For
Frances, Ruth and Rob...

...and with grateful appreciation to
the Polaroid Corporation,
who made this book possible

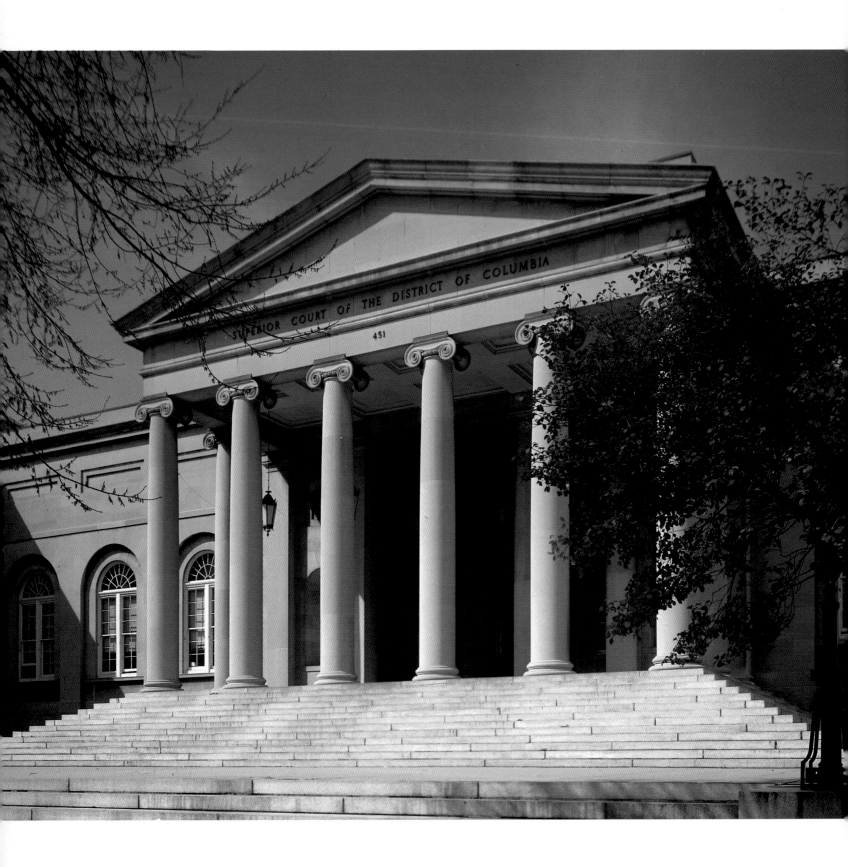

CONTENTS

INTRODUCTION

RECONNAISSANCE
OF THE TERRAIN

Architecture is always a public utterance. Willy-nilly, it conveys ideas. The American Greek Revival, however, was unusual for the forthrightness of its political statement, and unique in that it was so widely popular that it entered the vernacular.[†]

This had not happened before, and it did not happen again until our own time, when the Greeks themselves began building multitudes of houses reviving their ancient temple-forms, abstracted, simplified, and reduced in scale. If their terrain were not so different from that of upstate New York or the Western Reserve of Ohio, one might, in the moonlight, mistake buildings created on many an island in the Aegean in the 1970s for those of the American Greek Revival in the 1830s.

This is a book about the American Greek Revival, which flourished from 1825 to 1855; it is also about the political and psychological circumstances of a nation struggling to assert itself—and about the way in which it borrowed the means to make that assertion. Classical Architecture was deployed to proclaim American pride.

The American Greek Revival was not an expression of the founding fathers; it did not arise from any desire on their part to emulate the institutions of Greece or Rome. It was a statement on the part of the successors to the founders that was at once political and intimate, public and intensely private. The American Greek Revival arose as many Americans sensed the nation to be adrift after its heroic

† The Canadians understood the political significance of the Greek Revival in the United States, its close association with American nationalism, and avoided it almost entirely. It is true that if one never got beyond the Scottish stronghold of Montreal, it would be possible to think otherwise, for in the 1830s and 1840s, while that city was still the capital of the United Province of Canada, the Hellenizing of Edinburgh carried over into this outpost of Caledonian sentiment. The Old Custom House (John Ostell) of 1832, the Bonsecours Market (William Footner) of 1844–47, and the Bank of Montreal (John Wells) of 1846 suggest that pride in Scotland (specifically, among the directors of the Bank of Montreal, pride in its prototype, the Bank of Scotland) did, in that place almost alone, supervene the Canadians' general distaste for both the political and cultural ambitions of the United States.

As to a Greek Revival vernacular, some might say that a way of building that was broadly popular for only three to five decades would not qualify for that term, but in the American experience a half-century is a very long time, and thirty years a considerable one.

revolutionary accomplishments, feared its centrifugal disorder, but at the same time celebrated triumphs of their own. While their partisan battles became increasingly savage and were stated through the choice between classical forms, that partisanship did not prevent participation by people of all parties in a general classical revival that carried other more general messages.

When the circumstances arousing these feelings dissolved or resolved themselves, the Revival passed away, as quickly as it had come.[1]

Other Greek Revivals

The Greek Revivals of England, Italy, Denmark, France, Hungary, Poland, Finland, the Baltic states, and Russia, which appeared at various times between 1770 and 1840, were not nearly so complex as that in America. European Greek Revivals were the pleasure of—in some cases the affectation of—elites very small in number who did not display much passion for the political implications of the forms they were using, except in Germany and Scotland, which were the special cases, the one political but not popular, the other popular but not political.

Germany was still divided into a multitude of states, most of them small and politically impotent, though lively in music and literature. The temple forms of Greece and the Greek colonies were used to advance the claims of two German dynasties contending for predominance over the innumerable dukedoms, principalities, knightly estates, and bishoprics. The Hohenzollerns of Prussia and the Wittelsbachs of Bavaria, presiding over Berlin and Munich (still backwaters in comparison to Vienna, Paris, or London), summoned a competition in architectural Teuto-Hellenism. As Germans recovered from two centuries of French depredations that culminated in humiliations at the hands of Napoleon, their two chief ruling houses used columnar buildings to contend that it was not ludicrous to think of Germans as being as heroic as ancient Greeks.

Though Edinburgh delighted in calling itself "the Athens of the North" throughout the Revolutionary Age, Scotsmen, including scholars, are apt to look baffled or even annoyed when asked about the political implications of Greek forms. There do not seem to have been any; perhaps that is why the Acropolis of Edinburgh and that city's streets of Grecian town houses, though impressive, seem to an American to be somewhat heartless, dour, and cold. Nonetheless, Scottish archaeologists and philosophers, landscape designers and gardeners contributed considerably, by mail order, by example, and with their own hands, to the appearance of many American villages. The filaments of ideas tying the American Greek Revival to that of Scotland—the only nation in which it was as emphatic, conspicuous, and long lasting as in the United States—were not political.

Perhaps the two national architectures might have had more in common than coincident borrowings from the same sources had the prosperity of the two countries not only begun at the same time but also continued concurrently. Both the Scottish and American Greek Revivals arose as their economies reached a "takeoff" phase, but Scotland's growth slowed at the end of the 1820s, lacking natural resources to sustain it. In America an escalation commenced at the point when Scotland went into a decline. The boom that nourished the American Greek Revival only abated somewhat a decade later and was not truly arrested for many decades; indeed, that Revival was the most conspicuous means by which the newly rich celebrated their boom.

Yet, as paradoxical Americans, they kept glancing backward to the "Doric simplicity" of the founding fathers. The writings of the three decades before the Civil War are full of pride and—sometimes in the same sentences—of remorse at disappointing the frugal expectations of the founders. Americans knew they were engaged in a brash pursuit of riches, and they celebrated their successes. Yet they dutifully paid architectural tribute to two ideal societies, one ancient and distant, the other American and only a half century gone, both imagined as purer and worthier than their own, and left too quickly behind.

With a last good-bye, they then slung their bags over their shoulders and headed for the big city and the big stake and the big factory and the big multinational world and the check for the big deal—headed out to meet us, coming around the corner at the end of their century.

A Greek Revival Tour

We can set out on a journey across America to meet them, to accept their offerings to us: the buildings by which they told us what they wanted us to think of them—and what they thought of themselves. For though it is a public art, architecture is always an artifact of self-perception as well. It expresses either what one thinks one is or what one fears one will not be thought to be. The use of architecture to deceive is risky, for it sometimes betrays the deceiver. That is when it becomes most interesting, for, as Charles Sanders Pierce used to say about manifestos, "it is the belief men *betray* and not that which they *parade* which has to be studied."

What is betrayed by the delay in the arrival of a Greek Revival in America, and by its subsequent effulgence? What does the evidence of architecture tell us about the economic and psychological life of the citizens of the United States—about their self-perceptions and their perceptions of each other?

Their ambiguities can be felt, especially, in New England. Once a haven for Christian utopians, by the 1830s it was losing its energetic young to other utopias, some religious, some secular, and to the promises of the materialist West. The New England Greek Revival can be found in its most vigorous form in Maine, which, like the region beyond the Appalachians, had its boom in the 1830s. The race for the West sent Yankee emigrants across northern New York into the fresh-fledged states along the Great Lakes to create a Grecian Greater New England. This huge province had its entrepôt at Troy, New York, where Yankee merchants set out to seize control of the western movements of settlers and of the grain traffic pouring back through the Mohawk. In Troy they built in the Greek to differentiate themselves from the conservative taste of their competitors in the old Dutch town of Albany, across the river.

Greater New England, voting Whig (and, in the 1850s, Republican) and building in the Greek Revival, spread westward.[†] After Maine's great lumber boom collapsed in 1837–39, its sons and daughters took to the emigrant trail as well; their Greek Revival was suspended. The architects of Maine succumbed to Michigan fever and Texas fever and left their foundations, tools, and plans behind. Belfast and Bangor remained as gat-toothed as Chaucer's Wife of Bath. Bits of Grecian terraces shone white in the moonlight, just a bicuspid here and another there, with bankruptcy and vacant lots between. Yet, even in dereliction, Bangor shows how the architects of New England began the work they later carried on in Mobile, Natchez, Galveston, New Orleans, Cincinnati, and Milwaukee.[††]

Maine and Mobile had a good deal in common in the 1830s. Some of those commonalities survive, among them the most satisfying Free Classical churches in America. In the right light, the Swedenbor-

[†] Frederick Jackson Turner's maps of the congressional districts voting consistently Whig also serve as the best possible indicators of the concentration of Greek Revival houses.

[††] The Greek Revival was as much an urban as a rural or suburban phenomenon. New Orleans, for example, still possesses ranges of classical row houses, recalling those recently obliterated in Baltimore, New York, and Philadelphia. Providence and Richmond can boast of a few row houses that compare in elegance with those of Edinburgh or St. Petersburg. Once Mobile could, as well.

gian Church in Bath [33]* and the Government Street Presbyterian Church in Mobile [376] are so beautiful that you can imagine old Ictinus of Athens smiling upon them.

The Government Street Presbyterians of Mobile commissioned the design and construction of their church from the brothers James and Charles Dakin, of Massachusetts, and their partner, the cranky, Irish-born James Gallier (Galligher). So pleased were the Presbyterians with the results that the same architects were engaged by the Government Street Episcopalians to produce a Greek church for them as well (Christ Episcopal Church [54]), which is one of the very few built anywhere by communicants of the Church of England, who elsewhere embraced the Gothic. Gallier and the Dakins were wanderers, like Charles Bryant, who gave Bangor its Grecian look before he set himself to provoking little wars with the British and then went off to Galveston, to try little wars with Mexico, and died in a futile Indian skirmish. Galveston had an attraction for classically trained architects: Benjamin Henry Latrobe's respected colleague Bartholemy Lafon practiced city planning and piracy in Galveston. A little later, Henry Howard, another Irishman, and James Reynolds, a mystical New Yorker, passed through on their way to competing with Gallier and the Dakins for the burgeoning business of New Orleans.

As if anticipating the westering movement, the towns of the western slopes of New Hampshire and of Vermont are more Grecian than those looking eastward toward the sea and the past. Yankees who stayed at home were more cautious and more deferential toward eighteenth-century precedent than those who moved west. In Castleton, Vermont, lived one of them, Thomas Dake, whose caution was touched with genius. He never emerged from rural obscurity, but his work demonstrated that he knew as much of Regent's Park and the Palladian villas on the Thames as did Charles Bryant (who worked very comfortably in the London manner). For the most part, Dake approached the Greeks rather gingerly until, toward the end of his life, he found courage for a full-blown temple in Orwell [35], built for a sheep farmer who had successfully carried the enclosure movement into the nineteenth century.

Finally launched in the Greek, Dake became as uninhibited as the western practitioners of American Free Classicism. Both his shepherd's mansion in Orwell and his last work, a house in nearby Castleton, had porticos with an odd number of columns. Three-columned and five-columned houses had begun to appear as early as the late 1820s. Among the first of them was the tiny Brown-Simmons-Schug House, on the common in Monroeville, Ohio [226], which was perhaps in some roundabout way influenced by five-columned Oak Hill, completed in Loudon County, Virginia, in 1819 for the fifth president and eponym, James Monroe.†

The strict European tradition that had reached America a century earlier through the builders' guides issued by those English classicists who called themselves "Palladians" did not permit odd numbers, or oddities in general. They believed themselves to be preserving the canons of ancients, but in fact the canons were no older than the Renaissance. It mattered not that the Greeks had used odd numbers of columns, for the Palladians, like Palladio himself, were ignorant of Greece itself, and unaware of the frequency with which the Greeks themselves were "uncanonical."

The service of the Palladians to the Greek Revival was that they followed Palladio's injunction to publish, evangelize for the classical, and they led the way to the popularizing carpenters of the nineteenth century. The rediscovery of the Parthenonic temple form after 1750 was one of many discoveries published both by the so-called Palladians and by their competitors, including Robert Adam and James Gibbs. Popularization was then, as now, one of the noblest of human occupations; after 1750 it was given a coherent philosophy by Freemasonry, then at its most influential among architects, musicians, and laity.

The American Greek Revival was especially the beneficiary of this Masonic, popularizing tradition, a fact that is especially apparent in Utah, where it was sustained by the Mormon followers of Brigham Young, many of whom were, like Young himself, Freemasons before they were Mormons. Some, again like Young, were carpenter-builders by profession.

The American Greek Revival owes much to ancient forms—though by no means was it archaeological. It owes even more to ancient and Renaissance ideologies of building, to Pythagoras and Palladio, to such Masonic lodgemasters as Inigo Jones and Christopher Wren. Their impact upon Americans was felt even before the Brethren of the Workshop of Vitruvius were organized in New York about 1802; it did not end with the Mormon builders of Utah. Earnest carpenter-builders attending Asher Benjamin's classes in Vermont or studying at night in the library of Ithiel Town and the many makers of new carpenters' guides built a Free Classicism Greek only in detail. They wrote, thereby, the latest chapter in a classical tradition revived in the Renaissance and sustained to this day by people who take seriously the propagation of a gospel of beauty. That sort of statement makes cynics uncomfortable, but there have always been people who are serious about beauty and are prepared to go to considerable pains to help others attain it. Such people made it possible for the American Greek Revival to carry to a thousand hamlets the fruits of a tradition two thousand years old.

Asher Benjamin, at the end of his career, brought that tradition to the upper reaches of the Connecticut River Valley, from which the many other carpenter-builders spread its lessons south and west. The Dakins went to Alabama and Mississippi. Elias Carter went to Georgia, after giving his native Massachusetts valley six masterful churches, of which Templeton has one good example and Brimfield another. (Atop the church at Brimfield [36], a stuffed owl keeps the pigeons and starlings from the guttae

An Asher Benjamin design for
a church

and metules, reminding us that on more ancient temples the precedents for guttae and metules were portions of the anatomy of animals slaughtered in sacrifice—these architectural members were, in their way, "stuffed" as well.)

One of the great surprises in the study of this period in American architecture is the similarity of hip-roofed, cubical, columned houses in Natchez, central Georgia, and central Massachusetts, arising from two reciprocal feedback patterns, one from the Mississippi delta to the Georgia Piedmont, and the other from there to Carter's Worcester. Central Massachusetts has many towns that look Southern, but many portions of the South might be more truly said to look Yankee. In addition to the Dakins and Carter, the Greek Revival of South Carolina had the benefit of the presence of the Potter brothers and Russell Warren of Providence. Charleston was first given a Greek Revival cast by them and by the mysterious German, Charles Reichardt. Indeed, portions of South Carolina, Tennessee, New Jersey, and Alabama look Prussian. Reichardt was probably the designer of the most elegant Greek Revival mansion still surviving in the South, Milford [145–46], for which the Rhode Island trio were the contractors, as they had been for his work in Charleston.

Remote though it was and is, Milford was only one of a number of meeting places for the Yankee Greek Revival and the Prussian Greek Revival, as we shall see. Adolphus Heimann and William Strickland's Nashville was another, and a third was Gaineswood [149, 312–13], in Demopolis, Alabama.

Milford is a true country house, awaiting discovery at the end of a long red-clay road. It lies upon the brink of a wooded hill overlooking a vista that was first brown and dull green, sand plain and swamp; then it became white, planted in an expanse of cotton blossoms reaching to a bleached, heat-distorted horizon. Now it is abandoned to the green again, scrub pine and marsh. The prospect from Milford has become another portion of abandoned America, like the gnarled granite hill country of Elias Carter's central Massachusetts.

Milford, despite its name, has neither a mill nor a ford. Like the other buildings in a tight Greek cluster around Columbia, South Carolina, and the thousand or more columned, classical, but unpedimented buildings in Georgia's Piedmont, it is landlocked. In the West and North, however, the Greek Revival is, generally speaking, an aquatic architecture. It appeared along the upper Connecticut, the Mohawk, the tributaries to the Ohio and the Great Lakes, the rivers that offered access to the heart of the continent. It flourished as well along the canals that stitched the rivers together in the decades before the railroads, the Civil War, and the modern industrial world brought the Greek Revival to an end.

Yankees, carrying the Greek Revival westward, conquered western New York and left to us thousands of gabled white frame buildings, in villages and small cities as beautiful as any in the world, in sheltered places between ridges covered with wine grapes and apple orchards, sharing the valleys with broad, blue lakes.

Though larger in scale, the Yankee Lake District is more bucolic and densely settled than Wordsworth's, and blessed with better soil. It is strangely underappreciated by Americans, who may be drawn more to it if they become aware that it contains the best assemblages of Greek Revival buildings in their country.

Throughout the inland empire of New York and Pennsylvania, commencing in the 1820s, Irish and French-Canadian workers dug hundreds of miles of ditches that became silver strips uniting the Hudson, the Great Lakes, the Susquehanna, the Wabash, and the Ohio. These canals held the country together before it was bound by iron rails. Now the canal banks are giving way and the locks are rotting, and their brief moment as triumphs of "modern technology" lies forgotten except by the inhabitants of the nearly forgotten towns on their banks. Before the railroads, a hundred of these canal towns rose from the basin of the Mohawk to the flatter basin of the Raisin River of Michigan. Many were in the Grecian manner. They are still there, though to find them one must whirl about turnpike cloverleafs, abandon the east–west bias of modern transportation, and pursue the diagonals of the 1820s and 1830s.

Only the western fringes of the Catskills were touched by the Greek Revival, as emigrants eschewed its dank, narrow valleys and barren, bouldered hillsides. Such terrain was not enticing to people who could imagine fat meadows along the rivers on the horizon. Whereas much of rural New England has been abandoned, these unprepossessing upland pockets were never fully occupied. The West was there ahead, full of promises.

By the time canals had become disposable engineering and those who financed them had turned to railroads (more marketable to European bondholders), New York, New Jersey, and Pennsylvania constituted the richest group of states of the Union, and they were growing relatively richer. Nabobs of finance and transportation were competing in ostentation. The old brick cubic town house of the eighteenth century took upon itself a portico, a broad entablature, a fret or two, and spread westward from New York, Philadelphia, and Baltimore to Cincinnati, Sandusky, St. Louis, and, most elegantly, to Madison, Indiana. In New York itself, Town and Davis laid up a Greco-Roman domed palace for the Hoboken shipbuilder John Cox Stevens, on Murray Street.

Philadelphia entered enthusiastically into a competition in grandiosity; Quaker restraint vanished. Thomas Ustick Walter, brought to favor by Nicholas Biddle, provided a prototypical mansion, emulated as far away as New Orleans, for a clothing merchant turned railroad financier, Matthew Newkirk, at Thirteenth and Arch streets. Walter's mentor, William Strickland, designed a sprawling country seat for the Powels at Powelton. The "one-L" Powels were "old Philadelphia" (as the "one-eyed Gardiners" were "old Boston") which means that they had avoided the error most of their mercantile peers had made of siding with the losers in the War for Independence. Their chosen architect, Strickland, as clever a practitioner of the Greek Revival style as America produced, had been trained under Benjamin Henry Latrobe. Strickland was slick enough, in 1818, to best his mentor in a great competition for a headquarters building for the Second Bank of the United States [114–15]. Strickland's designs also included that for the remarkable Merchants Exchange [44], which can still be seen in Philadelphia, near the Second Bank (now a museum). This area near Independence Hall is the only portion of a major American city still displaying the Acropolean assemblages that dominated urban design in the antebellum years.

The Stevens mansion, the Newkirk House, and Powelton have fallen to the wreckers. Fallen, too, is the largest of America's Greek Revival palaces, George W. Carpenter's Phil-Ellena, with twenty-six columns, built along Carpenter Avenue in Germantown, Pennsylvania. Gone as well are Pittsburgh's entries in the contest for Hellenic show: Homewood, an essay in the heavy early Doric for Judge William Wilkins, and the superb Picnic House, for the heiress of the tough old Irish fur trader William Croghan.

There lies within that last paragraph a truth about the American Greek Revival distinguishing it from any comparable phenomenon in Europe, a matter of such importance that it requires this pause for emphasis. The largest, most ambitious, and most sophisticated houses built during the Greek Revival, and the best of its cottages, are known to us by the names of their owners, not those of their architects. Though this does not mean their architects, or designers, were unimportant, it does indicate that the American Greek Revival was the social and political statement of a popular state of feeling as much as it was an aesthetic phenomenon. It lies therefore beyond the scope of the kind of art history built upon the model of Vasari's *Lives of the Artists.*[†]

The aforementioned Picnic House in Pittsburgh is also gone, though its interior [314–15] had been spirited away, flown, indeed, heavenward in an apotheosis of urban renewal comparable only to the aerospace adventures of a Baroque ceiling. Now it roosts in a tower floor at the University of Pittsburgh—better there than not at all, of course. Still, to find grand-scale, residential Greek Revival in the central states of the eastern seaboard, one has to go beyond the reach of urban renewal, to the fringe of Philadelphia, near Valley Forge, where Fatlands still stands, or farther out, to Madison, New Jersey, and Altoona, Pennsylvania.

Altoona boasts rightly of its ironmaster Elias Baker, who brought Robert Cary Long, Jr., all the way from Baltimore to design and supervise a thirty-five-room house [236–37, 301] in the midst of a 3,500-acre estate in 1836. It is now being tended by the Blair County Historical Society. This is fortunate, for only one other grand-scale house of its period remains on the eastern seaboard between the Finger Lakes region of New York and Arlington House in Virginia [105–108]: The Forest in Madison, New Jersey [147, 148].

People willing to extend their experience of New Jersey beyond the bogs, refuse barrens, and commuter suburbs that occupy its northeastern corner can discover that the Greek Revival flourished as far as its opposite, northwest corner. This remote region is still remarkably rural, portions of it as serene as Vermont or Wisconsin. Flemington, for example, was the home of a master carpenter named Mahlon Fisher, who lined Main Street with Grecian houses and grew prosperous enough to put up one of the largest for himself. His counterpart in Princeton, Charles Steadman, built seventy or more houses, forty of which remain, most of them Grecian, providing America's most complete ensemble of small-town, middle-class housing during the reign of the Greek Revival. None of them, taken alone, is memorable, but as a group they are unsurpassed. And New Jersey has more to offer: hamlets such as Asbury, which boasts three Grecian houses well worth a detour. (Asbury does require a detour; it is across the state from all the traffic around the horses at Asbury Park.)

It is in small towns in the American countryside, such as Asbury—or Walpole, New Hampshire; Taylors Falls, Minnesota; Milan, Ohio; and Madison, Indiana—that one can sense what was best in the Greek Revival period. These accomplishments are felt most poignantly in the old Northwest Territory, the region south of the Great Lakes and north of the Ohio that was consciously and articulately shaped by the founding fathers. There, after 1788, they set out to build a new society. Their second chance might redeem the first, which, five years after independence, was already frustrating their hopes. In the West they might start anew; with fresh materials they might form a better reality than that possible within the

sands of buildings of the American Greek Revival.

The list of primary monuments of the Greek Revival includes Phil-Ellena, Fatlands, Roosevelt Hall, Whig Hall, Homewood, Ward Hall, and the New York Arlington, all anonymous and so, from Vasari's point of view, unworthy of note. They do belong in this book, however, though there is no virtue in anonymity. Indeed, we will try to identify the architects for four other masterpieces of the genre, because they were built by clients who knew a great deal about architecture and deserve credit for knowing enough to choose some very gifted architects—if the hypothesis developed herein is persuasive enough to give that credit. Two are Milford, the house on the isolated South Carolina hilltop, and The Forest, which may be overlooked, not because it is remote, but because it is too accessible. Underrating college administration buildings is as easy as underrating collegiate administrators, and The Forest is now the administration building at Drew University, in Madison, New Jersey. Though it has not worked its way into any of the standard histories of this period, it is very conspicuous: the columns across its 150-foot front are 36 feet tall.

It would be impossible for a book on this subject to remain of portable size if it were to be comprehensively anti-Vasarian; the vernacular of American popular classicism is too ample for a single volume.

refractory original thirteen states, cluttered and clogged by unexpungible bad habits such as human slavery and an unsuitable appetite for European luxuries.

Emboldened by such a prospect, they laid upon the land a grid, a geographic and psychological matrix into which their fellow countrymen might place schools and colleges and churches, villages for those who liked villages and plantations for those who wished to avoid coming together too much, but all in modest sizes. There was nobility in these plans, but, in retrospect, it appears as a flawed nobility. The founders shared in the human condition; though they had angels' dreams, their understanding was earthbound.

Even as they were laying before the world their exalted aspirations, they betrayed how indistinctly they discerned their own surroundings. It was enough for them to hope for a Northwest Territory populated by free men and women, but some of them did not like to think of that population including free people who were not white. (The Northwest Ordinance contained the nation's first Fugitive Slave Law.) And they neatly plotted towns and houses, gardens, farms, and burial places while disregarding the presence of a numerous people already there. The Native Americans had been present for some thousands of years. They already had houses and villages, fields and burial places, to whom township names drawn from the European classics and temple-form buildings had little symbolic significance.

From the 1820s onward, the region lying between the Ohio River and the Great Lakes received a rush of settlement from the east. The Greek Revival can be seen everywhere that settlement could reach. It can be found along the National Road, now Route 40, a straight path from Pittsburgh to the Mississippi.

The northern tier of this territory displays Yankee Hellenism, that is to say, a classic revival making use of the material used traditionally by Yankees—pinewood horizontals painted white, given Grecian heaviness and ornamental detail derived from Greek originals. When the usual materials were not at hand, they used such exotic materials as cobblestones, but white, wooden, gable-roofed rectangles with a pediment explicit or implied are the characteristic deposits of Yankee settlement in this Greater New England, which first extended only from New York's Finger Lakes and "Burnt Over District" into the Western Reserve of Ohio.

The look of Connecticut in Ohio is natural enough, for much of Ohio was originally the Western Reserve of Connecticut, which received the right to sell off this western colony soon after Massachusetts satisfied its western claims by exercising a similar option to sell, at a profit, that portion of central New York that even today shows similar Yankee qualities. After the Western Reserve filled up, the Yankees went west into the Firelands of Ohio, compensatory acreage for property burned out by British raiders scorching out resistance on the Connecticut shore.

Much of this settlement took place at the height of the Greek Revival period, as one can observe by following Yankee emigration into northern Indiana, around the corner of Lake Erie where Commodore Perry managed one of the few victories scored by the Americans over the British in the War of 1812, and on into a Greek Revival band of counties in southern Michigan and northern Illinois. From there Greater New England extended itself up across southern Wisconsin to the St. Croix River Valley, dividing Minnesota from Wisconsin, which became the *ultima Thule* of Greek Revival gentility in the contiguously settled United States before 1860. Taylors Falls, Afton, and Franconia in Minnesota and St. Croix Falls and Hudson in Wisconsin were the last outposts of Hellenic Yankeedom before it leapt a thousand miles of prairie and desert, eerie badlands, mountains, and western rivers. It came to earth again in its penultimate colonies in Oregon and Washington—the ultimate Yankee colony was on Oahu, where a palace (now the governor's mansion) became Polynesian-Greek.

Brick had been the material of choice in the Tidewater, the Upper South, and the central colonies, and it was generally found in a second band of settlement, descending the Ohio and penetrating its small tributary streams. The brick band has extensions northward into Illinois and Indiana and southward into Kentucky, swinging around the tip of Illinois and up to the Mississippi into the mining region of southwestern Wisconsin and northwestern Illinois.

Phil-Ellena, Germantown,
Pennsylvania

The brick tradition in the Midwest was occasioned by the declines of Virginia and Maryland and the inhospitality to agriculture of Appalachia. This migration was not accompanied by either the Yankees' shrewdness of mechanical invention or their sectarian utopianism, nor by their white frame, gabled tradition. But it did sustain certain habits of courtesy that expressed themselves rather subtly in an architecture somewhat more deferential to its neighbors than was likely to be found elsewhere in the North. It can be discerned in such beautiful villages as Vevay and Madison, Indiana, and in what is left of Lexington, Kentucky, and Galena and Shawneetown, Illinois.

It is arresting to note how differently these two bands of settlement evolved. The Butternut areas along the Ohio River, so-called because their people dyed their clothes with walnut or butternut oil, were dominated by the culture of the Upper South and Pennsylvania. They tended to produce corn, sweet potatoes, and corn-based whiskey. In James McPherson's summary of recent statistical studies, they were "positively correlated with . . . anti-bank and anti-black sentiments, illiteracy, and Baptist churches." They voted overwhelmingly for Democrats, while the Yankee counties voted Whig. These

Greater New England counties, which produced wheat, cheese, and wool, had higher farm value per acre and greater percentages of "improved land, value of farm machinery, banks and pro-bank sentiment, urbanization, population growth, schools, literacy, Congressional and Presbyterian churches, and temperance and anti-slavery societies." And greater enthusiasm for a Greek Revival.[2]

Madison, Vevay, and Shawneetown, which are in Butternut areas, are magnificent exceptions to a general rule that it is best to look to the northern and central, rather than the southern, counties of Ohio, Indiana, and Illinois for the Greek. But the Grecian Butternut migration also flavored Galena, a red-brick, templed little town far to the northwest of its main current, and Mineral Point, just across the border in Wisconsin, which was largely built of stone by Cornish tin miners. Even those Butternuts who settled Wisconsin did not favor wood sheathing, as did the Yankees, and they did not talk like Yankees. Many were Celts, trained for centuries to resist the English and the bland, nasal way of speaking inherited from the English by the New Englanders.

At the time temple-form houses were going up in Michigan and New York—a decade, in fact, before they were essayed along the St. Croix—Greek Revival houses were being built by Yankees who had crossed the "sea of grass" in "prairie schooners," all the way to Port Angeles and Port Townsend on Puget Sound.

As suggested earlier, like all things American, the Greek Revival was never, anywhere, "pure." It had too much to do, too much symbolic freight to carry, too many cultural pressures to accommodate. Along the California coast and in the Southwest, it actually revived the real Greece, from life rather than archaeology. Dwellings that might appear to an Englishman to be strange admixtures of the Greek and the Hispanic were, in fact, adaptations to a climate and terrain similar to those encountered by the ancient Greeks. These were courtyard buildings, turned inward around patios, with fountains and colonnaded passageways leading directly to interior rooms. This is how the Greeks lived—not in temples presenting columns and porticos to the world.

Mexican-American Texas made similar rediscoveries, but the Texas Greek Revival came with the leaders of the Texas Republic from Tennessee. The Jeffersonian-Roman-Tennessean mansions built in Austin by Abner Cook [242] and the simple "Grecian" houses of the Texas cotton country mark the limits of upland cotton-country Greater Tennessee. Such towns as Austin, Hills Prairie, San Augustine, Mount

Enterprise, and the Washingtons of Texas and Arkansas became anglicized and Greek while Mexican rule weakened and Texas became independent.

There are differences between Greek and Roman forms, and both were combined in the creole cottage, a form that owed nothing to the Greeks or Romans. It could be found even in East Texas and the adjacent hilly, red-dirt interior of Louisiana (which contains towns named Athens, Sparta, and Homer), but it came from the indigo-, rice-, and sugar-producing lowlands of the Mississippi delta, the fringe of the Caribbean.

From the West Indies and Brazil came a wet-and-hot synthesis to contrast with the dry-and-hot synthesis of Texas and California. The dry-and-hot model had been that of the Mediterranean house, hollow at the center, built around the courtyard. The wet-and-hot creole cottage was a house within a house, hollowness turned outward, with a colonnade representing a balconied courtyard, like that of the Roman *villa maratima*, flipped inside out. After William Nichols showed them the way at a house called Forks of Cypress, built before 1830 and burned in 1966, scores of creole cottages employed pillars and doorways with bold, heavy Greek proportions. Some even made use of iron ornament shipped from manufacturers in Cincinnati and Philadelphia, who based them upon English and French patterns, which in turn drew upon archaeological reports of Athens or Delphi or Bassae.[†]

† Nichols himself did not favor Greek doorways; his characteristic entrance, as at Forks of Cypress, was a semicircular transom in blocklike segments.

There are other, quite different hot-country floor plans to be found along the American fringe of the Caribbean. Among them is the T plan of the Gulf Coast, which provides as many rooms as possible with cross ventilation, and the U plan of South Carolina, which splits the central passage just inside the front door and sends its arms akimbo to embrace the breeze. Wherever one finds either of these floor plans— even in Madison, New Jersey; Madisonville, Ohio; and Trumansburg, Constableville, and Auburn, New York—one can be fairly confident that a trail will be found to the West Indies.

The Greek Revival only penetrated deeply into Florida in its northernmost province, as far as Tallahassee. Most of the state remained a fearsome frontier in the 1830s and 1840s. The Seminoles, like the Maroons of Jamaica, were very accomplished in their use of the natural defenses of a dense, hot, humid terrain. Florida's islands and saintly fortress towns were equally intransigent, remaining Spanish or British-Loyalist. They were as unaffected by the "gusto-Greco" as was Canada, and for the same political reasons. The Revival was seen as an American patriotic statement, distasteful to the descendants of Tory emigrants resettled in Ontario and to Spaniards who were citizens of the United States by conquest. The handful of houses in Florida that could be described as sharing in the Greek

Revival are all in the Marianna-Tallahassee area, centering upon the mansion built by the Jacksonian governor, Richard Keith Call, who, like Sam Houston, his counterpart in Texas, opposed secession in 1860. Call's Tallahassee, like Houston's Austin, marks the farthest reach of Greater Tennessee and of the Jeffersonian-Roman-Tennessean strain in American Free Classicism.

The chronology of all this can be a little confusing: despite proto-Parthenonic buildings such as Peter Harrison's Redwood Library in Newport, Rhode Island, and Prince William's Church in Sheldon, South Carolina (both of the 1750s), and Thomas Jefferson's (Roman) temple form for the Virginia capitol [359] of the 1780s, the American Greek Revival did not get underway until the 1820s, when temple-form buildings appeared in the West—as in Monroeville, Ohio—before they existed in coastal Maine. Though the movement petered out in the 1860s elsewhere, there was vigorous Mormon Hellenism in Utah in the 1870s, and two great, anachronistic public buildings appeared in the style of the 1850s—Addison Hutton's Ridgeway Library in Philadelphia (1874) and Arthur B. Mullet's San Francisco Mint (1870).

A few columns doth not a Greek Revival make. More elaborate definitions will come later, but it is important now to note that when we are willing to look beyond the Redwood Library and Prince William's Church, the two chief predecessors of the Virginia capitol as temple-form buildings, and examine a list of American buildings with monumental porticos two stories or more in height (leaving aside churches built with porticos in the Wren-Gibbs style), we find these porticos all merely additional to, not integral to, the shape of the buildings upon which they appear. This list includes Whitehall (1753–69), Governor Horatio Sharpe's banqueting house near Annapolis, Maryland, the central Roman pavilion of which *was* almost a temple form, but the rest of the house spread away from it in the Palladian manner.

James Madison's home, Montpelier, near Orange, Virginia

Other such examples are Hampton, on the Santee in South Carolina, its portico having been added about 1790; the Morris-Jumel House in New York City, with a portico of unknown date (probably added after 1788); The Woodlands in Philadelphia, whose portico was added in 1788; Montpelier, James Madison's house in Virginia, with a portico added in 1793; and Farmington, near Charlottesville, where the portico covers rooms of only one story, but is twenty-seven feet high—which could lead us toward Thomas Jefferson's smaller one-story Anglo-Palladian porticos at Monticello, Edgehill, Poplar Forest, Amthill, and Barboursville.

But the Greek Revival in America begins in earnest with Latrobe's north portico of the White House in 1829 and William Nichols's Forks of Cypress in the same year.

A Few Distinctions by the Roadside   We are now at a point where some distinctions among these strains may be useful. We have come this far together without much use of technical terms or taxonomies of style. More of that sort of thing will be necessary in the final section of the book, which is intended to offer some of the sequences inherent to old-fashioned architectural history narrowly considered. Even there, however, technical terms are used only if they are shorter, less repetitious, and more precise than would be the equivalent description.

Few readers will go about America with measuring devices to see how many times the diameter of a column must be repeated to reach its height, though distinguishing a Roman from a Greek form often does require calipers and tape. Few, indeed, may care very much whether an American capital, column, or frieze is drawn from one ancient temple or another, unless the trail of such selections leads to something more interesting—which, from time to time, it does.

The American Greek Revival was seldom very Greek and almost never scrupulously exact in its use of antique models. That is one reason too much pedantry about its sources would be regarded as ludicrous by its best practitioners. That is why the term Free Classicism is used herein to describe this phenomenon; it would be used even in this book's title were that term already sufficiently current to suggest what to expect within these covers. But some general rules for distinguishing the various strains may be useful.

Even without calipers, one can observe that Greek columns were stubbier than their Roman counterparts, and that American designers, from the eighteenth century onward, showed a marked tendency to attenuate even Roman forms. Americans also tended toward Roman siting: they, like the Romans, more often than not placed columns and whole buildings upon artificial elevated platforms. The Greeks created a sacred precinct around their temples, and when an elevation like the Acropolis or a rocky headland provided such a precinct naturally, they rejoiced in it, but their earliest columns, in the Doric mode, were not platformed, or to put the matter in another way, they were baseless.

There is no difficulty in distinguishing between Arlington House—which a hundred million Americans have seen, with its unmistakably Greek Doric portico and baseless columns—and any of the pavilions at the University of Virginia [370–71], which are Roman, by way of Palladio, his British or French revisers and simplifiers, and the team of architects working in Charlottesville to assist Thomas Jefferson.

From Jefferson's anthology at Charlottesville came a whole succession of Roman-Anglo-Palladian progeny, especially in Greater Tennessee, with its offshoots in Alabama, Texas, and Florida. From time

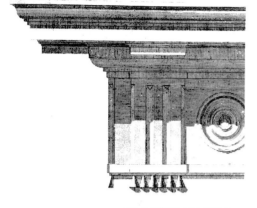

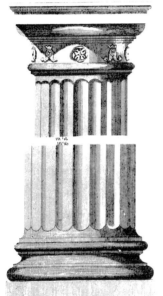

to time they cross-pollinated with Ionic Greek precedents (especially those of the Temple on the Ilissus, which had a large, though infrequently acknowledged, American following), and as they reached the Mississippi delta, were repollinated with both Greek and Roman forms introduced by a group of English, Irish, and German architects. Everybody in that flat and fertile region felt free to mix all these classical ideas with ornament invented in New York on Grecian themes and to apply the admixture to the raised and colonnaded format of West Indian cottages.

And, for leafing through the illustrations, it may also be useful to bear in mind that:

- the Doric is the simplest and stockiest of Greek column forms, and the most inanimate; its capitals are plain.
- the Ionic column capital is the one with whorls, like the horns of a mountain ram, at the corners. It is the most animal, recalling the use of Greek temples as places of animal sacrifice. Ionic columns are thinner than Doric columns.
- the Corinthian column capital, with its foliate effusions, is the most elaborate and botanical of the three.

So much for style, for the moment. Let us get back aboard the Greek Revival (Free Classical) tour.

The Doric order

Rejoining the Tour In Georgia, just over the original borderline of the United States from Florida, there appeared suddenly, in the boom years of the 1830s and beyond, thousands of hip-roofed, colonnaded houses in a creole-Hellenic format. Very few carried pedimented porticos, and of those few all were of Roman proportions—like the characteristic Romanism of Tennessee—not Greek. This profusion of Free Classicism was not, despite our Hollywood-encouraged expectations, predominantly rural. This fact was established thirty years ago by Wilbur Zelinsky, who drove every passable road in Georgia, noted on his map every house that he could find bearing columns, and found them concentrated densely in villages at the fall line. (My own survey demonstrates that the same clustering in urban or suburban knots occurred in Mississippi and Alabama, where single staple crops were produced by gangs of slaves for an international market, but not in Tennessee, where the economy was more diversified. There was an association between protective, reaffirming huddling and upland cotton, as opposed to a more scattered and confident settlement pattern where cotton, tobacco, horses, cattle, and wheat were grown together.)

That is not to say that Athens and Sparta, Washington and Madison, Milledgeville and Augusta, Macon and a dozen other clusters of Georgia's Grecian houses are not surpassingly beautiful. They are, even in the heat of summer. These are places made to be pleasing. They were the headquarters-compounds of a culture that deployed only the aesthetics of necessity on the plantations themselves. Overseers' cottages are admirable only in the most severely utilitarian way. Plantation owners gathered for mutual reassurance in small towns, where they could be safe while their overseers and slaves engaged in a long contest for survival that exhausted the soil and the slaves. White-colonnaded Southern towns were relatively removed from that contest. They were refuges, *bastides* without walls. As one travels from Savannah all the way to Natchez, one can observe that however ugly an economy may be, it does not always produce ugly buildings. And here it is helpful to recall that the Georgia "Greek Revival" is unlike any other *except for* that of the Mississippi delta between New Orleans and Natchez *and* for that around Worcester, Massachusetts, from which and to which there was traffic in architects and carpenters.

The little group of columned houses in up-country South Carolina around Columbia, including Millwood, share some characteristics of this hip-roofed and colonnaded style, probably because the Hampton family, which built these houses, shared with the Georgians ownership of huge holdings of delta lands from which this creole Hellenism emerged.

The Ionic order

In these villages lived the upland cotton planters, who remained secluded together even after a Yankee tinkerer named Eli Whitney exploded the cotton belt outward by inventing his gin, a machine to rake the seeds from the rough fibers that would grow beyond the sheltered sea islands. Whitney had been marooned on a plantation owned by Mrs. Nathaniel Greene, a Rhode Island lady who had been given the place by a legislature grateful for her husband's success in drawing Lord Cornwallis out of Georgia and all the way to Yorktown.

Before Whitney, the western claims of Georgia and South Carolina, reaching all the way to the Mississippi, had little attraction to those practicing European agricultural methods—that is to say the

The Corinthian order

cultivation of crops for sale to world markets. Moreover, this relatively unappealing terrain was already occupied by intelligent native agriculturists with no interest in world markets, whose military prowess had held the Europeans within seventy miles of the shore for a century and a half. Something extraordinary was needed to draw Americans into a long campaign to conquer the region above the fall line and to bring it within the international market system. Whitney provided that something, and the Greek Revival belt of Georgia, Alabama, and Mississippi was the result.

Few architects' names come to mind when one thinks of the thousands of buildings created to serve the settlers who drove the Native American occupants out of those regions after 1830. None can compete with the true architect of the Southern Greek Revival: Eli Whitney.

Like Florida, the Carolinas were little touched by a residential Greek Revival (there are many churches and other public buildings in the Carolinas in the Grecian style, as there are in Virginia, but very few houses). This is because the Greek Revival came along too late. The Carolinas and Virginia were in decline by the 1820s, their boldest spirits moving westward, their soils exhausted, their spirits weighted by the burden of disappointed hopes. It was commonplace for their statesmen to lament their diminishing power in the nation. It is noteworthy that in these states there is not a single house surrounded by columns, while there are hundreds in Georgia. Charleston produced Hellenic Baptist and Methodist churches and a superb synagogue [380]. But not even Charleston's native son, Robert Mills—the first of two American-born architects to work confidently in the Greek style, the other being William Strickland—could persuade clients there that the Greek was the proper thing for residences. The city does have a handful of large porticoed houses of a strutting vulgarity worthy of New Orleans's Yankee-built Garden District, but they are not really Charlestonian. They were built by rough, up-country planters endeavoring to make a mark among the old Huguenot and Barbadian families. The Greek Revival was a statement of power, and aside from the idiosyncratic Arlington House and Berry Hill, pedimented temple-form houses are not to be found in Virginia or either of the Carolinas.

Berry Hill, isolated near the Virginia–North Carolina line, is, aesthetically, not Southern at all. It owes its form to Philadelphia, especially to Nicholas Biddle's Andalusia [109, 110–11]. Like the Baptist churches in Virginia designed by Biddle's architect, Thomas Ustick Walter, the temple complex at Berry Hill demonstrates how thoroughly Virginia had fallen under the aesthetic shadow of Philadelphia by the 1830s. Thomas Jefferson had not been successful in his effort to instruct Virginians in classicism. His Roman Virginia capitol building of 1789 and his anthology of Roman forms around the lawn at the University of Virginia erected thirty years later had little influence in his own state, or in its sister to the south, North Carolina.

Berry Hill

Beyond the aging Piedmont and beyond the Smokies—in Alabama, Tennessee, Mississippi, Arkansas, northern Louisiana, a bit of Florida and Texas—is Greater Tennessee. This is the cotton kingdom—where up-country, long-staple, sticky-seed cotton gave rise to the brick Roman Revival of the New South. This is sometimes called Greek Revival country, though its houses (not its public buildings) might have looked as they did had Greece never been rediscovered. South and west of Berry Hill, not a single house has the form of the Parthenon. In this huge stretch of land reaching to the Rio Grande, there are not even Greek churches, beyond a handful in Alabama—the two finest are Yankee-built, in Mobile. There are about as many Grecian bank buildings, the two best in Natchez.

Many planters in the transmontane South took their cue from Andrew Jackson, whose followers loved to observe that he was an old Roman. Though fashionable taste in Jackson's cotton South was Roman, it was so by way of many intermediaries, the most important of whom was Palladio.[†]

And what has this to do with the Greek Revival? A sound question, the sounder for being too seldom asked. For Thomas Jefferson developed his taste wholly in disregard of the rediscovery of Greece. So did his beloved Palladio. Consequently, those portions of the United States, especially in the Jacksonian South, that took architectural cues from Jefferson and Jefferson's un-Hellenic Virginia never had a *Greek* Revival (excepting, once again, Arlington House and Berry Hill, plus two banks in Natchez and two churches in Mobile).

On the contrary, it was the *Northern* tradition in American architecture that showed the benefits of the direct observation of the work of the Greeks. For this we can be grateful to George Hadfield, Benjamin Henry Latrobe, Nicholas Biddle, Ithiel Town, and to scores of carpenter-builders who worked from Maine to Wisconsin.

The Philadelphia buildings in which Biddle took an interest and those of Hadfield in Washington do bear a family relationship to the Parthenon and to the temples at Paestum. The columnar residential

† In truth, Palladio was himself not very Roman; he earned the adjective *ingenious*, which is commonly coupled with his name. He professed to be re-interpreting the Roman critic Vitruvius, and Americans, following Jefferson, reinterpreted the British who reinterpreted Palladio. Palladio's architecture was unknown to Jefferson except as reduced to folio size in British and French eighteenth-century interpretations, which took many liberties with the originals. Since none of these interpreters knew what Vitruvius himself had drawn— only his prose survived—the connections of Rome to Nashville were somewhat tenuous.

architecture of the Upper South does not. The creole cottages of the Mississippi Valley compose their own genre, distinct from the Jeffersonian-Tennessean-Jacksonian progression. They are even less Greek than the Romanoid mansions of Greater Tennessee.

Following patterns set in the nation's first capital, Philadelphia, and its second, New York, and in its new, third, and (so far) final one being created on the banks of the Potomac, the classic revival swept across the North from Maine to Oregon and even to Hawaii (with a thousand miles of unconquered plains omitted). The work of Hadfield and his followers, Town and Alexander Jackson Davis, is inconceivable without the benefits of the rediscovery of Greece. Twenty thousand Northern buildings, perhaps more, bear the indelible imprint of the form of a Greek temple.

Even as late as the 1840s, however, an exhausted "Adamesque" building, with its swags and fanlights, was still fashionable in the strongholds of the old anglophilic order, Charleston and Boston. When the flowering of New England occurred, its ingenuity did not rush into architecture; it gently flowed, instead, toward the introverted arts, literature and philosophy. Antebellum Massachusetts was not bold in architecture, nor was South Carolina, nor Virginia. For a Roman Revival of a swaggering sort, one looks to Greater Tennessee; for a more Grecian Greek—and in the United States one cannot be too strict in such matters—the traveler turns to the Finger Lakes, the western slopes of Vermont, the coastal villages of Maine and Ohio, the riverbanks of Indiana, Wisconsin, Michigan, Minnesota, Connecticut, and Massachusetts. This book is intended as an incentive to the exploration of these beautiful places and of a few general ideas that arise when one asks questions about them.

THE MYTH OF
CLASSICAL EMULATION

Contrary to a once fashionable notion, the founding fathers were not eager to copy from the ancients either the government they founded or the buildings they erected. They had been *too* well trained in the classics to have emulated the practices of antiquity in any field. They knew too much. None of the relatively few public structures they were able to build during their lifetimes revived Greece or Rome—the closest was the Virginia state capitol of 1789—nor did any of their houses (Arlington House, of 1804–19, was of the second generation, and it was unique). Their other buildings were firmly frozen in European, eighteenth-century practice; that is why the Capitol in Washington could be adapted so readily to modifications made by a series of architects trained in England, Germany, Italy, France, and Russia, and why the White House might have been plucked from the banks of the Potomac and deposited in Gloucestershire or the suburbs of Dublin without seeming out of place or out of time in 1760 or 1770.

A Greek Revival would have been shocking to the founders' taste, requiring of them a completely fresh appraisal of classical architecture. Though twentieth-century writers have asserted that the men who won the Revolutionary War were ready for an abrupt break with their English past, they had spoken of their fight as being for the restoration of the rights of Englishmen; it was only as the struggle became more bitter and was joined by England's enemies, France, Holland, and Spain, that it became inevitable that there could be no turning back.

What they had done so reluctantly in politics, they had no mind to do in architecture. The founders had adhered to a continuous tradition, filtered through ten generations of Renaissance refinement and adjustment. Not until thirty years had passed did Americans have the confidence to make use of ancient forms directly, basing architecture upon their own observations of the ruins of antiquity. This was a large distinction, almost a revolutionary one. The founders drew upon the ancients only with the permission, so to speak, of the British and the French. The revivalists used them more closely, as models. The difference was one of archaeological directness (never merely copying) versus Renaissance intermediation. The founders had enough to do in the creation of a new political system; besides, they knew the Romans only by way of the Renaissance, and they did not know the Greeks at all. The Greek Revivalists knew the work of both directly and used both.

This all seems rather obvious, but it is important to pause for a moment to reflect upon the implications of the fact that the founders knew Greek and Roman *history* very well indeed. As a result, they did not choose to emulate either Greek or Roman political institutions, for their thorough understanding of the experience of the ancients left them with few illusions. "Greek democracy" and the Roman "Republic" offered a catalog of experiences to be avoided.

John Adams spoke with "horror" and Alexander Hamilton with "pain and disgust" of the "factions and confusions" of Greek politics in the classical age. Thomas Jefferson, James Madison, and Peter Livingston, of New York, saw in "the Republics of Greece" admonitions to escape such a fate. They were, said Livingston, "destroyed by the wealth of the aristocracy bearing down the people." From the opposite end of the political spectrum, somewhat later, Edward Everett invoked the ghosts of the two most celebrated orators of the classical age to warn of Jacksonian despotism: "Greece cries to us by the convulsed lips of her poisoned, dying Demosthenes, and Rome pleads with us in the mute persuasion of her mangled Tully." Americans generally had "interest in the scenes of antiquity, only as lessons of avoidance of nearly all their examples."[3]

Despite the explicit views of the founders, some who wrote about them in the 1930s and 1940s treated the 1790s as a time in which politicians were seeking to model the United States upon Greek or Roman practice. It was often implied that men as sophisticated as Jefferson nevertheless naively confused the Athenian and Roman republics and wished to re-create either. In the absence of supporting data drawn from the founders' words or their practice in architecture or government, pre-war scholars habitually made lists of place names, averring that "the evidence of that [classical] influence lies all around us," as Howard Mumford Jones put it. We were presented with catalogs of towns—Rome, Athens, Sparta, Ithaca, Corinth. We learned that colleges had been laid about in *campi*, attended by *sophomores*, *juniors*, and *seniors;* likewise, our country was governed by *Republicans* and *Democrats*, each seeking to gain the office of *praesidens*, gathering in a *con-gressi* whose *senior* branch was the *Senate*, in a building called *Capitol*, using Roman language and Roman symbols. There was a Roman goddess on our coinage and our seal, *et cetera*. All this was accomplished, it was averred, despite a classically impoverished terrain: "The New World was no part of the Roman Empire. . . . Americans do not, like Europeans, drive over highways originally laid down for the legions of Caesar, nor in the midst of cities or on some nearby hill see ruined temples from the time when Zeus was father of gods and men."[4]

Making the best of things, "the young nation . . . accepted a set of classical coordinates to particularize components of its government and its republican culture."[5]

Did it really? If so, it "particularized" very selectively. Jones intoned that the "young nation . . . [was driven by] an instinctual feeling that its official expression should begin with the Greek temple style (as in Jefferson's capitol at Richmond) and then slowly develop into the splendors of Imperial Rome." But it was not driven hard enough to do anything about it, for no American governmental building was built in a temple form for forty years after the Virginia capitol went up in 1789.[†]

It is still sometimes said that Jefferson was the father of the Greek Revival. He was, at most, its very skeptical grandfather, making use of classical models in politics for delight, not for utility. In his lexicon, much of it drawn from the Scottish Enlightenment, *delight* meant pleasure, or recreation. *Utility* meant practical use.

The distinction between pleasure and use was important to him. He spoke of "the luxury of reading . . . the remains of the Greek and Latin languages, . . . [indeed, to] read the Latin and Greek authors in the original is a sublime luxury; and I deem luxury in science to be at least as justifiable as in architecture, painting, gardening and the other arts. I enjoy Homer . . . I thank on my knees him who directed my early education [his father] for having put into my possession this rich source of delight."[6]

The Scottish scholars who initiated the pan-Hellenic tradition imparted to Jefferson in Williamsburg in the 1760s used classical languages "as models of pure taste in writing," for polish, not for shoes. It was their manner, not their matter, that was instructive, and even that instruction was not so important. When Benjamin Franklin and Benjamin Rush proposed to end instruction in Latin and Greek, Jefferson conceded that, compared to French and Spanish, "I think Greek the least useful."[7]

"Remains" of ancient buildings might be delightful as well—and useful in elevating the taste of a young nation. Neither Jefferson nor any of his contemporaries showed any desire to live in temples, differing in this way from the Greek Revivalists after 1825.

[†] (Jones, p. 270) The Virginia capitol was Roman, not Greek, very gingerly derived from the Maison Carrée in Nîmes by two good Renaissance scholars, Thomas Jefferson and Charles-Louis Clerisseau. Another fine prose writer of Jones's generation, Van Wyck Brooks, was equally eager to find an instant Greek Revival in the early years of the republic, and marred an otherwise splendid book, *The World of Washington Irving*, with the same insistence upon the prepotency of Jefferson's capitol (p. 61). Brooks says that Benjamin Henry Latrobe's remodeling of Kalorama, the Washington residence of the epic poet Joel Barlow, produced a building like the Virginia capitol. This is simply not true; Kalorama was nothing of the sort. It was a pleasant, cubical, Regency villa, bearing no relationship to a pedimented rectangle with porticos and columns.

The founders *did* freely adapt ancient models for the design of public buildings, but neither because they were so illiterate in ancient history as to think "the real analogy with the infant Republic lay in Rome" (as charged), nor because they thought Rome to be "a glorious model."[8]

American architecture, statecraft, and religious practice did not pedantically duplicate the forms of the past, not in constitutions, buildings, or bibles. Franklin revised the Book of Common Prayer for cold climates, and Jefferson felt entirely free to cut and paste the New Testament into his own, revised version. The Sage of Monticello spoke of the Declaration of Independence in terms he might have used, with only minor amendments, for the composition of the plan for the University of Virginia: "Neither aiming at originality of principle or sentiment, nor yet copied from any particular and previous writing, it was intended to be an expression of the American mind, and to give to that expression the proper tone and spirit called for by the occasion."[9]

Univeristy of Virginia, in Charlottesville

It is not true that he was "infatuated" by the Maison Carrée, though it is true that once, when writing in code through the Bourbon censors to a fellow radical in Paris, he said so. Having made sure his reader would know what he intended, by telling her earlier that he would throw off his police "tail" by pretending to visit Roman remains, he was using the temple as a cover and rendezvous for a meeting with a Brazilian insurrectionist against the Spanish Bourbons, José de Maia. It is true that Jefferson went to the trouble of asking Charles-Louis Clerisseau to create a plaster model of a Virginia capitol vaguely based upon the Maison Carrée. The temple model was intended to reassure skeptical Virginians on the building committee that they should desist from using Williamsburgian colonial models for a newly independent commonwealth. Jefferson and Clerisseau borrowed what they wanted from the Romans in order to enlarge the available stock of architectural forms, broadening "taste in this beautiful art . . . in our countrymen." How else might this be done "unless we avail ourselves of every occasion when public buildings are to be erected, of presenting to them models for their study and imitation?"[†]

It is quite natural for devotees of the classics to want to push beyond the evidence; it is their profession to argue the importance of a direct knowledge of ancient languages, literature, and architecture. But Jefferson is not a useful exemplar of their ideal, for he took none of his ideas directly from the very few Roman buildings he observed, never saw a Greek one, and was no more likely than his peers to search the classics for architectural or political examples: "So different was the style of society then, and with those people, from what it is now and with us, that I think little edification can be obtained from their writings on the subject of government."[††]

† (Jefferson quoted in Wright, p. 232) Jefferson consistently advised his countrymen that when a man or a nation becomes mature, in "conditions of life to which [classical models] . . . must be estranged," attending to them except for delight "would be a great misdeployment of time. Their acquisition should be the occupation of our early years only." (Quoted in Wright, pp. 226–27)

†† Jefferson expressed no regret that "the political writings of Aristotle, or of any other ancient, have been lost, or are unfaithfully rendered or explained to us." (Quoted in Wright, p. 230)

The Greek Revival, when it arrived in the 1820s and 1830s, did not revive antiquity. It revived something closer to hand, the reforming zeal of the 1770s and 1780s. After 1832 Robert Mills, studiously avoiding Roman excesses, created a Greek Revival capital city for Andrew Jackson in Washington, D.C. George Hadfield, the architect of Arlington House, had, it is true, used some Greek column capitals—from the Erechtheum, in Athens—to give Georgian dignity to his design for the War Department Building of 1796–97. But that building, a traditional brick rectangular block, presented its portico centered on its long side, sufficient for dignity but not for making the composition, as a whole, any more Greek than The Vyne, a Hampshire house that acquired a portico in 1654. Except for this tentative reference to Athens, the War Department Building bore closer resemblance to its contemporary, Samuel Blodget's First Bank of the United States in Philadelphia (which no one has designated a Greek Revival building), than to any of the temple-form structures of the 1830s.

A competition drawing by Thomas Jefferson for the White House

The impression that the founders commenced a Greek Revival requires the compression to the twinkling of an eye of a "classical lag" that actually lasted three decades, during which there was no Greek Revival. Nonetheless, some twentieth-century rewriters have depicted them as swept away by a "cult of Greek democracy," and housed accordingly.

An early view of the White House

The most frequently cited source of this notion was a careless phrase of a great intellectual historian who died before he could explain himself. Vernon Parrington wrote, in an unguarded moment, of the South's adherence to a "persuasive ideal of Greek democracy." He went on to assert that John C. Calhoun had "yielded to the seductions of a Greek republic."[10] By a further fusion of false images, Calhoun was presented as the founder not only of a cult but also the designer of its temples. Though a dour Calvinist who lived very simply in a non-Greek house in the eighteenth-century mode, Calhoun somehow became associated with the white-pillared Southern plantation of Darryl Zanuck's dreams.

The cult must have been kept secret, for there is little evidence for it in the written record and none at all in architecture. Calhoun gave only the most glancing mention to Greece; he was no more seduced by the ancients than any other educated man of his generation. But Parrington's unsupported statement was, like a piece of thistledown, caught in other hands, planted, and nurtured into a thorny thicket of misunderstanding. Its propagators included Clement Eaton, Rollin Osterweiss, Edwin H. Miles, and Harvard's Dean Charles Gummere.

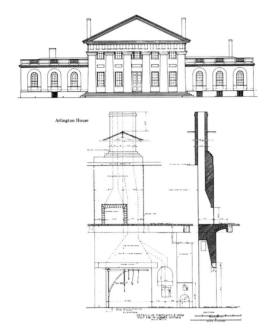

Arlington House

Arlington House

Miles was wont to insist that "many Southerners were . . . drawn to a cult of Greece . . . attracted to ancient Hellas with its system of small independent states." Eaton's "dream of Greek democracy" was inserted by Osterweiss into the subconscious of George Washington, despite the unavailability of his dream records and his preference for Romans. The "cult" and its myth (or "dream") now in place, cubical Southern cottages, under hipped roofs, could be presented as its sacred buildings, modeled upon "classic ideals of architecture." Howard Mumford Jones provided the final, fetching and fallacious metaphor, repeated in countless guidebooks: "in the Deep South . . . the plantation owner . . . required a house that was, as it were, the capitol of a small kingdom, stately pedestal and portico announced dignity and authority within. . . ."[11]

This was Reconstruction reconstructed. After a century and a Civil War, John C. Calhoun was vindicated. His image of the plantation as an independent kingdom was fused with Periclean Athens. Perhaps the doubling of analogies was needed to compensate for their remoteness. Athens had its own tragedies, but they were utterly unlike those of the dependent, colonial, unstable, and violent reality of the Southern planters. Imbedded in the popular mind, however, the myth and the white-columned cinematic image, have confused both architectural and political history. Quite aside from their pernicious racial and political implications, they have created false expectations as to the chronology, the form, and the symbolic content of the Greek Revival.

Fortunately, it is not necessary to unwind the entire tangle. A mere glance across the face of the antebellum South is sufficient; the myth dissolves in the presence of the constructed evidence. As suggested earlier, the founding fathers built no Greek Revival houses. Even if time constraints are distended a bit through the first half of the nineteenth century, we find only two temple-form residences constructed in the South, the region supposedly gripped by a temple-building "cult."

There *is* Arlington House, a memorial to a founder—George Washington. But it was not completed until nineteen years after his death in 1799. Its owner-curator was his adopted son, George Washington Parke Custis, and he chose a style that never commended itself to the founder himself. And if Calhoun asked that each plantation headquarters be the "capitol" building of an "independent kingdom," this was Custis's suburban villa—his major plantations were elsewhere.

Furthermore, Custis and his architect, George Hadfield, chose a form then associated not with Athenian political devices but with individual character—Doric simplicity. Custis expressed no admiration for Greek political forms, certainly not with any "cult" connected with Calhoun, whom he loathed. Nor did he intend a symbolic message in support of slavery or Southern separatism. He opposed Southern separation and sought every means within his comprehension to bring slavery to an end.

The other Greek temple-form house in the South is Berry Hill, built at the end of the 1840s when all the founders were dead. It was the home of Nicholas Biddle's friend James Coles Bruce, who, like Custis, was a Southern Unionist Whig who regretted slavery and whose cousin was an abolitionist governor of Illinois. Bruce too abhorred the doctrines of Calhoun.

Like all educated gentlemen of the time, the founders, their sons, grandsons, and great-grandsons made frequent classical references in their speech and writing. But they were not naive, and until the 1840s and 1850s, no educated person made the error of suggesting that Greek politics had a happy outcome or that Greece offered a desirable model for imitation in its treatment of slaves. It was only very late in the antebellum years that a classical justification for Southern slavery was found in some pamphlets of Thomas Dew, George Fitzhugh, and M. R. H. Garnett. They were writers of the 1850s, three sparrows of late November. They did not make a spring; they came too late to effect the Greek Revival. Seeking Greek precedents for their behavior in the final, desperate, degenerate days of the Southern garrison-state, fanatics such as Dew *did* attempt to cobble up apologia for a society based upon slavery. But they had only a tiny following, which included neither Custis nor Bruce.

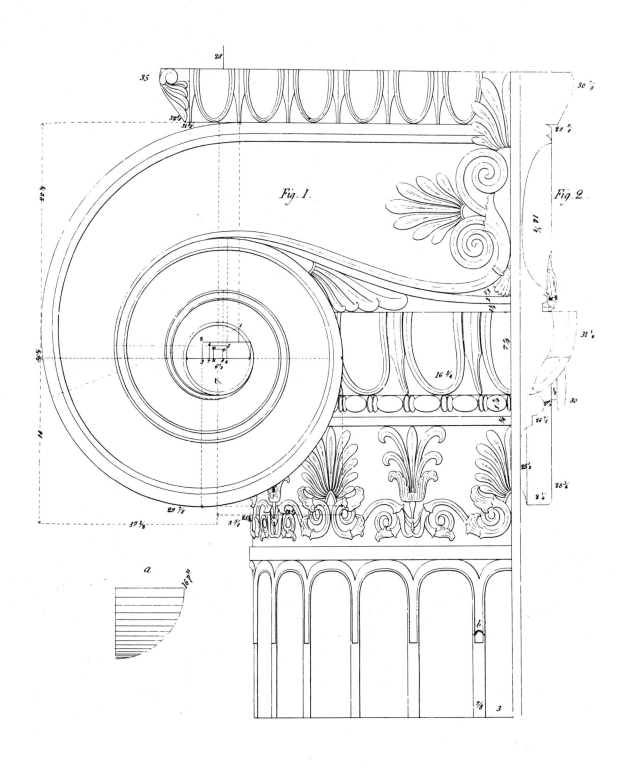

Fig. 1.

Fig. 2.

A detail of the Ionic order, by
Minard Lafever

10   20   30

Page 33: Swedenborgian Church—now Church of the New Jerusalem—in Bath, Maine (1843)

Opposite: The Jonas Cutting–Edward Kent House (1833), designed by Charles G. Bryant, is found in Bangor, Maine.

Left: The Wilcox-Cutts House in Orwell, Vermont, also known as Brookside, was originally built in the 1790s; Thomas Dake revised it in 1843.

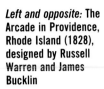

Left and opposite: The Arcade in Providence, Rhode Island (1828), designed by Russell Warren and James Bucklin

Page 40: House in Mystic, Connecticut (1833)

Page 41: Federal Hall (formerly the Subtreasury Building), in New York City (1842), is the work of the firm of Town and Davis.

Sailor's Snug Harbor,
Richmond (Staten
Island), New York
(1831), by Martin E.
Thompson

House in East
Randolph, New York
(c. 1840)

Opposite:
Philadelphia's
Merchants Exchange,
built in 1835 to designs
by William Strickland

Left: The Old
Courthouse in Dayton,
Ohio (1850), by Howard
Daniels

Opposite: Ohio State Capitol in Columbus (1839–61). Designers who contributed to the creation of this building included Henry Walter, Thomas Cole, Nathan B. Kelly, Isaiah Rogers, and the firm of Town and Davis.

Left: Kentucky State Capitol, Frankfort (1830), by Gideon Shryock

Two houses in Marshall, Michigan: The Fitch-Gorham-Brooks House (c. 1840) (*right*), and the 1842 Daniel Pratt House (*opposite*)

Opposite: Clifton Place (1839), Mount Pleasant, Tennessee

Left: Barton Academy, Mobile, Alabama (1835–37), designed by James Gallier and Charles and James H. Dakin

Opposite: Auburn in Natchez, Mississippi, created in 1812 by Levi Weeks; subsequently remodeled

Left: Edward Belo House, Winston-Salem, North Carolina (1848–58)

Page 54: Christ Episcopal Church in Mobile, Alabama (1836–37), by Charles and James H. Dakin

Page 55: Jefferson College—now the Manresa Retreat House—in Convent, Louisiana (1831)

Page 56: Temperance Temple at Bremo, Virginia, designed by Alexander Jackson Davis in 1849

PART ONE
THE POLITICAL ECONOMY
OF THE GREEK REVIVAL

THE WORLD
OF THE FOUNDERS

The political and economic record of the founding fathers after the founding is the essential backdrop to any discussion of their architecture. They were not, as has often been claimed, a band of consistently fortunate heroes, steeped in classical learning, presiding over an unbroken series of successes, building a government modeled upon Greece and Rome, who smugly had themselves sculpted in togas and housed in temples modeled on the Parthenon. Their speech *was* full of allusions to classical heroes, inviting the attribution of classically heroic qualities to themselves, but the rest of this picture is false.[†]

It is false—though if some professor of classics in the sky had arranged the time and place of a revolution to offer the greatest possible opportunity to display his wares, he could not have done better than to choose British North America in 1776. Never before or since have statesmen made such conspicuous and frequent display of their acquaintance with the ancients.

From the outset they used architectural metaphors to describe their political undertakings—and their countrymen appear to have found these figures of speech so compelling that they quickly converted them into figures drawn as cartoons. Federalists spoke of the need for "a firm and substantial roof . . . uniting the strength of the 13 rafters"; anti-Federalists replied that the national government was so rickety that "walls have fallen away." During the Constitutional Convention, the state legislatures were described as the "pillars" of the Congress, and newspapers referred to the Constitution as a "heaven-descended

† This is how this myth was presented by Major: "After the separation from England, America naturally turned more to the continent than heretofore and particularly to the ancient republics of Greece and Rome for inspiration in architecture as in government." (p. 17)
    Hamlin was only a little more wary: "The revolutions in France and America brought a quick rush of new life to . . . enthusiasm for the classic. The Roman citizen became the ideal of the perfect Republican, the Roman tribune the great leader, the Roman general the ideal of all generals. . . . Architects . . . followed the inspiration of Rome and Greece. . . . A new nation was being born, and Washington and Jefferson realized that the buildings that were to enshrine its activities must also be new. . . . For classicism was the 'modern' in that period." (*Greek Revival*, pp. 5–21)

DOME." Engravers composed woodcuts showing pillars rising as each state ratified "the GLORIOUS FABRIC," under "the beauteous dome . . . of the GREAT PALLADIUM." And, when the eleventh state, necessary to stabilize the structure, came into place, the classical references were completed with the motto "ACTUM EST." The "FEDERAL EDIFICE" was in place; toasts were drunk to "the grand Federal Temple"; and the carpenters and architects of Philadelphia turned out for a parade behind a "float" with thirteen Corinthian columns and a dome ten feet in diameter.[12]

The founders were classical gentlemen. Their verbal and visual metaphors were derived from the Roman and Grecian past, and of the two traditions, they had good reason to prefer the Greek. The American Revolution was a revolt against empire; imperial Britain had costumed itself in Roman architecture and argued in Roman rhetoric; the extinction of the Roman republic by Julius Caesar and his successors was a familiar cautionary tale. Then, as if to remind them in case they had forgotten, the new usurper, Napoleon, made use of a full panoply of metaphors to Rome to gratify his own regime: his Arch of Triumph echoed the façade of Keddleston Hall, the most Roman of the works of Robert Adam, echoing in turn the arches of Roman emperors. The columns inscribing Napoleon's victories repeated a phallic display the British had copied from the emperor Trajan. Bonaparte brought to ultimate degradation the benign possibilities of a French Revolution that to the founders had, at first, seemed to echo their own. He was the new Caesar. So, by the end of the 1790s, while many of the American founders were happy to speak of the Roman republic as an analog (though never as a prototype), it was to Athens that they were more likely to look for metaphorical and symbolic guidance.

Founding an independent American republic required, first, the defeat of an enemy superior in military technology, numbers, wealth, and experience in the organization of warfare. The leaders of that revolution then created a hardy new government, combining practical devices discovered in their own special history and a few lessons—largely negative—from the ancient past. These they learned in scholarly exertions unique among the founders of nations. Scholar-kings the world had known, but a scholarly and revolutionary oligarchy was unprecedented. On top of these achievements, the founders were remarkably alert to the psychological potency of architectural symbols: it is safe to assert that no large body of political persons since the time of Pericles has included so many with a passionate delight in the art of building.

It therefore seems strange that they made so little use of the Greek Revival, then fashionable in Europe from Moscow and Stockholm to the Pyrénées. This absence of a Greek Revival in the generation of the founding—it did not flourish until after most of the founders were dead—requires considerable explanation. It can tell us a good deal not only about the mindset of those founders, but also about their actual experience in the years after the founding.

The American Greek Revival, when it did arrive, coincided with individual "foundings," with the bringing of order to the first frontier regions conquered and settled by citizens of the United States. After the lapse of a generation from our political founding, an ambitious, truculent set of symbols finally came to suit the American mood. In part, this delay was occasioned by the lamentable political record of the founders after they had accomplished the task of founding. Such a record had not encouraged that sort of celebration.

The establishment of the American republic was a success; that statement requires no further amplification amid the bicentennial events of the late 1980s. But the luck of the founders did not hold; the confidence, credibility, and credit of the nation had dissipated by 1815. Their successors were more fortunate; their victories, celebrated in a Greek Revival, commenced with the defeat of the elite regiments of the British army before New Orleans in 1815 and progressed through a series of economic and diplomatic accomplishments in the following decades.

These were public triumphs, sufficient, perhaps, to produce public monuments like those that appeared in Copenhagen, St. Petersburg, Edinburgh, and along the Danube. But in America, unlike any other country, even Russia, there was a widespread individual commemoration of triumphs by private citizens. After 1825 the public mood and the private mood coincided and seized upon the Greek Revival, one of a number of competing styles of architecture available at the time, as the appropriate celebratorial architecture of the nation.

There are many reasons for this constellation of emotions around a single style in a period otherwise remarkable for its eclecticism—that is what this book is about. But they all fell within two broad themes, one private, one public. The energies of the people, on the frontier and in a rising economy, had led to innumerable victories over chaos and wilderness. And the collective anticipations of the Declaration of Independence were beginning to be redeemed. Perhaps, not long after its fiftieth anniversary, in 1826, a New Order of the Universe might be achieved.

America in 1800

"Nearly every foreign traveller who visited the United States during those years carried away an impression sober if not sad. A thousand miles of desolate and dreary forest, broken here and there by settlements; . . . no arts, a provincial literature, a cancerous disease of negro slavery, and differences of political theory fortified within geographical lines."[13]

Not all foreign travelers who came to inspect this scene were so charitable as to be either sobered or saddened. Some were delighted. The American revolutionaries had made large claims. Now their performance lent itself to scorn, and scorn could be profitable. Ambitious scriveners, seeking to curry favor with reactionary noblemen in Europe, advanced their careers by voyages to America to harvest derogatory anecdotes. Their ensuing verses and memoirs reassured the Old World that it was no worse than the New.

As the Virginia dynasty became painfully aware after 1800, humanitarians whose comforts were provided by black slaves could be easily lampooned. Thomas Moore, the Irish poet, called their regime "the piebald polity that reigns in free confusion o'er Columbia's plains . . . where bastard Freedom waves her fustian flag in mockery over slaves."[14]

Moore's view of the founders was shared by another poet, William Wordsworth, who wrote with "poignant scorn" of the "motley spectacle" of American post-heroic politics, denouncing it as "big passions strutting on a petty stage."[15]

In the 1760s Boston, New York, and Philadelphia had seemed like Moore's briefly radiant Dublin, but that urbane elegance had fled with the Tories. Moore was offended by the ensuing drabness, especially since it seemed to him compounded by affectation. The leaders of the new republic fell short of his standards oratorically and sartorially. To him, and to others with a refined sense of hierarchy, or even of propriety, all that was left was "one dull chaos, one infertile strife betwixt half-polished and half-barbarous life."[16] America had lost 100,000 of its most eminent men and women, emigrés more numerous, as a proportion of the population, than those forced out of France by its revolution.

The issue was one of authority—and with authority, class. This is a term uniquely discomfiting to Americans, who are prone to pretend that they do not know what it means, except when applied to distinguishing a bad from a worse vaudeville act. But this is a book about classical architecture; *class* and *classical* have a common root, together with *classification*. They all have to do with hierarchy. Buried in this etymology is an important clue to the reluctance of Americans to use classical devices until their jumbled social structure began to form its hierarchy anew.

Leaving aside for the moment any further distinctions between Greeks and Romans, we may note that the latter inadvertently bestowed upon us an etymological abundance when they chose to use a trumpet called a *classus* to call together their equivalent of a militia muster, a *classis*. Each of the orders of society assembled in rough divisions, or classifications, according to wealth. The first and wealthiest of these were the *classici*. Since very early in the literary life of Rome, it became conventional to distinguish things from each other in the manner of this "classification" of citizens—though without trumpets. Critics began ranking poets, and even vases, by calling the best "classics." In the Middle Ages, scholars who studied the very best precedents began to call each other "scholars of the classics." And so they do today.

Lafever's elevation of the Temple of Minerva, the Parthenon

Thus it has become a general practice to bundle together under the term *classical* such associated concepts as high quality and antiquity. More precisely, we denote as "classical antiquity" that period between the overrunning of the Minoan civilization in about 1200 B.C. by one set of northern tribes, the Dorians, and the overrunning of the western portion of the Roman Empire in about A.D. 450 by another set, the Vandals and the Goths. As a result, *classic* connotes gabled rectangular temples, surrounded by columns white from the bleaching of the sun.[†]

† A semantic wilderness lies outside these temple precincts, where paradoxes snarl at each other and all definitional footing is treacherous. There lurk the "unclassics"—Romanticism, Gothicism—the uncanonical, and the organic.

In early-nineteenth-century America, the term *classic* had additional implications: simplicity, austerity, and heroism. The founders narrowed their use of the term to describe the art of two episodes in the classical period. The first began in about 600 B.C. and ended with the advent of Alexander the Great. The second was the brief republican experiment in Rome, an admirable episode interrupting the progression from tribal kingship to international empire.

The reason for this foray into the etymology of words is to highlight the associations of *class* (meaning hierarchy), classical architecture, and *order*. I want to concentrate here primarily on the use of *order* among economists. Order and disorder are subjects of intense interest to those who strive to turn the incommensurable into numbers; they are consoled by placing fluctuations on graphs and measuring them.

By assigning a "beta coefficient" (a term drawn, appropriately, from the Greek) to disorder, it may be equated to unpredictability, and unpredictability thus to risk. In a way, risk and disorder and unpredictability can be tamed, retrospectively, by measurement. As an economist knows, and any eighteenth-century American familiar with Burkian theory knew, risk can be diminished prospectively by the maintenance of political hierarchy and continuity.

Economists have an important psychological lesson to teach architectural history; they know that when disorder and unpredictability are high, elevating the beta coefficient, then risk is seen to be high and evaluations of assets tend to be relatively low. Among those assets are self-esteem among those who think themselves responsible for leadership.

Eighteenth-century Americans talked and wrote constantly of order. It was very important to them; they worked diligently to achieve it in their domestic life. They hacked away at the random growth of forests and undergrowth and replaced randomness and wildness with walls and fences in rough rectangles; they had learned from the Native Americans how to tame, or domesticate, the growth of wild crops, including corn, squash, and beans; they introduced domesticated animals, once wild and random, and placed them in paddocks and yards, thereby adding more rectilinear precincts. They planted the trees in their orchards in rows, like columns, and finally they advanced so far toward classical architecture as to replace a sprawl of outbuildings with a graduated hierarchy of structures laid symmetrically in rows, as Palladio had taught them.

But in one area of their lives they had assaulted order and invited chaos: their politics were at variance with their domestic behavior. They had committed symbolic patricide. The king is the father of his people, and they had rebelled against their king. They mustered their arguments to assert that they had committed their ancient crime for good reasons, but they were close enough to medieval concepts of kingship to know that a crime it was. They did not pretend to take lightly to rebellion against their king.

They had committed the ultimate act of public disorder. And they knew from their Shakespeare and from their consciences that, though Englishmen had a long tradition of deposing and murdering kings, they were always remorseful about doing so, and generally left the task to the aristocracy. The French, by contrast, were amazingly deferential toward kings until 1789; when it came, French decapitation seemed especially shocking because it was not performed by gentlemen.

Reminded by the guillotine of 1793 of their own rebellious violence a decade earlier, the founders could not avoid recognizing that the beheading or the rejection of a king truncates a hierarchy and destroys order at its apex. It is likely that the founding fathers were, like King Henry IV in Shakespeare's play, uneasy in their own fatherhood. They were anxious about their own New Order of the Universe and diffident about proclaiming, in large, public forms, that it was fully achieved.

So four decades passed before there was a Greek Revival in the United States. The qualities it asserted had been torn from the fabric of life by the Revolutionary War and its unruly aftermath. At the end of the eighteenth century, those societies that built residences for the gentry in temple forms, thereby expressing without embarrassment a classical achievement, were those showing the most intense respect for hierarchy and the maintenance (or, as in Germany, the restoration) of order. This, the founding fathers had conspicuously failed to do. As members of a transatlantic community that knew precisely what classical forms implied, they abstained from vain pretense.

I have found no explicit, written confessions confirming the guilt I have attributed to the founders; I am arguing that *unconscious* diffidence made them reluctant to use temple forms. A few more paragraphs detailing their behavior and its consequences to order, continuity, and hierarchy may give some weight to the argument.

The Patricidal Fathers   Since any revolution against a king is a symbolic act of patricide, any action against the king's agents is a rending of order and hierarchy. In America especially, the king's party, otherwise known as the Tories, had been the principal custodians of each of the institutions representing order, predictability, and authority: the law, the church, the management of public business, the ownership of land, and sponsorship of the arts. This patriarchate was displaced by the patricidal founding fathers. Even in Virginia and New York, otherwise the great exceptions to many of these general observations, many of the most ancient and honored families stood with king and parliament. When they were forced aside, their places were taken by new men, not from the *classici*, the first tier in colonial society.

George Washington

Americans began disputing how revolutionary the Revolution actually was as soon as the last echoes of gunfire faded. The argument still sputters at scholarly conferences. It is fundamental to the hypothesis of this book that the Revolution was, in fact, revolutionary, that it was the nation's first defining trauma, with the Civil War its second. The term *patricide* may seem excessive for a revolution that never laid hands upon King George or his parliament, but the founders themselves were fully conscious of the shattering impact of their actions. Oedipus was familiar to them, thanks to Sophocles, though Freud was yet to come. When the British evacuated Boston, 1,100 refugees sailed away with them. "These eleven hundred, and the thousand or more who subsequently followed them, bore away perhaps a majority of the old aristocracy of

Massachusetts. . . . The loss of this important element, cultivated, experienced, and public spirited, was a very serious one. . . . In New York . . . in the height of the war . . . the bulk of the property-owners belonged to the Tory party."[17]

In the eighteenth century, the ownership of land conferred authority as no other possession, except, perhaps, a bishopric did. J. Franklin Jameson once observed that "multitudes of squires had been driven into exile or dethroned from their high position of dominance over the community," snapping lines of authority and terminating ancient habits of deference.[18] The Tories included the Penns of Pennsylvania, Sir John Wentworth of New Hampshire, William Byrd III and the sixth Lord Fairfax of Virginia. Among them would have been Sir William Pepperrell of Maine, who once could ride the thirty miles from Kittery Point to Saco without leaving his own land. But Pepperrell died, just in time to avoid the worst.

In New York the great landowners were divided by the Revolution. The Livingstons, Schuylers, and Van Rensselaers were with the winners and were well rewarded for being so. The Phillipses and Robinsons in Putnam and Westchester counties, and the only true rivals to the Livingstons in the colonial period—the extended family grouping of Johnsons, De Lanceys, and Warrens—saw their tens of thousands of acres transferred to new owners; one De Lancey estate was distributed to 275 people.

It is difficult for urbanized Americans of the twentieth century to imagine how close to decapitation it was for these agricultural communities when their squires were displaced and forced into exile. Eighteenth-century culture was intensely conscious of hierarchy and sensitive to its loss. Even if the winners gobbled up some of the lands of the losers, the loss was felt; a hundred years of deference, of kindnesses exchanged, of protection offered and solace provided, are not transferred so quickly by erasing the name on a title deed. And the Warrens, De Lanceys, Penns, and Johnsons had been good landlords.

(In New York, it is true, the old regime lasted longer than elsewhere, and the Revolution was not so much that as the successful rebellion of one set of squires and merchants against the English parliament, which was defended by another set. The Schuylers, Livingstons, and Van Rensselaers took the side of the rebels and were able to sustain the old order upon their holdings. Patricide was only partial, and the crypto-feudal regime of the Van Rensselaers was not disrupted until the 1820s.)

When authority based upon the land declines in significance, some other kind of authority is needed to take its place, and in some places, that authority is held by those who write and administer the laws. A society that drives out its lawyers—those who best understand the rules by which conflict is to be resolved and who hold the records of previous resolution of conflict—and, as revolutions often do, substitutes for them people less experienced, worse informed, and more erratic in judgment, is a society that has put itself at great risk. Citizens are likely to take the law into their own hands if they have little reason to defer to those into whose hands it has been given. John Adams reported that of the eight lawyers who had important practices before the Superior Court of Massachusetts in 1770, only he and James Otis were left after March 1776.[19]

Making laws is one thing; administering them is another. After the Revolution, many parts of the new nation could no longer count upon the services of those who had learned the ways a country can be governed, for many of them had been officers of the Crown; as such, their allegiance was to that Crown, and they were not available after 1783. Even the "patriot" Jeremy Belknap of New Hampshire remarked upon "the deficiency of persons qualified for the various departments in the government," regretting the loss of Tory experts, and his views were shared "by none more than by those few who know how public business ought to be conducted."[20]

The authority of government decreased as its competence decreased; Devereux Jarratt wrote in 1794 of the loss of that "due subordination . . . requisite in every government."[21] The franchise had been extended, as one conservative lamented, to "every biped of the forest." Many a man who was "only fit to patch a shoe" thought himself "fit to patch the State," and fancied himself "a Solon or Lycurgus."[22]

Theodore Roosevelt (in an unguarded moment) later called this moment the onset of "the millennium of the minnows." Fewer people doing the public business of each county and village knew how to do whatever the "bipeds" or "minnows" wanted done. After a decent interval, there was a reluctant turning to Tories or equivocators, such as Thomas Gibbons of Georgia, Wade Hampton of South Carolina, and William Constable and John Thurman of New York, to fill the void. But though they were competent, these were not always the most admirable or idealistic of the elite; there was much bitterness that the new order could do no better than to turn to them.[23]

When one father figure is rejected, all others are at risk. King George was rejected; General George stood in his place, and sedition coiled and reproduced itself in the shadows of the Revolutionary Army itself. As early as 1778, cabals of disgruntled officers attempted to replace Washington as commander-in-chief, first with Horatio Gates and then with Charles Lee. Lee began private negotiations with the British, anticipating the betrayal of the cause of independence by Benedict Arnold.

A Very Wintry Season   With the squirarchy of many of the colonies having been divided and many of its Loyalist wing driven off, the people of the coastal cities of Massachusetts, New York, New Jersey, and Pennsylvania observed their leading merchants and lawyers choose to go into exile rather than submit to

† One can lean too much upon the Anglican–Loyalist connection in the mountains. Even on the seaboard, an association of Cross and Crown reinforced the hostility of many country squires to the new government. "Sure I am, that no gentleman will choose to go to Heaven otherwise than by the way of the established church," said one Virginia gentleman (Jameson, p. 86), and the established church did not think highly of a regime led by such men as Thomas Jefferson, opposed to "establishment" on principle. Jefferson and others had good reason, therefore, to pursue even more relentlessly the termination of an "establishment" that had proven itself hostile to their designs.

†† In Maryland, where there had been 44 parishes with incumbent Anglican clergy, less than half that number could be found. In Virginia, there had been 95 parishes with 104 churches and chapels served by 91 Anglican clergy. Most of the churches were destroyed or injured beyond repair. Twenty-three parishes were extinct and 34 without clergy; only 28 clergymen were willing to remain in service. (See Jameson, p. 94) Rhys Isaac (p. 132) tells of two Virginia parishes during this "wintry season"; at Pope's Creek, near the ancestral home of the Washingtons, the old church was deliberately burned "in order to prevent injury, from the falling of the roof, to the cattle which were accustomed to shelter there." The morale of the other congregation was so low, and "so few were disposed to respond [to the responsive readings, that the minister] used to read only such parts as required no response, and not all of them. [Everywhere] broken down, neglected churches . . . [and] those pillaged for momentary gains . . . imprinted unmistakably on the landscape the collapse and abandonment of an ideal of society as a network of coercive but inclusive communities."

††† Presbyterian church buildings were treated as if they were centers of rebellion; fifty were destroyed across the thir-
(continued)

the new regime. The survivors of such a trauma might have turned to the churches for continuity and authority, but there were few sanctuaries and little solace to be found.

In colonial days, the Anglican church had been "established" in the South. Its priests were dependent upon the Crown's appointed bishops and archbishops for promotion and support. Until the middle of the eighteenth century, rural and frontier regions relied upon the clergy sent to them by the Society for the Propagation of the Faith. By 1779, the society had become fiercely partisan, serving as a corps of chaplains to the Loyalists. Though dissenting preachers had already begun to penetrate the mountains, persuade the unchurched, and convert the barely churched, and though Presbyterians, Baptists, Lutherans, and others had immigrated from Pennsylvania down the great valley of Virginia into the highlands, Anglican faith conjoined to loyalty to the Crown kept some frontiersmen hostile to independence until the very end of the war.†

After the war, returning Anglicans found their parishes dispersed or impoverished, and many of the clergy gone. In Richmond, with a population of three or four thousand, Presbyterian and Anglican services were held only on alternate Sundays, and—to the dismay of some—in a room in the "apostate" Jefferson's state capitol.††

Disestablishment also took place in New York, Maryland, and the southernmost colonies. William White was the only Anglican priest left in Pennsylvania; there were only five priests in New Jersey, four in Massachusetts, one in New Hampshire, and none in Rhode Island or Maine. The Methodists, relatively recent sprigs of Anglicanism, cut themselves off from the strict patriarchy established by John Wesley, and the Methodist Episcopal church was established in 1783.

The Presbyterians were the opposite case: their losses had been at the hands of the British and Tories. It was said that "if British soldiers discovered a large Bible and a metrical version of the psalms of David in any house, they took it as *prima facie* evidence that it was the home of a rebel."†††

Anglicans and Presbyterians, often antagonists in a bitter civil war lasting more than eight years, suffered most. The Methodists and Baptists were increasing in numbers, but all Christian denominations felt the demoralization of so long and so vicious a conflict. As it was said of the Baptists of New England at the time: "The war, though very propitious to the liberty of the Baptists, had an opposite effect upon the life of religion among them. . . . Certain it is, that they suffered a very wintry season. . . . The love of many waxed cold. Some of the watchmen fell, others stumbled, and many slumbered at their posts. Iniquity greatly abounded."[24]

Despite the onset of a swelling in Methodism, Baptism, and Presbyterianism that would become a boom in the Greek Revival period, Sidney Ahlstrom, the great historian of American religion, depicted the decades immediately after the Revolution as a time of "distraction, disruption and decline. . . . The churches reached a lower ebb of vitality during the two decades after the end of hostilities than at any other time in the country's religious history."[25] Church affiliation in America reached its nadir during this "critical period"—some estimate that no more than one in ten of its citizens was connected to a congregation in 1800. Some put the figure at one in twenty.

Dispirited Times and Spirituous Liquors   The wintry season lasted another two decades, an alcoholic's winter. The religious torpor of the American republic was sodden with whiskey and hard cider. Never, before or since, has so large a proportion of its men, women, and children gone to bed drunk. George Washington feared that addiction to alcohol would be "the ruin of half the workmen in this Country"; John Adams thought it "mortifying . . . that we . . . exceed all other . . . people . . . in this degrading, beastly vice."[†]

Because it wished to tax sales of distilled beverages, the United States began early to keep statistics on the matter that can be turned into graphs and charts. They corroborate the testimony of innumerable biographies: alcoholism was an American epidemic in the first decades of the nineteenth century, until the Second Great Awakening of religious fervor had fully permeated the life of the nation, and, I suggest, its self-confidence began to be restored. Temperance became America's first great crusade, anticipating abolition.

Thereafter, per capita consumption declined with astonishing rapidity, as a lagging response to recommitment to religious communities, to temperance, and to national pride. Temperance had immediate effects upon the landscape, as farmers cut down their apple trees, urged on by those who had seen hard cider intoxicate hundreds of thousands of country people from dawn to dusk.

As Thomas Jefferson's first term as president began, annual per capita consumption of alcohol exceeded five gallons, three times today's rate. Rum declined as the depressant of choice when the West Indies became less accessible and St. Domingue was devastated by civil war and French invasion, but hard cider and whiskey replaced it.

Whiskey was a portable and concentrated product of the first fields cleared on the frontier. So economical was fermented grain that it was used as currency in transactions remote from money centers.

teen colonies. The British sawed off the steeple of the church at Newtown, Long Island, and tore down the whole building at Babylon; in New Jersey, they burned churches at Elizabeth, Crumpound, and Mount Holly, and stripped the Kirk at Princeton of its woodwork and galleries for firewood. In the city of New York, Presbyterian churches were used for prisons or stables; Old South Church in Boston and a Dutch Reformed church in New York were used as riding schools. (See also Jameson, pp. 91–92)

† Thomas Jefferson observed it "spreading through the mass of our citizens" at a rate that led George Ticknor to fear that in "thirty years . . . we should be hardly better than a nation of sots." Since no records were kept by the colonial governments in comparable detail to those of the republic, W. J. Rorabaugh, the leading expert on this subject, has had to be content with the sense imparted by the founders themselves that things were getting worse in their time; he has supplemented these impressions with extrapolations of spotty records (largely for rum) and literary evidence, and concludes that, in general, their dismay was justified. (Rorabaugh, pp. 5–6)

It was also the means by which lonely people elevated themselves above the barest subsistence, amid their stumps and swamps and girdled trees. This they did by consuming large quantities of it themselves, to produce an artificial and temporary high (actually, of course, a depressant's low), and by selling it to others for a little cash, a few store-bought tools, or a bolt of calico.[†]

In the 1820s the American Temperance Society estimated that three million men drank sixty million gallons of liquor; one in eight Americans was a confirmed drunkard, and another eighth were occasional drunkards. By comparing the American experience to similar phenomena in Russia, Germany, England, and Sweden, W. J. Rorabaugh has developed the general thesis that agricultural surpluses, produced by surpluses of agricultural*ists*, precede the development of industry, in the presence, of course, of technology that can be used by abundant labor. Alcoholism accompanies that transition, as part of the same "economic crisis . . . brought about by the waning of traditional, agrarian society."[††]

But it was not, apparently, the industrial workers who were most conspicuously turning to whiskey. Life on the frontier was notoriously alcoholic. And on isolated, lonely plantations, amid a hostile work force of slaves, the julep was not a joke to many Southerners but a palliative; over time, it became a curse. One Florida planter wrote: "We have nothing . . . but whiskey." Lumberjacks, riverboatmen, canal builders, stage drivers, all the professions of rootless people on a frontier, became famous for alcoholism on the job and off, while the saloon became the sanctuary of the cowboy.[†††]

Individual anxiety has as many causes as there are individual biographies, but collective anxiety is an outcome one might expect among people who have observed the collapse of traditional authority and, soon thereafter, have attempted a sudden and very rapid change from rural to urban and industrial life.

Temperance and Confidence   In the 1820s and 1830s, anxiety of this sort diminished, as ruptured rural patterns of behavior and industrial growth no longer merely collapsed into disappointed hopes and offsetting industrial decline. Technological innovation now produced riches for some inventors, while westward expansion yielded crops whose prices were sustained by the demands of growing populations in industrial cities at home and abroad. People found support in temperance societies, in religious communities, in Bible societies and Sunday schools; they campaigned for abolition, prison reform, for national expansion—and a few even took women's rights seriously. "Young Americans . . . dismissed the older generation's views of equality and liberty as impractical abstractions," says Rorabaugh, "rejected the independent man's quest for those elusive ideals, and placed their confidence for attaining happiness in a combination of enterprise and evangelical religion. . . . Materialism was coupled with spirituality."[26]

[†] The Whiskey Rebellion of the middle 1790s was a protest against the taxation of all this. When the whiskey tax was repealed in 1802, many more acres of frontier land were used for whiskey production. Though Lancaster County, Pennsylvania, had no distilleries as late as 1786, there were 611 in 1814.

[††] In New England William Ellery Channing spoke of the new working class as exhibiting "a tendency to self-contempt and self-abandonment among those whose lot gives them no chance" of becoming either independent yeomen or capitalists. (Rorabaugh, pp. 88, 132)

[†††] Western movies and julep romances have glamorized this, but as Rorabaugh notes, "the primary reason people drink is to relieve anxiety; where there is heavy drinking there is significant underlying anxiety." (pp. 135, 146)

While they were making a mass commitment to temperance and to evangelical religion, some Americans built temples in which to worship and to live, expressing a new self-confidence in architecture. As the Greek Revival swept the nation in the 1820s and 1830s, indeed, within a decade after July 4, 1826, per capita alcohol consumption fell to the levels it has sustained ever since, about a third of what it had been at the peak; church membership multiplied by four to five times, as a percentage of the population (and, of course, vastly more in absolute numbers). The upsurge of religious commitment in the 1820s, especially among Presbyterians, Methodists, and Baptists, was explicitly associated with a decline in that propensity for slow suicide that is the identifying quality of the alcoholic. With renewed hopefulness for a dignified individual life and that collective pride that flows into patriotism came an architectural expression of both: the Greek Revival.[†]

† Any doubts as to the reinforcement given by temperance activity to classical ordering in architecture—and the passionate commitment by the revivalists to the recovery of order—fade when one reads the biographies of the Greek Revivalists themselves. Herman Camp of Trumansburg, New York, is one who comes to mind, but particularly in Camp's "burnt over" region and in the "firelands" of Ohio, the fire of religion was at war with that of spirituous liquor, and a columned, quiet architecture marked its private triumphs.

After 1825, temperance meetings and church congresses were often indistinguishable from patriotic assemblies. Reform, redemption, and reaffirmation were sung, a cappella, in thousands of enthusiastic voices. "On this day . . . did . . . a later generation . . . declare and maintain a SECOND INDEPENDENCE," proclaimed a Fourth of July orator, referring to independence from alcohol.[27] The Declaration of Independence was read at another meeting, with Prince Alcohol substituted for King George. Perhaps it was not sophisticated, but neither was the Greek Revival.

In 1800 all this was yet to come; to understand fully how it came, another survey is required of portions of the terrain already traversed, but from another point of view. At the end of that second sweep, certain conclusions, already apparent, become inescapable.

The Era of Halting Effort

Let us retreat a few decades to observe the forces seeking American independence. Having created an army before they created a government, these forces had to wait eight years until that army achieved victory. Five years more were required before a competent government emerged, as the first Confederacy was abandoned to make way for a federal Constitution. Even after George Washington transferred his prestige from military command to presidency, confidence in the capacity of the founding fathers to govern was slow to grow.

Public regard for the founding patricides, however impeccable their own behavior might have been, was diminished by the flagrant duplicity of those with whom they consorted. Benedict Arnold's late partners in traffic with the Tories, William Constable and William Duer, both adept in corruption, traded openly and notoriously with both sides. After they left Arnold in the mire, their offenses were indistinguishable from those of other commercial leaders of postrevolutionary New York; they were welcomed as major figures in its countinghouses.

Confidence in the New Order of the Universe proclaimed in Latin upon the Great Seal of the United States was diminished when Duer became Alexander Hamilton's deputy at the Department of the Treasury, and it diminished still more when he used his office flagrantly—and unsuccessfully—in schemes for private gain. Finally, despite his Old Etonian charm, he was dismissed and later jailed, but too late to keep Hamilton's own reputation unspattered.

The founders had attempted "a grandiose and dangerous experiment." For us, it is "difficult to appreciate their sense of the precariousness of what they were attempting,"[28] and the dismay with which some of them, and many of their successors, observed the collapse of their ideals into a squalid scuttling after riches.

From Georgia to Maine, a second revolution erupted. Unlike the first, it was quickly and effectively put down. The artisans' revolt in Charleston, the Whiskey Rebellion in Pennsylvania, and Shays's Rebellion in Massachusetts were only the most conspicuous of many outbreaks of violence in the cities and countryside, as people sometimes lumped together as "anti-Federalists" arose in impotent wrath against the disappointment of their revolutionary hopes. James Otis had warned in 1776 that "when the pot boils, the scum will rise." The "scum" did not share in any celebratory mood for the reaction, which some have called an American Thermidor, which they felt settling in all about them, but, as early as 1786,

Benjamin Rush was able to assure Richard Price that "the scum which was thrown upon the surface by the fermentation of the war is daily sinking."[29]

It was a bitterly divided country that went into the Constitutional Convention, and an even more bitterly divided one that wrangled over the document that emerged. The Constitution was opposed by many men of considerable standing, who saw in it a re-creation in Philadelphia of what they had rejected in London, men such as James Monroe, Patrick Henry, George Clinton, and Richard Henry Lee. Even they did not find among their peers in the revolutionary gentry, the patricidal fathers, adequate substitutes in virtue for the imperial statesmen from whom they had cut themselves adrift. Thomas Paine went so far as to ask of George Washington "whether you have abandoned good principles, or whether you ever had any."[30]

There was no consensus, no smooth progression from victory to victory. One revolution, which became a civil war, almost degenerated into another, and there was no general air of rejoicing of the sort that might lead a nation to elevate the precarious victors into heroes in togas. That could only come much later, when tempers had cooled and memories dimmed.

The question of slavery was at the core of these disputes. It was embedded in the new Constitution; some of the anti-Federalists opposed its acceptance on that ground. The scandal of slavery could not be hidden; it was a central subject of public discourse, and there was angry discussion of the subject in ratification debates of the 1780s and during the state constitutional debates of the 1820s. The South was riven by racial conflict and by disputes arising from a "system of labor" that was felt to be an abomination by many (perhaps, for a time, most) white Southerners. In this antebellum South, architecture undeniably evoking Greek and Roman precedents was never the popular *residential* form it was in the North. Instead, temple forms were reserved almost entirely for the official architecture of town halls and state capitols, bespeaking an order imposed from above. And, as is true of all such circumstances, whether in czarist Lithuania or Stalinist Leningrad or Albert Speer's Berlin, it could be seen as an importunate classicism, a frozen deference required of a people, not a celebration offered by them.

Slavery divided a community which was, at the same time, stretching itself to a breaking point. Two million people, already scattered across an immense area, now commenced a western migration spreading them farther still. A turbulent nation became less governable still.

Yankees abandoned bleak hills and flinty fields to settle the bottomlands of western New York and Ohio. As the Boston Chamber of Commerce complained: "There came over New England an era of halting effort, due to a loss of primal vigor to the West . . . a drain of New England energy and initiative. . . . The wholesale and continued transfusion of her best blood to the veins of the newer states could only mean the weakening of her own constitution. . . ."[31] The businessmen of Boston called this the "era of halting effort"; intellectuals such as Charles Francis Adams described the thirty years from 1790 to 1820 as "the ice-age—singularly barren and dark . . . this was the time when, as Emerson said, looking back . . . there was not a book, a speech, or a thought in the state."[32]

In fact there were speeches, angry speeches, in the farm areas left behind by the westering movement. The farmers who remained were little more tractable than the westerners; too old, too proud, or too poor to move, they remained to "delve among the snows and rocks and worn-out, sour old fields," resistant to taxation.[33] They were neither willing to liquidate the war debt nor to accept the returning Tories who claimed lands upon which some veterans had settled. Rebellions broke out in Massachusetts, Vermont, Pennsylvania, Rhode Island, and New York. Along the Mississippi frontier, in that region its enthusiasts called "the great west" and the Boston intellectuals derided as "the Poland of the United States," the ties of kinship to the original thirteen colonies became frayed.[34] Constant conspiracies tended toward secession. So feeble was the hold of the new government upon its nominal possessions across the Appalachians that British garrisons retained forts and trading bases deep into territory conceded in the treaties of 1783. For thirty years thereafter, British governors of Canada stirred up alliances of Native American tribes against the Americans.[35]

Thomas Jefferson

An inconclusive naval war with France at the end of the 1790s was followed by another, against the Muslim states of North Africa. American merchants discovered painfully how dependent they had been upon the protection of the British fleet during the colonial period. But the nation was not ruled by merchants. Especially after 1800, the Virginians who occupied the presidency steadfastly refused to pay the price required to protect American overseas commerce, or even to defend its coasts.

Mercantile necessities were not enough to overbalance old anxieties brought into the present by elderly statesmen. Fears of any strong central government, traditional among British subjects, and the recollection of the damage done by the British standing army in the 1770s led Jeffersonians to reduce American armed forces to a few ill-equipped militia brigades and a flotilla of gunboats. Britain was the only world power capable of invading and conquering the United States, so the central premise of Jeffersonian foreign policy became the avoidance of further tests of strength with Britain—at almost any cost. This was the sort of passivity to which the nineteenth-century British responded with tigerish delight. Out of such invitations elsewhere, they took an empire; they did not seek to reclaim the thirteen lost colonies, but they ground the Americans through a series of humiliations.

American seamen were kidnapped, American vessels boarded and searched. Jefferson justified his most supine concessions to the English, from 1800 to 1806, on the grounds that the people wanted peace. Writing of the period, Henry Adams was moved to observe that "many an American President who yearned no less passionately for the people's regard would have died an outcast rather than have trafficked in their dignity and his own self-respect in order to seek or save a personal popularity . . . the truth must be admitted that in 1808—for the first and probably the last time in history—a President of the United States begged for mercy from a British minister."[36]

We have difficulty imagining Jefferson as a supplicant; he was so towering a figure in American politics, so remarkable in his range of talent and interest, and so deeply admirable for his architectural achievements that it would be pleasant to assert that Adams was writing as an Adams first, a historian second, and therefore wrong. But the two presidential terms of the Sage of Monticello were not heroic. Nor were those of James Madison and James Monroe, who succeeded him.

The condition of Adams's own section, New England, in this period, as reported by the Boston Chamber of Commerce and by Charles Francis Adams, has already been noted. The son of Charles Francis, the saturnine Henry, gave this picture of Virginia in 1809:

> *Jefferson's reforms crippled and impoverished the gentry, but did little for the people, and for the slaves nothing. [The end of the slave trade in 1807 was ordained by the Constitution.] . . . [As for] the middle and lower classes of Virginians . . . their character was stereotyped, and development impossible . . . intellectual activity was confined to the hereditary commonplaces of politics. . . . Debarred from manufactures, possessing no shipping, and enjoying no domestic market, . . . the Virginians concentrated their thoughts almost exclusively upon politics [and agriculture].*[37]

In a nation that was becoming absorbed in private economic activity leading to the urban development of industry, those arcadian fascinations were becoming detrimental to the South, though Jefferson imposed his embargo to keep American vessels out of European waters and European goods out of American hands. Much of the burden of the embargo

> *fell on the Southern States, but most severely upon the great State of Virginia. Slowly decaying, but still half patriarchal, Virginia society could neither economize nor liquidate. . . . No episode in American history was more touching than the generous devotion with which Virginia clung to the embargo, and drained the poison which her own President held obstinately to her lips. . . . The embargo . . . shattered Jefferson's power, . . . emptied the Treasury, bankrupted the mercantile and agricultural class, and ground the poor beyond endurance. . . . Morally it sapped the nation's vital force, lowering its courage, paralyzing its energies, corrupting its principles, and arraying all the active elements of society in factious opposition or in secret paths of treason.*[38]

When Abraham Lincoln was born in 1809, the year in which Jefferson left office, the American economy was prostrate, and, as Adams observed, "American character stood in its lowest esteem."[39]

Not quite.

There is no need here to rehearse in detail the history of the administration of James Madison (1808–16), reaching the true nadir of the post-heroic age. Administratively incoherent, embarrassing in foreign policy, it was unprepared for war, and when the war with Britain did come, the American armed forces were in such a sorry condition that the president and his cabinet were forced to scuttle about the countryside while the smoke of their burning Capitol filled the horizon.

Jefferson became so dispirited that he could write of "the useless sacrifice of themselves by the generation of 1776, to acquire self-government and happiness to their country." Though he laid the blame upon "the unwise and unworthy passions of their sons," those sons did not see it quite that way. Few were so impolite as to attack their fathers directly; they merely rejected them in favor of "those men who did *not* go on to have national and controversial careers after the Revolution." As Michael Kammen has put it: "Men whom we now regard as figures of secondary importance were thought of as immortals during the first quarter of the nineteenth century; John Paul Jones . . . Francis Marion . . . Patrick Henry . . . James Otis and Richard Henry Lee . . . became the undisputed heroic luminaries."[40] "Only later," says Kammen, "did those whom we think of as being in the first rank outshine them and take their permanent places in the firmament of founders." In the interim, a giant figure occupied the stage, though he had been ignored by Washington and underrated by both John and John Quincy Adams. More than any other man, Andrew Jackson restored America's self-confidence. In the process, he carried back upward with him, into the firmament, those who had once been in "the first rank," but had "performed badly in their own controversial careers."[41]

Andrew Jackson was the most "controversial" of all those who had shed blood in the Revolution (he was only thirteen years old when he was wounded for the first time). The Cincinnatus of Tennessee, also known as "the Bonaparte of the forests," had a profound instinct for heroism. In 1815, he was a presence upon a distant horizon, gathering his forces for the defense not only of New Orleans, but also of America's pride.

A memorial tribute to
Washington

In 1797, on the occasion of his retirement from the presidency, George Washington, the Cincinnatus of Virginia, returned to Mount Vernon. After his death there was a flurry of monument building to him, but it was a remarkably halfhearted affair. The best of his monuments, until the marble shaft on the Mall in Washington, D.C., was completed nearly a century later, was George Washington Parke Custis's residential reliquary at Arlington House. But none of his co-heroes was memorialized in temples by their immediate posterity. Jefferson, for example, had to wait for his until 1943.

Why the delay? To find the answer, some myths must be brushed aside. These explanatory traditions turn out, upon examination, to be false to history.

During recent decades, after anthropology pounced with delight upon the concept of "cultural lag," historians have often written as if the founders were incapable of producing art in the latest fashion because Americans, in general, were laggard provincials. Yet the most cursory scouting of newspapers and library lists, to say nothing of buildings and gardens, is rewarded by ample proof that Philadelphia in 1780 was as well informed as Edinburgh and Charleston as sophisticated as Bristol. Transatlantic trade in goods and ideas was brisk in the eighteenth century. Americans were constantly traveling back and forth to Europe. Several American patrons of architecture maintained houses in London and Paris. In the 1770s the Izards were at Paestum, and in 1806 two sophisticated collectors, Nicholas Biddle and Joseph Allen Smith, were busily measuring the buildings of the Acropolis and wandering across the Peloponnese with Pausanius in hand. To judge by the lists made by revolutionary authorities in 1792, several hundred Americans were resident in Paris, and many more were living in London.

A sophisticated English traveler in 1797 found squires leading secluded lives in the woods of Virginia perfectly *au fait* as to literary, dramatic, and personal gossip of London and Paris. He was not speaking of globe-trotting cosmopolites such as John Quincy Adams, Thomas Jefferson, Benjamin Franklin, Gouverneur Morris, or John Jay. He was observing a phenomenon that would have seemed obvious in Philadelphia, Boston, or Charleston, and was worthy of note only in the backcountry.

As to architecture, the Renaissance style of the Restoration reached Boston before the 1680s were spent. The John Foster House preened its pilasters and smiled in classical pride just as early as similar houses in Dorset or Cornwall. (It was, it is true, not favored sufficiently to supply many progeny, and there was nothing templar about it.) And by the 1770s there was nothing laggard about high-style taste in Pennsylvania, Virginia, or the Carolinas until—and this is my point—the 1780s first marked a recidivism, which advanced only as far as laggard provincialism by 1820.

European talent, trained in the latest fashions, was certainly available to assist in construction in America. There were so many French architects in New York in the 1790s (Pierre Pharoux, Charles L'Enfant, the two Mangin brothers, Adrian Boucher, and Etienne Hallet among them) that Manhattan looked, for a while, like a newly rebuilt capital of a French *département*, not a state. After two of London's best—Benjamin Henry Latrobe and George Hadfield— arrived to augment the number of practicing architects during that decade, there was ample talent and ready money in New York and Philadelphia to create a Greek Revival if their citizens had been ready to construct one.

Robert Mills's Washington Monument, Baltimore

There must be other reasons why the heroic generation did not build in the then-fashionable Grecian style, why the transition from the red-brick Georgian colonial to the Grecian was delayed. In the United States, the Federal style, delicate and provincial, omitted the Doric grandeur that was to be seen in Europe at that time. (The symbolic intent of that grandeur was, of course, different in the Old World than it probably would have been then, or was, later, in the New.)

"Probably" is all that can be said, for it was absent—and its absence is not well explained by a second once-popular canard, which is a variation of the first. We still hear occasionally that America produced no Greek Revival during the incumbency of the classically conscious founding fathers because it could not afford it.

There is virtue in the assumption behind this assertion: that building in the very latest fashion requires a sudden rush of money, a set of nouveau riches avid for display, and an audience eagerly appreciative of extravagance. But in America, between 1790 and 1825, it was probably the presence, not the absence, of a series of booms, each producing a new crop of nouveau riches, and the sheer profligacy of expenditure during these booms, that militated against a classic revival of the sort then briefly flourishing in Europe.

Americans did not feel heroic.

Republican Simplicity   John Adams, Thomas Jefferson, and John Dickinson of Pennsylvania were all the authors of eloquent statements of the virtues of self-abnegation. Adams, on his farm in Braintree, was willing to include even bustling, cynical Boston in a dream of semirural, plain-living bliss, if its citizens were willing to live as if in "a Christian Sparta." The way was open for it to begin to look Grecian too, even if one had to turn from the unknown and, it is said, quite undistinguished architecture of frugal Sparta or abstemious, Catonian Rome. During the Revolution, a nonimportation meeting had congratulated Dickinson for his "Spartan, Roman . . . virtue."[42]

Robert Mills

The leaders of the revolt against parliament and luxury in the northern and central colonies wrote as if they regarded austerity as a revolutionary virtue to be carried over into peacetime. (Revolutionaries often assuage their guilt about symbolic patricide by assuring themselves that they will not enjoy its material benefits.) One of their weapons against the British parliament had been a refusal to consume; abstaining from tea and other luxuries marked a man as a patriot.

Congruent with, though not identical to, Puritan and Quaker aspirations to austerity in the North was Jefferson's ideal of a rural simplicity in the South. That simplicity, though his ideal, it is true, was supported by the greater austerity of life among slaves. It was a little late, in Virginia, for all citizens to be yeomen; plantations worked by slaves stretched over thousands of acres.

The disappointed, nagging ideal remained even after the war. Successful rebels no longer contended against British corruption imposed upon them, but sins of their own. A falling away into luxury was lamented by the surviving founders, who had much to lament. Their countrymen were scolded as "a Luxurious, Voluptuous, indolent, expensive people without Economy or Industry." They recalled the warnings of George Washington that "we have, probably, had too good an opinion of human nature in forming our confederation." John Adams (to whom the tone of Jeremiah was as natural as was that of Tacitus to Adams's great-grandson Henry) lamented: "Oh my country, how I mourn over thy follies and vices." Benjamin Rush wrote Adams in 1808 that the nation was becoming "bedollared." And Adams asked Jefferson: "Where are now . . . the perfection and perfectability of human nature? Where is the amelioration of society?"[43]

James Warren, of Plymouth, Massachusetts, coupled two observations: his countrymen were falling away from republican simplicity, and the postrevolutionary elite were a vulgar lot. He described imported fashions and luxuries pouring in, vitiating those "Ideas of Frugality which Necessity had before given." What was especially galling was the shameless display of "British Frippery" by the leaders of the new nation: "Are not our mushroom gentry . . . introducing every species of foreign luxuries, not only in dress, but at their tables?" Sam Adams, puritan to the last, spoke of the public as "bewildered, and stupefied by dissipation and extravagance." Like the Quakers and Puritans, he used the example of Rome to remind his lay countrymen of a republic degenerating into "dissipation . . . extravagance [and] effeminate refinements."[44]

(In the language of early republican economics and aesthetics, Doric architecture and "republican simplicity" were always attributed to a male gender. This is a matter of considerable importance to the rise and fall of the American Greek Revival, to which we will return.)

Though Sam Adams never received a visit from the grandest of the "mushroom gentry," William Bingham and his beautiful and fashionable wife Anne, the Binghams did call upon cousin Abigail Adams. They seemed to her . . . abandoned. They were rich and immensely enjoyed it. Abigail declared herself "stupefied" by Anne Bingham's "stile of dress . . . really an outrage upon all decency. . . . A satin petticoat of certainly not more than three breadths gored at the top, nothing beneath but a chemise . . . over this a thin coat, a muslin . . . made so straight before as perfectly to show the whole form. The arm naked almost to the shoulder. . . . To do justice to the other ladies . . . most of them wear their cloths too scant upon the body and too full upon the bosom . . . like nursing mothers."[45]

These were the ladies of Boston, no longer a Christian Sparta, now a boom town. The "great number of new and elegant buildings . . . strikes the eye with astonishment, and proves the rapid manner in which the people have been acquiring wealth."[†]

It was clear that the ideal was present, but, with increasing vehemence, so was republican prodigality.

Dispiriting Times   The shadow side of speculative cultures is an unwillingness to invest in projects that require tending over a long period. That unwillingness was—and is—a blight upon genuine inventiveness.

We have been schooled to think of America in the early nineteenth century as bursting with energy and innovation; it was, but its population was growing at such an enormous rate and spreading westward so

[†] (North, p. 47) And an old Whig reported dourly: "Our catalogue of merchants was swelled much beyond what it was entitled to be from the state of our population. . . . The most adventurous . . . spirit of that time has had a powerful effect in determining the spirit of the rising generation. . . . The brilliant prospects held out by commerce caused our citizens to neglect the mechanical and manufacturing branches of industry; fallacious views, founded upon temporary circumstances, carried us from those pursuits. . . . Temporary benefits were mistaken for permanent advantages; so certain were the profits on the foreign voyage that commerce was only considered as an art; all the knowledge that former experience had considered as essentially necessary, was now unattended to; the philosophy of commerce . . . was totally neglected. . . . The most adventurous became the most wealthy, and that without the knowledge of any of the principles which govern commerce under ordinary circumstances. . . . The less experienced considered the newly acquired advantages as matters of right, . . . they did not contemplate a period of general peace." (Ibid., pp. 47–48)

rapidly that prosperity did not work its way into per capita income as rapidly or as steadily as was true after 1830. There were endless delays in consummating the benefits of innovation, as mechanics of genius found to their dismay. Oliver Evans developed the high-pressure steam engine in 1802 and was ready to build steam locomotives (really trucks for roads) in 1804, but like John Fitch's and James Rumsey's steamboats, they could not be financed.[†]

† Evans "was not rich, and he failed to interest merchant capitalists" (North, p. 32). He developed a semiautomated grain mill, which likewise failed to find support. Had his innovations in metalworking—or those of Nathan Sellers—found adequate capital, steam locomotives might have appeared twenty years earlier. Rumsey died before he got money together even to construct a working prototype, and Fitch's steam-powered passenger boats were commercial failures. Philip Schuyler had imported a Newcomen steam engine as far back as 1757, but it languished, undeveloped, in the presence of plenteous water power and cheap wood for fuel. The Arkwright water-powered frame for spinning thread was developed in England at around the same time; it was finally brought to the United States twenty years later, but it, too, failed to attract capital.

This was an economy more conducive to real estate speculation than to industrial growth. This is not to say that there was none of the latter but, rather, that there might have been considerably more if Americans had not been so long conditioned to quick gratification. Booms threw up mushroom gentry and upstart merchants, but soon all came crashing down again. Amid the wreckage, whatever was left standing was just where it had been before. Ordinary folk were suffering, however; some very sorely. Fishermen of New England and indigo growers of the Georgia and Carolina coasts never recovered the West Indies markets once assured them by British imperial preference.

During the Confederation period (1783–87), more Americans than at any other time in our national history sought employment in foreign trade. Coastal towns were becoming crowded. But exports were no greater than they had been two decades earlier.

Since the population rose by at least half again, per capita exports fell by 59 percent and coastal living standards declined precipitately. Across the board, losses arising from "adjustments to independence . . . surely outnumbered gains."[46]

The smuggling boom, largely sterile economically, even when euphemized as "re-export," swelled in volume from zero in 1790 to $45 million in 1800. After 1793, Britain and France were at war; goods that would have been contraband in ships of French or British registry sailed upon American bottoms to Europe. It thereby nurtured a new crop of mushroom gentry in the 1790s, who were especially conspicuous amid the declining living standards of their fellow citizens. These were not conditions conducive to Spartan habits, settled communities, or even capital investment; riches seemed to be the flowers of evil, growing out of the troubles of others. This impression was reinforced when the flowers wilted in peacetime: when Britain and France did arrange a truce in 1802, "re-export" fell to a third of its volume.

After Europe went back to war in 1804, "re-export" flourished briefly again, until all trade with Europe was forbidden by the policies of Thomas

Jefferson. Many New England ports never recovered from the effects of his Embargo Act of 1807. With the purchase of European luxuries denied them, supporters of the embargo cried: "Let us unanimously lay aside foreign superfluities. . . . SAVE YOUR MONEY AND YOU WILL SAVE YOUR COUNTRY. . . . Homespun clothes are all the armor, spades and ploughshares, all the weapons we need in this holy war."[47]

But once again frugality was a failure—Americans refused Sparta as they had refused Arcadia. Instead, they abandoned themselves to fancy goods of all sorts, including luxuries smuggled in from Britain. Henry Adams had this to say of a foreign policy that sought to punish the British by refusing to exchange goods with them: "The American tended already to become narrow in his views and timid in his methods. The great issues of 1776 and 1787 had dwindled into disputes whether robbery and violence should be punished by refusing to buy millinery and hardware from the robbers."[48]

Self-denial did not persuade the British; the War of 1812 became necessary instead. Thereafter, Americans reverted to conspicuous consumption. Their abandon was not, however, shameless; they did and do indulge in the rueful and continuous comparison of their actual behavior to the frugal ideals of the fathers. Each generation felt itself less simple than the previous one, each more heedless, each less noble. And among the classically educated, Americans got the worst of comparisons to the Roman republicans of whom later Romans had written in elegant self-reproach, as repentant, almost, as the Americans.

"Re-export" had been legal in American jurisprudence; "nonintercourse," as Henry Adams observed, merely "sanctioned smuggling, and was intended for no other purpose. [Secretary of the Treasury Albert] Gallatin in his disgust flung open the doors to illicit commerce."[49]

Legitimate shipping activity fell from an index point of more than 120 in 1806 to 65 in 1809. One historian reported that "newspapers were full of insolvent-debtor notices. . . . At New York during 1809, thirteen hundred men were imprisoned for no other crime than being ruined by the embargo . . . it looked like a town ravaged by pestilence."[50]

The prosperity of a nation in which many people are living by subsistence agriculture cannot be judged by its exports. In fact, it is very difficult to support general statements about living standards by useful statistics in such a society. But many Americans did make their living in shipping, and Henry Adams, always ready to describe with verve any Jeffersonian disaster, recounted the results of cutting it off:

> *Every artisan dropped his tools, every merchant*
> *closed his doors, every ship was dismantled. Ameri-*

can produce—wheat, timber, cotton, tobacco, rice—
dropped in value or became unsalable; every imported
article rose in price; wages stopped; swarms of debtors
became bankrupt. . . . A reign of idleness began; and
the men who were not already ruined felt their ruin
was only a matter of time. . . . The embargo opened
the sluice-gates of social corruption. At every point
along the coast and frontier [the military and cus-
toms services were exposed to the benefits of bribery];
while every man in private life was placed under
strong motives to corrupt. Every article produced or
consumed in the country became an object of specula-
tion; every form of industry became a form of
gambling.[51]

The nation's leaders, ruining honest merchants and tolerating corruption, could no longer be trusted, nor could the mushroom gentry. Commercial life became characterized by a ready avoidance of obligations. From 1795 to 1825, bankruptcy was as frequent as "junk bond" financing in the 1980s. Merchants, plungers, and share-jobbers (sellers of equity securities) compiled a sorry record; while some survived personally, their abated ventures destroyed the savings of those who had invested in them. Reminiscing, New York businessman Nathaniel Griswold said that only seven of a hundred men he knew in this period had completely avoided failure.

Some economic historians of our own time take a hard-boiled view of all this, arguing that "failure was largely a matter of shifting accounts, [so] continuous new starts set a trend of innovation in the economy, [and] . . . more than compensated for any stalling due to temporary misallocation of money that resulted from insolvency." They further contend that "the fact that nearly half of [the banks] . . . that opened between 1810 and 1820 had failed by 1825 was not as serious as it may sound. The physical improvements remained, and only a group of entrepreneurs and stockholders lost money . . . ," and that "many of those [factories] organized in the previous decade failed. . . . Yet there was a considerable increase in the number of men with manufacturing experience."[52] But what does this "shifting of accounts" do to habits of deference, to mutual respect, to self-esteem? Perhaps only those whose impressions of economic life were formed during a depression, amid the debris of bankruptcy, bank failure, and "out of business" signs, can sense what it was like to live in America in its wintry season.

In such times, architects, whose business it is to create very large faces, are not often asked for images noble, heroic, or even cheerful. As Latrobe noted at the time, in a letter to Dolley Madison, there was little work for him amid "a general feeling of frustration, national dishonor, and dissatisfaction."[53]

Disappointment deepened in the continuing presence of the Revolution's heroes, who became inescapably besmirched by that disappointment. Jefferson's abortive efforts to revive austerity, Madison's incompetent economic policy, and Monroe's indifference to corruption and to the mechanics of government deepened the nation's self-disdain into self-disgust.

The consequences of that self-disgust had been, predictably, alcoholism and dishonesty. During this period the republic had little reason to be proud of itself. Robert Remini has recently surveyed the moral tone of its public life and concluded that "sufficient evidence exists, both public and private, to prove that . . . the years 1816–1828 . . . generally known as the Era of Good Feelings . . . instead . . . deserve to be called the nation's first Era of Corruption."[54]

The Architecture of Unrepentance

Until they had nearly fifty years of independence behind them, Americans did not become thoroughly inured to their unheroic nature. Only then did they abandon, finally, all pretense of being simple, austere republicans. Only then did they reconcile themselves to living as opulently as they were able, without rueful reference to their shortcomings, conscious of the private victories over nature—and over their worst selves.[†]

Until the middle 1820s, aged heroes still teetered about, chiding and remonstrating, themselves a remonstrance. When they were gone, Americans became comfortable with themselves and were free to embark upon a Greek Revival. The "classic," in America, had until then still carried some inhibiting association with republican simplicity and with austerity.

Arlington House, the nation's first temple-form residence, was the temple of this cult of republican simplicity. George Washington Parke Custis began its construction in 1803 or 1804, to plans by George Hadfield. Custis made it clear from the start that he intended it to serve as the first Washington monument. It was to be the shrine of the elusive dream of a chaste republican order, which conveyed

Benjamin Henry Latrobe sketch of Washington

qualities attributed to Hadfield himself: "a lofty, unbending spirit of independence, . . . the simplicity of republican institutions."[55] Its stark, Doric grandeur was intended to remind his countrymen of the example of the General-President-Father, whose special accompanying adjective was "austere."

Washington, a man of great theatrical talent, had two favorite roles. The first was Cincinnatus. The second was Cato, not the Cato of Rome, but the hero of Joseph Addison's play of the same name, in which austerity was treated as a synonym of probity. Washington was not alone in taking Cato as mentor. *Austerity* became a political catchword, though only infrequently and partially a policy.

Until the 1830s and 1840s, amid striving and jostling and getting ahead, amid the guzzling and gluttony and chink of precious metals, it was an embarrassment to be forced to think of Catonian virtue. Even more embarrassing had been the faint sound of an even more ancient recollection, a panpipe, the shy anthem of Arcadia, faint but noble, calling the people out of their feeding frenzies of acquisition. Its notes could still induce remorse if not repentance.

But by 1830 the withered laurels of the founders lay upon their tombs. The prayer at the grave sides of Jefferson and John Adams in 1826 might have commenced: "We, thine unworthy children," as the mourners recalled, for a moment, the days of heroic self-abnegation. But soon enough the bowed heads rose, and the crowd dispersed at a quickening pace. Into their saddles they sprang, spurring their mounts, and plunged post-heroically ahead. Even those lagging at the cenotaph might hear a sermon like that of a Fourth of July orator: "The dead cannot save the living. They . . . received their reward. We and our successors have also a part to act, . . . [we must no longer] grope among the dry bones of the past."[56]

Still, these were Americans, and paradoxical. Though the Greek Revival seemed to strut and swagger in unabashed capitalist pride, it was always shadowed by a sense of having forsaken a simpler and nobler world. Sparta and Arcadia were never completely out of mind, even at Belle Grove, Phil-Ellena, and Belmont [318, 319].

The Age of
Jackson and Biddle

In September 1814 the British were reconsidering their campaign against Baltimore. Having so low an opinion of the Americans as to be surprised by any show of firmness or military competence, they were annoyed that their probes of the city's defenses met serious resistance. There was, during the pause, an exchange of prisoners. One of the American commissioners seeking to arrange such a transaction was a lawyer from Georgetown named Francis Scott Key. He went aboard a British warship to secure the release of a harmless old physician who had been captured while trying to prevent the marauding of some British stragglers.

Key was waiting for those negotiations to be completed when the British concluded that they had chastened the Americans enough. They had burned their capital city and sent their president, James Madison, into the underbrush. Up went the sails of His Majesty's warships, and they set out for the open ocean, leaving the young negotiator free to set in verse this picture: through the mist and rain squalls, at six o'clock on the morning of September 4, Key had seen through his telescope, above the battlement of Fort McHenry, a flag presciently ordered to be outsized by its commander. Baltimore was safe, and Key began the composition of the verses of the "Star-Spangled Banner" that gave him immortality when set to the tune of an old English drinking song.

(History loves irony. Key, though a patriot, was a Federalist, with a low opinion of Madison and "Mr. Madison's War"; he regarded both as "abominable." And, incidentally, Fort McHenry had been named after the secretary of war fired by an earlier president, John Adams, for incompetence and personal disloyalty.)

At almost the same time, a small American victory near Plattsburgh, New York, provided some respite from the long season of humiliations, but neither the British withdrawal from the Chesapeake nor a skirmish on Lake Champlain assuaged the disgrace at Washington. It was not until Andrew Jackson led a polyglot force of French professional soldiers, city sportsmen, poets, architects, Kentucky riflemen, pirates, and economists to victory in the suburbs of New Orleans that the long depression began to lift. Said one observer: "we can hide our shame . . . in the smoke of Jackson's victory."[57]

Rising Glory of the American Republic!

So sang the headlines. In the House of Representatives, the theme of redemption was taken up by Ingersoll of Pennsylvania: "The victory at New Orleans has rendered...glorious and honorable" a generally inglorious war. Even Jackson's lifetime antagonist, Henry Clay, commented from Paris, "Now I can go to England without mortification."[58]

An old Indian fighter, land speculator, and slave trader whose previous appearances in Washington, as a congressman and senator from Tennessee, had been unprepossessing, now took the national stage as a redeemer, promising to purge the people of "shame and frustration," and to restore their "sense of national prowess and destiny."[59] He scarcely missed an opportunity to accept the projections of a nation desperate for a hero, and a classic one at that. Sometimes he was Spartan—Leonides—sometimes Roman—Cato or Cincinnatus—but always he was virile, in a Doric, fatherly way.

Unless selected for camouflage, these were strange heroes for an ambitious frontier politician. Fortunately, Jackson's constituents included few who knew much about Lucius Quinctius Cincinnatus, according to legend a crabby snob who steadfastly refused to brook the inclusion of the plebeian-born among the voting gentry. Cincinnatus did live in poverty though bringing spoils to the state; he did return to his farm twice after being called to be dictator of Rome and leading it to victories.

Marcus Porcius Cato (234–149 B.C.), soldier and writer of maxims, histories, and a treatise on agriculture, was most famous as censor of the Roman republic. In this role he ejected from their status as knights or senators those who were excessively luxurious or who had lost their money. He was, himself, cruel in warfare, nasty to his family (especially the women), and, says the venerable *Encyclopaedia Britannica*: "continued to distinguish himself as the persistent opponent of the new ideas. . . . He had a horror of physicians. . . . It was not until his eightieth year that he made his first acquaintance with Greek literature."

Certain qualities carefully selected from admiring accounts of these two Romans were stressed and restressed in Jackson's own utterances and in those of his closest followers.[†]

Representative Troup of Georgia responded to the news from New Orleans by telling the House that Jackson was "a fit subject" for either Greek or Roman analogy, "for the genius of Homer," or for recollections of Cincinnatus, "fresh from his plow."[60]

† In another age they might have been called his "handlers," and in another *case* than Jackson's one might speak of them as his "managers." But whatever else he may have been, Andrew Jackson was never a man to be managed by anyone else, not by John Quincy Adams, nor by James Monroe, though both made the attempt.

It had been a long time since the general from Tennessee had actually touched a plow—his slaves did that sort of thing—but the Cincinnatus image had splendid dramatic possibilities. Consider what Booth or Forrest might have done: a quick costume change, and the star could be back on stage to play the last military politician of whom Americans were justly proud, George Washington. Then, recalling Washington in full tableau amid the officers of the Order of the Cincinnati, it would require only a minor adjustment of the lights to convey the audience all the way back to 458 B.C., to the original role player, the reluctant hero Cincinnatus.

Symbol for an Age As one of Jackson's eulogists put it at the time, he "was the embodiment of the true spirit of the nation. . . . He put himself at the head of the great movement of the age. . . . Because his countrymen saw their image and spirit in Andrew Jackson they bestowed their honor and admiration upon him."[61]

What was that spirit, that "great movement"? Michael Kammen tells us that "most interesting about the 1820s, perhaps, is the fact that many Americans became engaged . . . upon a quest for political order, social stability, and national identity."[62]

Jackson personalized, in his own career, both the process of striving and the monumental, indeed lapidary, benefits of success. He was at once in constant motion, assaulting the edges of the possible and, somehow, longing for repose in his colonnaded mansion in the Roman mode. The Hermitage [112–13] was not built all at once. It grew along with Jackson's fortune; trees went down and columns went up, but once up, it looked to Amos Kendall, one of Jackson's cabinet, "perennial, perpetual."[63] That was Jackson's paradoxical charm; he belonged at once to the backwoods and to the ages.

Andrew Jackson Jackson was timeless, but in some ways the past was his province. Despite his rhetoric and his reputation, he was very conservative, perhaps one might even say retrogressive, in his politics. In his western political career, he had been attorney and friend to an elite of speculators and bankers. As his circle of supporters widened, it drew in the cotton nabobs of Tennessee and the fur magnates of St. Louis. Although he waged war against Nicholas Biddle's Bank of the United States, he did not in fact hate all banks or bankers; two members of his own cabinet had been bank directors. One of them was Martin Van Buren, his self-appointed successor.

Intellectuals are often thought to be prone to radicalism, but the most famous of the writers who came to power with Jackson were even more conservative than he. Chief among them were James Fenimore Cooper, Washington Irving, and James Kirke Paulding. Cooper, early on, had applied to George Washington the adjective *Doric*, to elevate to the heroic the first president's republican simplicity. Now he presented this package of associations to Jackson. The literary squire of Cooperstown said of the master of the Hermitage that he possessed "the virile qualities of decision, courage, and patriotism, joined to simple courtesy and stout independence . . . the stronger image of the Doric model."[64]

As we shall see, George Washington Parke Custis had already transferred to Jackson the symbolic potency of the Doric portico of Arlington House, previously dedicated to Washington. Cooper was merely confirming the transaction in writing.

Rehearsal for the Second Washington: Lafayette's Return In the 1820s America was charged with a powerful field of yearning energy for a Senex—a leader virile, wise, elderly, but potent. Elderly men can be very attractive in politics; but seldom do their ascendancies coincide with periods of expansiveness and growing confidence. So it was in the period in which the people of the United States turned to Andrew Jackson (born 1767, elected 1828), and to William Henry Harrison (born 1773, elected 1840), who was a sort of Whig parody of Jackson. It seems reasonable to suppose that there was an eagerness abroad in the land to find a place to ground deep feelings for founding fathers. Old Hickory was in fact only a little older than all but one of his predecessors had been at inauguration—he was sixty-two, and John Adams had been sixty-two as well—but he *seemed* old, and was so depicted after his scarred and emaciated frame carried him past fifty.

If Andrew Jackson had any doubt about the electricity in the air, he had only to observe the lightning surrounding the 1824 return of the marquis de Lafayette (born 1757). Sustained by a patriotic rapture lasting thirteen months, Lafayette made a slow triumphant tour as "the nation's guest," visiting every state in the Union and collecting a large cash grant from Congress (plus a township of speculative land). Each step of his progress was reported; he was the despair of other public figures seeking notice.

Except, perhaps, Jackson, who benefited from Lafayette's testing of the themes developed thereafter in his own living myth. That myth became for Jackson the most successful political device created for any American statesman, far transcending the bully-boy image contrived by Theodore Roosevelt and his pamphleteers.

† (Theme of ingratitude, Somkin, pp. 137, 138, 142) The first orator to address Lafayette, as he stepped ashore on Manhattan, repeated the denial, though no one had yet made the charge. At Lafayette's next stop up the Hudson, in Athens, a town once known as Esperanza, the refrain was the same. So too was the motto on his triumphal arch in Albany, endlessly repeated thereafter.

†† In a sense, he was more than a catalyst, he was a conduit. For he was the first "second Washington"; many were not yet ready to elevate Jackson to that heroic status. After President Horace Holley, of Transylvania University in Kentucky, said to Lafayette: "We identify you, as we do WASHINGTON, with the cause, the sentiments," it was then easy for others to make the "identification of Lafayette . . . with the most potent father image in American history." (Somkin, pp. 148–49) Lafayette rejoiced in the appellation and picked it up in his speech in Camden, South Carolina, where he proclaimed himself to be "Washington's adopted son." Custis, who actually *was* that adopted son, did not seem to mind; he stepped aside as the people of Charleston welcomed Lafayette with a placard calling "WASHINGTON, our Common Father— *you* his favorite *son.*" The Grand Master of New Jersey's Washington Lodge of the Masons made it official, presenting to Lafayette a gold medal inscribed: "LAFAYETTE . . . a second Washington." (The process of Lafayette's adopting Washington is detailed in the works of Louis Gottschalk, cited ibid., pp. 149–50.) *Niles' Register* was generally known for its acrid tone, but in Lafayette's case all was solemn deference: "To us he is like a venerated father, returned from the grave, to bless and receive the blessings of a mightily increased and joyous posterity." Other venerated fathers may have overstayed their leave-taking, but Lafayette did not— quite—make that mistake. After thirteen months as guest, he departed, described by the *Virginia Herald* as "our father, the good Lafayette." (Ibid., pp. 153, 156)

The mood was elegiac:

> *Of the great actors on our stage,*
> *Of warrior, patriot, statesman, sage,*
> *How few remain, how few remain!*[65]

These were people aching to adopt a new father, yet not quite willing to admit they wished to reject the old. The theme of ingratitude was first denied, then proclaimed by exhortation, and finally engraved upon the public consciousness by classical analogy. Schoolbooks warned anxiously: "Let it never be said of us, as of Rome and Athens, that ingratitude is the common vice of republics." What was troubling the sons of the fathers? Was it, as the editor of *N.Y. Literary Gazette* was so cruel to admit, that "heartless neglect which the nation has exhibited to its early protectors and benefactors"?[†]

When they were not apologizing for classical sins not yet—quite—committed, Americans in the 1820s were reasserting classical virtues they projected onto Lafayette: as a result, "the dominant motif of the Lafayette celebrations was heavily Roman." Lafayette was the catalyst for the transfer of Cincinnatus-Washington to Cincinnatus-Jackson; true to the ethics of catalysis, he obligingly withdrew after the chemical reaction was complete.[††]

In a final ceremony at Mount Vernon, the classical synthesis was nearly completed: Cincinnatus, Lafayette, and George Washington were brought together. In his bold, chocolate-brown baritone, George Washington Parke Custis told the audience that Lafayette's national tour was of "the splendor of a triumph greater than Roman consul ever had."[66]

It was only necessary for Custis to anoint Andrew Jackson as Washington's successor and for Jackson to connect Athens, at Arlington, to Rome, at Mount Vernon. To the Doric virtues were added the *gravitas* of Rome.

The second coming was followed by a second going. One of the most popular cartoons of the period had depicted Washington disappearing into the heavens swathed in a rainbow. Lafayette's departure from America was a cartoon of a cartoon. After a final visit to Mount Vernon, "the sun burst forth . . . and formed a magnificent arch, reaching from shore to shore, the barque which bears the venerable chief being immediately in the centre."[67]

The visit presented Jackson's rival, John Quincy Adams, with a problem. His career was inextricably intertwined with those of the failed fathers; as Levi Woodbury wrote Van Buren, their opponents included almost all the old leaders of both parties. The key word was *old*. The "professor" could not be taken by anyone as Cincinnatus or a second Washington, but Adams had no wish to be consigned to the geriatric ward. Even he had spoken of "indolence" and of "palsied . . . will." Now the wind was rising: "The spirit of improvement is abroad upon the earth. It stimulates the heart and sharpens the faculties."[68]

A memorial tribute to the Marquis de Lafayette

The Roman Façade   At the Hermitage, Cincinnatus-Jackson began writing of himself as "a plain cultivator of the soil," though he had recently completed laying in $1,500 worth of fine cut glass and lining his walls with French hand-printed wallpaper. Democratic meetings in Philadelphia and Cincinnati affirmed the Cincinnatus-Washington-Jackson theme; Robert Rantoul, one of the party's most effective propagandists, told the people of Massachusetts that Jackson "has more of the Roman in him than any other man now living," comparable only to Washington.[69]

Rantoul mentioned Thomas Jefferson as well, but only in passing. The direction of Jacksonian propaganda was retrospective, but it did not pause long in honoring the surviving founders; there was no glory to be borrowed from them. (Washington was an exception, having removed himself from the embarrassing foreground in 1799.)

This progression backward, toward an acceptably heroic past, can also be observed in Jackson's architectural associations. The façade of the Hermitage had always been a part of his rhetoric; in his final, Cincinnatian phase his constructed persona became explicitly Roman. He had arrived there in stages.

First, he had been content with the assemblage of frontier cabins he inhabited while establishing himself in a headquarters complex south of Nashville. When he and Rachel, his wife, were in Natchez after their marriage, they observed, but apparently rejected as beyond their current aspirations, the "high-style" classical buildings that were beginning to appear in such fashionable places, especially those of the first classically trained architect in Natchez, Levi Weeks, of New York's Brethren of the Workshop of Vitruvius.

Weeks was a Burrite. So were his chief clients. So had been Andrew Jackson. But after the failure of Burr's "conspiracy," his man Weeks had few attractions to the Jacksons. Besides, his use of "the orders," meaning grand-scale porticos, was expensive; moreover, Weeks was too free with remarks about Virginians and Carolinians. Jackson was one of the latter and wished to be considered fit to associate with the former. The Jacksons eschewed Weeks and "the orders" and built a brick house of a type common on the seaboard in the 1770s.

But classical images even more elegant than those contrived in Natchez might have been lingering in Andrew Jackson's memory, images of a grandeur that had eluded him in his first effort to attain the culture of cities. Long before he met Rachel, he had squandered an inheritance from his grandfather in Charleston, South Carolina, among the cockfighting, horse-racing young gentlemen in a city where the pride of the town was the brick mansion of Miles Brewton. Its rural counterpart, Drayton Hall, could be seen along the road from Charleston to Jackson's native Waxhaw district. These were good models to any aspiring squire; they were not carpenter-Vitruvian but quietly and surehandedly Palladian—a temple front atop an arcade.[†]

† This is a real distinction, though Palladio often pretended there was not. He invented the biloggial form that one could see at Drayton Hall, three centuries later. It placed a loggia with one set of columns under a pediment, and another below.

By the time Jackson became middle-aged, the Piedmont had adopted the style set by these Palladian mansions and turned the biloggial device into a trademark of gentility—one that was backward-looking, as are most such trademarks. In Natchez they were emulated at Linden, too grand for the Jacksons at the time but very much admired by Rachel. There is no way to establish the exact date of its construction, but it was available for the Jacksons' scrutiny in 1818.

It is not unreasonable to believe the Natchez tradition at Linden became associated in Jackson's mind with his beloved Rachel and their honeymoon in Natchez. Though it did not affect the first house they built together nor the second Hermitage of 1819–20, after Rachel's death and his own election to the presidency, Jackson returned to the past, to the memory of Natchez and of Charleston. The third Hermitage, of 1831, incorporating the first and second, included a biloggial portico, designed by David Morrison under Jackson's supervision. Together, they created two memorials to Rachel; the first was the house itself, a close representation of Linden. The second was the temple and monument in the garden, a Roman design drawn from Vitruvius.[70]

†† One could follow a Virginia biloggial tradition as well, from the Governor's Palace, as remodeled in Williamsburg, Shirley, and Teddington, all roughly contemporary with the Miles Brewton House, but I doubt they were very influential upon the Carolina stream of migration exemplified by Jackson. Contrary to what I stated in *Architecture, Men, Women and Money*, this is not really a sign that might indicate Jefferson's influence in Tennessee. I was thinking of his design for the first Monticello, but who would have known of that? And of his subsequent suggestions to friends and relatives, only Annfield used the motif. It was already well established before Jefferson took a hand in propagating it.

Jackson heard of the destruction by fire of this third Hermitage in October 1834 and was at first intent upon reconstructing it. But with him in Washington was Robert Mills, architect of the imperial public buildings of Jackson's regime. Probably guided both by his own masterful symbolic sense and by Mills, he moved on—or rather *back*—to an old form, one associated with Lafayette and with Washington. The final Hermitage was an inescapable statement that Andrew Jackson *was* a second George Washington.[††]

The fourth Hermitage was laid up in a trumpeting Roman style, with full colonnades front and back, stretched completely across the façade. Robert Remini, Jackson's most comprehensive biographer, tells us: "It is very probable that the restoration of the Hermitage borrowed much from George Washington's home at Mt. Vernon, especially the monumental colonnade and the shape of the driveway leading to the portico."[†]

There were little details to underline the point; the unpedimented colonnade was the most obvious, but it is poignant to observe Jackson's replacement of the "very splendid French paper" in the hallway with a scene from the *Odyssey*.[71] Washington had favored one father-and-son tale from the *Aeneid*, Aeneas and Anchises; Jackson chose Telemachus and Odysseus.

And there was a little Jefferson there too, the Jefferson of the Roman pavilions at the University of Virginia—two-story columns, big and proud. But Jackson and his Tennessee carpenter-builders, Joseph Rieff and William Hume, created their own fresh fusion of Mount Vernon and Jefferson's university, with column capitals invented, it seems, on the spot to be as much Jackson as either Washington or Jefferson.

From Jackson's point of view, the handclasp of Jefferson may have been welcome, but not his embrace. It would have been unwise to adopt Jefferson as father. Despite the acquisition of Louisiana, the philosopher at Monticello was not universally admired on the frontier, as Aaron Burr had demonstrated when he easily drew both Jackson and Clay into his western contest against Jefferson. They had both aided his "conspiracy" in 1805–1806.

Those who admired Jackson's machismo could easily contrast his impetuous and successful exploits to Jefferson's propensity to follow bellicose words with timorous action. The Sage of Monticello had weakened the nation's armed forces and had left it exposed to the humiliations that befell his successor, Madison. Neither he nor Madison mustered the will to take Florida; Jackson did that, as one orator said, "without sixteen years of negotiation." In Cincinnati, Jackson was pointed to as a "soldier whose hobby it is always to conquer," in contrast to such intellectuals as Jefferson and John Quincy Adams. The saying was: "Jackson made the law, Adams quoted it."[††]

Many Federalists were irked that Jackson was called "the modern Cincinnatus" and "the second Washington." "What an abuse of language," sputtered one anonymous pamphleteer. But Jackson knew what he wanted. It was the mantle of the Great Old Man—the American Senex. Anchises was a little feeble, but certainly Odysseus would do. He became solicitous and courtly with George Washington Parke Custis and with Custis's sister, Nellie. He took to voyaging to Mount Vernon in full view of crowds on the riverbank and commenced his presidency with a national tour modeled expressly upon that undertaken by Washington. The ultimate tribute was the Hermitage—wearing the old man's architec-

† (Remini, *Jackson*, vol. 3, p. 333) Mills may or may not have suggested to Jackson the Tower-of-the-Winds capitals and Roman proportions that gave antique dignity to the portico of the Hermitage. The most obvious aspect of that portico was that it was unpedimented like Mount Vernon's (and unlike the little pedimented porticos of the octagonal "tower" built in Athens to observe the weather). All we have to suggest that he did is a letter (February 16, 1836, in the David Paton Papers in the North Carolina state archives), in which he told a colleague that he had recommended a tin roof for the Hermitage and "sent a model showing the mode of putting on the sheets." He may well have sent other models or drawings, but they have been lost. It is very doubtful that he ever went to Tennessee for the purpose; we need not take seriously a charge brought against him by his competitor, William Elliott, that he had gotten federal jobs by moonlighting for the president personally.

†† (Ward, pp. 61–62) Jackson's biographers do not entirely agree upon the opinions of Jackson and Jefferson of each other. Marquis James asserted that Jackson thought Jefferson "a feathery doctrinaire; Jefferson looked on Jackson as a border ruffian." (James, p. 415) Though Arthur Schlesinger, Jr. (a hundred years after the event and intent upon preserving the apostolic succession) cast doubt upon their testimony, Daniel Webster and George Ticknor reported that, over dinner at Monticello, Jefferson spoke of Jackson as "unfit for the presidency . . . a dangerous man." (Schlesinger, p. 37; see also the remarkable brief essays on these characters scattered throughout his text, especially pp. 308 ff.)
    Similarly, John Quincy Adams reported that Jefferson warned James Monroe against Jackson as a begetter of needless quarrels. Jefferson had reason to be sensitive to Jackson's quarrelsomeness, for in 1806 Old Hickory had been a close associate of Aaron Burr, *(continued)*

tural clothes, somewhat Romanized. Custis, enraptured, welcomed Jackson to Arlington House, abandoned Federalism to support Jackson against the "little men" who opposed him, and named one of his real estate speculations "Jackson Village."[72]

While enthusiasts for Jackson talked of him as a second Washington, the first Adams, the first Jefferson, the first Madison, and the first Monroe were still alive, hanging around in the new day. Their presence was a problem.

The Great Divide

Not wishing to show ingratitude, even in the face of overwhelming evidence that the results of the founding had been somewhat disappointing, editors of the 1820s observed the founders "still walking among the people; lingering a little as if to give their farewell benediction to the nation they had baptized with their blood," and dutifully insisted that, while they lived, "still the golden age . . . continued . . . [as if] the brazen age of the commerce of the people had not opened."[73]

John Quincy Adams

The difficulty was that the heroes had been lingering for half a century, occupying themselves with harder work than giving benedictions. They governed the country until 1824, when John Quincy Adams proclaimed himself, in his Inaugural Address, to be the first of the *sons* of the fathers.

Then, as if to demonstrate that the heroic generation had life left in them, Adams was dumped from office by old Andrew Jackson. Jackson's successor, Martin Van Buren, attempted to correct Adams's timing by making himself the first of a (generously expanded) second generation, using his own inaugural to proclaim: "I feel that I belong to a later age."[74]

But, leaving personalities aside for the moment, Adams was more right than Van Buren, for the economic, psychological, and architectural life of the United States *did* start its second phase on or about the Fourth of July 1826, the fiftieth anniversary of the Declaration of Independence, and the death day of both Thomas Jefferson and John Adams.

This was a great divide. Edward Everett declared the heroic age closed and was echoed by Daniel Webster, who noted somewhat impatiently that it was ready to be closed. It did not seem to matter that Aaron Burr, James Madison, James Monroe, and the marquis de Lafayette lived on. As for the apparently immortal Charles Carroll of Carrollton, the only surviving signer of the Declaration of Independence after Jefferson's and Adams's deaths, only Jackson saw the value of his presence. Though Webster dismissed him as a relic of the past, Jackson stage-managed a grand presidential visit to the old gentleman at Carrollton in September 1831, to add yet another founding endorse-

Martin Van Buren

ment to his list, Arlington House and Mount Vernon having been captured. Nonetheless, it *was* time to move on.

The prepotency of July 4, 1826, was irresistible. Other earlier division points now wilted by comparison—1799, for example, when George Washington died with the eighteenth century, taking with him the last realistic aspirations to the presidency on the part of the Federalists. But the economic history of the full span of time between the Revolution and the Civil War reveals no significant change in direction in 1799.

In about 1825, however, there was a shift—a fault line, between two distinct phases. The first, from independence until the middle 1820s, was an extended and dispiriting oscillation of spurts of energy and equally sharp declines, without any sustained upward trend. Thereafter ensued a sharp escalation of business activity, which held and increased its gains despite disappointments along the way. After 1825 or 1826, the people of the United States emerged from the doldrums, and in a long surge coincident with the Greek Revival, delivered per capita wealth very much greater than that known in the nation at any earlier time.

It is no longer fashionable to write of takeoff points in development economics, so to put it more modestly: July 4, 1826, is close to the point at which the American economy began to move sharply upward in activity. It is also the takeoff point for the Greek Revival.

The world was changing on July 4, 1826, changing in subtle ways that overwhelmed politics and all individual biography. Though we cannot know precisely when these changes began and when they ended, it is certain that the use of that date comes in very handy.

The "Period of No Progress" Ends

The nation's long, trendless, economic turmoil came to an end in the 1820s. The preceding decades had shown productivity gains, but population growth had been so rapid and the descent of that population into frontier conditions had been so extensive that those gains were swallowed up. The average person was probably no better off in 1820 than he or she had been in 1790 or 1795.[75]

After the Revolution, as people turned from military to domestic exertion, they produced progeny in sufficient number to survive pestilence and malnutrition and to replace the many that died in wars. Eighty new people were added to every one hundred every twenty years. Human fertility outstripped agricultural fertility and the other capacities of the economy. As a result, per capita *income* was probably no higher in 1825 than it had been in 1800. But it did not remain low, even though the population continued to explode and new land continued to be occupied.

The people who occupied it must have had both courage and a full sense of their own potentialities to improve their lot; they willingly accepted lower standards of living, tactically, because they had confidence they would "win," strategically. But there was much travail along the way; they did have the resources to spend in celebration with large-scale architecture but little success worth celebrating until, after 1815, the great postwar rush westward paid off.

In the 1820s a long period of ups and downs gave way to sustained growth. Now, finally, all the promises seemed to be kept: "real per capita income more than doubled . . . in sixty years, and increased . . . sixfold in 120 years." Per capita *output* had declined from 1800 to 1810, as the emigrating population struggled to bring new farmlands under cultivation, and according to the best estimates, it only increased by a little over 9 percent between 1810 and 1820. Then it began to ascend rapidly. It increased by 24 percent between 1820 and 1830, and by 18 or 19 percent on average during the three decades preceding the Civil War.[76]

But what happened during the depression of 1837–43, so often compared to that of 1929–33, and called, in a standard text, "the worst depression of the century"? Nine states defaulted upon the interest on their bonds; credit markets were in disarray. Monetarists, observing that the money stock and price level fell even more in 1837–43 than in 1929–33, might characteristically equate the paper economy with the real economy. But there is real doubt that a depression—as distinguished from a deflation—was occurring.[77]

Business activity declined, and there was real distress; the laments of businessmen and bankers were loud. But there is little evidence of unemployment on a large scale, and real consumption and real gross national product actually increased—this is not what happened from 1929 to 1933. Peter Temin, to whose analysis these paragraphs owe a large debt, gives this table of comparisons of changes in real values (percent):

	1837–43	1929–33
Gross investment	−23	−91
Consumption	+21	−19
Gross national product	+16	−30[78]

Neither the psychological climate of the Age of Jackson nor its economy were like those of the 1890s and the 1930s, when prices fell and brought production and employment down with them. In the 1830s far more people were still engaged in subsistence agriculture and were still in occupations for which access to money and credit was not nearly so important as it became as the nation was tied together, tasks became more specialized, and the joints between parts of the apparatus became much tighter.

One last series of statistics may be useful in illustrating the breadth of this sweep, contrary to the expectations one might have of a depression of 1837–43. It was not limited to the investing or owning classes. Its psychological effects would have included those rising from the mudsill, those artisans becoming contractors and builders, and those builders becoming architect-builders.

The Index of Money Wage Rates paid for common or unskilled labor, which takes the year 1860 as its standard at 100, shows an uneasy rise and fall in the first two decades of the nineteenth century. Its abysses are in the Jeffersonian years, 1800 (60), 1803 (57), 1805 (62), and 1808 (68), then a swelling that receded in 1820 (67), 1822 (68), 1825 (68), 1828–35 (67–62), and then, when one might expect an abrupt falling off, there was none. Instead, there was a steady incline, with a pause in 1843 (68), and no other values below 71 in the 1840s and none below 82 in the 1850s. And the purchasing power of those wages increased, slowly, erratically, but ineluctably from 1820 to 1860.[79]

So, as recent research has demonstrated, there was no depression of 1837–43. "Investment was down . . . but the flow of goods and services to consumers did not fall. It did not even seem to slow its growth, and we can infer from this that discomfort was not widespread. . . . Farmers, textile workers, and others found their money wages reduced. They were not unemployed, however, and their real incomes may not have fallen. . . . Agricultural production was unaffected by the deflation, and the growing industrial sector of the economy continued to expand."[80]

This new perception of the American economy from 1783 to the Civil War is crucial to our analysis of its psychological and architectural results. A graph of its progress would show a horizontal pattern, erratic but flaccid, during the period when the country was being governed by the leaders of the Revolution. They went to their laurel-bedecked graves by the end of the 1820s. Then, ungratefully, the nation experienced an abrupt upward movement, sustained until the Civil War, though somewhat diminished in pace during the deflation of 1837–43. The whole population was carried along in its exuberance except the original occupants of the continent and those brought to it in servitude.

What has all this to do with the Greek Revival? The economic conditions that came to nurture it were not dissonant with the political history of the time. The reign of the American heroes had not been like that of Pericles; their revolutionary triumphs were followed by bitter disappointments, until the last dregs of disgrace were drunk in 1814. Then a new dawn opened over New Orleans, one presaged on Baltimore Bay. It slowly brightened the scene. Americans at first seemed transparently truculent to foreign observers, but from the middle of the 1820s until the end of the 1850s, they were justified—both economically and politically—in celebrating their achievements in a grand, ceremonial architecture.

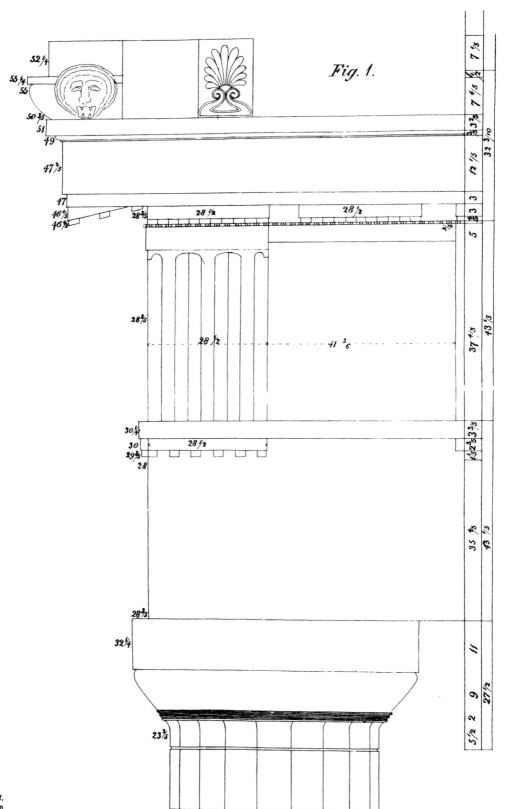

Fig. 1.

A detail of the Doric order,
by Asher Benjamin

Pages 105–108: Arlington House (1808–18), in Arlington, Virginia, is also known as the Custis-Lee Mansion. It was designed for George Washington Parke Custis by George Hadfield.

Pages 109 and 110:
Andalusia (1798), in
Philadelphia. Nicholas
Biddle commissioned
Thomas U. Walter to
remodel this building in
1835–36, at which time
the Greek Revival
portico (*opposite*) was
added.

Left: An outbuilding on
the grounds of
Andalusia

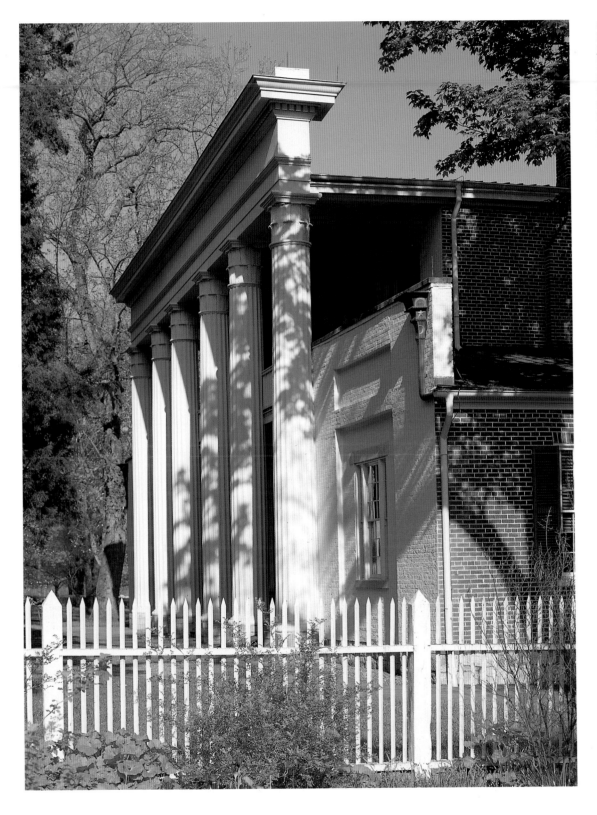

Opposite and left: The Hermitage, Andrew Jackson's home in Donelson, Tennessee, was redesigned three times—in 1819, 1831, and 1836. David Morrison was responsible for one revision, and Robert Mills may have contributed to the last.

Right and opposite: The Second Bank of the United States (1824), in Philadelphia, designed by William Strickland

The Commercial Bank in Natchez, Mississippi—now the First Church of Christ, Scientist (*opposite*) was built in 1838. Living quarters for the president and cashier were included (*right*).

Opposite and left: The Fairmont Waterworks in Philadelphia (1812–22) were designed by Frederick C. Graff.

Page 120: Founders Hall at Girard College (1833–47), in Philadelphia, is the work of Thomas U. Walter and Nicholas Biddle.

PART TWO
A CASE STUDY:
THE FOREST AND MILFORD

Old heroes surviving from the revolutionary generation found good works yet to do. Fifty-three years after he signed his name to the Declaration of Independence, Charles Carroll of Carrollton turned the first shovelful of earth to commence construction of the Baltimore and Ohio Railroad. In 1820 Albert Gallatin, summoning up the Jacobin idealism of his incendiary youth, urged an American expeditionary force to aid the Greeks in their revolt against the Turks. James Madison and Aaron Burr lived until 1836. Madison welcomed the ageless naïf, the marquis de Lafayette, to America in 1824, but declined Burr's invitation to effect the sort of literary reconciliation to which John Adams and Thomas Jefferson had come; Burr was beyond the pale.

Hellenic Whiggery

Even while Jefferson and Adams, Carroll, Gallatin, and Madison were still about, even while James Monroe creaked about the White House in his knee breeches, other men were setting another tone—ruthless, morally adaptable, and avaricious. Most conspicuous among these freebooting founders of private fortunes (rather than benefactors of the public weal) were Thomas Gibbons (1757–1826) and Wade Hampton I (1754–1835). The political founding fathers did not, as we have noted, produce a Greek Revival, but these fortune builders endowed sons and daughters with wealth which was deployed in building the greatest of America's Greek Revival mansions.

Gibbons's The Forest [147, 148], built in 1832–36, the Hampton's Milford [145, 146] of 1838–41, and Houmas House [151] of 1840, still exist. The Hampton's Millwood of 1841–44 was burned by Sherman's men during the War between the States (sometimes known elsewhere as "The War of the Great Rebellion"). The stubs of its columns, identical to those of Milford, are all that remain.

These were very large buildings, stately and grave, marching across the landscape with great arcades of columns, set under flat entablatures without pediments. The rhythm of that march was set in Berlin in the 1820s, was picked up in London, and began to dominate whole blocks of Manhattan in the 1830s. The Altes Museum in Berlin was the prototype; the British Museum, the endorsement; and Lafayette Terrace the New World resonance of that beat of stylar *gravitas*. The Hampton and Gibbons houses were its residential, yet still public, statements. Whereas the Altes Museum set forth in stone the pride of the resurgent Hohenzollern dynasty after humiliations at the hands of Napoleon, it is not accidental that its echoes could be heard in such remote places as rural New Jersey and up-country South Carolina.

The Forest has 36-foot columns across a 150-foot front. Thomas Gibbons, its founding father, was big as well—he weighed more than 400 pounds. Wade Hampton I, the man who endowed Millwood, Milford, and Houmas House, was smaller but produced even more columns than this list of houses might indicate if one were to count all those his children built in Louisiana, Mississippi, Alabama, and North and South Carolina. However, they might not number a tenth of the number of his slaves.

It was a cruel system that made all this construction possible, yet in the years just before the Civil War, its cruelties were moderated by the sons and daughters of these founders. The difference between their life-style and that of the senior Gibbons and Hampton, though shadowed by the source of their pride, does mark the rapid progression from the brutality of the frontier to a kind of civility that was symbolized by a columnar stability.

Wade Hampton I and Wade Hampton II   Both Gibbons and Hampton began the Revolutionary War as Tories, swearing loyalty to king and parliament. After supplying the British forces as a sutler, Hampton made a timely switch and commenced the same profitable service to the forces of independence. But he was more than a merchant with an eye to opportunity and a smooth-functioning wind gauge. He became an able field commander in the Revolutionary War, in a series of race wars in Louisiana, and in the War of 1812. The race wars demonstrated his ferocity; he decorated a mile of the River Road south of New Orleans with stakes upon which were impaled the heads of slaves who had lost their fight for freedom.

After Hampton had engorged himself on Tory confiscations in Georgia and South Carolina in the 1780s and 1790s, he extended the reach of his speculations from the Carolinas into Louisiana and those western lands of Georgia that eventually became the states of Mississippi and Alabama. He and his friends suborned the Georgia legislature into making grants of millions of acres, and the famous Yazoo frauds were born. So important was the continuity of contract to the fragile economy of the nation that, despite clear proof that they were secured by bribery, these grants were given constitutional protection by the United States Supreme Court in its decision in *Fletcher v. Peck.*[81]

Wade Hampton I

Neither Wade Hampton I nor Thomas Gibbons bothered to adopt the demeanor of squires, though between them they owned three or four million acres of land at one time or another. They both grew cotton on an immense scale, but neither agriculture nor nurture of any sort engaged their primary exertions. They were men of the industrial age, turning land speculation into cash with which to buy machinery. As relentless modernizers, they exemplified the adversarial rather than the nurturing style. Hampton bragged that he had had an agent dress in women's clothes and hide in an outhouse to steal the plan for a cotton gin from Eli Whitney himself, and that he had made the process industrial by linking it to a steam engine. He might have gone on to build textile plants, had he lived, while Gibbons abandoned the South to its growing obsession with agriculture and sailed into New York harbor with all his ambitions blazing.

Some further biographical detail about these two will be forthcoming, but our real interest is in their sons. Neither of the patriarchs was responsible for the creation of any significant permanent legacy beyond money, but their sons left us architecture. The character, taste, and accomplishments of these fathers and sons illustrate the transition occurring in America in the time of Andrew Jackson and Nicholas Biddle.

Wade Hampton II

By the time the Greek Revival swept across America, Charleston and Savannah were past their prime. Up-country planters kept houses there, but political power had shifted to the Georgia and Carolina Piedmont. Around Sumter and Columbia, South Carolina, were the head-quarters of the Hamptons, over which Wade Hampton II (1791–1858) pre-sided after his father's death. Though a gentle soul, not given to self-assertion except architecturally, this son of one general and father of another was so powerful politically that he was called the "Warwick of South Carolina" (a nod to Shakespeare's "Warwick the Kingmaker," in *Henry IV*). Moderate Whig statesmen became accustomed to seeking his support; Henry Clay made his pilgrimage to Millwood in April 1844, and Daniel Webster, his, three years later.

Like all those who built major Greek Revival houses, in the South as in the North, Wade II was an opponent of the reopening of the slave trade and a staunch foe of secession. The nullification crisis of the 1830s made obvious the distinction between unionist Southern Whigs such as Hampton and Clay and the radicals, including John C. Calhoun and, later, Jefferson Davis, who put the preservation of Southern economic interests ahead of preservation of the Union. The threat of disunion became coupled to the claim that slavery was a "positive good," a statement never made by Wade Hampton II.

Well before these controversies led to Calhoun's doctrine of nullification, the Gibbonses had followed the economic energies of the nation northward, from their plantations in Georgia (centered upon a tract that is now the Savannah airport) all the way to New Jersey. There they too had become potent in politics. Indeed, their power was nearly as great as that of Wade Hampton I in Alabama, where he had an honorary seat in the legislature though he had never been elected to it, and in Georgia, where his desires were followed to the letter and the dollar until he, like Gibbons, fell out with an antagonist worthy of the steel of either of them, James Jackson. (The consequences of Jackson's enmity to Hampton were financial—the reversal of the Yazoo favors; Gibbons felt them more directly, upon his person.)

Thomas Gibbons The influence of Thomas Gibbons upon the New Jersey legislature, and their determination to contest the power of the Roosevelt and Livingston clans in the legislature of New York, produced a battle of legislation that approached armed conflict.

William Gibbons (1794–1852), the son of Thomas, followed his father's lead and diversified into steamboats, iron manufacturing, hotels, and banking. Though Wade Hampton II placed modest bets in banks and railroads, his heart remained where his hearth remained, in agriculture and in the South. Neither he nor his brothers-in-law followed the Gibbonses very far out of agriculture. As a result, the second-generation Hamptons stood for the old order, the Gibbonses, father and son, for the new.[†]

† Contrary to many myths about the great antebellum planters of the upland South, Wade Hampton II, like James Coles Bruce, did diversify regionally—Hampton was seen at land sales in Wisconsin and Illinois. There is a good deal more about this in *Architecture, Men, Women and Money*.

Thomas Gibbons was as familiar with the dueling pistol, the bludgeon, and the horsewhip as with the lawsuit. He was short, squat, at first burly and later obese, looking out upon the world with hostile eyes under heavy lids. Shrewd, eloquent, charming when he needed to be, brave to the point of foolhardiness, Gibbons's career led him toward the future of the nineteenth-century New South. Yet his behavior was characteristic of the origins of the seventeenth-century Old South, of the brawling planters who transferred their ambitions and their first squads of slaves from the islands of the West Indies to those off the Carolina coast. His grandfather made his beachhead on Wadmalaw Island, South Carolina; the son of this pioneer married well, moved to tidewater Georgia, and accumulated rice and indigo land through royal grants and purchases. Thomas, his eighth child, was born in 1757, twelve years before his father's death. He did not acquire an endowment or many illusions, but he was given a sound legal education in Charleston.[82]

Gibbons, though personally even more fierce in his antipathies than Wade Hampton I, did not compile a military record. The British took Savannah in 1778; he was still a Tory when they evacuated it in 1782. Gibbons was arrested and his estates offered up to those like Hampton, who were now buying up confiscated property.

Thomas Gibbons

But his brother, brother-in-law, and uncle had kept their lines to the "rebels" open. He married Anne Heyward in 1780, and her family, who had been from the outset "rebellious," also aided him in recovering from a deprivation of citizenship and a ban from public office that was to have lasted until 1796. Gibbons went to court, won back citizenship after only a year, and became mayor of Savannah in 1791, commencing three terms that ran through most of the 1790s.

By the end of that decade, Thomas Gibbons and Wade Hampton I were powers in the land (while Charles Carroll rarely emerged from squirely contemplation between his last encounter with politics, in the eighteenth century, and his first with steam in 1829). Legislatures toadied to them, took their bribes, lavished favors upon them, and created a maze of constitutional questions that required the wizardry of John Marshall to refine the pure gold of constitutional law from their squalid jobbery. Hampton won *Fletcher v. Peck*, which arose from the creation of special legislative favors for his syndicate. The victory of Gibbons in *Gibbons v. Ogden* ensued from the plaintiff's muscling into such favors previously granted others.

In Savannah Gibbons's fellow citizens kept him in office as a Federalist, though the courts voided the election to Congress of General "Mad Anthony" Wayne after a campaign managed by the mayor, when the loser, James Jackson, convinced the jury that Gibbons had found "more votes than there were voters." Jackson went on to the governorship of Georgia, pausing on the way to deprive his old foe of a seat in its legislature, charging that Gibbons's own election had been as fraudulent as the one he had conducted for Wayne.

Wayne was turned loose upon the Indians, winning the Battle of Fallen Timbers and becoming a national hero. President John Adams rewarded Gibbons's faithful services to the Federalist party by including him in the list of "midnight judges" named in the last hours of his presidency, but Thomas Jefferson's new Congress refused to honor those appointments.

James Jackson and Gibbons confined the violence of their feud to a bloodless duel, though one of Jackson's lieutenants, Henry Putnam, horsewhipped the mayor on the street. It seems that Jackson and Putnam had discovered Gibbons's transmissions to the national capital of slanderous allegations against Jackson, for use in the halls of Congress. This discovery was possibly facilitated by the discreet application of steam by agents of the postmaster-general and chief of Jefferson's intelligence, Gideon Granger.[†]

† Granger was a loyal Republican, but also one of Hampton's partners in the Yazoo affair and one of the losers after Jackson's opposition to the Yazoo concessions.

Gibbons may have felt Georgia insufficiently appreciative of his talents; South Carolina had sent Wade Hampton to Congress as a Republican, though his chief interest was protection for his Yazoo claims. Jackson's supporters dominated Georgia, and there was little room for Gibbons. So he began acquiring property in New York and New Jersey, beginning with service facilities useful to travelers, such as turnpikes, taverns, stage lines, brothels, and steamboats.

Though he was about to enter the most contentious period of a quarrelsome life, he was not merely a wrangling, egocentric buccaneer; he took great risks protecting underdogs. When Savannah was held by the British, he defended imprisoned rebels against the Tories; after the British evacuated Savannah, he defended imprisoned Tories from Whigs. Other recipients of his solicitude were blacks and architects.

Gibbons's Taste Thomas Gibbons and his son were avid for architecture. In the Metropolitan Museum in New York is a fragment of the Roman Ionic doorway of their town house that once stood on Savannah's West Broad Street. The house, judging from ancient photographs, was a simple, large, white frame building, upon which a little neoclassicism was applied around the doorway. This probably occurred in 1797 or 1798, when Gibbons was still mayor, and when another, similar doorway was added to another frame mansion, on Reynolds Square. This house too is gone, demolished in 1920, but Historic American Building Survey photographs show that it had the first neoclassical groin-vaulted passageway in the city. The architect was the French-trained Adrian Boucher, formerly a draftsman with the celebrated Mangin brothers in New York.†

Boucher was the first of the Gibbonses' architects. He arrived in Savannah in February 1797; in 1802 he announced a school for "civil and Modern architecture, and the properties of the five Orders." In between, thanks to the mayor, he was busy.[83]

He built a New City Exchange in 1799, under the patronage of Gibbons and other merchants. He also kept a "porter house" on Broughton Street, of which the mayor may well have been a part owner. (Gibbons was soon to be proprietor of another, in Elizabethtown, New Jersey, where the name of the landlady was Mrs. Cornelius Vanderbilt.) Boucher's tavern was popular with free blacks. When one of them, named Jim, wanted to hold a party there after the curfew, Boucher followed what was apparently his practice and made them welcome. He "held . . . the dance with the permission of the Mayor." Some of Gibbons's enemies called for William Smith, "whose duty it was to guard against insurrection or insubordination on the part of the Negroes."[84]

Smith closed the "riotous house . . . [and] the whole assembly of blacks was carried to gaol . . . near midnight." Then, "in spite of the hour," he remonstrated with the mayor, who, according to Smith's account, "attempted to break my head with a club." So fearsome was the mayor's wrath that no one was prosecuted, and it is unlikely that Boucher and Jim ceased their cheerful relationship.[85]

Though Thomas Gibbons transferred his primary energies to New York and New Jersey thereafter, he maintained the house in Savannah, to which Boucher added the neoclassical doorway, as well as more than 10,000 acres of rich rice plantations in Georgia. William Gibbons was, apparently, staked at the northern end of the axis of the Gibbonses' interests, setting up his household at 1 Greenwich Street in New York even before he went off to complete his education at Princeton. He was forced to leave college to oversee the family's Southern interests as well, after his father was diagnosed as diabetic, then a disease without remedy. After 1818 the family turned back to Savannah as a field for investment, this time in urban development. They were wisely wary of going deeper into agriculture.

Boucher had died in 1804, so the family turned to others to design their new ventures in Savannah. William Jay was there by 1817, adding a Regency flair, and was still available in 1820 when William

† The Historic American Building Survey photographs are supplemented by those in Nichols (p. 48). Nichols saw in the grainy photographs "a beautifully proportioned example of the Doric . . . used on the tabernacle doorway." I do not see them that way. The house was known as the Houston-Johnston-Screven House.

Another architectural mystery, the French classical design of South End House, may be resolved somewhat by the notation in Granger et al. that Thomas Spalding of Sapelo Island was apprenticed in the law to Thomas Gibbons during the last years of the 1790s when Gibbons was also the patron of Boucher. Spalding was a remarkable man, quite capable of the kind of amateur architecture another planter, Dr. William Thornton, produced farther north, but he may have learned from Boucher some things useful to him in designing South End House in 1810.

Gibbons added massive stone Regency-Baroque stables to the family town house. He also built an entire block of brick stores and houses on Market Square that remained into the 1970s, pilastered and elegant, even in a dilapidated state.[†]

Though their Savannah town house had been built of white frame, brick and stone now became Gibbons materials, in keeping with "the principle laid down" by Thomas to his son: "in living, live as if each day were the last but in building [as, apparently in testamentary draftsmanship] build as if I was to live forever!"[86]

More Litigation   Thomas Gibbons was a destroyer as well as a builder. He turned upon his daughter, charging in court that she had lived openly with John Trumbull, whom he loathed, before they were married. But Mrs. Trumbull had inherited his spirit, and she gave as good as she got: she replied that his efforts to deny her property on grounds of immorality should not be taken seriously because he was keeping the Union Hotel in Elizabethtown as his personal bordello. His aversion to Trumbull apparently arose from pique; her husband was no stable boy; he was the nephew of painter John Trumbull and of Governor Jonathan Trumbull of Connecticut, sons of an earlier governor of Connecticut also named Jonathan Trumbull. His vendetta against the Trumbulls was as unrelenting as that against James Jackson, but neither quarrel had the constitutional consequences of his long contest with Aaron Ogden.

William Gibbons did not seem to hold his father's grudges, for he happily turned to members of the Ogden tribe to assist in his business transactions and he did not become estranged from his sister, Mrs. Trumbull.

Gibbons's obituary in the *Savannah Georgian* called him "arbitrary, impetuous, vindictive, but courageous and brilliant." Vindictive he certainly was. His will carried language as close to a bill of attainder against his daughter and son-in-law as any private document in American history: "I do pray to God, before whom I am shortly to appear, that I have been enabled to so devise and bequeath my whole estate. . . that no event may or possibly can arise. . . that will enable John M. Trumbull, or any one of his children, or any person descending from them to be benefited one cent, or the value thereof, from my estate. . . to the end of time."[87]

This prayerful document also provided $40,000 to pursue a contest against Aaron Ogden to the bitter end. The story of their litigation is one of the great dramas of the American bar. In the end, by his famous disposition of the matter, Chief Justice John Marshall cleared the way for a more rapid expansion of capitalism, striking down the attempt of any state to erect a barrier against the free commerce of others in interstate waters—or, by extension, across state lines, enabling the steam engine's next progeny, the railroad, to operate without restriction between states. This was the fundament upon which American entrepreneurs commenced their operations across the continent. The Gibbonses grew considerably richer; their steamboat business, their real estate, their turnpike and banking ventures, and their rice lands in Georgia increased, and with them, the purse available to pay for architecture on a grand scale.

The elder Gibbons had shown no greater interest in building stylish plantation headquarters than had Wade Hampton I, but the next generation was more ambitious. The Forest is larger than any house attempted even by the baronial Hamptons—so large, in fact, that it has eased very comfortably into its present role as the administration building of Drew University.

The Architects of The Forest

William Gibbons made his first stake in New Jersey in the wilderness lands "west of Bottle Hill" (now within the township of Madison), far enough from the port of New York to be free of its noise and jostle but close enough to supervise youngsters such as Captain Vanderbilt. At the end of 1832, he wrote that he expected construction to start in the following spring. But there seem to have been delays, perhaps arising from the appearance on the scene of a strong-minded architect—the last bills were not paid until 1836. Who might that architect have been?[†]

My hypothesis is that there were two, Russell Warren and Charles Reichardt, a hypothesis based upon evidence of their presence in the area at the time, upon their associations then and their formal, contractual associations elsewhere somewhat later. There are bits and pieces of compelling information as to their character and habits, as to the relationships between them both and the Hamptons, and between the Hamptons, the Gibbonses, and horses. There are, as well, concurrences of timing too compelling for coincidence and some likenesses in plan and principal elevations between The Forest and the Hamptons' Milford.

Between 1832 and 1836, Reichardt and Warren were in New York, available for the work, and moving in circles where Mr. Trumbull and Mrs. William Gibbons might easily have encountered them. The two architects later worked as partners in South Carolina, though it is important to note at the outset that there was a difference of status between them. Reichardt was a glamorous foreigner, known as a professional architect. Warren was an American carpenter-builder who, though widely known in the area around Narragansett Bay, had not yet found clients among either the fashionable New Yorkers who turned to Ithiel Town and Alexander Jackson Davis or the Charlestonians who later rushed to engage Reichardt.

Dozens of Warren's works are still to be found around Providence, Bristol, and Warren, Rhode Island, and in New Bedford and Fall River, Massachusetts. His bridges spanned streams from Georgia to New Brunswick. He was fifty years old in 1833, an established but provincial figure, still casting about to find partners with whom he could work and from whom he could learn. He seems to have found one in the mysterious Herr Reichardt.

Warren had built a good practice in Rhode Island, but he chose to move to New York, where in 1835 he formed an alliance with the younger, less experienced, but extravagantly talented draftsman Alexander Jackson Davis. There was much combining and regrouping among a small group of architects and

† Gibbons's correspondence is scattered, though much of it can be found in the Drew University Library. In Cunningham (pp. 47–48), it is said that the bricks for The Forest came from Benjamin Lum's brickyard in nearby Chatham, the mahogany from Santo Domingo, and that mahogany for interior trim together with the "stout wooden pillars for the front piazza were designed and carved in London." This is the sort of tale that was often told in the early nineteenth century. A Mr. Jenkins of New Brunswick, New Jersey, "assembled the materials," so we have at least a clear indication of the identity of the contractor, and the Ionic pillars were almost certainly local, though it is possible, but scarcely likely, that the capitals were carved abroad. After comparing these columns with those used by Russell Warren in his frequently illustrated John Avery Parker House in New Bedford (1833) and elsewhere, as well as with scores of other progeny of Ithiel Town's Bowers House (1826–27) and George Hadfield's Washington City Hall (1818–21), I am certain that they are all using the same Ionic format. That being the case, there was no need to send to England for carvers to reproduce what was becoming a very common form. At one point I thought that an early and rather indistinct etching reproduced by Cunningham indicated that the house originally had Corinthian columns of the Lysicratean, or as I call it, Reichardtian, order. It would be gratifying to my hypothesis about Reichardt's association with the house if they did.

draftsmen at this time, who made many variations and adaptive reuses of each other's ideas. At one stage Davis shared an office with James Dakin, who, in illustrations for the architectural handbooks of Minard Lafever, was showing Americans how exciting so-called Greek ornament could be. (Though Warren and Reichardt later made ample use of Dakin–Lafever ideas, this ornamentation's full, flowering profusion was not yet fully developed when The Forest was built.)†

Asserting that he had been trained by the renowned Karl Friedrich Schinkel, architect to the royal court of Prussia, Charles F. (Karl Friedrich?) Reichardt was in New York by the early 1830s.†† He too came into the orbit of Ithiel Town. Town and Davis had already assimilated the lessons of English neoclassicism as demonstrated in America by Latrobe and by Town's friend George Hadfield, whose work had been assiduously studied by Davis; they were quite capable of drawing out of Reichardt whatever might be useful in the Prussian imperial style.[88]

Americans were still seeking instruction in neoclassical architecture and were well aware of the magnificent examples provided in Berlin by Schinkel. His Altes Museum was one of the wonders of the world; from 1825 to 1828 the construction of its enormous colonnade, emblazoned against the greenery of the Lustgarten, was observed by traveling Americans. Its imperial message was as clear as the fanfare of massed military bands. Schinkel gave the resurgent Hohenzollerns an awesome march of columns under an entablature—a "beam" of stone—two blocks long.

The first American residential colonnade in that style was, it happens, built as a tribute to a Frenchman, the marquis de Lafayette. It was a row of town houses in New York City still sometimes called Lafayette Terrace [i] and sometimes by the name of his country seat, La Grange. (Some bays still remain, but they have been miserably manhandled.) This Prussian ensemble went up, without a pediment, in 1831–32. Why the stress on the pediment or upon its absence? Because unpedimented colonnades were new in America, and because we are searching for the architect who may have designed one for The Forest, Milford, and Millbrook, which were among the first American houses to display one.

Russell Warren and James C. Bucklin had put a row of columns upon one façade of their Arcade (a prototypical shopping mall) in Providence in 1827–28 [38–39], but the magic of the Altes Museum was absent. Warren and Bucklin's columns were stiffly restricted within a heavy frame—tight, Yankee, and despite their technical proficiency, dull. Lafayette Terrace was something grand and challenging, an unconstrained sequence of pillars giving the impression that, if enough tenants could be found, they could march on all the way to the Harlem River. It was New York at its booming, blustering best.

† Lafever came to New York in 1827 and provided drafting services and carpentry to John Haviland, to Martin Euclid Thompson, and to Thompson's partner from 1827 through 1828, Ithiel Town, who had arrived in the city in about 1825 from New Haven and Washington.

Town was in partnership with Alexander Jackson Davis from 1829 through 1835. James Dakin joined them as a draftsman and became a partner in 1832. Lafever listed himself separately as a builder and then as an architect after 1829, but was in frequent professional association with Dakin, Davis, and with James Gallier, who arrived in the city in 1832 and was hired as a draftsman for Town, Davis, and Dakin. J. F. Rague, the architect for the Illinois and Iowa state capitols, worked in Lafever's office in 1828, 1831, and 1836.

The younger Robert Cary Long of Baltimore was in New York and may have worked with Thompson, Lafever, or both together in the early 1830s. Reichardt was there by summer 1834 and remained until the end of 1836.

Dakin withdrew from the Town and Davis partnership in November 1833, not long after his brother Charles entered the office in training. Gallier left also, to join Lafever, but not for long. In October 1834 he departed with Charles Dakin for Mobile and New Orleans.

In 1835 Lafever abandoned the Grecian in his practice, and Davis left Town. Davis was joined in August 1835 by Russell Warren, who remained for a year. Warren had worked in South Carolina in the 1820s, as a contractor, and while he also produced buildings in Providence and Bristol in 1836, it seems likely that he made what Alexander calls his "usual winter trip" to the South that fall (Alexander to the author, letter dated September 21, 1987). It seems likely that he accompanied Reichardt in December, for they were soon at work jointly, in Charleston, for Wade Hampton II.

†† The shipping notices of the early 1830s and the city directories seem to show no notice of Reichardt's arrival in New York.

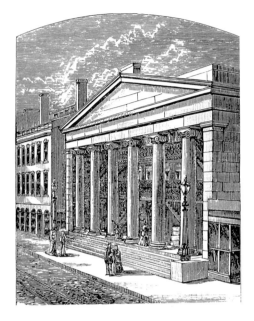

The Arcade in Providence, Rhode Island

New York City's Lafayette Terrace

† Similar colonnades soon appeared elsewhere, by Isaiah Rogers (the New York Merchants' Exchange), Robert Mills (the Treasury Department in Washington), and in a series of works by members of the Town circle. The chief practitioner of the form in Louisiana was James Dakin.

Warren had also used columns to give a touch of grandeur to his Rhode Island mansions as early as 1808. Until the 1830s, however, they were of attenuated, Roman, pattern-book proportions, like those drawn by Asher Benjamin. Later, after the success of the Arcade, they became Greek, though always overweighted by peculiar, blocky attics (as if Warren felt he had to give his clients more space and did not know how to do it without the loss of grace).

Lafayette Terrace was begun in the early 1830s, soon after the completion of the Altes Museum. Its architect has never been established, though it is known that Town, Davis, and James Dakin were at work on its interior arrangements by 1834–35. Perhaps it was the first American work of Reichardt.

Prussophilia Reichardt was a restless sort, leaving only a few wisps of information with which to compose the fragments of his biography. By March 9, 1835, he had been in New York long enough to be announced as one of the prizewinners in the competition for the prison that became known as "the Tombs." By December 6, 1836, he was important enough to be listed among the handful of masters of the profession who came together at the Astor House Hotel to organize the Architects Association, prototype of the American Institute of Architects.[89]

The colossal portico of The Forest was built during the tenures of both Warren and Reichardt in New York. Like the Altes Museum, but unlike any earlier work of Warren, it was without a pediment or blocky attic.†

Reichardt shrewdly advertised himself in the newspapers to be "an architect from Germany, a pupil of the great Shinkle [sic]."[90] Prussia, like the United States, was a rising power in the world, and the Hohenzollerns were famous builders. Obscured behind the clouds of cordite smoke of two twentieth-century world wars is the remote world of the 1830s, when the United States and Prussia had much in common. Americans and liberal Germans saw each other as fellow contenders against the smug British and the unreliable and predatory French.

Even among those whose sentiments were not liberal, Americans and Prussians seemed formed by similar circumstances. The sandy uplands of the American South were like the pine plains of East

Prussia; the villages where plantation owners gathered, from Natchez, Mississippi, to Athens, Georgia, were like the garrison towns of the Junker provinces, where Poles played the roles of blacks. Polish and Prussian travelers often expressed a sense of déjà vu when they arrived in Alabama and Mississippi. Northern merchants had their German affinities as well, for, as Samuel Eliot Morison was wont to point out, "German erudition entered New England" as part of the smuggled cargo from Hamburg and Lubeck during the Napoleonic Wars.[91]

A variety of Americans therefore felt a kinship with the Prussians, whose royal family, the Hohenzollerns, seemed until 1848 to be relatively benign, built grandly, admired Greece, and spoke of a "New Europe." On his way to Greece, Jefferson's young friend George Ticknor sojourned in Germany, from whence he reported, "all is still new & young," as if he were talking of Ohio. Ticknor felt in Berlin "the workings of its untried spirit . . . free, & philosophical," and of the Germans' "unwearied activity with which they push forward."[92] Likewise, German travelers were inspired by the Americans. It was to be nearly a century, after the best of German liberalism had been exiled after the uprisings of 1830 and 1848, after Prussia became more like imperial Rome than Peisistraten Athens, that both sides in this admiring dialogue came to see how little they had in common.

Prussophilia was at its height before the repression of the liberals made it unwise, thereafter, for the hundreds of Americans attending the great German universities to speak of a common "contempt for ancient forms" of government. But in the 1830s and 1840s, liberal exiles from Germany reenacted the vivifying role of the French emigrés of the 1790s. This was especially true in architecture. Reichardt was merely the first of a succession of German emigrés to contribute to the American Greek Revival.

Colleagues   The cachet of an association with the great Schinkel would not have been undesirable to the ambitious and architecturally sophisticated Gibbonses, a family that, since 1798, had made use of the best neoclassical talent available. By 1830, Adrian Boucher was dead and William Jay exiled to Mauritius, so a new designer had to be found to announce the presence in New Jersey of country gentry who could afford to live on a grand scale. If not a Frenchman or an Englishman, why not a German, even if available only at the last minute, even if the house were already under way? The Gibbonses were most unlikely to leave themselves at the mercy of a local contractor-builder, or even of Warren alone.[93]

When the work was done, the Gibbonses had an impressive house. The Forest is miraculously preserved in the midst of the oaks and elms that suggested its name a hundred and fifty years ago. It is now known as Mead Hall, the centerpiece of Drew University, a complex of white-columned buildings looking out across broad green lawns puddled, in midsummer, by the deep blue shadows of its forest. This might be an unusually prosperous Southern town, centered upon the bronze equestrian statue of a general, such as Wade Hampton I or Wade Hampton III. It is, instead, a Methodist campus; the statue is of a circuit-riding preacher.[†]

The interior of Mead Hall is capacious; on the main floor, the ceiling is 18 feet above the black-and-white marble floor. The hall extends about 60 feet from the front door, to open into a suite of large rooms giving access to a veranda overlooking the park. At the doors to those rooms, one turns right or left along a hall, still 20 feet wide. This lintel of the **T** is nearly 110 feet long, leading to more rooms and offices in the wings. The interior ornament is sparing, as if the architect were not yet well enough acquainted with Lafever and Dakin.[††]

Like Milford, it was brick, painted white; the paint has been sandblasted away, but the building stands, a remarkable survival. Most of its peers in grandeur have vanished from the American scene; only Milford matches it as an evocation of the great American Greek Revival estate, and Milford is far less accessible. Both houses owe much to the Altes Museum, but The Forest also shows in other aspects—its plan, its "order," the blocky details around its front door and windows, and its ornament—the well-developed routines of Warren. He had refined these elements in his work upon a mansion of equivalent scale (now gone), for John Avery Parker of New Bedford (1833), one of his last major residential commissions before he moved to New York.

Warren was always ready to welcome colleagues, especially in design. Trained as a carpenter by his father, he knew construction but was not too proud to ask for help from a young, well-trained German who knew how to handle an international clientele. Thereafter, the two men might have been introduced by John Trumbull. (Ann Gibbons Trumbull died in 1817.)

There is hard evidence that Trumbull was acquainted with Alexander Jackson Davis, who knew both Warren and Reichardt. William Gibbons could have been drawn into the circle of Town, Davis, Warren, and Reichardt through his sister; her husband was very active in the artistic life of New York, which was being crystallized in such organizations as the Architects Association.

Or, possibly, Warren and Reichardt were introduced to the Gibbonses by the Wards, who were kin to the Gibbonses and clients of Warren's partner, Alexander Jackson Davis.

Thomas Gibbons died in the same year as Thomas Jefferson and John Adams, though accompanied by somewhat less elegiac an obituary; he was too much a man of the present and, in a sense, of the future. Industry was commencing its ascent to dominance of the continent, and in the next decade, the Age of

[† In addition to the ghost of Thomas Gibbons, another may be present at Drew University: the endowing founder of the university, Daniel Drew, arch-scallywag of stock-jobbing and fraud in the postbellum period. Drew, with Jay Gould and Jim Fisk, pillaged railroad companies. He got his start in transportation driving pigs to market, then cattle, and then by running a tavern frequented by other pig and cattle drivers. It is pleasant to think of Gould, in the Age of Grant, ensconced at Lyndhurst, and Drew, at The Forest, hatching ways to bait the trap that drew Commodore Vanderbilt into investing in their Erie Railroad. It is pleasanter still to recall that Vanderbilt, well trained by Thomas Gibbons, beat them at their own game. Despite losses suffered in wars against him, they were rich enough to endow universities.

†† Alexander, in his thesis "The Architecture of Russell Warren" (New York University, 1952), makes it clear that there is nothing specifically "Southern" about the deep hall with corridors running off to wings, though it once was conventionally thought to be. In Rhode Island and Massachusetts, Warren used the same format.]

Jackson and Biddle, new centers of finance were arising. New York, the new power base of the Gibbons family, was chief among them, and at the apogee of the New York banking world was Samuel Ward.

Ward was the leader of the shrewd and politically resourceful New Yorkers who conducted a war against Biddle and Philadelphia that was as ferocious and successful as Gibbons's against Ogden. This was the bank war, in which Wall Street had Andrew Jackson as an ally. While often depicted by Jackson and some subsequent historians as a war between the president and "the banks," it was, in fact, a contest in which Jackson successfully opposed the rechartering of "Biddle's bank"—the Second Bank of the United States, situated in Philadelphia—and distributed the government's deposits elsewhere. It was as much a conflict *among* banks as against banks. Few of Jackson's supporters, and certainly not Jackson himself, opposed banks in general; among his closest advisers and cabinet members were men heavily invested in the stocks of state banks, especially those financed in New York City.

Clues to architectural history can often be found in the sort of financial history that eventuates, as it often does, in "society," the natural habitat of people such as Samuel Ward McAllister. That charming man married William Gibbons's daughter and was thereby unable to laze through the rest of his life as a "society man." Even though he enjoyed a certain sort of fame as inventor of the term (and of the qualifications for inclusion within) "the 400," for our purposes he is of considerably more interest as a signpost pointing toward other connections, for he was the nephew of Samuel Ward, whose firm, Prime, Ward and King, built a handsome Greek temple headquarters at the end of the 1820s.

The bank building was fine enough, but not nearly so impressive as Samuel Ward's own mansion, which was completed to the designs of Town and Davis in 1831–34, just as The Forest was getting under way. Known as The Corner, it stood at Broadway and Bond Street (the site later occupied, for a time, by Brooks Brothers) and boasted a library nearly as large as that of Ithiel Town himself.

The Gibbonses were clients of Prime, Ward and King, whose principal partner was a client of Alexander Jackson Davis, friend and sometime partner of Russell Warren. Therefore, a circle was completed when Samuel Ward married the sister of Louisa Cutler McAllister of Georgia, whose son, Samuel Ward McAllister, married Sarah Gibbons, William's daughter. This was as it should be, for the McAllisters had been partners of Thomas Gibbons years before in Savannah.[†]

The Route through the Stable Yard   Though the Hamptons and Gibbonses built similar houses and had some concurrent agricultural interests, no evidence as yet has demonstrated that they had business interests, literary affinities, or lawyers in common, nor were they intermarried. Their orbits did intersect,

† It is possible that the Wards were led to the Greek by Nicholas Biddle, for Biddle and Prime, Ward and King had been equally dependent upon good relations with the Baring Brothers and the Bank of England. There was a time, before the bank war, when Biddle took affectionate note of them in verse, twitting John Jacob Astor for expressing anxiety that he was more interested in poetry than in banking: "I prefer my last letter from Barings or Hope/To the finest epistles of Pliny or Pope . . . /One lot of good bills from Prime, Bell or the Biddles/To whole volumes of epics or satire or idylls."

Biddle was becoming unwary; one did not cross John Jacob Astor without unpleasant consequences. Prime, Ward and King were the paymasters of the Barings in America and, hence, very powerful in controlling the money supply of the United States. They were also, like Astor, New Yorkers. Biddle's friendly verse could not have been written after the fall of the Second Bank, for Samuel Ward was the leader of "the monied junto in New York" that arrayed itself against him in the bank war. These New York houses preferred no national bank at all to one in Philadelphia and contributed heavily to the coffers of Martin Van Buren and Andrew Jackson.

There is lively dispute as to how much truth there was in the widely circulated stories that the New York bankers had joined with Van Buren's Albany junto in a war against Philadelphia. As Van Buren wrote Jackson, "the opposition . . . [attribute] the removal of the Deposits to the solicitations of myself, and the monied junto in N. York." Robert Remini, a biographer of Jackson who denigrates the story, quotes Jackson's friend Silas Wright as denying, a little too fiercely perhaps, the existence of "'some cursed wall street operation' to ruin the Bank and snatch financial leadership in the country for New York." (Remini, *Bank War*, pp. 115–16) Remini refers darkly to "some historians . . . identifying . . . hidden conspiracies . . . Wall Street bankers and conniving politicians in Albany. . . . But the evidence is overwhelming that *(continued)* the killing of the BUS was primarily the work of one man, and that man was Andrew Jackson. True, he had essential support from a great corps of friends, most of them named above." (Ibid., pp. 42–43) I cannot prove a flow of funds from Ward to Jackson's campaigns. Remini does not deny the possibility. Thomas Govan, Biddle's biographer, identifies Prime, Ward and King, along with Brown Brothers, as leading the New York interests against the Bank in Philadelphia. (Govan, p. 175)

It is likely that there was as much British and international money committed to the New Yorkers against Biddle in that fight as there was for him. Arthur Schlesinger, Jr., no admirer of Biddle, told a part of this story from a Jacksonian point of view: Ward, aligned with Albert Gallatin and Jackson, favored the resumption of payments in gold upon the currency, to restore the credit of the Jackson administration. Biddle feared another round of Jacksonian improvidence and communicated his feelings to others, who felt another kind of fear, "the fear of Mr. Biddle," who made at least one country banker behave "like a frightened schoolboy." Schlesinger asserts that "there can be no doubt that Biddle planned raiding the New York money market and forcing the New York banks to close their doors again; but Samuel Ward in the nick of time negotiated a loan of five million dollars in gold bars from the Bank of England, and Biddle was frustrated." (Schlesinger, p. 253) When the silver kings of Denver lost their battle against the international gold standard fifty years later, their motives for supporting William Jennings Bryan would have tested no purer than those of Prime and Ward in rallying behind Old Hickory. Jackson was saved, and the way opened for Wall Street to replace Chestnut Street as the chief money market of the nation.

however, in the stable yard. These families were as likely to exchange horses as architects, and with equal enthusiasm.

Documents tying the Gibbonses and Hamptons together can be found where an antebellum Southern gentleman might expect them, in studbooks. Horse racing was an enthusiasm approaching obsession among them in the 1830s. While many of the architectural documents of the South, and some of its architecture, went up in smoke between 1860 and 1865, studbooks were kept at both ends of North–South transactions.

At The Forest, William Gibbons built the largest Greek Revival house still left to us north of the Mason-Dixon line—and also one of the nation's finest stud farms. It was rivaled only by that of Nicholas Biddle and his brother-in-law, John Craig, and in the South by that of Wade Hampton II. The founding Hampton had been a sharecropper's son whose precise date and place of birth are unknown, whose chief acquaintance with the equine species was with the mules he followed down the furrows as a boy. The immense riches he later accumulated made it possible for his son, Wade II, to become "the impersonation of Carolina chivalry, the embodied spirit of Carolina blood and honor . . . the main contributor to . . . the improvement of the breed of horses." This devotion was so profound that it was said at the time that "no pilgrim ever knelt at the shrine of My Lady of Loretto . . . with more devotion than does Col. Hampton when he visits his stables in the morning."[94]

And no other horse owner except, perhaps, William Gibbons was so successful in enlarging a personal hobby into a community cult, with its rituals and celebrations. The Charleston racecourse became known as Hampton Park. In New Jersey the neighborhood observed that Gibbons's "racing victories brought joy to the mansion. Gibbons gave his servants [read, slaves] a new suit of clothes or a new dress for every triumph." Starting in 1829, he began acquiring horses and building his private racecourse. In 1834 Gibbons joined the national horse-breeding circuit by acquiring the racing mare Bonnets o' Blue from Craig and Biddle. She was "a prime filly," bred and raced by Colonel William Ransom Johnson of Virginia, rivaled only by Bay Maria, sold by Johnson at about the same time to Wade Hampton II.[95]

In 1837 Bonnets o' Blue produced the chestnut mare Fashion, and Alexander Mackay-Smith, who knows as much about this subject as Samuel Eliot Morison did about maritime Massachusetts, reports that from 1840 to 1848 Fashion "raced on Long Island, in New Jersey, Baltimore, Washington and Alexandria, and I find it impossible to believe that Col. Hampton did not watch her race, probably several times, and thus knew William Gibbons." He adds that "the French painter Henri deLattre from 1838 to 1839 painted a number of horses for Col. Hampton. After his father's death in 1853, William Heyward

Gibbons [son of William] commissioned deLattre to paint a number of the horses he had inherited, including Fashion and Bonnets o' Blue. He certainly raced horses in Savannah and Charleston."[96]

Colonel Johnson was the switching station for Greek Revival architecture as well as horses. He was present at the apparent coincidence that occurred when a student of the court architect of Prussia was brought to South Carolina to design a columned racecourse pavilion at a time midway between the creation of a Prussian arcade for one horseman/planter in New Jersey and two more for horsemen/ planters in South Carolina. One might encourage a gentlemanly interest in either a good house or a good horse—as frontier businessmen became genteel.[†]

William Ransom Johnson was known as "the Napoleon of the Turf." He was "a plunger . . . a bundle of nerves . . . suave of manner . . . ready to resent an insult, and a man of the old school." He was well known to many of the great Greek Revivalists, to Nicholas Biddle of Andalusia, to the Hamptons of Milford, Millwood, and Houmas House, to William Gibbons of The Forest, and to James Coles Bruce of Berry Hill, the author of the above opinion.[97]

Berry Hill was created for Bruce by William Johnson's son, John, an architect, a decade later than these other Greek Revival houses. Bruce said of the senior Johnson "I detest his character," but he could not resist his charm. Bruce lent him money, and more to the point, introduced John Johnson to the Biddles at Andalusia, upon which Berry Hill was closely modeled. The Bruces and their cousins, the Coles, were often present at Biddle's estate on business—political, equine, and financial.[98]

So far as we know, John Johnson never visited either Milford or The Forest; the latter was being completed while he was still a student. His father, "the Napoleon of the Turf," may well have done so, though he generally arranged his exchanges of horseflesh and patronage without straying far beyond the shelter of the portico of his mansion at Oakland, the first Grecian design of his son. (Henry Lewis only recently discovered that Grecian portico—the house is gone, but an image of it appears as background to a picture of a horse.)

† It would be a great convenience if the paternity of architecture were as easy to follow in this period as that of horses. But research into the latter may aid in solving this conundrum: The first house in America to be completely surrounded by a classical colonnade was The Forks of Cypress (the name of a creek, which came together there), built before 1830, probably to designs by William Nichols, near Florence, Alabama. The second was probably Houmas House, built by Caroline Hampton Preston and her husband John, on the Hampton Louisiana lands in about 1840. Caroline was almost as avid for horses as her brother, Wade II, and James Jackson of The Forks were. In the 1830s Jackson built stables and a regulation racecourse in the meadow below his house and capped his acquisitions of horseflesh by buying the famous *Glencoe* in 1835. It is almost certain that Milford and Millwood were built with Houmas in mind and I would be willing to enter a horse-racing wager that the Hamptons knew The Forks as well.

At the end of 1836, Russell Warren ended his formal association with Alexander Jackson Davis, and Charles Reichardt threw over his own New York endeavors and headed for Charleston. He arrived there at Christmastime; the appearance of the student of the celebrated architect of the Altes Museum was noted in the newspapers. Reichardt may have been traveling with Warren, who landed unannounced by the Charleston press, probably because the Yankee carpenter-builder was not a new face in town, having worked there, from time to time, for more than a decade, building up-country Carolina courthouses as early as 1824.

Reichardt immediately set to work on two commissions arising from the passion of Wade Hampton II for horse racing. The young German probably came to Charleston on the strength of those commissions, and the connections to the Hamptons he formed thereby probably explain why he remained.[99]

Who recommended Reichardt to Wade Hampton? The answer may lie embedded in a story told in Charleston that Hampton was especially eager to give the city a racecourse of appropriate grandeur because he had just become a little richer from the winnings of a mare named Kitty Heath. She leads us back toward the Gibbonses, by way of "the Napoleon of the Turf."[100]

The colonnaded grandstand for Hampton Park was in place by 1837. Then, to provide accommodations for the visitors during race weeks, there followed (1837–39) "the architectural symbol the city needed,"

† (Ravenel, pp. 177 ff.) In the initial building, Reichardt's partner was Jacob Small of Baltimore, who had been trained by Latrobe while working on the Merchants' Exchange. Warren may not have been available or, perhaps, was not low bidder.

The Charleston Hotel

the Charleston Hotel, subsidized by the railroads, of which Wade Hampton II was a director. Charleston was striving to tie itself into the nation's expansion by building a line to Cincinnati, the metropolis of the West. Hampton was the leader in this venture. The hotel was finished in 1837, "the plan . . . by Mr. Reichardt having been chosen." It burned in the next year but was completely rebuilt in 1839, by the partnership of Reichardt, N. F. Potter, James A. Potter, and Russell Warren. The Potter brothers and Warren were already accustomed to one another, having worked together on many commissions in Providence. The hotel was a monument to Charleston's silver age until it was torn down in the 1960s. It had "fourteen colossal Corinthian columns . . . unsurpassed in taste and elegance with any similar building in the United States."†

This was a feverish period of investment in Charleston; patronage was still munificent. Reichardt rushed on to remodel the interior of the old Bank of the United States, to build an Ionic New Theater (1837) modeled on the Hohenzollerns' Royal Theater in Berlin, a new steeple for Robert Mills's Circular Congregational Church (1838), and the Guard House (a Charleston euphemism for a police station) on Meeting Street with fifteen Doric columns. Another colonnade around the corner, Reichardt's Vendue Range, had fifteen more. The Apprentices Library Company was yet another example of this Teuto-Hellenism, and there is evidence that the Potters and Reichardt were responsible for the shaping of one of Charleston's Doric masterpieces, the Beth Elohim Synagogue [380]. He left unexecuted projects as well: a mariners' church, a Masonic hall, and alterations to the city hall.[†]

Their German architect was now fully tested. The Hamptons could be confident he could add a cosmopolitan refinement beyond the reach of Warren alone to the mansions they had in mind as headquarters for their imperial holdings in the Piedmont. As contractors, Warren and the Potters had shown their competence in Charleston. There is a tradition that, for years, Warren had "wintered" in Charleston. With a little social deflation one may deduce from this that when the building season shriveled in the New England winter, he went south for work. He appeared in the Charleston *Directory* of 1821 as a "carpenter" and owned two houses there in the following decade, both for speculation. But he is *not* recorded as the architect for any buildings in Charleston; perhaps he had become typecast there as a carpenter-contractor, just as the Potters remained brick masons however many bricks they may have ordered others to lay. Warren was thoroughly competent as an architect, but the Hamptons did not turn to him for the design of either the grandstand or the hotel.[101]

The destruction of the Hampton records has left no document tying Reichardt to what were probably his greatest commissions, a new creation, John L. Manning's Milford, and Wade Hampton's remodeling of Millwood.

They had an affinity for Germans; they were already collecting German furniture. Folk-memory in the region of Sumter, where these houses were built, attributed Milford to "the German-born architect Niernsee."[102] Niernsee was, in fact, chosen by Wade Hampton II to work on the South Carolina state capitol in the 1850s; but he was a child when Milford was designed. Some German, however, *is* likely.[††]

Milford, the residence of Hampton's brother-in-law, Governor John L. Manning, is similar in plan and many details to The Forest, but it makes use of the full panoply of the new Lafever–Dakin ornament, as it had been developed in New York in the interim. Though begun in 1838, its completion dragged along

† (For Reichardt's Charleston work, see Ravenel, except for the evidence for the synagogue, for much of which I am indebted to Mills Lane's *South Carolina*.) In November 1838, soon after he had arrived in Charleston, Reichardt delivered to the congregation "a plan of the Exterior & Interior of the Synagogue." Three local builders also submitted plans at the time, which were apparently rejected. Two more local builders offered more detail, which was accepted, for a building "with a Greek & Doric portico" like that Reichardt had provided for Vendue Range.

In May, while Reichardt was presumably up-country working for the Hamptons, "Mr. Potter, the builder of the New Hotel" told the committee of the congregation that he needed more-detailed working drawings, and in July Cyrus L. Warner, a draftsman in New York, delivered them, profuse with the Lafever–Dakin ornament deployed at Milford. The shallow coved dome is an enlarged variation of the stair-hall dome at Milford. The building contract was awarded in October 1839.

Why did Reichardt not stay closer to the job? Possibly because he was too busy with commissions for the Hamptons, anticipating a departure, which may have occurred as early as the late summer or early fall of 1839. He was no longer available in 1840; the cornerstone was laid, without him, in January, and the building was dedicated in March.

†† There is yet another German tendril twining about the columns of Milford, which stretches all the way to Tennessee. Belle Meade, the Harding house built outside Nashville in the early 1850s, was probably designed by Adolphus Heimann, who may have worked alongside his father and (if one believes Reichardt's story) Reichardt and the great Schinkel in Berlin. It is generally said that Belle Meade owes its façade to the choragic monument of Thrasyllus (319 B.C.); it seems *(continued)*

to me much more akin to a more proximate precedent, the recently completed Milford. Harding, another horse-breeder, had business connections to the Hamptons. (This choragic monument, one of many, did provide two sizes of square columns and a flat entablature to Louisiana houses such as Ashland [159] and Bocage, both built in the 1830s probably to designs by James Dakin, and later, to the Lincoln Memorial in Washington.)

until 1841. Scattered contract documents indicate the contractors were the Potters. Not a scrap of paper yet discovered shows plans, specifications, or elevations with a mention of Reichardt, though Warren was paid some small sums for plans he contributed or transmitted. But the columns are there, six of them, like those of Millwood and, more to the point, like those of Reichardt's now-departed Charleston Hotel, as it appears in surviving photographs. Those photographs show many other similarities between the hotel and Milford—in scale, proportions, and blocking courses. [103]

Millwood was reconstructed for Wade Hampton II, during the period from 1841 to 1844, around or as a replacement of an earlier cottage. No pictures of it exist, but its ruins remain; it was described at the time in this way:

Floor plans for The Forest (*top*), Millwood (*center*), and Milford (*bottom*)

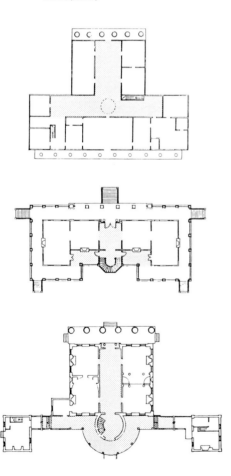

The front of the dwelling is very imposing as you ride up to it. A good deal of effect and character is conferred on the entrance by a very magnificent colonnade with its massy pillars of the composite order, which extends entirely along the whole southern front of the building. The entrance is in the center, by an easy flight of steps into a hall about sixteen by twenty, on either side of which are doors, opening into the principal suite of apartments. At the northern extremity of the hall, (the walls of which are adorned by highly finished colored portraits taken from life, of some of the favorite horses of the proprietor) is a sexangular projection for a staircase of much beauty of proportion, lighted from above by highly stained glass, producing a mellow and most agreeable form of light. At the front of the staircase on both sides are rooms opening on a veranda, extending around two wings of the edifice, in the rear, communicating with spacious dormitories, bath rooms, etc., etc., affording a delightful and umbrageous walk at all times, sheltered as it is, by embowering branches of tall forest trees. [104]

The "delightful and umbrageous" verandas along the back façades of The Forest and Milford are still with us, however, giving us a sense of what they were like at Millwood, where they were not merely piazzas but a series of open rooms. A veranda of ten single-story columns runs across the rear of The Forest; at Millwood such a colonnade was set all about the new mansion, which had engulfed the old cottage. This little "skirt" became, at the front, a grand portico like that of Milford.[105]

The "footprint" of Milford is almost identical to the front section of The Forest, and rather uncommon in the South. None of these houses has the conventional central hall of the Piedmont that proceeds completely through to a back piazza. Instead, the hall extends to a **T** crossing—a back hall. These crossings in the two houses are essentially congruent, though Milford's is made more sophisticated by a partition giving an apsidal end to one of its two right-hand drawing rooms. The Gibbons house allows for another range of rooms at the rear, including a ballroom (now boardroom) where Milford has an elliptical staircase and Millwood had its "sexangular" one. In order to accommodate its ballroom, The Forest has a wider back hall with a straight staircase, but all three houses have a domed cupola in roughly the same position. The Gibbons house has an ellipse cut through the floor of the hall on the second floor, in the place where stairwells were placed by the Hamptons (to accord with a Charleston tradition, it is said).[†]

More columns were to come: a set of three Hampton "cottages" went up at White Sulphur Springs, Virginia—eighteen pillars in sets of six, in 1838–40—to become known as The Colonnade.[††]

        In 1840, when the commissions for the Hamptons were nearly completed, Charles Reichardt disappeared, and Charleston ceased building in the Prussian style. The man responsible for its introduction there may have gone on to Central America, to look into places where German immigrants might settle and to examine the path of a potential canal across Nicaragua. Two volumes on these possibilities were published in Brunswick in 1850 and 1854; their author was "C.F. Reichardt."

And two volumes more, at least, would be required to seek out all the probable but not yet clearly established designers for the major monuments of the American Greek Revival. Many were left anonymous by the habits of clientage of the time. The architects for the Gibbonses and Hamptons have been pursued at this length because their stories illustrate the major themes of the Greek Revival, as well as suggest further inquiries into other intriguing instances. Clients, however, are often as important as architects—and sometimes more so.

† As was the case with The Forest, something seems to have intervened in the construction of Milford, for the original contract with the Potters, as contractors, called for completion by November 1, 1839; the last payments were not made until two years later. (*Newsletter of the Victorian Society of America* 5, no.7)
    It would be handy if a bill for plans from Reichardt had turned up as well, but such is not the case. I agree with Waddell, however, that "the outstanding features of both buildings [Milford and the Charleston Hotel] are surely by Reichardt."

†† Two Charleston houses with capitals like those of the Charleston Hotel and Milford have been attributed to Reichardt as well. One, at 172 Tradd Street, was built in 1836 by Alexander Hext Chisholm, a rice planter, miller, and business associate of the Hamptons. The other, now known as the Edmonston-Alston House, at 21 East Battery, was remodeled by the Hamptons' friend Charles Alston between 1836 and 1840, and given an upper piazza bearing a smaller version of the capitals from which to look out upon the harbor.

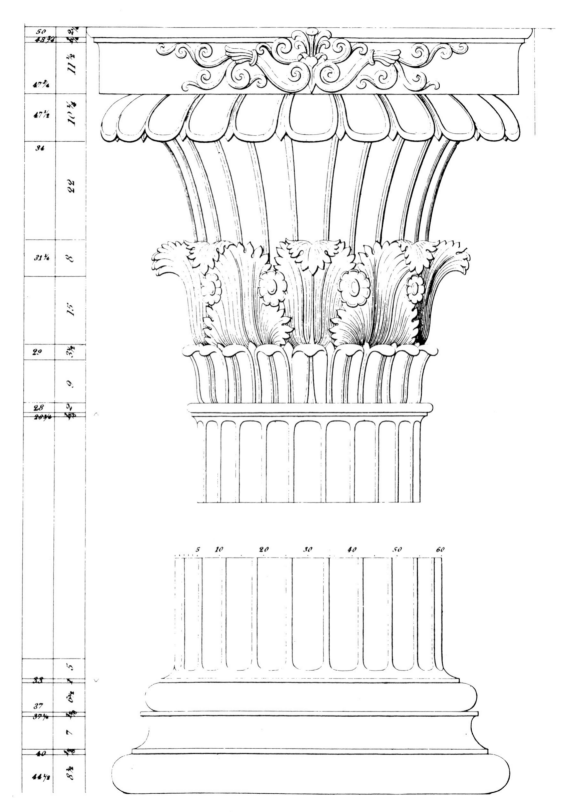

**Detail of a composite order,
by Minard Lafever**

Page 145: Milford (1838–41), in Columbia, South Carolina, was probably designed by Charles F. Reichardt and Russell Warren.

Right: The porch at Milford

The Forest (now Mead
Hall at Drew
University), in Madison,
New Jersey, was built
from 1832 to 1836, and
may have been the
work of Charles F.
Reichardt and Russell
Warren.

Right: The Forest (Mead Hall at Drew University)

Opposite: Gaineswood (1842–60), in Demopolis, Alabama; the amalgamation of designs from many sources accumulated by its owner, General Nathan Bryan Whitfield

Page 150: Waverly (1852) in Columbus, Mississippi, built by George Hampton Young

Page 151: Houmas House–Burnside, in Burnside, Louisiana

Right: Stanton Hall (1857) in Natchez, Mississippi, may have been designed by Thomas Rose and Lewis Reynolds.

Opposite: The New York architectural firm of Town and Davis created the Samuel Russell House (1828–30; now part of Wesleyan University) in Middletown, Connecticut.

Page 154: The Lanier Mansion, known today as the Lanier Historical Site, in Madison, Indiana, was built in 1840–44 to designs by Francis Costigan.

Page 155: George W. Polk's Rattle and Snap (1845) in Columbia, Tennessee

Page 156: The Varner-Alexander House (1854–57), in Tuskegee, Alabama, is now the President's House at Tuskegee Institute.

Page 157: Dunleith (1856) in Natchez

Page 158: Madewood (1846–48), designed by Henry Howard, is near Napoleonville, Louisiana.

Page 159: Also near Napoleonville is Belle Helene (or Ashland), designed by James Gallier, Sr., in 1840–41.

Page 160: The ruins of Windsor near Port Gibson, Mississippi

PART THREE
REVIVING GREECE

$\mathbf{A}$ncient Greece was not a nation-state; it was a constellation of towns, drawing upon flocks and herds, vineyards and orchards, and a few spare stripes of grain to support the real business of most Greeks, maritime trade. When the meager hinterlands of scores of independent, competitive, disparate, and abrasive little cities could no longer support their population, they sent out colonies. These colonies, in their turn, became colonizers, some of them anticipating the Northwest Ordinance of 1787 with rectilinear town plans.[†]

The Greeks tended toward rectangles; their characteristic house, city, and temple plans were so ordered from the Crimea to Portugal, beyond the pillars of Hercules. There are even hints of rectangular ruins along coves and beaches where Greek traders paused along their regular routes as far away as the coasts of the British Isles at one end of the world and the Red Sea at another.

This colonizing process produced larger cities outside Greece than in it; and after Greece lost its political independence to Macedon, it gained an artistic empire that produced a profusion of examples of the Greek way of building as far to the east as Afghanistan. The vehement export of Greek aesthetic ideals began under Alexander the Great; it lasted a thousand years, but its monuments were vulnerable and very few remained standing after barbarian invasions culminating in the fall of Byzantium in 1453. In out-of-the-way places in Sicily and southern Italy (especially amid the famous wild roses growing in

[†] Historians of town planning long attributed the origination of rectilinearity to Hippodamus, a Milesian architect of the middle fifth century B.C., suggesting that it thereafter became their universal practice. More digging has yielded a modified view, that its usage was gradual and spotty.

profusion upon the royal hunting grounds at Paestum), uncompleted and ruined temples whitened in the sun, waiting to be rediscovered. Southern Italy was a prize for which popes and emperors, Normans, Spaniards, Austrians, and the French contended. For centuries Italian peasants grazed their flocks amid the ruins, hoping to be left alone by these armored invaders on their fine horses.

In the early Middle Ages, Greece itself was held by the Byzantine Empire, successor to Rome and largely staffed by Greek bureaucrats. At about the time their cousins invaded England, Franks and Normans conquered Sicily and southern Italy and attacked Greece. With a fine indifference to religious prejudice, the allegedly Christian Franks and the allegedly Muslim Turks cooperated in the elimination of the last vestiges of the classic world. Then the predators fell out and fell upon each other. After centuries of warfare, the Turks prevailed over the Franks and Byzantines (sometimes called the Greeks), completing their conquest of Greece a few years before the voyages of Columbus to America.

The memory of Greek literature was kept alive by classical scholars, but the Renaissance took no interest whatsoever in Greek architecture. The Turks were not hospitable to Italian architectural historians, and the very name of Athens disappeared from the cartography of Western Europe: a map published as late as 1555 called it "Setines." Palladio, perhaps the most influential architect who ever lived, became so in utter ignorance of Greece and even of the Greek buildings in Italy. One might have asked Michelangelo or Leonardo in vain for opinions of the Parthenon or of Paestum.

After a century of vigor, the Ottoman Empire began its own long decline. During the decade of the 1680s (while the English formally acquired New York from the Dutch), the Venetians, summoning a last spasm of energy, actually managed conquest of most of Greece, including Athens, but so conducted themselves as to become no more popular than the Turks. In 1687 they lobbed shells to explode a Turkish ammunition dump on the Acropolis, indifferent to the fact that its precise location was inside the walls of a temple built by Pericles twenty centuries earlier. It was called the Parthenon, and they scored a direct hit. Because it had been well built, some of it remained.

By executions and deportations, the Venetians and Turks systematically deprived the Greek resident population of its leadership. They squeezed the peasants with land tithes extorted by corrupt local officials and expropriated their land to provide for their own settlers. The Turks carried off the sons of Greece to Istanbul, to serve as Janissaries (soldiers) or worse. Between the Venetians and Turks, the Greek population of the Morea (the ancient Peloponnese) was reduced from 300,000 to 86,000, impoverished and degraded.

The czarina of Russia, Catherine the Great, now entered upon this desolate scene. Her convenient theory was that she was the heir of the Caesars of Byzantium and Rome; so justified, her ventures into the Mediterranean began with an ill-supported expedition to the Morea in 1769 (while she was also tightening her grip on Alaska and probing both the California coast and the shores of Hawaii).

The leader of the Morean expedition was her lover, Count Orlov, who found the climate unpleasant and abandoned his troops. The Turks turned loose their Albanian allies, first upon the Russian remnant and then to ravage the countryside. Ultimately (during the period of the American Revolution) the Albanians were exterminated by Turkish regulars.

The Russians did succeed in extricating from the Turks a treaty under which the Greeks could ply their proficiency in ocean trade under protection of the Russian flag. They required that protection, in part, against the Greek pirates of the Aegean, while, on land, Greek bandits vied with *armotoles*, Christian warriors licensed by the Turks to "police" the farmers. As maritime prosperity increased, so did the spirit of revolt. Encouraged by the American and French examples, small groups of patriots rediscovered an ancient language and ancient pride.

THE BIRTH
OF THE GREEK REVIVAL

While these events were transpiring in Greece itself, other rediscoveries were occurring in "greater Greece"—the areas of Italy and Sicily still marked with evidence of Greek colonization. In 1751 and 1752, amid the roses of Paestum, Italian, French, and English travelers suddenly recognized the presence of a complex of magnificent Doric temples.

It is often said that the European Greek Revival was born in 1752, when the earl of Guilford, who often used his courtesy title Lord North, and his friend Thomas Major measured and sketched these temples. The meticulous notes of their observations, published in a report in 1768 under the aegis of Robert Wood, became one of the most important sources of Greek Revival architecture. Wood, Major, and North were eager young Hellenophiles and amateur archaeologists who went on to other things. Wood conducted the negotiations leading to the replacement of the French empire in Canada with a British one in 1763, and Lord North became the prime minister who presided over the liquidation of the Thirteen Colonies. It was he who exclaimed after Yorktown: "Oh God, it is all over!"[106]

In the meantime, American tourists had begun to arrive at Paestum, led by the Izards of Charleston, South Carolina, who were accompanied by the Boston-born painter John Singleton Copley. This party arrived in 1775. Copley spent the Revolutionary War years in Europe, taking Lord North's side of the matter, as did another Tory, the architect Gabriel Manigault, who married one of the Izard daughters.

It is worthy of note, in light of earlier remarks about Tory patronage, that every person practicing painting or architecture with any degree of professional skill in America in 1775, except Charles Willson Peale and Thomas Jefferson, was opposed to separation from England. So was nearly every patron of importance. Along with Manigault and Copley, there were Ralph Earl, Gilbert Stuart, and Benjamin West, all safe in Britain, Peter Harrison, whose library was burned by a mob of what the politically ambiguous John Trumbull called "dirt-bred patriots," and William Buckland of Annapolis, who died before he had to resolve his own political affinities.

For historians of the Greek Revival, however, Manigault was not nearly so important as another Charlestonian of conservative views, who enters our story shortly as Mr. Smith of Carolina.

Lovers of Greece   Though Lord North said it was "all over" in 1781, in Greece it was far from over. The emperors of Austria and Russia agreed (using the code-name "the Greek Project") to engorge themselves at the expense of the Turks, as they had at the expense of the Poles. Greece, to them, was a real estate transaction.

Idealists, especially classically trained idealists, invested modern Greeks with ancient virtues and rallied to the cause of their independence. As soon as the United States was free of Britain, Thomas Jefferson's thoughts turned to Greece. In 1785 he wrote from Paris, to Ezra Styles, that independent Greeks "would easily get back to . . . classical models. . . . We might then expect, once more, to see the language of Homer and Demosthenes a living language." Two years later, he said to George Wythe: "I cannot help looking forward to the re-establishment of the Greeks as a people, and the language of Homer becoming again a living language."[107]

† Latrobe's European travels are not well mapped, but his remarks about acoustics make it clear that he traveled extensively in Italy, and it seems most unlikely that he failed to make the obligatory expedition to see the Greek ruins at Paestum. Hadfield was born in Florence, educated as a child in Rome, and returned there for several years to study architecture. He produced a series of beautiful drawings of ruins in the region, though none specifically of Paestum. Yet no student in Rome for more than a few months would have been likely to miss the opportunity.

During the 1780s and early 1790s, both George Hadfield and Benjamin Henry Latrobe were in Italy, where Greek remains were being unearthed with passionate interest. We know from Hadfield's sketches, presented in London after his return there in the early 1790s, that he had made a careful study of the Roman monuments, and Latrobe later wrote of his own impressions of the Pantheon. Neither of them left any specific comments on visits to Paestum, but by that time its temples were a stop on the grand tour of every aspiring young architect. Greece was not yet quite accessible; it became so in the mid-1790s, but both Latrobe and Hadfield were by then in the United States (they arrived in 1795 and 1796).†

Even before architects' tours came to include Athens and Corinth, sensitive American travelers went abroad expecting to venerate the classical past but returned with a very negative view of the Romans, for political reasons. The word *Roman* came to connote contemporary Rome and other crowded, plague-ridden cities. London was by then full of imperial Roman allusions, and hostile to Americans; likewise (and competitively), Napoleonic Paris had become a sort of fancy-dress stage set, where the First Consul had declared himself "imperator" amid triumphal arches and columns that rivaled those of Trajan and Constantine. Americans who experienced all this pompous fuss developed an aversion to things Roman and a willingness to be convinced that Greek style was more becoming to a simple society. Their view was shared by revolutionaries in Paris itself, where a group of artists who called themselves "the primitives" created a Doric temple on the Champs-Elysées as a commentary on Napoleonic pretense.

When Nicholas Biddle arrived in Paris in July 1805, that temple of "the primitives" provided his first exposure to Greek architecture. In the Louvre, there were classical statues to be copied, in plaster, under the instruction of Jean-Antoine Houdon, the sculptor of Franklin, Jefferson, and Washington. Then Biddle went off to Rome and Florence under the tutelage of John Vanderlyn. So prepared, he set out for Greece.

His Hellenic journey was made from April through July of 1806. He survived the equal dangers of Greek plagues, rising from the swamps, and Greek bandits, descending from the mountains. He looked like Byron, and though his writing was stately rather than poetic, a passion for Greece equal to Byron's keeps breaking through. That passion sustained him amid flies and fools and petty larceny, as he searched for architectural symbols to proclaim his personal and political visions. Young, patriotic, and full of enthusiasm, he saw ancient temples set against a romantic landscape and wrote of them as villas in the Pennsylvania woods.

In Athens Biddle came under the wing of Louis François Sébastien Fauvel, the French consul and antiquarian, "the cicerone of every learned traveller in Athens."[108] Fauvel had created his own private museum of antiquities, like that being assembled by the comte de Marcellus, who purchased the *Venus de Milo* for France in 1820.

Nicholas Biddle

The purchase of individual works of art was a traditional means by which a gentleman could demonstrate that he was among the cognoscenti. But trucking away an entire assemblage—such as the frieze from the

Parthenon—seemed barbaric. Biddle was horrified that Lord Elgin had made off to England with the famous marbles. The ancient destruction of the temple of Ephesus by Herostratus was horrible, said Biddle, but "Erostratus burnt for glory, Elgin robbed for gold."[109]

Biddle himself hoped for glory gained in other ways. Walking in the footsteps of Pericles and Solon, his ambition swelled. He would become an orator and statesman (it is sometimes forgotten that he became a banker only when his political career foundered); he made his first reputation as a serious student of antiquity and translator of Greek.

It is a measure of the quality of the man that, though Biddle was hungry for adulation, he did not claim to be the first American in Greece. In one of his first reports to his elder brother, he noted that he was "the second of my countrymen who has been here, exploring the ruins of Corinth." Later, when he came to Ithaca, he "set off for the farthest part of the port," ascended a hill "through currant and vine fields" and came "to an ancient well in perfect preservation . . . called the well of Ulysses and justly for no doubt he made use of its water. It is excellent water and my pleasure in drinking it was heightened by knowledge that my countryman Smith of Carolina had discovered it for the benefit of the Ithacans."[110]

Biddle had heard from the islanders that an unnamed "Milord" had come to visit the mountain, and "after looking about [had] declared to the astonishment of the people that there must be water in such a place . . . he brought workmen and made them remove stones and dirt until water appeared. The man who lives near the well said it was an Englishman, an error I very patriotically removed."[111]

Joseph Allen Smith of Charleston had gone abroad for the first time in 1793. He looked about on his own, guided by his reading. Tiring of the obvious and accessible, he commenced adventures that took him first on a tour of the remoter reaches of Scotland and Ireland, and then farther afield, to Copenhagen, St. Petersburg, Moscow, Astrakhan, Persia, and Turkey. Somewhere along the line he was introduced to the Anglo-Irish Fitzmaurice family, and in 1800 and 1801, his traveling companion was John Henry Petty Fitzmaurice, son and heir to that earl of Shelburne (later marquis of Lansdowne) who took office in 1782 in the Rockingham cabinet, and later became prime minister on the condition that King George III recognize the independence of the United States. Quite aside from the entrée provided Smith by this friendship to the faction of the aristocracy of England friendly to Americans, it also led him into the circle of Scotsmen who were guiding the taste of that circle. John Adam, brother architect to the more famous Robert, and Gavin Hamilton, the painter, spent as much time in Italy, sending home essays on architecture, statues, casts, and antiquities, as they did in Scotland; both served to whet the appetite of the Fitzmaurices for the classic.[†] The statues, cameos, antique gems, and coins Smith sent home to the Philadelphia Academy were a direct reflection of the habits of his friends.[††]

† They were "cultivated" in a way somewhat more Scottish than English; the first marquis of Lansdowne was one of Robert Adam's most important clients for buildings reflecting the aesthetic theories being developed by his brother and by Lord Kames.

†† Unlike the Fitzmaurices and Adams, Smith did not limit his instruction in the Greek to Roman copies or the theories developed by Hamilton's acolytes in Rome. He was in Constantinople in May 1804 and obtained passage to Athens aboard a Russian warship. His brother, William, was living in Philadelphia, where he received dispatches from Joseph that might have been shown to Biddle before he embarked on his own voyage to Europe. Joseph Smith was back in Constantinople in October, on his way to Paris via Russia. That was also the month in which Biddle arrived in France, so they apparently overlapped, since Biddle did not leave France for Greece until the spring of 1806. There was plenty of time for Smith to regale Biddle with his own version of the tale of Ulysses' well. After Biddle's own adventures in Greece, they both returned to Philadelphia in 1807, perhaps together.

Upon his return to the United States, Smith slipped easily into the Philadelphia circle dominated by George Tucker, the chief apostle of Scottish Enlightenment theories in the United States, and Nicholas Biddle. Joseph Smith remained steadfastly an eighteenth-century man; his contribution to the American Greek Revival consisted of encouragement for Biddle, a few plaster casts, and after-dinner stories of his early travels.

Smith was not interested in a public reputation; he left only a little memoir of "The Present State of Athens," in the *Literary Magazine and American Register* of October 1807. (It is possible, indeed likely, that he contributed anonymously to *The Port folio* as well.) Even before he returned home, he had sent to Philadelphia engravings, paintings, gems, and plaster casts which, with Biddle's, formed the core of the collection of the Pennsylvania Academy of the Fine Arts. As Smith's gifts arrived, the grateful citizenry organized the academy to receive them.

Not long after his return, Joseph Allen Smith married "the other Izard sister" (his brother William had married the second, Gabriel Manigault the first) and commenced an agreeable life as a diner-out and source of anecdotes. The Biddles and Smiths were members of the same proud high-Federalist faction, with its headquarters in Philadelphia, where the Smiths maintained a residence. Like the Biddles, the Smiths came from a line of West Indies traders (Joseph Allen Smith's mother was one of the Barbadian Wragg family). Except for Biddle, the circle's taste was as conservative as its politics; as the nineteenth century proceeded, they continued to favor the villa forms of the last decades of the eighteenth, though they had residences in London and Paris and knew that things were changing. It did not seem to occur to any of them that the Smiths or the Izards might have responded to the power of Greek example, rather than following French and British fashion. Biddle, alone among them, did so.†

The lavish ornamentation and flamboyant color of the Greek Revival succeeded the tamer Federal period, which, while rooted in mid-eighteenth-century English and Scottish practice, did not dare to use the brilliant "Palmyran" colors of Robert Adam or James Wyatt and essayed only very muted color and derivative ornament. When interiors grew more colorful at the end of the 1820s and when, a decade later, American Free Classicism developed its own riotous ornament, the surviving members of this high-Tory-turned-Federalist faction did not take part.

Instead, they looked backward. They did not cotton much to Latrobe's suggestions for color, nor did they employ experienced colorists like Joseph-Jacques Ramée, who were available, to work in America as vigorously as they had in Europe.[112] They did not do much to encourage American-born artists in independent development, nor even adjust to Biddle's Whiggish Hellenism. The Society of Artists, in Philadelphia, to which Latrobe gave his famous Anniversary Oration, was formed to contend against the

† The Izards and their Tory connections deserve a book of their own; though they did not move with alacrity into the nineteenth century, within the constraints of the old fashion they and their friends brought the American villa form to a state of elegance and geometric freedom that only Frank Lloyd Wright could match a century later. In 1801 Henry Izard introduced Christopher Gore of Massachusetts to Jacques-Guillaume Legrand in Paris, who worked on the "sketch" that became Gore Place, with its oval rooms and "perfect freedom from ornamentation," in conforming with the strict dictates of the neoclassicism of Kames and James Adam. (Gore to Rufus King, October 20, 1802, King Letters, James Gore King Collection, New York Historical Society; and November 24, 1804, Rufus King Papers, New York Historical Society. See also *Orders from France.*)

At the same time, Gabriel Manigault (Henry Izard's brother-in-law) was designing, for his brother Joseph, another villa, which is still standing, behind its little French entrance pavilion, at 550 Meeting Street in Charleston. It had an even more venturesome country cousin for, after The Elms, one of the Izard plantations, burned in 1807, Henry himself could indulge his architectural interests in the way he had encouraged Rebecca Gore in her role in the design of Gore Place, later built in Waltham, Massachusetts. He rebuilt the house with octagonal rooms fitted out with piano, guitar, lyre, and "the most superb Harp . . . in Christendom." Cosmopolitan as were these Carolinians, the same observer reported that their dinner consisted of "tea, hominy, John Cake, & meats." (See Lane, *South Carolina*, pp. 107 ff.) Later Henry Izard went even further in his adaptations: in a distant plantation reached at the end of "eight days travelling from the Elms," he planned (and may have built) a "wigwam," "Circular, & the stack of chimneys in the middle . . . of Cob." (Ibid.)

archaeological, reverential view of the classics on the part of the Pennsylvania Academy of the Fine Arts, centering upon Smith's Grecian collection. So, in a way, that oration was directed against Smith—or people like Smith.

Biddle the Nationalist

Though Biddle was stereotyped by the Jacksonians as the financier of "the British party," he saw art, architecture, and much of literature through French spectacles, amusing himself by translating French verse and playing charades to French words. Biddle's experiences in France were very much like those of Jefferson, and they even knew some of the same people: Biddle visited Lafayette, dined with Madame de Staël, and flirted with Caroline du Sait.

These flirtations did not make him any less a nationalist than Jefferson or, indeed, Jackson. Despite their reciprocal loathing, the Philadelphia financier and the Tennessee general—"Nick the Greek" and "Old Hickory," rebuilders of American self-esteem—shared much the same opinion of the British. Both were sensitive to the patronizing airs of the "Milords," and though Biddle had not paid in blood for a refusal to put up with their pretensions (a British officer slashed the young Jackson for refusing to black his boots), his Greek journal is full of prickly nationalist asides.

He had "trodden the Roman forum and breathed the air of Grecian eloquence," but he had not lost his interest in people, living people, and present needs. In this he felt superior to "English travellers, assiduous hunters of curiosities, riding day and night to see an old wall or column, . . . but careless about any inquiry with regard to the people, their character, their usages, laws, etc. There is a sort of brutal coldness about them which forbids them from mingling with, or deriving information from foreigners. Every man is estimated by the distance of his birthplace from Hyde Park."[113]

He rejoiced in representing "the new and only republic . . . [amid] the ruins of the old." He was not intimidated by the ghosts of the past, for he came from a country "more civilized, more moral, more enlightened, better than any whose exploits have been transmitted by history." He was willing to admit that there was an argument for a nobility, but only one: "Its giving to the state citizens who are not always bent upon making money." He himself was never so bent; he sought power, not money, and in fact, after his marriage, had no need for "surplusage."[114]

Biddle's ambitions centered on public service through politics; he studied ancient oratory, "at once the engine of power, the road to fame and the means to fortune." All his life he referred to himself as a "republican," even after his political ambitions were frustrated by republican processes. Though he did succeed in election to the state legislature, he made the mistake of associating with the slimy but charming James Wilkinson, who betrayed everyone he knew, including a second friend of Biddle, Aaron Burr. The Biddles gave Burr shelter and legal business even after the collapse of Burr's contest with

Thomas Jefferson and his western adventures (sometimes called his "conspiracy"). Jefferson was sufficiently affronted to preclude any possibility that Biddle would have a career in the Jeffersonian party. (It is of some incidental interest that both Biddle and Jackson were supporters of Burr.)

Biddle was later an important source of funds for such Whigs as Webster and Clay, but he clung to the Federalist party much too long, abandoning it only when the New England Federalists outraged his nationalist principles by their cabals and threats of secession during the War of 1812. When he finally joined the Whigs, it was too late. Yet he never gave up his pride in a political system that offered an "avenue which leads to glory—wide and easy to Americans." As he groomed his oratorical skills, he reminded his brother that in "Europe there is no eloquence. Language is everywhere prostituted to adulation, and even in England oratory is paralyzed by venality, or trammeled by royal privilege, or chilled by the cold immoveable habits of the people."[115]

Here is the voice of young America, not at all overwhelmed by contemporary Europe or by ancient cultures. He was unperturbed by the "sneer of satire, the illusions, and that miserable cant which induces us to decry everything around and to bewail the degeneracy of men." The ancients were admirable, especially for their architecture, but "strip . . . the glare which renders them dazzling" and the modern citizens of Pennsylvania emerged very handsomely by comparison.[116]

Especially handsome was Biddle himself. He deployed his personal charms and his classical scholarship to reinforce nationalist stirrings in James Monroe, who was representing the Jefferson administration in Paris. He traveled with Monroe to London and Cambridge, where he performed the feat of confounding a group of dons with his knowledge of both ancient and modern Greek idioms. Monroe pronounced it to be "a kind of American triumph."[117]

When he came home, he prevailed upon his mother-in-law, Mrs. John Craig, to permit him to build a memory of Greece in the form of a little Doric pavilion at Andalusia, then a Craig estate. Next, in 1833, the other trustees of the estate of Stephen Girard were persuaded to use much of it to construct an entire temple compound for a school to serve, primarily, orphaned sons of seamen.† Finally, when the Craig estate became the Biddle estate, its new master caused the villa that Latrobe had remodeled for Craig to be remodeled again and encased by a massive Doric colonnade.[118]

The Financial Regents

When the trustees of Girard College [120] agreed to the displacement of the eighteenth-century aesthetic of their founder by the Greek Revival of Nicholas Biddle, they were also marking another stage in the transition of American finance. In the West, militant American nationalism expanded with cotton wealth across the upper South, and aspired to expand into Texas and Cuba as well. The militants did not speak very much of their dependence upon British markets and British money. Nor was it good form to remind the Jacksonians among them that while Old Hickory was restoring the nation's confidence, in the East, Nicholas Biddle (having learned in his youth how to negotiate the Louisiana Purchase loans in Paris and London) was restoring its credit.

The United States had borrowed foreign talent to conduct its financial affairs, as it had required French and British emigrés to get it started in architecture. These two sets of "trustees" or "regents" helped it to maturity—to become truly independent economically and aesthetically. The financier of the Revolution, Robert Morris, was born in Liverpool; Alexander Hamilton, the first treasury secretary, on the Caribbean island of Nevis. French lenders, led by Jacques Leray de Chaumont, joined with syndicates of Dutch bankers and the Spanish government to provide the funds Morris required. The Hopes of Holland and the Barings of Emden, Exeter, and London lent the money to buy Louisiana and sent David Parish, of Antwerp, to Philadelphia to arrange the massive shipments of Mexican silver to Europe in 1806–1808, shavings from which permitted Secretary of the Treasury Albert Gallatin, originally of Geneva, to rescue the fragile finances of the Jefferson administration.

Thereafter, the French-speaking Parish and Gallatin, together with Stephen Girard, born in Bordeaux, joined John Jacob Astor, whose written Anglo-German was barely legible (though good on a check), in finding the money to pay for the War of 1812, including provisions for the campaigns of Jackson, and for the capitalization of the Second Bank of the United States, without which the career of Nicholas Biddle might have been confined to the role of editor of the Lewis and Clark papers and *The Port folio*. They secured most of the money from American sources, and from that base Biddle slowly built the bank into an American institution.

While Biddle was advocating Grecian architecture as an expression of American nationalism, he was also busy espousing the cause of nationalist-classicism in literature. He defended Joel Barlow's epic poem *The Columbiad* against British critics on the ground that it showed an American language to be evolving. He served as editor for the Lewis and Clark papers and gradually took over the leadership of *The Port folio* as an American response to the *Edinburgh Review*.

Girard College

In that role he used every means to propagandize for a Greek Revival, publishing Latrobe's Anniversary Oration and a series of articles by George Tucker. Tucker braided together Greek ideas of architecture, American nationalism, and Scottish common-sense frugality. He rejoiced a decade early, in 1814, that the influence of "the numerous marble structures" of Athens from "the quarries of Pentelicus" could be seen in America, as the "marble of the Schuylkill manifested a propitious influence on architecture and the kindred art of sculpture in Philadelphia."[119]

What the Monroe Doctrine Did Not Include

Architecture as a public utterance is not always a statement on the part of an entire public, or even of a large majority. But when a way of building commends itself to such a large majority, rather suddenly and all at once, it is likely to express a set of feelings widely shared. The Greek Revival proclaimed a renewal of American pride after the mid-1820s. In this way, it was an American revival.

It is an irony of history that one of the clearest indications of the depths to which American pride had fallen was the federal government's lack of a commitment, morally or rhetorically—even in the absence of a show of sympathetic force—to the revival of Greece as an independent nation, and to the struggles for independence on the part of the Latin Americans.

The cosmopolitan spirit of the Declaration of Independence had not been a universal passion among the founders, though it was keenly felt by many of them. After 1820, those who kept that faith were reduced to an impotent handful. Once, the hope of "inalienable rights" had been held out to all mankind. A fleet was mustered in the Mediterranean to contend against "Barbary pirates" interfering with commerce, but no American frigate sailed in the Aegean. Though a series of secretaries of state blustered against Spain in support of the expansion of plantation slavery, there was not the energy to support Latin American independence with so much as a token expedition of the sort embattled France gave the Irish in 1798.

The Holy Alliance, despotic and otiose, presided over the cripples and cynics who had survived the Napoleonic wars and the decay of the Spanish Empire. At the extremes of the world that came easily within the American vision, the peoples of Greece and Latin America exerted themselves, and looked in vain for aid to the United States. This was a problem of conscience, and the failure of an American response showed how low the nation's self-esteem had fallen. To those living upon the shores of the Aegean and La Plata, the American revolutionary success and American revolutionary doctrine seemed universally applicable. But when put to the test, Americans no longer seemed to recall the principles of the Declaration; in their despondency they recoiled from exertion, except in commerce.

As if to comfort themselves for the moral stinginess to which all but a few had declined, they tried to persuade themselves that those now aspiring to freedom were unworthy of their aid. This, to Latin Americans, was the message of the Monroe Doctrine. While the European powers were warned that the United States would "consider any attempt on their part to extend" their colonies as "dangerous to our peace and safety," the forces of the region seeking independence were also warned, in the next sentence, that "with the existing colonies . . . we have not interfered and shall not interfere."[120]

In these balanced words, John Quincy Adams, the chief draftsman of the doctrine, told all who would listen that the United States had "no community of interests" with revolutionary forces in Latin America, which, he said, did not "possess the first elements of good or free government. Arbitrary power, military and ecclesiastical, was stamped upon their education, upon their habits, and upon all their instruments. Civil dissension . . . war and mutual destruction" were their habit.[121]

Adams's policy for Latin America was to keep the French, Russians, and British out, not to raise the Latin Americans up. His view was shared by Edward Everett, who expressed doubt that frugal Yankee yeomen had anything in common with the plantation owners of the Southern Hemisphere, who, as he put it, sat on horseback to fish.[122]

Henry Clay, as usual more generous in his views, damaged his presidential chances by losing his temper on the floor of the House of Representatives when he heard the contention that foreigners were unworthy to be free. He denounced as cowardly, "low," and "debased" those who would risk nothing to aid them. His colleague from Kentucky, Richard M. Johnson, though a man well ahead of his time on racial matters, did not extend himself far in foreign policy. Johnson derided Clay as imprudent, and it seems probable that even Nicholas Biddle, a chillier personality though a friend to Greece, concurred. Biddle was an Eastern aristocratic republican, Clay a Western one. Biddle admired Clay as he admired the highlanders of Arcadia, while viewing the rabble of cities, whether Athens or Philadelphia, as "little superior to the beasts they drive. . . . Unable to act, they scarcely dare to think freely. . . ."[123]

Clay was not alone for long, however. Albert Gallatin, in Paris, wrote President Monroe that the United States should send a naval expedition to aid the Greeks. From Indiana William Henry Harrison was heard to proclaim "the Star Spangled Banner must wave in the Aegean."[124] Many humbler Americans began volunteering to fight for Greek independence, and James Madison roused himself to tell Monroe it would be appropriate to recognize the Greek insurgents as an independent government. Monroe actually readied language to that effect for a presidential message, and Daniel Webster introduced a resolution to send an agent, or "commissioner," to Greece. For a moment it appeared that Monroe, prodded by Gallatin, Madison, and the Whigs, would do so.

Secretary of State John Quincy Adams stood firm, however, refusing to go even so far as the policy stated in the last lapidary utterance of the founding father—the Farewell Address of George Washington.

George Washington did not encourage his countrymen to be so rash as to think they were strong enough to be of much practical help, at the official level, to Latin American aspirations. Yet, though his Farewell Address firmly admonished his countrymen to eschew involvement in European wars (several of his

American-born officers had joined the French revolutionary armies in Flanders), it omitted any similar restraint as to private military or commercial intervention in Latin America.[†]

Both Washington and Hamilton gave support to Francisco de Miranda, the "precursor" of Venezuelan independence, though not so much as that recommended to them by the painter John Trumbull.[††] Miranda is one of those protean figures in the history of this period whom one encounters in unexpected ways. Among Trumbull's papers is a handsome sketch described in the handwriting of his old age (about 1840) as "General Miranda's plan for an Athenian house, 1797."[125] Miranda had passed Greece and, perhaps, visited Athens in 1786, on his way to seeking aid from Russia for his revolutionary activities. The house was not for Athens, of course, but for some American location; perhaps if Miranda had been more fortunate, it would have been the Venezuelan White House, the first true Greek Revival residence in the Western Hemisphere.[†††]

Trumbull and Rufus King, the American minister to London, were urging Washington and his successor, John Adams, to send military expeditions in support of "the emancipation of Mexico and South America." Trumbull wrote scores of letters describing the citizens of those Spanish colonies as exposed to the threat of "the Pollution of debauched and decrepid Old" Europe. Here was a theme familiar in American architectural theory and political theory; what was remarkable in Trumbull's formulation was that Latin Americans were included among those whose "Charms of youth & Health & Innocence" should be protected. Trumbull did not see things as did John Quincy Adams or Edward Everett, who did not acknowledge the Latinos as "youthful, vigorous, uncorrupted neighbors."[126]

Miranda died in a Spanish dungeon, having failed to secure sufficient support from the United States to give him a better chance of success when he finally made his expedition to liberate Venezuela. But it was not to be. The United States did not play the role for him that France had played for Washington, whose successors in the Virginia dynasty, Jefferson, Madison, and Monroe, were diffident in their support for revolts to the south.[127]

That diffidence was apparent in the cabinet infighting that preceded the promulgation of the presidential dicta that became the Monroe Doctrine. John Quincy Adams, then secretary of state, mobilized every argument he could muster to induce Monroe to go no further than a reaffirmation of a special interest on the part of the United States in Latin America. Adams especially sought to delete any commitment to the independence of either the Latins or Greeks.

Monroe's original draft had included such a passage; he had come so far as that with the new mood of confidence in the country. He had been congratulated for doing so by Madison and had received no

† Alexander Hamilton and George Washington, though more friendly to oligarchic Britain than to Jacobin France, did not wish the influence of either to grow stronger in the Western Hemisphere. There were expanding markets in Latin America, and there was, for some Federalists, a genuine sympathy for other Americans seeking independence, even those led by blacks, such as Toussaint-Louverture, in the West Indies. Hamilton himself supported Toussaint, helped write the constitution for his black republic on Hispaniola, and aspired to lead American expeditions to "liberate" the Spanish borderlands in the 1790s.
  John Adams, Washington's successor, actively deployed the United States fleet in support of the revolution of Toussaint. This policy was reversed by Jefferson, after 1800, for fear of the spread of slave insurrection and for love of France.

†† Trumbull was an arch-Federalist (ambiguous only as between Whigs and Tories at the time of the Revolution) who saw Miranda's aversion to Jacobinism as a guarantee against the spread of radical ideas and the reappearance of a French empire in the Americas. After Jefferson became president, he put Adams's inept son-in-law, William Smith, on trial for actively supporting Miranda by furnishing military supplies in New York.

††† Miranda had a good eye for palaces; we are indebted to him for some of our knowledge of French gardens for, when he paused in North Carolina for recruits and supplies, he saw the estate of the British colonial governor, William Tryon, and observed amid the ravages of revolution vestiges of an elaborate garden plan. He made inquiries, and as a result it was established that Claude-Joseph Sauthier of Strasbourg was the designer.

objection from Jefferson. Adams talked him out of it, to the latter-day approbation of the devotees of *realpolitik*. To such men as Hans Morgenthau or Henry Kissinger, Adams demonstrated "statecraft in an atmosphere saturated with Jeffersonian [meaning vaguely idealistic, apparently] principles." But others have regretted ever since that he abandoned "the innocence of Old Republicanism, . . . the belief of the cosmopolitans among the founders that it was the mission of the United States to transform the Old World, not by fleets and subsidies but by the magic of example and the force of morality." In the end Monroe permitted himself to relinquish even the mention of Greece by name and slunk behind vague references to Americans' viewing the struggle for freedom in Europe as "anxious and interested spectators," cherishing "sentiments the most friendly, in favor of the liberty and happiness of their fellowmen."[128]

Thus denatured of its cosmopolitan mission, Monroe's equally vague references to Latin America offered as little challenge to the reimposition of despotism in Latin America as to the maintenance of Turkish despotism in Greece. It appeared that all the United States desired was an open opportunity for trade.

Henry Clay was speaking for a new set of leaders who renewed the old cries for aid to the insurgents in Latin America and Greece. John Quincy Adams's statesmanship was no doubt prudent, for Monroe's armed forces were scarcely able to assure protection for American shipping beyond the mouth of the Mississippi. Yet it was demeaning to rely upon the British fleet to keep Latin markets open to British merchants and, incidentally, to American shipping as well. This dependency upon British commercial interest was characteristic of the dispirited times. The Monroe Doctrine is a product of America as it was pulling itself out of a trough. Had it been written by Daniel Webster or by Clay, rather than by John Quincy Adams and James Monroe, it might have included an inspiring manifesto for the Greek Revival.

Greek Independence

Meanwhile, the Greeks were going ahead, soliciting aid for the cause of independence from more vigorous "idealists." In 1821 the president of the international "Friends of Greece," Alexandros Ypsilantis, invaded Turkey from the north, and the archbishop of Patras rose in open rebellion in the Morea.

The Christian clergy of Greece were leaders of revolt; the Turks responded by trying to exterminate them. After the execution of the patriarch of Constantinople and the celebrated massacre of the inhabitants of Scio (Khíos), the Protestant and Roman Catholic West joined with the Orthodox East. The repressed liberalism of Western Europe found common cause with the residual evangelism of America. Though only grudging aid came to the Greek people from the reactionary governments of Britain, France, and Russia, individual idealists from those countries and from the United States joined the cause with passion and, in some cases, effectiveness.

Free spirits, religious zealots, and self-dramatizing men of letters joined in an outpouring of support for Greek independence. Some of it was merely rhetorical: one upstate New York braggart asserted that he could mobilize "five hundred men six feet high, with sinewy arms and case-hardened constitutions, bold spirits and daring adventurers, who would travel upon a bushel of corn and a gallon of whiskey per man from the extreme part of the world [presumably the region of Otsego County] to Constantinople."[129]

Americans were not very useful in Greece; but the old idealism of the Declaration began to reappear just as the Greeks themselves achieved their independence. Perhaps it was that independence that was useful in *America* instead. The Greek example roused thoughts like those William Gilpin expressed in 1846: "The *untransacted* destiny of the American people is . . . to cheer them upward . . . to regenerate superannuated nations . . . to dissolve the spell of tyranny and exalt charity . . . to shed blessings around the world." At least the spirit was willing. Theophilus Fisk proclaimed: "With friends of freedom throughout the world, let us be co-workers," and the full flush of the old enthusiasm was felt in Fanny Wright's slogan: "The People of the World have but one Cause."[130]

Other friends of Greece, such as Lord Byron, had not only stated the case more elegantly, but expressed themselves with action as well as ringing words. Byron's death in Greece in 1824 and Chateaubriand's famous question "Will Christendom allow Turks to strangle Christians?" led to a flood of volunteers; the commander of the Greek forces in 1825 was a former officer under Napoleon, and the conti di Santa Rosa, leader of the Piedmont revolution against the Austrians, died in Greece "as a simple soldier."[131]

The star-spangled banner never waved in the Aegean, but the French called for the "Standard of the Cross . . . [to] fly over the roofs of Constantinople or over the Parthenon." Since the Standard of the Cross had flown over the Venetian force that had sent shells into the Parthenon not too long before, that was an unfortunate turn of phrase, but all over Europe, Latin America, and the United States, there was an ebullience of genuine sympathy for Greece.[132]

The combined navies of Britain, France, and Russia eliminated the Turkish fleet at Navarino in 1827, though only for their own purposes. The British were freed of further threats to the puppet commonwealth they had established in the Aegean Islands in 1815, the Turks on land were deprived of their supply lines, and the Greeks had by that time achieved control of most of the mainland. In the end, it was "not the governments of Europe who saved Greece, but public opinion." And public opinion in the United States was not of much practical use, though it brought about the renaming of innumerable towns for Sparta, Athens, Corinth, Homer, and Ypsilanti.[133]

In March 1829 the powers of Europe went so far as to force the Turks to set a Christian prince upon the throne of Greece as a tributary to the sultan. Six months later, the Greeks were irresistible in their demands for full independence, though the intrigues of agents of the great powers rendered its throne unappetizing to a succession of potential princes. No one would take the job; the Greeks could not agree on anyone the powers could agree upon. Not until 1863 did a sovereign acceptable to the Greeks, British, French, and Russians appear. He was the first modern king of Greece, George I, who had been merely a Danish prince, William Ferdinand Adolphus George of Schleswig-Holstein-Sønderborg-Glucksburg.

Andrew Jackson and the Classics

In the 1780s, the Great Seal of the United States had proclaimed the arrival of a New Order of the Universe. In the 1830s, it seemed possible that such a new order had, at last, arrived in the United States.

Andrew Jackson, cleansed of the wild profligacy of his youth and purged of that love of luxury that marked his middle years, became the living symbol of a renewal of austere patriotism, while the Greek Revival provided the physical symbols of Jacksonian simplicity and "manliness"—the latter quality being defined in ways peculiar to the period. Like all symbols, Jackson himself, and the Greek Revival, had imparted diverse meanings to diverse people, but most of these implications were mutually reinforcing. Along with austerity, virility, and patriotism, the architecture (always a public art) and the man (increasingly a public figure) signified stability imposed by firmness, order instated, and independence. *Independence* meant something more than political self-government. True American independence meant, as well, freedom from the influence of Europe.

The founders had left their work incomplete. They had disrupted the continuities in the institutions of church, aristocracy, family, army, and squirarchy; they had risked dispensing with inherited forms and usages "which long experience had shown to be needed for the safety of society."[134] They established a new frame of government, but they did not succeed in filling quickly the void they had left. (It could be argued that void has never been filled.) Even their contemporaries were aware that though the "American War is over . . . this is far from being the case with the American revolution. On the contrary, nothing but the first act of the great drama is closed."[135]

As the decades proceeded, the brave new world betrayed the limitations inherent in any mundane reality, and those infirmities particular to the American situation. The heroes were shrinking to human scale. Because they were heroes, their failures became the people's failures. That is the way of heroes. But, shamefully, the people became ashamed of them.

Andrew Jackson positioned himself to gather the energy of this national chagrin and remorse, turning his back upon his own past as a gambler, land speculator, slave trader, and frontier entrepreneur avid for riches. He reappeared as Cincinnatus, the simple farmer, called from the plow to the presidency. He had often been called to heroism in war, twice against the British, once against the Spaniards, and innumerable times for skirmishes against the Native Americans. In the 1820s he responded to a nation's longing for a father of whom they could be proud, who might restore to them their own childhood.

In his Inaugural Address, Jackson commenced a contest against the forces of modernity. The recently converted frontier Calvinist did not go so far as to repent in public for his own youthful indiscretions, but he did call for a collective reformation. The frontier evangelists were calling for a Second Great Awakening; reform and repentance were in the air. All through the backwoods, preachers inveighed against drunkenness and indiscriminate sexuality; they had energy left to inveigh against the largely inaccessible sins of luxury and European vices. Jackson's contribution was a crusade against the financial means whereby opportunities for these exotic vices might be obtained. He attacked banks as agents of foreigners and of government policies that had lavished favor upon the corrupt and the already excessively blessed. In a campaign against deficiencies in virtue, he set himself to "revive and perpetuate those habits of economy and simplicity which are so congenial to the character of republicans."[136]

Taking up the ancient fight, he recalled that luxury undermined Grecian power and reduced to ashes the might of Rome; more recently, luxury had betrayed the hopes of the founders. But in the 1830s a Greek and Roman revival might meet and conquer luxury: "To build in the classic, to stress the simple, to emphasize realism in portraiture and geometry in architecture meant an eschewal of elaborate ornament and an avoidance of visual richness which to Americans . . . hung over the decayed Continent like the evil breath of tyranny."[137]

Jackson's constant use of classical analogies may surprise those who retain the impression that he was a heroic bumpkin, a sort of wise man of the woods, full of canniness but devoid of education, and that his administration was peopled by vulgarians top to bottom. It used to be said that, until his administration, the presidents were invariably gentlemen trained in the classics. Thereafter, it was implied, things descended to brawling bumptiousness. The myth persisted that the last of the classical gentlemen was John Quincy Adams, whose administration (1825–29) closed the era in which classical gentlemen set the tone. Adams, to give emphasis to the point, died amid the classical statuary of the Capitol.

But Jackson cleverly made a popular appeal to democracy, an invocation of the first, leveling stage of the frontier, and at the same time, gave subtle reassurance that he was a classical gentleman who would preserve order against nullifying states, unruly mobs, slave insurrection, or bothersome Indians. The disorder most white Americans feared did not arise from a little friendly politicking on the part of the unwashed; it was unfriendly sedition by blacks, Indian attacks, or the collapse of the Union into warring sections.

There was no doubt where Jackson stood; he was the president who first gave Washington City classical grandeur, and the first frontiersman to build himself a Roman mansion of international celebrity.

Besides, anyone who followed his politics closely knew that those who actually governed during his administration held more college degrees and came from a somewhat higher economic status than those in office under Thomas Jefferson. If one counts classical references in the utterances of the statesmen in the entourage of Jackson and checks the sociology of his appointments, it will be found that they confirm the constructed evidence: the Jackson administration *opened* the era in which the classical past can truly be said to have shaped American architecture. The Greek Revival, the most widespread, vigorous, and ingenious expression of the power of that past in any realm of American life, arose as Adams was on his way *out* of office and Jackson on his way *in*.

For Jackson, Robert Mills implanted a uniform, ceremonious Grecian style upon the nation's capital, as none of the "court architects" of preceding presidents had been able to do. And during the Jackson administration, the American public made the explicitly classical its predominant private architecture.

True enough, it was no longer so fashionable for politicians to deploy a patronizing and invidious erudition about ancient languages and classical references. Daniel Webster, acting as speech rewriter for William Henry Harrison, said he "slew seventeen Roman pro-consuls as dead as smelts," but only because he was updating Harrison's old-fashioned rhythms in the use of classical allusions.[138] While the Whigs were retrofitting that old Virginian gentleman into their answer to Jackson, a log-cabin-and-hard-cider frontiersman, the Jacksonians became profuse in classical allusions, both in language and in building. The triumph of the Greek Revival demonstrated that the use of classical forms was as popular in architecture as in rhetoric; its contours became a primary means by which the nation expressed both its recovered confidence and its commitment to orderly progressions in politics and the dominance of nature. Among other messages, the Greek Revival made the statement that Americans were coming to be—indeed, insisted upon being—*themselves*, neither effete Europeans nor savages.

Men still living in 1830 could recall that, since the 1790s, it had been conventional for politicians to issue periodic calls for patriotic austerity. The commissioners of public buildings in Washington City had said they wished to exhibit republican simplicity. Though that earlier era of simplicity hardly lasted to nightfall, it dawned again in the 1820s for Andrew Jackson with this difference: simplicity need not be small.

In that, Jackson agreed completely with Nicholas Biddle. Biddle's exhortation to another building committee, this one assembled for Girard College in Philadelphia in 1833, that they lavish millions of austere old Stephen Girard's bequest upon the construction of "simple" temples, was not hypocritical just because the results would be expensive. It may seem odd to urge such extravagance as patriotic thrift. But what he said to the committee was consistent with what he said and wrote elsewhere; though very

† (Biddle quoted in Gilchrest, pp. 23 ff.) Thomas Jefferson sometimes *wrote* as if he were making distinctions similar to those upon which Jackson acted: there was, after all, an overlap of thirty years in their public careers. His instructions to architects (such as Latrobe) sometimes used the adjective *Athenian* to describe the kind of public buildings he wanted, and he once demanded that Latrobe produce a column capital often used by English classicists and drawn from the Greek. But he never concerned himself with the differences between the domed and vaulted usages of the Romans and the post-and-lintel construction employed (aboveground) by the Greeks. More to the point, he was indifferent to distinct symbolic resonances of Greek and Roman forms. He showed no real interest in Greek forms in general, except when testing Latrobe as to the aforesaid capital and in a little interior ornament at Monticello.

large, and therefore expensive, these new temples in the "chaste" Grecian style would carry the meaning of "austere" simplicity and show that Americans could eschew the "gaudy profusion" of the Old World.[139]

Biddle did not, of course, suggest a return to nature. Though Europe may have been overripe, Philadelphia should not be raw. There should be no lapse in taste to mark its citizens as coarse and unlettered. The Greek Revival would be a civilized separation from degenerate Europe, not a retreat into barbarism. For nationalist Americans of Biddle's taste, the Grecian was the only proper style for either public or domestic use; for those who followed Jackson, it was employed only for public buildings. They preferred something more elaborate, the Roman, in private.†

Nicholas Biddle and an Ideology for the Greek Revival

Under Nicholas Biddle's aegis, the journal *The Port folio*, in Philadelphia, began in 1811 to offer a bracing sequence of essays upon nationalism in architecture, literature, and banking policy. It had been edited by his friend Joseph Dennie, but Dennie was alcoholic and erratic, so Biddle increasingly took responsibility for its content. His two chief architectural writers were George Tucker, the American best qualified to carry into "the western wilds" the pan-Hellenism that had flowered in Edinburgh in the 1760s, and Benjamin Henry Latrobe.

Latrobe and Tucker enjoyed the sponsorship of Biddle in *The Port folio* and, at the same time, were friends and protégés of the aged Thomas Jefferson. Latrobe had so endeared himself to the Sage of Monticello that, even after his dismissal from the superintendency of public buildings in Washington (the post to which he had been appointed by Jefferson), the former president, in retirement, sought his advice as to the architecture of his beloved University of Virginia, while he selected Tucker to occupy one of the first faculty posts for the university. As professor of moral philosophy, Tucker imparted to students, in the Greek Revival period, the Scottish "Common Sense" philosophy that had been so important to Jefferson in his own youth.[140]

American philosophy, aesthetic, economic, and political, had deep roots in Edinburgh. Gavin Hamilton, Lord Kames, David Hume, and Adam Smith had their own effects upon the American scene, though transmuted into American forms. In the 1760s and 1770s these men combined a profound enthusiasm for Greece with a sophisticated view of "liberal" economics. They reinforced in each other, and in their colleague Robert Adam, a due respect for the discoveries of the young Scotsman James Stuart and his friend Nicholas Revett. Hamilton and his patrons, the first and second marquises of Lansdowne, are the links between Edinburgh and the first great American painters, John Singleton Copley and Benjamin West, as well as to the first great American antiquary and Hellenist, Joseph Allen Smith.

Tucker did not subscribe to Jefferson's hostile view of banks and bankers; nor had the Scots, but their enthusiasm for banking had not seemed important in Jefferson's Williamsburg of the 1760s and 1770s. Until the death of the Sage in 1826, Tucker was careful to keep anonymous most of his writing on that subject when the publications were those of Virginia, for his views, drawn from those of the Edinburgh circle around Adam Smith, were entirely harmonious with those of Biddle. Anonymous too, after 1814, were his contributions to the pages of *The Port folio*. "On Style" was followed by "On the Future Destiny of the United States"; "On Architecture" and "On Beauty," by "On Banks of Circulation." Then came "On Simplicity in Ornament" and "On Rhyme," followed by "On National Debts."[141]

The Port folio carried only one signed article by Latrobe—though its policy of anonymity may cloak other entries—a restatement of his Anniversary Oration to the Society of Artists, in Philadelphia, which had been delivered in May 1811. Latrobe gave America its first clear statement of pan-Hellenism of the Scottish variety—and, incidentally, of a friendly connection between bankers and Greek Revival architecture.[142]

Latrobe distinguished between Athenian buildings and those of the Romans, created for "the indulgence of popular pleasures . . . by the most tyrannical emperors . . . monuments to the departed liberty of the people," which were emulated in eighteenth-century France. There was nothing vague about his knowledge of the differences between Greece and Rome; nor did he share his patron Jefferson's aversion to either merchants or bankers. He contrasted Rome to "Florence under the merchants, the Medicis" and urged Philadelphia to rejoice in its similarities to the latter. It was not "the corrupt age of Dioclesian, or the still more absurd and debased taste of Louis the XIV" that Americans should emulate, but the simple tastes of William Penn and his merchant successors, who erected the "first building in which marble was employed as the principal material of its front, . . . the Bank of the United States."[143]

Latrobe proudly noted that his first large commission in America, the Bank of Pennsylvania, "a pure specimen of Greek simplicity in design," came only a year after the Bank of the United States. "The existence and taste of this building," said he (with modesty so rare as to be almost certainly sincere), "is due, not to the architect, but to . . . the late President of the Pennsylvania Bank, Mr. Samuel M. Fox. . . . Had this city been Athens, he would have been a Pericles."[144]

Biddle solicited Grecian works for Philadelphia, to make it the "Athens of America" (perhaps he may have heard that Adams aspired to make of Boston a "Christian Sparta"). Biddle's purpose was not, however, to emulate the ancients; his nationalism was as powerful as, indeed indistinguishable from, his pan-Hellenism. For *The Port folio* he solicited American epics of "the revolutionary contest" from "our young poets," and Latrobe's address, with its rejection of archaeological exactitude or replication, was reprinted in its entirety as soon as it was delivered, the first statement of an American ideology—a mythic framework—for the American Greek Revival.[145] It was a little premature in 1811, just as the Bank of Pennsylvania had been premature in 1798. But its principles were taken up after 1825 and came to dominate American discourse about architecture for the thirty years thereafter.

The Anniversary Oration   In the accents of David Hume, Latrobe told his audience that classical architecture arose in Greece, to which "the civilized world has been indebted for more than two thousand years, for instruction in the fine arts."[146] This seems a blandly conventional statement to us, but much of eighteenth-century English architectural theory was based upon the idea that the Romans brought architecture to perfection and that the Greeks lacked elegance and grace. Imperial England saw itself as the successor to imperial Rome, not to republican Greece. So Latrobe was speaking for the nineteenth century, not for the eighteenth, and for his new country, not for that he had left behind.

"Greece was free," he said. That was her chief claim, "the source of her eminence. . . . In Greece every citizen felt himself important . . . the path of glory was equally open to all." The analogy to the United States was obvious, and the subsequent subjection of Greece to Rome was a sober warning "to guard well the liberty that alone can produce such wonders."[147]

From its pristine "Attic Simplicity," Hume, and the pan-Hellenic Scots, had seen the ancient world decline from Greek simplicity into Hellenistic "complex and profuse ornament," and ultimately into the "Asiatic Complexity" of Rome, as it sank into imperial despotism.[148] Latrobe asserted that the buildings of republican Rome had included some "of the best taste," but "the monuments . . . during the reign of the emperors, grow into colossal size and expense . . . dwindle into absurdity in the style of their decorations . . . a crowded patchwork of parts, pillaged from the trophies of former conquerors."[149]

Latrobe was politicizing architecture, pointing to a reciprocal relationship between public art and the public that at once nourishes and is nourished by it. "Greece was free when the arts flourished, and that freedom derived from them much of her support and permanence." It was only natural that there should be a revival of Grecian forms in America, where freedom and openness to talent had been revived upon "soil as congenial" to the arts "and as favorable to their growth and perfection, as that of Sparta, Thebes, Delphos, or Athens." Perhaps "the days of Greece may be revived in the woods of America, and Philadelphia become the Athens of the Western World."†

Literal-minded contemporaries were as quick to mistake his meaning as literal-minded historians a century later; Latrobe became quite cross when his critics seized upon his unfortunate use of the term *specimen* of classical architecture to mean *replica*. The British and French antiquarians had indeed made replicas, and he had no desire to be confused with them. "The grossest ignorance alone could assert that the Bank of Pennsylvania is the copy of a Greek Temple. All that is said on this subject is as absurd as it is false—even the Porticos vary in every part of their proportions of columns and entablature from every temple in existence."[150]

This much he had in common with Jefferson who, twenty-two years earlier, explained what he meant when he offered the Maison Carrée, a Roman temple at Nîmes, as the model for the Virginia capitol. He

† (Latrobe, *Papers*, vol. 3, pp. 67–91) Latrobe was not as well acquainted as George Hadfield with the recent discoveries of Greek ruins in Italy, but he had considerable firsthand knowledge of Roman architecture, especially the Pantheon. Like Jefferson, he was forced to depend upon secondary sources as well as the sometimes unreliable impressions of intervening critics and historians. He had toured Italy with Antoine Desgodetz's guidebook that attributed the first-century A.D. amphitheater at Verona to the Roman architect and writer Vitruvius, citing Perrault, who was the editor, it happens, of the first book on architecture owned by Jefferson. As a result, he repeated a tiny mistake by Desgodetz in his Anniversary Oration. (The Vitruvius at Verona story appears, with all appropriate citations, as note 17 to the Anniversary Oration, ibid.)

Latrobe was not impressed by Vitruvius, despite what Jefferson, Palladio, or Piranesi had to say. "The book of Vitruvius, a Roman . . . is of very inferior rank . . . in its . . . taste, and its science, and is not now entirely intelligible." (Ibid.)

did not suggest that it be copied and, in his own free transcription of its form, came no closer to copying it than did he, and contemporaries, reproduce either Greek or Roman political institutions.

Latrobe, Tucker, and Jefferson were repeatedly and customarily in advance of their countrymen. But the American Greek Revival did, ultimately, advance along the lines they laid down. When that occurred, after 1825, it partook in their nationalist and republican symbolic intentions and was, therefore, quite a distinct phenomenon from its closest physical counterpart, the Scottish Greek Revival. Though all three of these aesthetic philosophers used the verbal rhetoric of Edinburgh for part of their arguments and displayed the benefits of Scottish learning, they added an American political emphasis. The Scots, under the British Crown, could not be expected to deploy their pan-Hellenism in the same way as the Americans; and though the Scottish Greek Revival was conspicuously more ambitious than the English, it was nonetheless closer to the labored antiquarianism of London than to the less learned and more ingenious Free Classicism of the new towns of the American West.

In the 1830s Robert Mills took up Latrobe's job as superintendent of public buildings (with a slightly different title) in Washington, working as court architect to Andrew Jackson as Latrobe had served Jefferson. He took up the theme developed by both the mentors of his youth, Jefferson and Latrobe: while expressing respect for "the Greek masters," he was firm that Americans should "learn principles, not copy shapes . . . let us imitate them like men, not ape them like monkeys."[151] Though Mills worked for Jackson and Thomas Ustick Walter for Biddle, Walter also repudiated the "popular idea that to design in Grecian taste is nothing more than to copy a Grecian building." This notion was "altogether erroneous. . . . Even the Greeks never made two buildings alike. . . . If architects would more often think as the Greeks thought, than to do as the Greeks did, our columnar architecture would possess a higher degree of originality and its character and expression would gradually conform to the local circumstances of the country and the republican spirit of its institutions." To a glorious degree, they did—and it did.[152]

Nicholas Biddle caused a series of essays on this theme to be printed in *The Port folio;* after those of Latrobe and Tucker came others by William Strickland. Philadelphia and Athens—even today a coupling of the two does not seem altogether foolish, as one looks up from one's *Wall Street Journal* soon after the train leaves Thirtieth Street for New York and sees the little succession of temples along the Schuylkill. Though they compose only a waterworks [118–19], and not so Hellenistically dramatic a waterworks as that composed a little later for Louisville [368, 369], they will do. Even the engines of an industrial society accommodated themselves to the ideology of the Greek Revival, for a while.

Like Latrobe, Nicholas Biddle saw nothing presumptuous in setting temples, even temples for banking, shining white upon the banks of American rivers. He assured the citizens of Philadelphia that they were worthy successors to the Greeks—and to the Florentines as well. "There is not a more picturesque or poetic region than our own—Arcadia itself is no more beautiful, nor yet more sonorous, than Pennsylvania; and the Thames, or even the Arno, are insipid brooks, by the side of the Hudson or the Schuylkill." The use of a Greek form, untainted by the decayed fashions of Europe, would ensure that "no country on earth can boast a purer specimen of architecture . . . to convey to distant ages the 'spirit of the time.'"[153]

Fairmont Waterworks, Philadelphia

His critics responded that it ill became a banker-dilettante to place his inky fingertips upon poetry or architecture. Latrobe was forgotten, and so was Samuel Fox. How could a man of commerce speak so proudly of "the spirit of the time"? But it was precisely because commercial America was coming to think more proudly of itself—as Fox and Biddle thought more of themselves than could be conveyed in any shriveled stereotype of a banker—that nothing short of the Grecian and the heroic would do.

The times . . . the times . . . let us consider *time*, like *order*, as a term carrying more meanings than were dreamt of by Nicholas Biddle's detractors. They did not pause to consider what is meant when one says that money is a "store of value." Money resists time, especially if it is redeemable in specie—silver or gold.

In the Greek Revival period, when American banking was first taking shape and assuming its architectural expression, Americans, as now, were obsessed with the passage of time and gained some comfort, as Fred Somkin has suggested, from the possibility that "by cleaving to the primitively old . . . [they] gained the possibility of continuing to be always new. . . . In the classic, archetypal forms of political life . . . [or of architecture] were to be found . . . a kind of rebuke to time."[154]

All architects who have brooded much upon the relationship of classical architecture to time, from Jefferson and Latrobe to Le Corbusier, have seen the temple form as architecture aspiring to longevity. Jefferson wrote Latrobe that he wished to see the national Capitol as "the first temple dedicated to the sovereignty of the people, embellishing with Athenian taste the course of a nation looking beyond the range of Athenian destinies."[155†]

The Romans had their own Greek Revival, and their temple-form structures—firmly anchored by columns—looked, felt, and were massive, dense, and stable. Their columnar buildings gave comfort

† (Jefferson quoted in Paul F. Norton, "Thomas Jefferson and the Planning of the National Capitol," in William Howard Adams et al., *The Eye of Thomas Jefferson.* Washington: National Gallery of Art, 1976, p. 227)

Similar classical themes dominated drama and opera. The solemn stateliness of Cherubini and Gluck carried the implication that the more things changed—even with apparent violence and with bewildering rapidity—the more they remained the same. When a rebellious genius such as Mozart made bold to trifle with these grand themes in *The Magic Flute,* his comic relief was of an ancient, almost liturgical, kind. Though Papagena and Pagageno spoke in German, classically trained members of his audience would know that the ritual purpose they served was older than any modern language.

When Jefferson wrote to Latrobe about the importance of making the Capitol "a durable and honorable monument of our infant republic," he required not only that it would be soundly constructed, but also that it invoke a sense of duration, like "the remains of the same kind of the ancient republics of Greece & Rome." "To embellish with Athenian taste" meant providing symbols to imply that the American republic might last as long as the Athenian republic—and longer.

against chaos in A.D. 300 as the Greeks' had in 400 B.C. and as the Americans' would in 1824. To virility and simplicity, purity and republicanism, was added pertinacity as a virtue of the Greek Revival.

T he Greek was new in 1800; still new, because rarely seen, in 1830. It was both ancient and new, because it was free of contemporary European corruptions. It was not in that way distinct from the uncorrupted, or precorrupted, state to which Henry David Thoreau urged his countrymen to return. He did not endorse simplicity of the Doric sort, but he did tell them to "keep the New World *new*, preserve all the advantages of living in the country. . . . Sin . . . is in proportion to the . . . degree to which our elements are mixed with the elements of the world."[156]

Thoreau and his contemporaries were finally piercing the mystery of Lafayette's irresistible attraction; his was the biography of a search for redeeming newness. Lafayette had repudiated Old Europe when he was young, voyaging to America in a quest for an unspoiled Eden:

> *The old world's night he leaves behind;*
> *The morn of the New is before him.*[157]

He was the perfect herald to the Greek Revival, as well as the perfect schoolmaster for Andrew Jackson. Though Thoreau and Walt Whitman had very little in common, they were concerted in admiring the beauty of gestures like Lafayette's rejection of Europe and his embrace of young, bold, fresh, innocent, decent America: "Let the Old World wag under its cumbrous load of form and conservatism."[158]

Though their country was civilized, it inhabited a border province of the Atlantic community. *Behind* was the Old World, afflicted with cynicism and tyrannous exploitation. *Ahead* was the wilderness, savage and demoralizing.

This picture, a little simply stated, was widely believed in the Age of Jackson and Biddle. The Greek Revival was set before such a backdrop. When Americans thought and wrote about their architecture, they had this "middle state" in mind. Nicholas Biddle had already used that term to describe Pennsylvania when he wrote home from Greece. Other traveling Americans followed Biddle to Greece, and there they saw temples, bleached white by the years, defying time and tyranny. Amid roses and olives, these eternal symbols stood at the end of one kind of history. American temple-homesteads might stand at the beginning of another. Ancient Greece seemed closer to their own isolation and *relative* simplicity than the intervening stews and confusions of Britain or France. White temple ruins, defying nature, became white temple-form houses, defying both contemporary Europe and nature.

The Europe most proximate to them historically was Great Britain. The wilderness most on their minds was the untamed West. (Yankees looked to the north toward wilderness, and Georgians to the south as well, but the West was a universal synonym for the wild.) To stand between corruption and savagery meant a choice between the forms of architectural necessity on a frontier (such as log cabins, soddies, or caves) and the Greek.

Not all Americans chose the Greek, of course; the force of other traditions was, and is, very powerful. But it is remarkable that as soon as new building devices made mass production of housing possible on the frontier, as with the balloon frame in Chicago in the 1830s, they were immediately employed to build Greek Revival houses.

Biddle and His Buildings

With patriotic conviction, Nicholas Biddle turned his countrymen toward the elevation of the national credit and of the national taste—Thomas Jefferson had attempted only the latter. As Latrobe had reminded Philadelphians, the First Bank of the United States had a portico, ill formed as it was, and that portico was of marble. His Bank of Pennsylvania, in 1798, came closer to the Greek, despite its dome and vaults. There is no clear evidence of Biddle's opinion of Latrobe, but there is a good deal of documentation of his support for the new generation, his own generation, of architects then benefiting from Latrobe's example.

Second Bank of the United States, Philadelphia

Among these were John Haviland, who completed the first Greek Revival pattern book in 1817; Latrobe's student, William Strickland; and Strickland's student, Thomas Walter. When the Second Bank of the United States held a competition for the design of its headquarters in Philadelphia in 1818, Haviland, Strickland, Latrobe, George Hadfield, Robert Mills, and Robert Cary Long, Sr., made submissions. It appears that Biddle placed his influence behind his friend and close contemporary, Strickland, rejecting the older men. Besides, Latrobe was Jefferson's friend, and Biddle was a Burrite. Biddle discussed his opinions with many people, almost certainly including the directors of the Second Bank, all of whom were known to him. In the end, Strickland's Greek design was chosen for the headquarters for the rechartered bank.

A decade later Biddle made an irresistible combination of offers to Walter, a man with talent for architecture and—as he demonstrated throughout a long and richly rewarded career—for his "main chance." The first was to sheathe Biddle's famous country house, Andalusia, with columns carrying allusions to classical heroism, to be modeled upon those of a temple to Theseus. The other was to be weaned from the plan for an old-fashioned, English-derived composition with which Walter had won the competition for the most celebrated public-building scheme in Philadelphia, the campus for Girard College.

There is no evidence that Biddle pointedly linked the two; they merely became available with intriguing simultaneity. Andalusia was already conspicuous as the seat of the president of the Bank of the United States. And Biddle assured Walter that a reconsideration of the design for the college was a "rare opportunity of immortalizing himself by a perfect, chaste specimen of Greek architecture." Soon, the building committee came around to the conclusion that "all the plans which had been previously offered . . . should be set aside, and that the Architect be directed to prepare a new design . . . after the manner of a Greek temple."[159]

Thereby they set aside, as well, Philadelphia's long, stubborn resistance to the classic. Latrobe, Strickland, and Haviland had tried sweet reason and carpenters' guides; now, in the 1830s, Biddle used more persuasive means. Walter's conservative winning design, a competent reiteration of the habits of his fellow artisans in the powerful Carpenters' Company, was replaced with something more to Biddle's liking—and less, one can be quite sure, to the decedent Girard's. As Walter abandoned his first plan, the hold of colonialism and of the eighteenth century had finally been broken. Long stale, the Georgian, the Adamesque Federal, the Roman, and the eighteenth-century French had finally become politically unsavory.

Jacksonian Gothic

American temple builders lived during an era in which literature and architecture were twin muses, not easily separated. If one chose to build in the Greek style, one might be expected to be able to explain why, and in respectable prose. The explanation might include the reasons one was not building in the Gothic, for any competent architect was trained to work in both (Latrobe initiated the Gothic Revival in America with his William Crammond House in Philadelphia). Famous writers had made the case for each, at length. In England the eighteenth-century "Gothick" had been the playful indulgence of the cheerfully morbid imagination of novelists such as Horace Walpole and William Beckford. Their buildings and their stories were extravagant and fanciful confections, free of the dampening effects of historical exactitude. In the nineteenth century, the Gothic lost a *k* and gained the patriotic fervor of both the English and the Scots. It was adopted in North America by anglophilic Canadians and by literary people hoping their neighbors would mistake them for Walpole, or later, for the squire of Abbotsford, Sir Walter Scott.

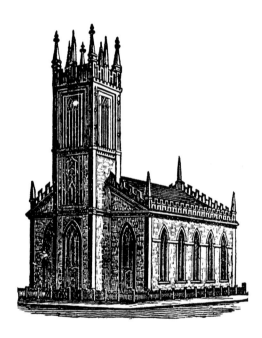

St. Paul's Church, Troy, New York

The Gothic was also adopted by some Jacksonians whose pantheons were commodious enough to accommodate both the Senex father and the Mother country. These were the Gothic Jacksonians, tame in their nationalism, natural Tories drawn to Jackson largely out of a love of drama. The largest of their houses to survive to our day is Lyndhurst, in Tarrytown, New York, built by William Paulding at the urging of his brother James, a Jacksonian pamphleteer. The Pauldings were Northern men, but so reactionary that James had already written a passionate defense of slavery. He moved even farther right in the course of his life; Martin Van Buren made the mistake of naming him secretary of the navy, a post in which he was both a functional failure and a political embarrassment.

Paulding's popular reputation rested upon his *Life of Washington*. He liked generals and swooned before Jackson, "the only man I ever saw that excited my admiration to a pitch of wonder." His wonder degenerated into the submission of an intellectual faced by a Natural Man. He said of Old Hickory: "To him knowledge seemed entirely unnecessary. He saw intuitively into everything."[160] (It is probably unfair, but one is tempted to think that Paulding might have been equally submissive to a fierce fellow of a later age, as unkempt as Jackson but quite as forceful: Jay Gould, who became the owner of Lyndhurst later in the century.)

The responses of Washington Irving and James Fenimore Cooper were only a little more chaste than Paulding's. They were not quite so prone to the vapors in the presence of a strong man; their passion for Jackson was more like the father-substitution practiced by George Washington Parke Custis. But none of them had any commitment to Jacksonian revolution. Their affinity to the general was personal, not ideological. They were nostalgic for a romanticized past, and such people are seldom very revolutionary. They expended much energy searching for better countries, better architecture, and better ancestors.[†]

† Cooper was joined in the New York Jacksonian party by the Albany junto of squires and "solid citizens," and when the squires were attacked by the rabble in the rent wars, "it was the Whigs who played up to rebel feelings and the Democratic administration which acted sternly in behalf of order." (Ward, p. 59)

Irving began his tour of Europe in 1815, accompanied by an engineer named James Renwick, whose son was to become one of the foremost American Gothicists. In Europe, where he spent seventeen years, Irving admired ruins considerably younger than those he might have found in the Spanish possessions of the Southwest or among the mounds and ruined fortress-temples of the Ohio Valley. Then he returned to join a little choir of dilettantes lamenting the lack of antiquities in America, who did not explore widely enough to discover the slumbering examples of American Gothic, such as the early parish churches of rural Virginia. But these native antiquities were unrecognized and largely untended in the 1830s.

After writing of hoary cathedrals, turreted strongholds bearing the "rust of barons' wars," and creeper-covered mansions, including expensive new-fledged pseudo-antiques such as Walter Scott's Abbotsford, Irving returned to Gothicize Sunnyside, his house on the Hudson. His friend Cooper added ersatz antiquity to the headquarters of his own father's holdings in central New York. Thereafter, Cooper and Irving raised the embarrassments of provincials to the level of belles lettres. Images of transition from log cabin in a clearing to temple in a tamed landscape did not persuade Paulding and Irving, and Cooper was only a little more willing to sing the praises of change. These literary Jacksonians did not choose to live on the frontier. They were men of the suburbs and the settled, bucolic scene.

Following their lead, some Americans, taking shelter in the colonial past from the prevailing nationalist and Hellenic winds, reverted to English religion and English architecture. Taking instruction from the Ecclesiologists, a cool, antiquarian, hierarchic response among Anglicans to revivals among the Methodists and other "nonconformists," stressing rood screens and incense and esoteric medievalism, they produced some very beautiful though unoriginal buildings. (Perhaps the best is St. James the Less in Philadelphia, the first church since colonial days to take pride in being built "under the direct supervision of the English." The Cambridge Camden Society had recommended its prototype, St. Michael's, Longstanton, as appropriate for all the "colonies," including the aberrant ones between Maine and Florida.)[161]

The American Gothic Revival became drier and more exact as it progressed from the provision of gazebos to Gunston Hall, through Latrobe's unconvincing pointed arches for the disagreeable Mr. Crammond and the early Regency churches of Latrobe, Godefroy, and Ramée, into the full-tilt, archaeological nostalgia of the Ecclesiologists. The Jacksonian Gothic was literary and quite out of character with Jackson himself. By the time he died in 1845, it had moved wholly beyond his nationalist influence and was enthusiastically neocolonial.

The parents of Andrew Jackson Downing bestowed Old Hickory's name upon their son, but as he grew to manhood in the post-Jacksonian world, Downing became enraptured by what he called the "wonderfully captivating . . . idea of a battlemented castle," or the "peculiar and interesting associations . . . of the Middle Ages," and unashamedly yielded to the "home-whispering voice" of Old England. Besides, Downing called it as "absurd for the critics to ask for the *American style* of architecture as it was for the English friends of a Yankee of our acquaintance to request him to do for them the favor to put on his savage dress and talk a little American."[162]

The watchwords of the Gothic Revivalists were continuity with the past (even a manufactured continuity—like a false family tree) and assimilation with nature. They did not approve of white temple-form houses set in nature, demanding attention. They noted quite fairly that the Greek Revival seemed very little interested in what was done around it, with the result that it can be associated with no school of landscaping, while the designers of the Gothic Revival were often landscapists first and architects second.

American Practice and Scottish Theory

More than thirty years ago, John William Ward spied the paradox in the relationship of Old Hickory to Cincinnatus. Americans "rejected Europe" in the Jacksonian period, but their imagery, verbal and architectural, was "saturated" with classical references implying "an obeisance to European tradition rather than alienation from it. Americans were so fond of classical imagery because they imagined themselves to constitute a return to the uncorrupted state of the past, before the fall, so to speak, while contemporary Europe seemed a corruption of the virtues of *its own* past. [It was] logically possible for Americans in their rejection of Europe as degenerate to have become antiquarians and to have exemplified Europe's present fall from grace by reference to a golden past."[163] Ward summed up with a line written by a Jacksonian dramatist and put into the mouth of one of the victors at New Orleans in 1815: "Our western wilds preserve the ancient glory."[164]

Here was a good summary of the myth supporting the Greek Revival. It might have been a line from Latrobe's Anniversary Oration or from the aesthetic philosophy of George Tucker and the Scottish Enlightenment. Stuart and Revett had gone forth to inspect and report upon the antiquities of Athens, carrying in their pack-train easels, painting and sketching materials, calipers and linear measures, surveying instruments, and a set of expectations about art that led antiquaries, painters, architects, and archaeologists to look at ruins in the same way. It was not our way, though it bears some family relationship to what has subsequently been called "the romantic view" of art. It was one element of an American compound made up of what Geoffrey Scott, who was hostile to it, called "the ethical fallacy," and what might be called "the political fallacy," if it were a fallacy at all.[165]

The Americans, even more than the Scots, did not consider fallacious the viewing of architecture as potent with symbolic meaning, political and psychological, though later writers might denigrate that sort of thing. They brought to ruins an expectation that the experience would stimulate feelings as important to them as any dead facts to be learned from archaeology. The "awful dignity and grandeur" of the Doric temple excited with "sensation"—that was how it instructed. The Parthenon "struck" them with feelings of admiration arising both from its density and its pertinacity. During the Greek Revival period, those who encountered the Doric temple, with its appearance of eternal duration, responded with a "solemn and majestic feeling."

The key words here are *sensation* and *feeling*, which, especially in the writing of George Tucker, were taken directly from the aesthetics of the Scottish Enlightenment. Though Tucker's language may seem archaic or sentimental (in our modern usage of that term), his psychology was sound. Without sensation, the Greek Revival would have lacked the energy that comes from the unconscious. The "character of durability" was as important as the "characters" of virility and simplicity. The power of feeling arising from these "characters" resonated with the psychological needs of the Age of Jackson. The simple and durable temple was "felt" to be standing apart from nature, "felt" to be dominant within its precinct, "felt" to be containing, against that world, a contra-world of its own.

The myth of the Greek Revival had a field of energy that drew to it an entirely different set of clients than that of the contemporary American Gothic Revival. The Gothic house assumed the colors of the fields and trees, of copses and bosky shadows, lying half hidden, inviting discovery but not demanding it. It never fully emerged from the earth; never was it fully "brought forth," in Abraham Lincoln's words, by the power of the sky, to sit on a templed hill.

The Gothic Revival of the 1840s was gaining its own strength and sending its own message, implying responsibility to the land and to those who will occupy it after the receiver has gone on. This was the sort of feeling that led Lincoln to speak of his countrymen as "the heirs of a great estate," trustees of the fertile continent, theirs to be transmitted undebased, indeed, enriched and husbanded, to future generations. The term *husbanded* is not accidental; it signals an attitude toward "mother earth" and an attitude about manliness somewhat at odds with the heedless, burly rip, reap, and run of the stereotypical frontiersman. The Gothicists had more in common with modern ideas of a respectful relationship between nature and architecture than did the builders of the Greek Revival: "The Gothic house could be harmonious with nature because its shapes were natural, its rooflines pitched in parallel to arching trees, its eaves carved like vines . . . its chimneys prominent like ancient cottages, its colors . . . chosen to blend with the natural hues all about. It did not sit, as a Grecian house did, glaring out upon its surroundings, daring a vine to touch it with a tendril. It invited nature to enshroud it."[166]

Yet the idealists of the Greek Revival did not intend any less permanent relationship to the land than the Gothicists. Though they implied dominance, they also required of the husbandman that his commitment, and his symbols, signal permanence. Longevity and stability are expressed in both a Gothic cottage, so old as to be indistinguishable from the landscape, and in a Greek one.

The creation of a precinct of artistic order to "instruct and persuade according to the classical rhetoricians"[167] has been called world-making by writers of the 1980s. This term, taken from the Greek, was put back in modern coinage in 1834, by Harriet Martineau, the abolitionist economist. She wrote of the Jacksonian Americans as embarked upon "the process of world-making," creating a new society, longing for symbols of permanence amid constant "mobility," forcing themselves "incessantly to work, to undertake, to spread, create, produce."[168]

The poignancy of these efforts fascinated Martineau and her contemporary, Alexis de Tocqueville. The defiant temples then set upon the American land carried and still carry some of the same force as the Parthenon when Le Corbusier saw it in the 1930s, "stark, stripped, economical, violent; a clamorous outcry against a landscape of grace and terror. All strength and purity."[169]

Corbusier saw the Parthenon in its bleached state, as a ruin, "stark, stripped" of color, and more "violent" in its apartness, therefore, than it might have been originally. But it is true of classical art, in general, especially within the sacred precinct, that it arouses an echo of the trumpet call—the *classicus*—proclaiming the moral function of art to make small pockets of order in a disorderly world. This is not as appealing a kind of art as is one more participatory with the natural, one less insistent, more diffident, more, perhaps in this sense, "romantic." But the classical impulse is courageous; it contends against both chaos and boredom, perseveres against the disruptively unexpected while refusing to be weighed down by what is merely to be expected.

The term used in ancient Greece for the precinct within which a temple was to be found was the *temenos*. It was to be sanctified by sacrifices and rites of purification. Greece itself was like that—a place ravaged, pillaged, and burned, but retaining a numinosity that was felt—and is felt—by each generation of visitors from Western Europe and the Western world. The suffering of its population has been like the ritual scourging of the acolytes of a temple. Though its sacred sites might appear to be abandoned, to a person responsive to such things they are alive with unseen presences. In places such as these, Plato's goddess Diotima still "seeks the sun, . . . though the sun of the spirit, the more beautiful world, has sunk."[170]

Even the cold, appraising, commercial eye of the early nineteenth century saw Greece as "a land set apart." Not only were its temples "approached by a portico and surrounded by a consecrated enclosure, [but] . . . the whole land of ATTICA itself was a sacred TEMENOS."[171]

When Americans came to Greece, they were ready to plunge into the experience of that sacredness, bringing with them the hope and enthusiasm "of the new and only republic to the ruins of the old." Nicholas Biddle was only the first to articulate the "melancholy satisfactions" induced by an intense scrutiny of its temples.[172]

Biddle's "melancholy" was a direct consequence of his juxtaposing a realistic assessment of the squalor of modern Greece with the remnants of its past glories. By "satisfaction," he meant a combination of pride and opportunity. There was opportunity to aid in the resurrection of Greece. There was opportunity, as well, to aid in the creation of an America worthy of Greece.

Biddle was a hopeful man. Americans might yet deserve comparison to the Athenians in the days of Pericles, might come to live aptly within symbolic structures all the world might read as proclaiming them to be worthy successors to the ancients. This hope became the spirit of the 1830s and 1840s; the whole nation seemed to share Daniel Webster's impatience to get on with world-making. As Biddle himself put it, "we shall all die, and there we shall be quiet enough. . . . Whilst we . . . live it is better to go forward. . . . Go ahead! is the order of the day."[173]

There was only a seeming paradox in a "go ahead" generation's use of an architectural vocabulary that required it, simultaneously, to look backward. The bleached purity of the Greek Revival, its sun-washed, time-washed new-oldness, seemed uncontaminated by the immediate European past, yet ennobled by the common past of them all. They had forced themselves upon a continent unknown to their ancestors; some of them, like Irving and Cooper, reached back toward Europe for reassurance. But, though their European connections of commerce and culture throbbed with life, many others retained the revolutionary sense of a special mission or, at least, a special situation. So they embraced the primitively old while insisting that in America everything was always new.

The baggage of Europe no longer needed to be carried—Lafayette had helped make that clear. The Greek Revival was a light burden, new because it was so very old. Better yet, for restless Americans, it was timeless, as free floating, as bold as they themselves sometimes felt.

Regional Variants

The heart of the new empire created west of the Appalachians was in bluegrass Tennessee. Though in that heartland itself agriculture was diversified, elsewhere in Greater Tennessee, this was the empire of upland cotton, and of affluence displayed in an architecture at once Jacksonian and Roman. Its proportions taller, its members more ornate, its balances more daring than the Greek of the Whigs and the North, it extended its sway beyond Nashville, beyond the bluegrass counties of Maury and Columbia, westward and southward into that deep-soil crescent of northern Alabama lying north of the Tennessee River, down the Natchez Trace into Mississippi and Arkansas, across the red-dirt region of northern Louisiana into Texas.

At its farthest reaches, its scale reduced and its components simplified, this architecture seemed almost Greek again, as, for example, it gathered itself in southwestern Arkansas, along the Red River, for campaigns against Mexico. There, in the hamlet of Washington, remain a dozen "Greek" buildings marking the edge of American nationalism of the 1840s in forms quite similar to those to be found along the St. Croix River in Minnesota and Wisconsin. Arkansas was still too poor to be Roman.

The Greek Revival was also coming under other influences. In Louisiana, the cotton South began to be absorbed into another tradition, that of the Caribbean. Indeed, the study of the architecture of this period is like the study of oleaginous substances that ooze into each other, borrow qualities reciprocally, and swirl backward into the source of each. When Carolina planters accumulated lands across Alabama, Mississippi, and Arkansas, they learned new ways to build, and when they came to Louisiana, they encountered concentrations of cubical raised cottages under hipped roofs, with pillars all, or part way, around, and gardens designed along stately, axial French patterns. The Hamptons, for example, classicized Houmas House, a big creole cottage, to serve as headquarters for their largest Louisiana plantation, and carried its garden plan back with them to follow in redesigning the grounds at Millwood. Classicized creole cottages set in French gardens soon appeared from Piedmont Georgia, across the Black Belt (the term refers to the color of the soil, not of the labor force) counties of Alabama and Mississippi, all the way to Shreveport.

The diversified planters of Greater Tennessee were almost as prosperous as the sugar growers of Louisiana, though much less interested in heavy tariffs on foreign-produced sugar and therefore less likely to vote Whig. In the 1830s Piedmont South Carolina and Georgia experienced a brief period of prosperity as well, but by the end of the 1840s, that region was exporting capital, slaves, and managers to the West. This brief Piedmont prosperity permitted a few newly rich planters to remove themselves downhill, against the stream of westering history, to Charleston itself, where Roman-columned houses marked the advent of the newer rich.

The "Greek Revival" of the cotton kingdom is best observed in palatial form in Greater Tennessee, and in its urban format in a dozen very beautiful towns such as Athens and Sparta, in Georgia, where the Gulf Coast "house within a house," set all about with columns, became the standard "Greek" format of Georgia planters. There seems to be nothing remotely Hellenic about these houses, except for the presence of columns. They can, however, be seen as Greek houses turned inside (atrium side) out. These Southern forms were different from those in common use in the North, where the Greek Revival came more directly from old Athens, by way of Philadelphia and the District of Columbia. (The region lying about Worcester, in central Massachusetts, was the Georgia of the North, for special reasons to which I will return.)

The Parthenonic form lent its gable front and portico to the architecture of the American North and its screen of white columns, all around, to the South. No residences built at that time in the North have columns set before all four sides. Only a handful of gable-fronted Grecian houses were built in the South: if one is strict about proportions, there are only two, Arlington House and Berry Hill. And the former was only secondarily a residence, while the latter was more Philadelphian than Virginian.

The influence of climate upon this distinction has been overstressed. The architectural line is sharp at the Mason-Dixon line, though the climate changes only in imperceptible gradations from north to south. There are good reasons to lift a house off the damp ground, north or south, and to provide a refuge from the ferocious North American summer, north or south. No one who has endured the Minnesota prairie in August, before air conditioning, doubts the blessings of a "front porch" any more than a Mississippian questions the beauties of a "veranda." The Greek Revival provided "orders" in both places, to dignify porches and verandas, as it did in giving "piazzas" a classical cast (should that be "caste"?) in Boston. [†]

The reasons for the differences in the predominant styles in the two regions are complex; they arise from the differing traditions of the people who trooped westward to replace the Native Americans who had inhabited those regions. A key difference was in the organizing principles of the states and territories north of the Ohio River, as opposed to those applied to the south of it.

The Northwest Ordinance did not go so far as to prohibit slavery from the entire trans-Appalachian region; that had been attempted in 1784, at the high point of Thomas Jefferson's willingness to take political risks to prevent the spread of the South's "peculiar institution." It had failed; the 1787

[†] Between Boston and Springfield lie nearly all the peripterally colonnaded houses to be found in the North—the work of Elias Carter [245]. Which he built before, and which after he lent his talents to the construction of similar houses in Georgia is unknown. So it cannot be determined when this canny Yankee builder first learned to apply the lessons of the Mississippi, as transmitted to Georgia, to benefit his clients on the shores of the Barre, the Prince, or the majestic Barnshirt, the streams along which the work of Elias Carter can be observed to this day.

ordinance left slavery intact where it already existed, south of the Ohio, and included the first fugitive slave provision enacted by Congress. But it did forbid slavery north of the river.

Acquiescence in the existence and spread of slavery westward seemed a compromise required to hold the Union together. The power of that expansionary force was shown two years later when North Carolina set its terms to acquiescence in the passage of the great congressional cleavage that sliced diagonally across its territory, leaving the western half to organize its own affairs as the territory of Tennessee. The Statute of Acquiescence did so with these words: "Provided always, That no regulations made or to be made by Congress shall tend to emancipate slaves, otherwise than shall be directed by the Assembly or legislature of such State or States."

So, instead of the familiar image of the frontiersman hacking his way through the underbrush to establish himself and his family in new, free homes in the West, an image Northern stories have set in our minds as universal on the Western frontier, we must substitute a more complicated picture on the southwestern frontier. Though yeomen there were unaided by slaves in their exertions, creating a new culture west of the mountains, beside them the old culture settled in as well.

"Here the covered wagons had been followed by long lines of slaves; here, as Jefferson Davis observed in 1861, it was slaves not freemen who had made farms out of the wilderness; here the structure of power was aristocratic and not egalitarian; here the effect of frontier life was to coarsen and brutalize the peculiar institution; not to humanize it."[174]

Greek Whigs v. Roman Jacksonians

In the interval between the completion of Arlington House in 1817 and the early 1830s, Nicholas Biddle became master of Andalusia, and Mrs. Biddle inherited John Craig's fortune, providing the funds to Hellenize it. The temple form began its conquest of American architecture with the aid of Biddle's enormous energy and skill. As suggested, after 1834 it became emblematic of Whiggery—and of banking.

And it conveyed something else, something sexual. Banking was a profession completely closed to women. In Biddle's time it might have been said to have been the most masculine of professions—a realm of abstractions and of a grasping for power. Many of us today would dispute the attribution of those affinities to males, or their opposites, invidiously, to females. But it was no accident that, from the outset of professional commercial banking, in Philadelphia in the 1790s, and especially after Biddle's influence was felt after 1818, it was columnar to a degree uncontested by any other profession.

Affluent Americans who became acquainted with Biddle on his home ground—in his temple house or his temple bank or on the precincts of his temple college (though this last bore Stephen Girard's name)—felt the potency of a powerful architectural imagination. A profusion of temples arose from the stimulating effects of his new commercial power upon the delayed flowering of the Grecian aspirations of Latrobe (who had been drawn away to New Orleans and died there in 1821). Latrobe's students, Robert Mills and William Strickland, remained in Philadelphia, as did Strickland's pupil Thomas Walter. They were joined by an Englishman nearly as gifted as Latrobe or George Hadfield, and even more devoted to the Greek: John Haviland.

Haviland had arrived from England just in time to renew the Grecian impulse withdrawn by the departure of Latrobe; he issued his manifesto immediately and in the 1820s was at work upon temple-form churches. Walter's remodeling of Latrobe's earlier villa at Andalusia established the residential style, which both Haviland and Strickland followed quickly. Walter and Biddle's Girard College was the nation's most complete temple compound; Latrobe's Bank of Pennsylvania and Strickland's Second Bank of the United States became "mother-houses" (in the monastic use of that term) for bankers.

Some who operated in the state banking systems found it expedient to be Jacksonians, but the architectural evidence suggests that the representatives of the Bank of the United States, in its branches, were Whigs and Grecian to a man. Biddle was the spider at the center; his influence, in banking and architecture, extended throughout the web. The structures housing the bank's branches made this clear. None went up in other than Grecian form after he became president of the system.

From Maine to New Orleans, bankers did their business in temples. Some lived in other temples built nearby. In Natchez, Mississippi, Tallahassee, Florida, and Cazenovia, New York, living quarters were attached to the back of the temple bank; Erie, Pennsylvania, had a temple for the bank, another for the president, and the cashier had his own Greek house next door. In Savannah William Jay had already provided the branch bank there with his only full-scale Grecian design. Contemporary with Jay's Savannah branch, Strickland provided a temple for the headquarters of the Second Bank of the United States, where Biddle himself was installed. Bankers, though few in number, wielded much influence. Following their lead, Whig manufacturers, merchants, and squires fervently embraced the Greek.

A correlation of the political preferences of the builders of the houses depicted in these pages with the building styles they chose indicates that preferences for Greek and Roman architectural forms were beginning to divide along party lines at this time. Most of the planters who ruled the latifundia of Greater Tennessee built in the Jacksonian-Roman style; those who did not, and turned instead to the Grecian, knew Biddle through banking, horse breeding, Whig politics, or all three at once.

Berry Hill, near Halifax—the only residential Grecian temple, aside from Arlington House, in Virginia—was built by James Coles Bruce, whose ties to Biddle were financial, political, social, and equestrian. And but one more Greek Revival house, in a strict sense, was built in all the territory between the Blue Ridge and the Mississippi: Levin Marshall's Richmond. Marshall was Biddle's representative in Natchez, Mississippi, paymaster to Henry Clay, and the sponsor of the Agricultural Bank, which, with its twin, the Commercial Bank [116, 117], remain with Richmond to remind the citizens of Natchez of this remarkable, sardonic, handsome, and inscrutable man.[175]

A single residence in Tennessee has a portico of unequivocally Grecian dimensions, Cleveland Hall, near Nashville, built by Stockley Donelson, nephew of Andrew Jackson. Why did a young man, who was close to Jackson for many years, build as if he were close, instead, to Nicholas Biddle? As is so often the case, the architecture inspires a deeper look at the biography, and vice versa. Cleveland Hall was built between 1839 and 1841; Donelson had just abandoned Jackson and, with his brother William, had become what the general called "worthless Whig scamps." A drunken brawl among Donelson's and Jackson's slaves had led to a murder. While Cleveland Hall was under way, Donelson's insistence that Jackson's "people" were guilty led the general to charge Donelson wanted "political revenge . . . [in a] cruel and vindictive display of spite."[176] A portico evoking Andalusia ensued.

And so it was in many other instances in which a trail of influence led to Nicholas Biddle; his political, architectural, and financial messages were often carried in the same saddlebags. He had other means of extending his influence as well: he learned from Jefferson a device well known to tribal chiefs in feudal

Europe and central Africa. They took as "secretaries" the sons of useful potential allies. The consequences of Biddle's and Jefferson's interests in architecture can often be found by following the later careers of these young men. Biddle found quadrupedal means at hand as well; horses could also be exchanged for the periods of time necessary to improve the breeding of the next generation (of horses, that is).

Jackson, Julius Caesar, and the Whigs

When Andrew Jackson became president in 1828, some might have said: "The hand that grasped the plow now holds the mace of empire." But the old façade builder would have used other terms. He was meticulous about his classical references, avoiding those implying that he aspired to establish an empire. He drew, instead, upon republican Rome, before Caesar: "I thought with the ancient Romans, that it was right never to cede any land or boundary of the Republic, but always to add to it by any honorable treaty."[177]

Cincinnatus and Cato. He had been scrupulous about which Romans were his Romans, and as we have seen, he had contrived to merge his Romans with George Washington Parke Custis's austere Greeks. But the Whigs wanted to link with another tradition, that of Julius Caesar and Napoleon Bonaparte.

When Jackson talked of aggrandizing not himself but the republic, Henry Clay hastened to remind the audience that Caesar had talked that way too as he returned from conquering Gaul to bring the Roman republic to its end. Said Clay: "Remember that Greece had her Alexander, Rome her Caesar, England her Cromwell, France her Bonaparte, and . . . we must avoid their errors."[†]

The Whig linguist in the Senate, George P. Marsh of Vermont, fluent in both ancient and modern Greek, hotly responded to Jacksonian attacks on the Whigs as "the English party"; the Jacksonians, he said, were not only Caesarean-Roman in their leader's similarities to Caesar and Bonaparte, but imperial-Roman because *their* intellectuals were anglophiles. He might have added that several of them were Gothic anglophiles, to boot.[††]

England, said Marsh, was "Roman by adoption . . . her grasping ambition, her material energies, her spirit of exclusive selfishness, are due to the Roman nurse." Jackson and Jackson's Greater Tennessee were, by this description, Roman too. The rising young Charles Sumner of Massachusetts, "with his broad cosmopolitan culture, his Alpine elevation, his friendship with Brougham, Grote, Macauley, Longfellow, Prescott and Tocqueville," was contemptuous of Cincinnatean bullies, with their "Roman patriotism . . . and . . . exaggerated prejudice of country."[178]

Classical references were still rhetorical weapons on the floor of the U.S. Senate: during the debate on Biddle's bank, Jackson's spokesman, Thomas Hart Benton, lost patience with noisy Whigs in the gallery. Deriding them as "bank ruffians," he cried out: "Seize them, sergeant-at-arms!" This was what

† (Clay quoted in Ward, p. 187) Clay eschewed the Roman style for his own house, Ashland, near Lexington, Kentucky, turning to Latrobe for a sober Regency design, and few Whig nabobs, even in Tennessee, followed the Roman fashion.

†† A strange cult of Romantic Gothicism began to take hold, even among former Whigs in the South, on the verge of the Civil War. Berry Hill, which is Greek, and Staunton Hill, which is one of the South's relatively few Gothic mansions and was the last of the great Bruce houses in "southside" Virginia, exemplify this phenomenon of the 1850s.

the Whig senators were waiting for. They replied: "Remove us. Turn us out. Expel us. . . . Call in the praetorian guard. Take us. Apprehend us. March us off!" Caesar was on the doorstep.[179]

Though Jackson's domestic architecture, like Napoleon's, was Roman (though a little different in scale), and though planters who admired both Jackson and the Hermitage followed him toward the Roman, he did not carry that politically vulnerable affinity out of Tennessee. In Washington, he sought to secure his merger of the Cincinnatus-Washington role with the Arlington House set of Greek virtues by agreeing to Robert Mills's Hellenizing of the capital. Under Mills's direction, Jacksonian Washington became a city of Greek public buildings to rival Helsinki and Edinburgh.

Outside the home states of Jackson and Biddle, however, gratifyingly neat distinctions between the Whiggish Greek and the Jacksonian Roman appear only in those few cases in which both political sentiments and aesthetic preferences are clear. In 1845, a builder who knew a client to be a Whig—rich or poor—could be reasonably certain he would want a Greek house—especially in the North. If he knew him to be Jacksonian he could be quite sure he would not—especially in the South. I have found no important lieutenants of Biddle in the South who built in the Roman style, and a goodly number who put the Grecian to their service. Likewise, I have found no major Jacksonian politicians in the North who built in templar Grecian forms, though thousands of their neighbors did so. (There are probably exceptions to be found—there usually are.)

Mills affirmed Jackson's second-father role in Washington. Biddle's public buildings were banks; they and the residences constructed by his friends and allies in a multitude of outlying places mark the scattered but formidable power bases upon which he drew.

The Later Whiggery and William H. Seward

As the 1830s unfolded, a new Whig party was shrewdly built in concentric circles centering in western New York. One of its principal financial backers, the sanguine William Kerley Strong, had no need to make a pretense of republican austerity. Strong was not a candidate, though he was "boiling over with zeal" for Whig politics and its symbols (as he would later be for the defeat of the South in war). He had become very rich from banking and the wool trade, and his wealth went on display, in 1839, with his magnificently Grecian Rose Hill, outside Geneva, New York.[180]

Strong was working within a tradition commenced by George Washington Parke Custis. After celebrating Federalist ideals at Arlington House and the Washington city hall [iv], Custis went alone, unheeded, and anathematized by his peers for his subsequent endorsement of Jackson—and he did not, in fact, succeed in transferring the residential Greek to the Jacksonians. Nicholas Biddle had preempted it for his own use at Andalusia, Girard College, and for the branch banks of the Second Bank of the United States.

Arlington House and the Washington city hall continued to be Federalist-Whig prototypes, disseminated throughout New England and New York by the followers of Ithiel Town. Rose Hill is one of the finest expressions of their work, but there are a hundred others. While it was under construction, Strong was outdone by one of his partners, Richard De Zeng, now the Whig leader of Skaneateles. De Zeng found an earlier porticoed house too small for his taste and, in the dead of the northern winter, had it moved across the ice of Skaneateles Lake to crown the opposite hill. He then set about building the structure now known as Roosevelt Hall. The interior has been given the full twentieth-century classical re-revival treatment by the descendants of Benjamin Henry Latrobe, whose daughter married a Roosevelt. Arlington House, Rose Hill, and Roosevelt Hall, upon their hilltops, are the most impressively sited American Greek Revival residences.

Among his other undertakings, De Zeng had grown rich selling New York real estate to Yankee emigrants. He extricated himself from the land boom of the 1830s just as Nicholas Biddle was contracting the money supply and, with it, the capacity of speculators to pay for architecture. De Zeng and his brother had been in the banking and the glass business in Geneva, with Strong. No remaining records tie either of them to Town, or even to a set of plans, a plan book, or a graduated student from Town's atelier. But these are houses worthy of the masters of the form.[†]

In Ogdensburg, squire Henry Van Rensselaer was not so lucky in disposing of the 140,000 acres he had acquired through foreclosure from the founding family, the Ogdens. Between 1834 and 1844, however,

† The final section on architects and buildings will clarify how these mansions are derived from Ithiel Town's Bowers House of 1826–28, and will, I think, tie them ultimately to Town's exposure to George Hadfield and the Doric of Arlington House of 1804–19.
A smaller version of Rose Hill (four Ionic columns instead of six, but otherwise complete to the form of the little temple cupola) was built in 1835 by Elias Brown in Mystic, Connecticut. Four- or five-columned versions without cupolas appeared throughout northern New York from Cazenovia to Fredonia, and dozens of them are still there.

while his affluence lasted, he expanded an earlier house into a great Hellenic mansion very much like that of De Zeng.

The virtues of Whig Hall, in Lysander Township, west of Cicero, northwest of Syracuse, and north of Camillus and Marcellus (inserted between Clay and Van Buren townships), are more subtle. It is without porticos; its color is the buff of local brick and the gray of its granite lintels, not the glaring white of its competitors. But that stonework is ornamented with an elegance unrivaled in America, and its interior remains almost exactly as it was when built in the middle 1830s by a great landowner, Colonel James Voorhees.

It too stands proudly upon a hilltop, and it has the luxury of a rural setting, where its adjacent woodlot and park retain their ancient trees, and the view of deep-soiled fields along the lazily looping Seneca River is unsullied. The river, now again so pastoral, once provided a pageant of westering activity. It formed a link in the Erie Canal, which was enlarged and improved as it passed through this section of New York whenever the Whigs, who owned much of the landscape, were able to get control of the legislature (the canal was initially built, in the 1820s, before Whig–Democrat distinctions were clear).

The list of grand-scale houses built by the rising Whig leadership of New York, Pennsylvania, and Ohio could be expanded to such length that it might deaden rather than enliven a desire to travel to see them. Three more, as a package, may be permissible as examples of a Greek Revival sense of humor. "The Three Bears," in Ovid, New York, is a progression of brick-porticoed civic buildings of graduated size, from the sheriff's office to the town hall. A decision as to which is "just right" should be deferred to a sunny day, with time to ramble about Ovid, and with time to spare to descend upon neighboring Trumansburg to inspect the monumental Camp House, laid up in brick and granite in the middle 1840s, set amid enormous trees, with the vestiges of extensive Victorian parterres clearly visible, along with a recently restored gazebo.[†]

† The Camp House bears a considerable likeness in elevation, though not in plan, to The Forest in Madison, New Jersey. So far, no connections, economic, political, familial, or equine, between the Camps and the Gibbonses have emerged.

From power bases like these, a new kind of Whig leadership was asserted. Nicholas Biddle was gone, a victim of his own pride. He had retreated to a state bank, chartered in Pennsylvania, as his final redoubt in the bank war with Jackson. The president had seen Biddle and his bank as competitors for power, unendorsed by a popular mandate and drawing upon foreign investors for too much of their capital resources. Jackson assaulted the Bank of the United States, besieged it, impugned its legitimacy, asked Congress not to renew its charter, and then cut off its supplies by removing its federal deposits.

Biddle lost his battles in Congress, lost his power base in the Bank of the United States, lost his head, and then lost his fortune. He refused to recognize the limitations of a mere state bank, tried to support cotton prices, exceeded his resources, and took the Pennsylvania bank into bankruptcy just as his architecture was beginning to acquire a broad following.

The bank war was like more recent vendettas between Maoists and Leninists. It set two men in opposition who treated each other as heretics worthy of the stake. Anathemas were called down upon each by the other, and unimaginable horrors predicted if the other prevailed. So it is when people of essentially like mind have overlapping ambition. Each will loathe the proximate competitor more than a distant one.

If one were to list the fundamental political principles of Biddle and Jackson—their nationalism, their unquestioning belief in private property and a system in which class distinctions are to be observed but access to each class shall be open, their adherence to concepts that encouraged the growth of capitalism in their time—few fundamental differences seem to divide them. As to Jackson's charge that Biddle's bank was dependent upon foreign money—well, so too was Jackson's plantation, for without Manchester and Liverpool, the prices for upland cotton would have been lower, and Greater Tennessee poorer.

Between them, Biddle and Jackson were more responsible than any other Americans for providing the political, psychological, and rhetorical context and the symbolic statements of American Free Classicism.

Finally, America had a Free Classical style. Aesthetic fashion had held it in reserve until the psychology of the nation was ready for it. It is a characteristically American paradox that both Biddle and Jackson spoke for the past, not for the future. In the end, Biddle's squirely capitalism was more accommodating to that future than Jackson's plantation capitalism.

The New Whigs   After the fall of Nicholas Biddle, Daniel Webster, who had been on Biddle's payroll throughout the ebullient years of the Second Bank, became secretary of state but coldly refused to consider pensioning off his former patron with an ambassadorship. Biddle returned to farming at Andalusia, which had been redeemed from his creditors by his wife and son.

William H. Seward had lived in a Grecian house while he conducted his speculations in western New York farmlands in Chautauqua County, but when he returned to politics, he not only stressed democratic biceps, but also republican simplicity of an old-fashioned sort. His mansion in Auburn was very old-fashioned; like Henry Clay's in Lexington, Kentucky, it had nothing of Rome or Greece about it.

Seward had the political career to which Biddle had aspired—and he took up an issue that Biddle avoided, the abolition of slavery and the overthrow of the Southern plantocracy. Furthermore, Seward had a new style that Biddle could never have mastered. He went to extremities of modesty, preferring to appear at rallies in a rowboat, even when steamboats were available. And Seward turned back upon the aging Jacksonians their own rhetoric: "We should be degenerate descendants of our heroic forefathers did we not assail . . . aristocracy, remove the barriers between the rich and poor, break the control of the few over the many . . . and strengthen the democratic principles of our constitution."[181]

The "few" to which he referred were his local antagonists, the Albany junto surrounding Martin Van Buren. The contest for power had very little to do with class struggle. In Arkansas there was a Jacksonian hierarchy; in Florida his old cronies coalesced into the "Land Office Gang"; in St. Louis the "little junto," holders of huge Spanish grants and vast tracts of slave-driven plantation lands, supported Thomas Hart Benton, that stentorian Jacksonian. Everyone agreed upon the need for a new race of heroes, and among politicians, there was much scrambling for star billing. There was little dispute as to the desirability of social hierarchy; the only question was which few would be on top.

Though some of Biddle's Philadelphia group, such as Horace Binney, disapproved of this sort of scrambling and the sort of demagogic appeals that went with it, complaining that the Whigs were becoming "more democratic in their devices and principles than the Democrats were in the days of Jefferson," Seward eventually became secretary of state, but not in a Whig administration. He led the movement of Conscience Whigs into the Republican party and served under both Abraham Lincoln and Andrew Johnson.[182]

Architecturally, his taste migrated toward foreign affairs as well; it is possible to read in this a loss of youthful idealism, though neither his aesthetic interests nor his symbolic sense were ever strong. In such matters, he merely acceded to the fashions of his time. After 1848 Seward thought it wise to abandon the classic and join the rising fashion for the Gothic. His son wrote that their old house, like other "villas and rural dwellings . . . square . . . and . . . [in] a monotonous array of white paint and green blinds," had come to seem a little too "country." Rising international figures might observe "signs of change . . . near New York and Boston."[183]

Andrew Jackson Downing's "books and magazines found ready place on Seward's library table, and were always consulted when any improvement of house or grounds was talked of." The tower that ensued and the library were, of course, all for public business. "Novels occupied but meager space. . . . [Still, the] English poets he often read; Scott, Spencer [sic], Southey, Coleridge, Chaucer, and Burns were his favorites. . . . [But he] never lost his taste for the classic authors."[184]

Recalling Frederick Jackson Turner's maps of the elections fought between earlier Whig candidates (such as Clay) and Democrats (such as Jackson, Van Buren, or James K. Polk), and the marks upon them indicating the presence of Greek Revival homes, it is now easier to understand why the marks coincide so nicely with the districts that voted Whig. Later, as Seward became a Republican, the old distinctions between Whigs and Jacksonians were being shattered by the urgency of the debate over slavery. The Age of Hope and Reform, and of the Greek Revival, was coming to an end.

People still came to the polling place moved as much by habit and heritage as by doctrine; Whig districts in the North were now Republican in the outlying precincts of Greater New England. Yankees had traditionally built in white wood, and it was easy for them to add a few classical touches; they had traditionally regarded the wilderness as a place of bewilderment and bewitchery, against which to lay up defenses, and the classical temple was, psychologically, as much a defense as the blockhouse or the rectilinear meetinghouse form (which was, after all, protoclassical). The Gothic Revival did not appeal to Puritans.

Most citizens of Greater New England, extending as far as Franconia and Stillwater, Minnesota, still honored its white-painted-siding tradition. They persisted in covering brick buildings with white paint, though Downing now explained this practice to be foolish, when the good mellow tones of nature and of the Olde Gothick required less frequent coating and could be taken to be quaint even in decay. But this dialogue only occurred at the end of our period and anticipated the "Brown Decades" that followed the Civil War. Frederick Seward was correct; his father's was "an early effort. . . . Some years elapsed . . . before towers and [earth tones] . . . began to multiply in the land."[185]

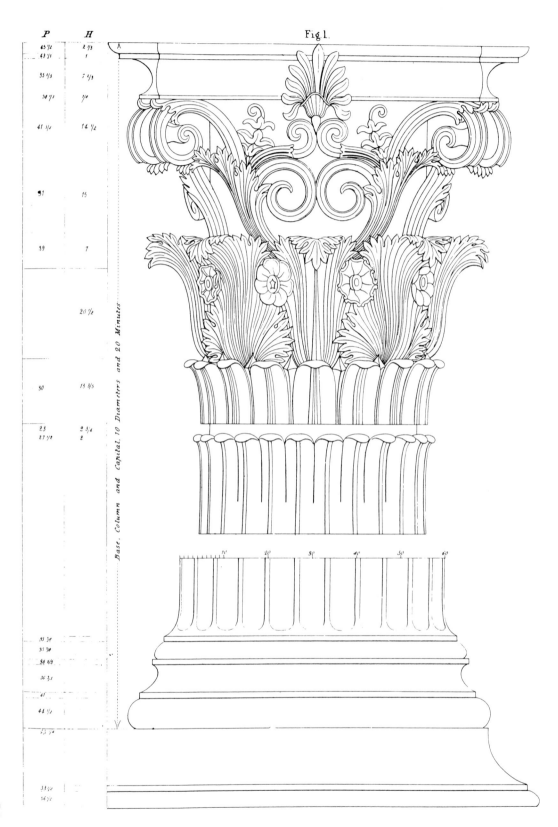

A detail of the Corinthian order, by Minard Lafever

Fig l.

P	H
45 1/2	2 1/3
43 1/4	1
35 1/3	7 1/3
30 1/3	1/4
41 3/4	14 1/2
31	15
39	7
	21 1/2
30	13 3/5
23	2 3/4
27 1/2	2
33 3/4	
37 3/4	
38 2/3	
36 3/5	
41	
44 1/2	1
43 3/4	
33 1/2	
36 1/2	

Base, Column and Capital, 10 Diameters and 20 Minutes

Page 217: Edmiston House (1845), in West Andover, Ohio, designed by Leverett Osborn

Right: Four buildings that demonstrate some of the applications of the Greek Revival style in more modest structures include doctors' offices in South Worcester, New York (*top, left*) and in Cooperstown, New York (*bottom, left*); a store in Breakabeen, New York (*top, right*); and the Caulkins law office in Grand Rapids, Michigan (*bottom, right*).

Opposite: The Alexander Wurts law office (1811) in Flemington, New Jersey, was remodeled by Mahlon Fisher in 1840.

Page 220: Gray-Thompson House (1846) in Glenwood, Indiana

Page 221: The Henry DeWitt Bennett House (1853), in Ann Arbor, Michigan, was probably designed by Arden Ballard.

Page 222: Also attributed to Ballard is the William Anderson House (1831) in Ann Arbor.

Page 223: Known as Stonehall, the Hays-Brooks House in Marshall, Michigan, was built in 1838.

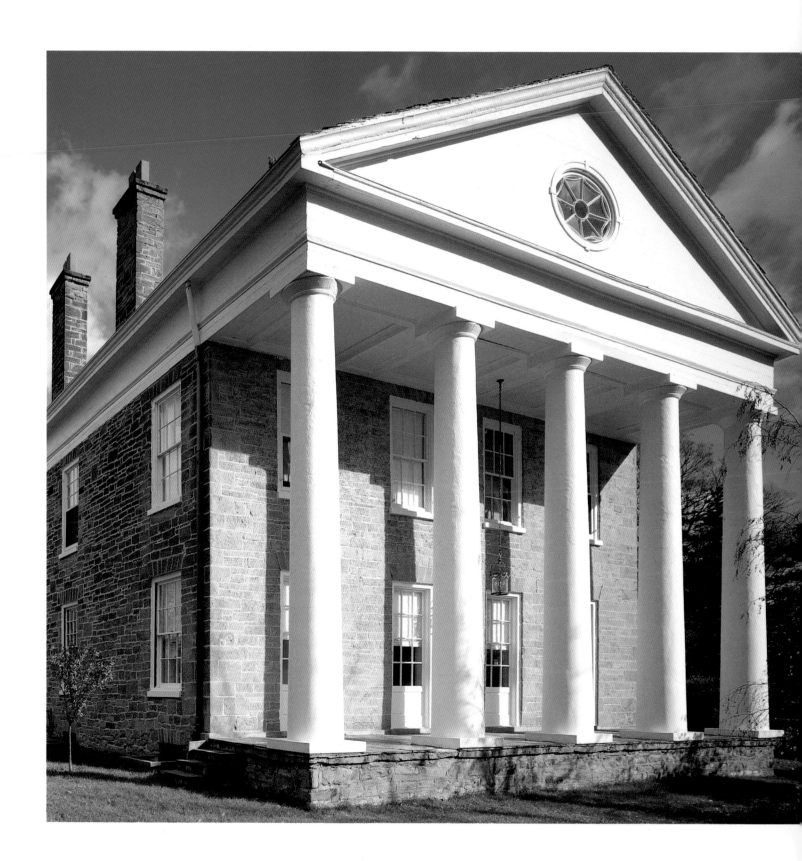

Right: (*Top*) The Brown-Simmons-Schug House (1829?) in Monroeville, Ohio; (*bottom*) the John H. Swartout House (1847)—now the Waukegan, Illinois, Chamber of Commerce

Opposite: a farm house in Meridale, New York, built around 1835

Page 228: The Ann Arbor House is now part of the Henry Ford Museum and Greenfield Village in Dearborn, Michigan.

Page 229: Oakleigh (1833–38), in Mobile, Alabama, also known as the Dennison House, was designed by James W. Roper.

Page 230: House in Poolville, New York, built about 1845

Page 231: The David Stearns House (1851–55) in Richmond, Maine

Page 232: Based on the designs of Minard Lafever, the Avery-Downer House in Granville, Ohio, was built in 1842.

Page 233: Mitchell-Turner House (1828) in Milan, Ohio

Opposite: A Greek Revival house in Maine on Route 201

Left: The Judge Robert S. Wilson House (1843) in Ann Arbor, Michigan

Opposite and left:
Robert Cary Long, Jr.,
designed the Elias
Baker House, in
Altoona, Pennsylvania,
in 1845.

Right and opposite: The William Risley House (c. 1837), in Fredonia, New York, is the work of John Jones.

Right: In 1840, Calvin A. Ryder designed the Captain James P. White House in Belfast, Maine.

Opposite: Kirkwood, or the Dr. H.A. Kirksey House (1850s) in Eutaw, Alabama

Opposite: The Governor's Manison (1855) in Austin, Texas, by Abner Cook

Left: (*Top*) Smith-Bly-Baxter House (1835) in Asheville, New York; (*bottom*) Edward Russell House (c. 1842) in Middletown, Connecticut

Page 244: The A. P. Dearing House (1850–56) in Athens, Georgia

Page 245: One of the many houses in central Massachusetts designed by Elias Carter

PART FOUR
A SECOND CASE STUDY:
THE INTERIOR

The Northern Greek Revival was at least as vigorous and diverse as that in the antebellum South; but all the great houses of the North that might have illustrated this part of the story have fallen victim to that region's industrial success. Those possessing a full panoply of interior ornamentation were built in and around cities—Philadelphia, Pittsburgh, New York, and Cincinnati—in areas that have been rebuilt several times since. Only the Croghan-Schenley rooms removed to the University of Pittsburgh's Cathedral of Learning, remain to remind us of scores of lost, high-style, Northern, big-city, Greek Revival interiors. The Campbell-Whittlesey House [300] in Rochester, New York, and the Avery-Downer House [232] in Granville, Ohio, are the best examples remaining of the somewhat more muted aspirations of relatively smaller places.

The plantation economy of the South did not build at its grandest in cities, but in clusters of headquarters buildings in the compound-communities of the Georgia and South Carolina Piedmont, around Columbus and Natchez, Mississippi, and in a few more dispersed groupings in Tennessee, Alabama, Mississippi, and upriver Louisiana. The most distinguished of these, aside from Milford and The Forest, are west of the Appalachians.

At the risk of reinforcing the obsolete notion that the Greek Revival was a largely Southern phenomenon, this second case study resumes a story we left in the first, and then moves west. Instead of introducing an entirely new cast of characters merely to make the point that there were other, Northern, stories to tell, this discussion follows the westering of some people to whom we have already been introduced, to find kinsmen creating the most interesting interiors remaining in America, which happen to be in the South.

As the presence of a gazetteer demonstrates, this book is intended to be an inducement to visit the places we describe, and that is another reason we move beyond Milford and The Forest. Milford is still in the hands of private owners, who are gracious but not willing to permit casual visits, and The Forest is a busy administrative building on a university campus. So we present Waverly [150, 310–11] and Gaineswood [149, 312, 313], which can be visited easily. As much as any buildings in the North, and even more than our earlier pair, they show us how strong-willed amateurs responded to the architectural ideas of their time.

Waverly and Gaineswood are peerless in expressing American ornamental and spatial ideas of this period. Although a bit more attention is devoted to them than to the houses of the Carolina Hamptons, the purpose has not been to write an extensive history of Greek Revival furniture or interior design (in the aesthetic sense), but instead to offer an outline of what might be included in such a history, drawing upon evidence inside Waverly and Gaineswood, which can be more easily found there than within any two other houses in the nation.

These two houses were built in the 1840s and 1850s by planters who, though residing eighty miles apart, were united by family ties and by the Tombigbee River. Access to the Tombigbee was important because this river conveyed their cotton crops downriver to Mobile, the Gulf, and ultimately to the waiting mills of Manchester and Lowell. Even "a most excellent piece of land . . . situated 10 or 12 miles from the river" [would be] "out of the way . . . out of the world," it was said at the time. It was a noble river, wandering through long, dark, leisurely loopings, as if seeking to avoid its ultimate dissolution in the waters of the Gulf of Mexico. (It has since been given bypass surgery by the Corps of Engineers, making it a prosaic "waterway.")[186]

George Hampton Young of Waverly, on the west bank, in Mississippi, was the son of Nancy Hampton, first cousin of Wade Hampton I.[†] Young and his kinsman by marriage—Nathan Bryan Whitfield of Gaineswood, downstream and in Alabama—had taken their squads of slaves west to occupy holdings in lands claimed as part of the Yazoo frauds in the 1790s (Hampton acquired a parcel, more than a mile in width, from the Tombigbee to the Mississippi). These lands were fought over by Andrew Jackson in his Creek Wars, and were taken by forced cession from the Cherokees, Creeks, Chickasaws, and Choctaws in the 1830s.

† Further genealogical information reveals that Wade's sister Elizabeth married James Harrison. The Harrisons' son Isham, also of the Columbus, Mississippi, group, begat Isham, Jr., who married Julia Whitfield in 1844. Julia Whitfield was the daughter of Governor James Whitfield of Columbus, who was a cousin of General Nathan Bryan Whitfield of Gaineswood, near Demopolis, Alabama. (James was the grandson of Luke Whitfield, brother of William, who was grandsire to General Nathan Bryan Whitfield.) To knit things together even more neatly, the two Whitfield families of Columbus and Demopolis were united by the marriage of Julia Whitfield's brother William to Nathan Bryan Whitfield's daughter Mary Elizabeth on March 3, 1847. That is, Elizabeth Hampton's grandson (Isham, Jr.) married Julia Whitfield, whose brother (William) married Nathan Bryan Whitfield's daughter (Mary Elizabeth), and Julia and William Whitfield also lived in the same Columbus–Aberdeen community as Nancy Hampton's descendants begat by George Hampton Young. Family papers tell us that "the first reference to the construction of the house known today as Gaineswood is found . . . [in] a letter from Mary Elizabeth and William." (Patton, p. 20) Finally, and after the fact, in the 1890s Elizabeth Hampton's great-grandson James Evans (of the Harrison line) married Emmy Young, granddaughter of George Hampton Young, of the Nancy Hampton line.

The western transfer of Hampton interests was extensive: about 1825, Wade Hampton II built Walnut Ridge in Issaquena County, Mississippi. About 1844, one of his sons, Wade III, built Wild Woods in Lake Washington, Mississippi, to tend that holding and others: Bayou Place, Otterbourne, Bear Garden, and Richland. About three years later, another son, Christopher, built Linden nearby.

Outside the Windows

A few comments upon the nature of the society being constructed in the Southern interior (in the geographical sense) may suggest some of the sounds and smells that passed through the windows into the opulent internal spaces of these houses.

Lest we bask too uncritically within, leafing through sentimental stories of their owners' lives, it is well to recall those who were driven from and driven to the fertile plains to provide the wealth to build such mansions. Family papers and letters from Whitfield to his wife give a series of glimpses of what immense human suffering went into the houses' creation. When Whitfield made a reconnaissance of Florida before settling in Alabama, his slaves went with him, "directed by a man named Fields." Directed, they were, thereafter, to work for others while their owner inspected the terrain: "Men . . . hire for 8 and 10 dollars a month boys and girls $4 and $5. Women about $5 and $6." The wages, of course, went to the owner, not the worker.

Cheaper land beckoned in Alabama. Though that already possessed by white speculators was priced "very high . . . and rising," things looked better across the fragile and porous lines drawn in Indian treaties. Whitfield knew that acquisition was somewhat impeded by the presence of Native Americans who had cleared some of the land and were raising crops upon it themselves: "I expect to go over in the Choctaw country to see what can be done there." Another set of treaties would be necessary, but thereafter he wrote his wife, "it is often the case . . . that one crop will pay for the land at $10 per acre."[187]

The rapid acquisition of hundreds of acres by cash-poor planters becomes more explicable when one perceives that, if they possessed slaves, that work force could be rented out to others at rates sufficient to buy an acre a month for a man and an acre every two months or so for a boy or girl. Upkeep, of course, had to be deducted, but turning slave labor into extensive plantations—and then into architecture—was within reach of the fortunate.

Whitfield's figures were good only for the savannahs, where the great trees did not have to be burnt out. In the forest, things went more slowly; deciduous trees were ringed to deprive them of the water to permit photosynthesis; their leaves dried and fell, causing winter to come upon them in midsummer, one by one. Below, however, corn could grow as the general summer settled in. After being left a year or so to dry out, these hardwoods were felled alongside the pines, and the woods came to be full of the scent of burning resin, the roar of flames, and the shouts of the men, women, and children doing the work. Henry

Morton Stanley, writing a few years later of such a scene in Arkansas (his African adventures came later), acknowledged the heat and the danger, but "the excitement of the gangs . . . had a real fascination for me."[188]

What it "had" for the gangs themselves we do not know, but for the Choctaws, Cherokees, and Chickasaws other fires were recalled at the end of the 1830s. By then, the architect William Nichols had produced a cool, serene, elegant, new Alabama capitol in Tuscaloosa. In its legislative chamber, Chief Eufula bade farewell: "The white man [in his pursuit of land upon which to grow cotton, has] brought burden and ache of heart upon my people in driving them from their homes and yoking them with laws they did not understand. . . . In these lands of Alabama, which have belonged to my forefathers and where their bones are buried, I see that the Indian fires are going out. Soon they will be cold. [Still,] I do not believe our Great Father means to harm his red children. . . . We leave behind our good will to the people of Alabama who will build great houses."[189]

The "removal" of the Native Americans was achieved by General George Gaines and Colonel James R. Bryan, the two leading speculators in the region stretching from Aberdeen, Mississippi, to Demopolis, Alabama, and southward along the upper Tombigbee. From their headquarters emerged a steady flow of encomia to the fertility of the shores of the Tombigbee and Black Warrior rivers. Corn and beans were already thriving at the hands of the Creeks and Chickasaws; how much better might such rich soil respond to the ministrations of experienced planters whose cotton lands in the Piedmont Carolinas and Georgia were already showing signs of exhaustion.

Gaines secured a final cession of this valuable real estate from the Native Americans in the "Treaty" of Dancing Rabbit, and commenced disposing of it, at a price, to his friends and their friends. Among the newcomers were Nathan Whitfield (a nephew of Colonel Bryan), his cousin James Whitfield, and a covey of Hampton kinfolk—including the Harrisons and Earles, descendants of Elizabeth Hampton, sister of Wade I—as well as George Hampton Young, son of the old general's cousin Nancy. The Columbus Whitfields were made kin to the Harrisons by marriage in 1844, and ties to their Demopolis cousins were reaffirmed by the marriage of Nathan Whitfield's daughter to William Whitfield of Columbus, in 1847.

These families are not only intertwined genetically, but sociologically and aesthetically as well. Nathan Whitfield and George Young were both born in 1799 of Piedmont planters, one in North Carolina and the other in Georgia. (Their heritage was the same: the diagonal migration along the eastern slope of the Appalachians. The Youngs had simply pushed south and west ahead of the Whitfields.) Whitfield came to Demopolis in 1833, at about the same time Young arrived upriver and across the Mississippi line. Both were exceptionally well-educated for the time—Young at the University of Georgia and Columbia University Law School, and Whitfield at the University of North Carolina, of which his father, General Bryan Whitfield, had been a founder.

As a result, they had become accustomed to observing the growth of an American classical revival. The University of Georgia at Athens was chartered in 1785, though its "Senatus Academicus" met in no deeper shade than that provided by a large oak on the bank of the Ocanee River until 1806, when Old College was built. This sober rectangle of brick, laid in Flemish bond, was followed in 1824 by Demosthenian Hall, still in the eighteenth-century manner, with plaster swags, Venetian window, and fanlit doorway. Then, while George Young was disposing of Georgia properties and consolidating his ventures in Mississippi, the Georgia Greek Revival got under way. Three superb buildings, the first two probably by Charles Cluskey, appeared: the Old Medical College Building [374] in Augusta (1835), the chapel (1832–33) and Phi Beta Kappa Hall (1836) in Athens.

The central rotunda of the Medical College presaged an even more magnificent interior Pantheon designed by Cluskey in 1837–38: the Executive Mansion in Milledgeville. When the mansion was finished in 1839 it was (and, after the destruction of some formidable competitors built subsequently, it is once again) the most impressive residence built in America bringing the Palladian villa format into the Greek Revival period.

At Waverly, the central space is almost all there is; the house barely seems to be able to hold together around that huge vacuity. Outside, front and back, there are two indented verandas with attenuated Ionic columns—not porticos, surely, but recollections of porticos, perhaps.[†]

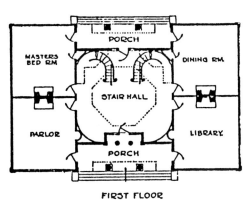

FIRST FLOOR

The rotunda dominated the architectural experience of George Hampton Young; on the other hand, Nathan Bryan Whitfield learned his neoclassicism from a more recent English school—one associated with the shallow domes of the Regency of Sir John Soane, though Whitfield was quite capable of picking up German massing and American ornamental ideas as well.

The campus of the University of North Carolina, Chapel Hill, where he was educated, and where his father was a major force, was undergoing completion in the early 1820s to designs by William Nichols, of Bath, the Regency watering-place in Somersetshire. When Whitfield served terms in both houses of the North Carolina legislature [354–55] before seeking a greater fortune in Alabama, he was also working within chambers designed by Nichols, who had already created the most imposing buildings around Edenton, the Whitfields' political base in that period.

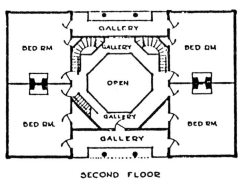

SECOND FLOOR

Floor plan of Waverly

Later, in Alabama, Whitfield was acquainted with Nichols's work as state architect and then as state engineer (1827–33), after which Nichols proceeded on to be state architect of Mississippi from 1836 to 1848. It was hardly possible to escape the Nichols manner when one traveled up the Black Warrior River to Tuscaloosa, the state capital. The Greek Revival, with a Regency dash,

† When Young took the lead in organizing the University of Mississippi in Oxford, from 1846 to 1848, just before Waverly was built, he and the other founders turned to Nichols again. The architect was "at the center of Mississippi's social and political life for over twelve years" (Peatross, p. 29) since he had also designed this state's capitol and executive mansion. Yet neither Young nor Whitfield displayed much deference to this overwhelmingly influential artist when it came to designing their own houses. It is noteworthy that neither of their idiosyncratic structures shows any desire to follow the rush of other planters to follow the colonnaded style Nichols probably introduced to the region in the late 1820s with his Forks of Cypress, not far away in Florence, Alabama. ("Probably" in the cases of Forks of Cypress and the James H. Dearing House because no written evidence corroborates the stylistic evidence and Nichols's known availability.) Furthermore, if Nathan Bryan Whitfield were as architecturally sensitive in his earlier as in his later years, he may well have been the person who introduced Nichols to his neighboring planters. Nichols's style was becoming old-fashioned in the eyes of a restless innovator like Whitfield, but not to the more conservative Glovers of Rosemount.

was established by his designs for the capitol, the state bank, the University of Alabama, the town hall, and both the Episcopal and Methodist churches. (None of these buildings survives; of all those that can be attributed to Nichols in the city, only the James H. Dearing House remains.)†

Not that Whitfield could be easily overwhelmed. He was vehemently original; though he played pianoforte, bagpipe, harp, and violin, he invented a keyboard instrument called a "flutina," which produced flutelike sounds from a cylinder apparently filled with air, by cranking it. Out of doors, his engineering was expressed on a larger scale, in a lock-and-dam system of canals to drain his plantations, and his own contrivances for lathes, power wheels, and construction machinery.

He was also a painter, and a sculptor of portraits in pinewood. He did not have an opportunity to be encouraged in architecture by either Latrobe or Soane, yet during the period he was shuttling between Edenton, Raleigh, and Demopolis, he was able to observe the manipulation of surfaces being carried on by Nichols's successor as architect of the capitol, the very skillful and ambitious David Paton, who had just come from training (1829–30) under Soane, in London.

The North Carolina capitol, like the Hampton houses in South Carolina, showed the early effects of another set of influences, American in origin though Greek in inspiration. This was ornament composed in New York by Minard Lafever, James Gallier, and James Dakin, marketed by the yard in papier-mâché, and presented for emulation in the builders' guides of Lafever, with illustrations often drawn by Gallier or the Dakins. The bare beginnings of this ornamental "school" could be seen at The Forest; it was still somewhat diffident in the rectilinear spaces of the Hampton houses in South Carolina, but it spread across entire ceilings, twining down along doorframes and over mirrors in its late-summer harvest amid the ambiguous and shadowy spaces of Gaineswood.

Whitfield provided there a greenhouse for the flowering of American ornament; in his house the spaces—one is tempted to say "its trellises"—are less important than the surfaces. And he kept tinkering with it: in 1861 he wrote of a "new portico" on the north, above a new "pond or lake." He had just built a "family bedroom" for his second wife, with a "circular gallery" straight from Regent's Park. "The parlor and dining room are also changed . . . by adding lights [cupolas?] to the ceiling, which are very beautiful."[190]

Waverly is an entirely different phenomenon. It does not display ornament except to impart piquancy to its changes of plane at doors and windows, cupboards and niches. It is not an essay about surfaces but about their absence.

Anyone who thinks the American Greek Revival lacked variety should experience these two houses within easy striking distance of each other. Aesthetically, either might have been better here and there, more coherent perhaps, if built all at once out of the single inspired moment of an experienced architect. But from a historian's point of view they are better as they are; resounding statements by confident amateurs who could have turned matters over to architects, but did not do so. They were well-acquainted with the fashions of their time, and chose what they wanted, leaving the rest aside.[191]

Visitors   They were not obstinate or solecistic about this; it is likely that Young and Whitfield, kinsmen and competitors in architectural experiment, were not loath to make use of general concepts they admired in the published work of others or to ask those architects who came their way to refine and extend their own ideas.[192]

† Adolphus Heimann, also trained in Berlin, was available in the area for consultation in the German style, but his own work is not as Schinkelesque as either Reichardt's or Whitfield's.

It is possible that the Schinkelesque qualities of Gaineswood, which have received much baffled comment over the years, arose from a visit by Charles Reichardt. The house required at least nine years in gestation (from 1833 to 1842) and another nineteen to be brought to completion in 1861. During that period, Whitfield may have gotten a sketch or two from Reichardt. One thing is certain: he built a more Prussian building than anything designed for the Hamptons.†

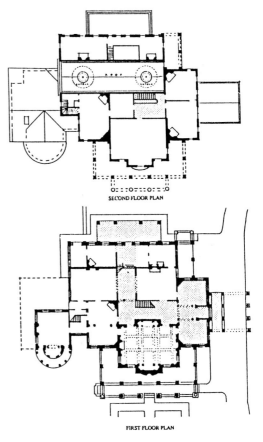

SECOND FLOOR PLAN

FIRST FLOOR PLAN

Floor plan of Gaineswood

While Whitfield was accumulating wealth and ideas for Gaineswood, the most conspicuous plantation houses in the South were being built to Reichardt's designs by Hampton kinfolk; Milford and Millwood lay on the route back and forth from Alabama to North Carolina. In 1840, Reichardt left the South Carolina Hamptons, and he might have paused among the Youngs, Harrisons, and Whitfields on his way to Mexico. There may even be an echo of such a visit in the report that George Hampton Young used the services of a "German gardener" to landscape the terrain between his house and the Tombigbee.[193]

Later in this book, the word *Regents* is used to describe men like Nichols, William Jay, Latrobe, and Hadfield, a usage drawn from American jurisprudence and architecture experience. This *American* Regency was under the tutelage of European architects who gave the craftsmen of the new republic guidance and instruction until American training caught up with American need. But the *English* Regency also contributed to American building; Gaineswood and Waverly are among those American houses most directly, and obviously, indebted to the villas sweetly dispersed among the newly planted copses and glades set before the enormous "sets"—continuous "flats" in the theatrical as well as the real estate sense—placed by the Prince Regent's architects around the periphery of his park in London.

In other sections of this book we will observe the American "Regency" in Indiana, Maine, Wisconsin, and Kentucky, as its lessons were transmitted and transmuted through the interconnected offices of Town and Davis, Dakin, Lafever, Gallier, Warren, Rague, and Reichardt (in New York) in the 1830s. In builders' guides and in person these men spread throughout America what they found exciting in the Regent's Park villas that a decade earlier had been placed by Decimus Burton and John Raffield upon the stage set created by John Nash.

These villas were depicted in British publications (like James Elmes's *Metropolitan Improvements* in 1819), which reached New York in the first steamers after publication; they went on to Alabama as soon as saddlebags could be packed. Minard Lafever reduced the complexity of those designs for his *Young Builder's General Instructor* in the same year, and in all his subsequent manuals of style until 1856. But the process did not stop with simplification; in the provinces, ambitious clients and architects recomplicated these designs in their own ways.

James Gallier, who had English training and was then working for Lafever, provided two successive stages of simplification of Burton's concept in two plates for *The Modern Builder's Guide* of 1833, which Whitfield embellished. Then he went back, it appears, to Burton for a final element, a curved colonnade and new bedroom wing for his second wife.

The pleasures of following the Regency of Regent's Park into the American interior, where it could merge with Prussian ideas of picturesque neoclassicism, are endless: Raffield's John Maberly Villa (St. John's Lodge) of 1819 was freely adapted by Lafever in Plate 44 of his *Young Builder's General Instructor*, "A Gentleman's Country Residence," then by Adolphus Heimann in his Nashville Masonic Hall of 1851, and, even more grandly, in Heimann's and Adelicia Cheatham's Belmont (a.k.a. "Belle Mont") of 1859.

At Gaineswood, Prussian ideas were admixed with a Regent's Park "original," Decimus Burton's villa for George B. Greenough (1824), and mixed again with American originations. Lafever's and Gallier's adaptations of Burton's theme can be seen in hundreds of fresh cadenzas across the Finger Lakes region of New York, and in southern Michigan, hearing its last echo in the Cooley House in Racine, Wisconsin. In the North, as in the South, few builders of Grecian houses had Whitfield's gift for creative synthesis, and tended to take their ideas either directly from pattern books or from local carpenter-builders who did. Though later we attend to the careers of a number of professional architects, most of the buildings in this book did not arise from their efforts, but from the diffusion of ideas through books.

But this was not new. It had been that way since Palladio himself demonstrated the benefits the printing press had on the reputation of architects with a gift for self-promotion, and on the quality of building. In Alabama, Minard Lafever, Asher Benjamin, and Chester Hill (*The Builders Guide*, 1834) provided a range of options for blocking out buildings and for ornamental detail, to which local or traveling craftsmen added their own distinctive fillips. And when the gifts of the bookmen and of the craftsmen were added to the anonymous contributions of "the folk" who had established local traditions, clients like Whitfield and Young were able to bring to the scene their own observations and instincts.[†]

Neither Gaineswood nor Waverly evidences much indebtedness in plan or elevation to anything of the Dakins, and only a few modest lines running to Berlin, London, New York, or Mobile—not enough to weigh down men and women of strong personality and great sophistication. Yet inside these houses one can discern some general imperatives in the organization of space during the Greek Revival period.[††]

† Whitfield's library is dispersed, so we can no longer be certain if he had his own *Metropolitan Improvements* or his own Stuart and Revett, or perhaps only the works of Gallier and Lafever. But in any case, Gallier himself was not far off—together with Lafever's other draftsmen, the Dakins, reinforcing the Regency ideas found in books. By 1842, when Whitfield was ready to begin construction, Gallier and the Dakins had nearly a decade of work along the lower Tombigbee behind them, having made timely departure from the crowded architectural competition in New York. They had become as dominant in the artistic life of southern Alabama as Nichols was in its northern provinces. Mobile of the 1830s was re-created by them in the Greek Revival mode, and Mobile was the seaport through which both Whitfield and Young sold their cotton.

†† Arthur Scully, James Dakin's biographer, calls attention to Dakin's first large residential commission, the Perry House in Brooklyn, New York (1832), as contributing some ideas which might have been interesting to Whitfield.
 In *Southern Comfort*, Starr emphasizes the importance of Regency influences upon Henry Howard and Lewis Reynolds, in Louisiana. Gallier and Howard, both Irish-born but both conditioned by residence in New York in the 1830s, applied their Regency in opposite directions—Gallier made it simpler; Howard made it more complex. Starr sees Howard's urban buildings (his chief focus) as less exuberant than those of either Howard's mentor, James Dakin, or his competitor, Lewis Reynolds. But the only American competitors to Gaineswood in fearless amplification of received Regency ideas are Howard's contemporary essays in Hellenistic excess: Nottoway [316–17] and Belle Grove.

Classical Space

In its first phase, the evolution of the American post-colonial interior could offer only uncertain and provincial decoration upon the inside of boxlike rooms. Too often, the American Federal offers bleached-out Adamesque swags, desiccated garlands, attenuated colonnettes, and a little finicking plasterwork here and there. As we have noted, there was very little aesthetic independence in the first years after political independence. In this febrile period, colors were muted, forms were nervous, and the eyes of most American clients seemed always to be fixed upon some other, more admirable place to emulate.

In a very few instances, bold spirits pressed floor plans toward the curves and polygons used thirty years earlier in the villas of Robert Adam and his British contemporaries. However, until the arrival of Benjamin Henry Latrobe and George Hadfield from Britain in 1795–96, and Joseph Jacques Ramée from France in 1811 or 1812, American interiors did not show much verve. With Latrobe, America entered its neoclassical period with an architect who knew how to use color and space to amaze.

Surprise and amazement had been desired by the architects of the Baroque a century earlier. To achieve these effects, they hid the sources of light, thrust towers and domes upward until ceilings disappeared into shadow, and confused and delighted with false ceilings, sculptured niches, and trompe l'oeil painting, though seldom, in England, in combination with plaster cherubs; the Germans and Italians amazed in ways which have only recently been surpassed by the inspired illusionists of Disneyland.

Latrobe was educated in Germany, and his early work in England—especially Ashdown, flamboyant with color and full of tricks with light and contrived gloom—stood in the Baroque tradition. And from the beginning of his American career, he delighted in its repertory of devices.

Latrobe's houses designed for Norfolk and Richmond, Virginia, at the end of the 1790s, brought into American practice the central tribune, an open well of space, lit from the top, and dedicated to eliciting a gasp of wonder from the visitor. It remained the most consistent element of his style, finding its ultimate expression in the Piranesian vastness of his Baltimore Cathedral. Awe and wonder were surely intended to be felt by visitors even to his chambers for reasonable legislators, in the national Capitol.[†] Latrobe would bury a Pantheon inside a Parthenon in order to surprise and impress those who came into a bank, a hall for a congress, a mansion, or a cathedral.

The desire to elicit Latrobian awe remained at the center of American Greek Revival practice until its end. Waverly is the nation's most extreme expression of the desire to hew out startling caverns, even from

† In Latrobe's absence, England's Sir John Soane continued his own independent development of sculptured space and illusionist tricks. Robert Adam had admired his great Baroque predecessor, Sir John Vanbrugh; Soane and Latrobe admired Adam, and combined his effects with those suggested by the terrifying and wonderful engravings of Adam's friend Piranesi.

relatively small structures. Its internal rotunda is a hidden wonder, not implied by its exterior form. The house looks fairly solid from the outside. Light streams from below through the windows of the cupola, but the great space from which that light comes is as unexpected as the central grandeur of Latrobe's banks.

However, the grand, neo-Baroque stairway within the tribune of Waverly comes from another tradition, one that was launched in America by the New York City Hall (1804) and carried forward in Kentucky by Gideon Shryock for the rotunda of the old statehouse in Frankfort, of 1827–29 [47]. George Hampton Young had adequate access to both; his cotton crop was sold through New York factors, and the Kentucky statehouse was famous—it was the first Greek Revival building west of the Appalachians.

The New York City Hall was the work of Joseph-François Mangin and John McComb, Jr., who drew upon French precedents such as the Hotel de Ville at Nancy (1752–56), and British ones including Wardour House, Wiltshire, built 1768–76 by the earl of Arundell to drawings by James Paine, and Robert Adam's wonderful design for the countess of Hume's house on Portman Square in London (now part of the Courtauld Institute), built in the same years. The form was widely disseminated: it appeared in the British residency in Hyderabad, George Hadfield's Washington City Hall of 1817–22, and John S. Norris's Savannah custom house of 1846–52.[†]

At Barton Hall [v], further north, along the Natchez Trace in Cherokee, Alabama, Armistead Barton entered this competition in Alabama amazement in 1849 with an awesome stair hall of a different sort, throwing bridges across a cavern. John Julius Norwich recently described its only English counterpart— that within Kingstone Lisle House, in Oxfordshire—thus: "It is a wild force of nature, leaping from wall to wall like a flying fox, taking space and span in its stride, breaking out and recoiling again and all the while creating perspectives that would cause Piranesi to blink his eyes."[194]

Barton Hall, like Waverly, holds its surprises in check until the visitor is lured within by hints of the Greek Revival upon a demure façade. It also illustrates the general principle that one should never assume that there was a "Greek Revival" floor plan to serve all clients. It was one thing to accept four walls, a ceiling, and a floor from the colonial period, to allocate to them whatever decoration one can afford, and to join one set of rectangular cells to another set above by a solemn, straight staircase. It was quite another to whip stairs about, throw them, like rope bridges, across domestic chasms, and mold space with the confidence of Barton and Young.

It is true that Greek Revival façades were often merely imposed upon older, four-square houses, and that new ones were built as if they were so remodeled. The number of spatial inventors is never great at any

† McComb knew Shryock's mentor William Strickland and, Clay Lancaster suggests, may have known Shryock too. (Lancaster in "New York City Hall Stair Rotunda Reconsidered," *Journal of the Society of Architectural Historians* 29, no. 1 (March 1970) pp. 33 ff.) McComb lived until 1853, and the reclusive Shryock outlived nearly all the characters in these pages, sending drawings to assist other architects and builders, such as those that shaped the state capitol in Little Rock, Arkansas [362–63], in 1833 and, we are free to speculate, a page or two of suggestions to George Hampton Young. Who knows?

† C. Ford Peatross suggests that Nichols designed Rosemount, on grounds of its resemblances to the Hayes Plantation, and the fact that Williamson Allen Glover, its builder, was the father-in-law of James I. Thornton, Alabama's secretary of state during Nichols's tenure as state architect, and who built Thornhill, which also bears Nichols's thumbprints. In family lore reported by Mary Wallace Crocker, Governor James Whitfield's Snowdoun is "attributed to William H. O'Neal, an architect originally from North Carolina." (*Historic Architecture in Mississippi.* Jackson: University and College Press of Mississippi, 1973. p. 121) William Nichols, who *was* from North Carolina, was in the neighborhood with his ever-ready set of pattern-book ideas, and many ideas of his own.

Octagonal central spaces attracted members of the Whitfield family as well as Young. Governor James Whitfield built Snowdoun in Columbus, Mississippi, two years after Waverly was completed. At the center of two splayed wings, and behind a recessed Roman Doric colonnade at their juncture, one finds an open, octagonal stair hall. Nichols assisted a number of local builders in their experiments with space, encouraging them to vary, somewhat, the generalities of builders' guides. If Nichols was offering suggestions to the Tombigbee experimenters in rotundal space, other possibilities arise. He is very likely to have known the famous interiors of Carlton House, the Regency palace that had recently been destroyed in London. If we imagine him visiting James Whitfield or George Young with some sketches in hand, we could also imagine his penciling together a fusion of the double, twisting staircase and the adjacent octagonal tribune in that amazing building and offering them up, in a minimalist abstraction, to his hosts. Of course one has to be wary of giving Nichols credit for all oversize cupolas; the old Iolani Palace in Honolulu, constructed in 1844–45, had a grand one, and so did Barton Hall before it was blown away by a tornado. Still, Peatross's idea opens some wonderful possibilities.
(continued)

time. The ambitions of some Mississippians were satisfied by putting three rooms behind each other in progression, along a central hall, instead of the customary two. But along the Tombigbee there were many who took a cue from another invention of William Nichols's, a huge cupola on the roof, into which interior space unfolded—blossomed.

Waverly has the most "organic" of these. Young created a great lantern, high enough to be seen a long way down the river. Rosemount, a house that lies about midway between Young's property and Whitfield's, brings a staircase into a rooftop ballroom that is so large it dominates the whole house, as did the one Nichols provided for Hayes Plantation, in Edenton, North Carolina.[†]

Were these ballrooms and professional staircases feminine spaces? Or were they spaces in which men might parade their women? (See Appendix A.)

Both William Nichols and Charles Reichardt could have visited George Hampton Young, Nathan and James Whitfield, Barton, or Williamson Allen Glover of Rosemount. But to enjoy their wonderful houses we do not require the casting offices of our imaginations to furnish such complete sets of characters playing out the full story. These clients were cosmopolitans who had made visits to New York, Philadelphia, Baltimore, and Savannah, and they were buyers of architectural books as well. So what they might have learned from Reichardt or Nichols personally, could also have been learned from examining their work—or Latrobe's, William Jay's (in Savannah and Charleston), Jay's successor, Charles Cluskey's, and the work of Latrobe's pupils: Robert Mills and William Strickland.[††]

In the Greek Revival period there were always amateurs emboldened to cut and chip and trowel and press sideways and upward, in order to create an impression, even in small houses, that their space had been hewn out of solids, rather than created merely by adding modules of ceiling, walls, and floor. One does not expect such ingenuity in out-of-the-way places, and one can be even more surprised by what can be found in the use of color. At Gaineswood, General Whitfield deployed a full palette upon his repertory of Lafeverish ornament, upon which played mysterious light from the crowns of his domed rooms.

Furniture

When Elbridge Gerry entered the White House in 1813, he was captivated by the effects achieved by Latrobe. It was, he said, "a perfect palace. You enter the front door and are at once in a large hall. . . . Pillars of immense size are dispersed thro' this." After Mrs. Madison's sitting room, one came into a chamber that was not very large to us but, at the time, "immense and magnificent . . . in the oval form. . . . The windows are nearly the height of the room, and have superb red silk velvet curtains . . . the chairs are wood painted, with worked bottoms and each has a red velvet cushion."[195]

Among the paradoxes of the paradoxical time between the arrival of Latrobe and Hadfield in the 1790s and the appearance of an architectural Greek Revival in the 1820s is that while exteriors were not Greek (with the handful of exceptions noted), furniture often was.

Later, as exteriors assumed Greek and Roman forms (though often modified enough to escape any attribution, except to American ingenuity), interiors ceased to be derived directly from ancient forms, and came instead to be modeled upon the intervening styles of the eighteenth century.[†††]

American furniture in its neoclassical phase, as it anticipated the Greek Revival, was first created by Latrobe. His furniture for the White House was burnt by the British in 1814, but it had its effect upon American furniture builders: Chief Justice John Marshall owned a "klismos" chair made in Philadelphia around 1820, from which he may have read his decision in *Gibbons v. Ogden*. One of his predecessors, John Jay, later had three such chairs made, bearing his coat of arms, in high Federalist style. Manufacturers such as Duncan Phyfe of New York modulated their earlier French designs into the new style. Along with French politics, the style thickened from Directoire into the burlier Empire, though it was not any more French than English.[††††]

American design was first encouraged when scores of French furniture makers arrived in New York, New Orleans (from which Andrew Jackson procured pieces for the Hermitage), Baltimore, and Philadelphia, in refuge from revolutions in San Domingo and France itself. The Empire or Napoleonic style received an additional impetus when the Emperor Napoleon's brother, Joseph, arrived in Philadelphia in 1816. The former king of Naples and Spain brought a large collection of furniture, sculpture, and paintings with him, which he abandoned occasionally to visit his hundred-thousand-acre hunting preserve in the Adirondacks, though he never ventured to pay a state visit to his loyal followers in Alabama. Finally, domestic ingenuity was stimulated by the tariff of 1820, which imposed a surcharge of 30 percent on furniture and 50 percent on clocks.

Glover and Nathan Whitfield were close friends and business associates as well. Local tradition attributes to Whitfield the Glover Mausoleum built in the 1840s by the widow of Allen Glover. But it might as well be Nichols's work. So might Allen Glover's Demopolis house, long vanished, next to Bluff Hall, the Greek portico for which was added (possibly by Whitfield or Nichols) in the 1850s. The Allen Glover House, judging from the old photograph in Robert Gamble's *The Alabama Catalogue*, bore a biloggial portico of Nichols's North Carolina pattern.

†† Nathan Whitfield has left us reports of visits to New York in 1842, and a series of visits to Philadelphia, where his son attended medical school.

††† In 1985 the Philadelphia Museum came into possession of a few of Latrobe's Grecian tables, chairs, and a sofa from the Waln House, on which he was working in 1808. A fine exhibition thereafter gave us a sense of the space he created around these sleek, trim pieces. The museum even created replicas of the stenciled friezes, derived from Greek vases by the English artist John Flaxman, that he prescribed to go with them.
The Valentine Museum in Richmond has succeeded in recovering some similar scenes that once animated the walls of their Wickham House, designed three years later by Alexander Parris with advice from Latrobe. Parris learned to work competently in Latrobe's vaulting tribune-centered mode, as his Sears House (now the Somerset Club) in Boston demonstrates, but he was not the virtuoso sculptor of space that his mentor was.

†††† It was imported largely by British publications such as those of Thomas Hope and George Smith—and especially by the monthly guidance received from Rudolph Ackerman's magazine, published from 1809 to 1828.

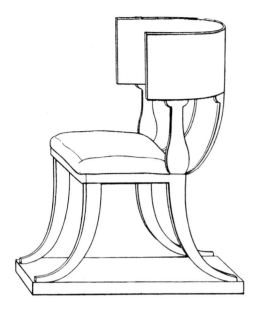

Thomas Hope design for a chair

While the Latrobe-Hope-Phyfe style was often elaborate with inlays and gildings, it was never heavy; heaviness set in with Bonapartism. Then the Greek Revival became imperial, giving way to scrolls and columns, to thickening and weightiness. Clothing thickened too as ladies replaced the gauzy, high-waisted, zephyr-catching frocks with ever more layers of fat and fabric.

As the 1820s led into the thirties, forties, and fifties, interiors became more somber, language more refined, and manners more mannered. Brilliant colors of floral carpeting, laid wall-to-wall, made the old floor-cloths seem primitive, but it was difficult to discern color amid the murk, for natural light was hidden behind a vast inventory of curtains.

After Empire came the Rococo Revival, of which the restored interiors of Rosedown Plantation in Louisiana and the Richmond Room at New York's Metropolitan Museum of Art offer good examples. The Rococo Revival was redeemed by the technical virtuosity of John Henry Belter in the 1850s, for Belter offered ingenuity in lamination to satisfy an insatiable public yearning for complexity and opulence. American taste had come a long way from the spare, Hellenic, "republican simplicity" of Latrobe and Dolley Madison.

As early as 1840, at least one English visitor had remarked upon the strange progression from the stripped clarity of American exteriors into the ambiguous spaces and profusion of objects within. That observer put the matter in sexual terms, speaking as if the columnar Greek Revival outside was masculine, and the interiors feminine, full of "little tables, looking and smelling like flower beds, portfolios, knickknacks, bronzes, busts, cameos, and alabaster vases, illustrated copies of lady-like rhymes bound in silk, and, in short, all the pretty coxcomalities of the drawing room scattered about with . . . profuse and studied negligence."[196] Mirrors had replaced stenciling, and sturdy portraits of founders had been replaced by pictures of anonymous, button-eyed ladies in bonnets gazing reverentially at the heavens or at bassinets. This was the world we glimpse in the tarry background of photographs of a house dominated by a woman, Ellen Carpenter's Phil-Ellena.

An inside–outside, feminine–masculine distinction is on its surface offensive, and is far too simple, and there is too much complexity in the power relationships between the sexes to permit full treatment here. (I have offered a hypothesis about one element of that complexity in Appendix A, entitled "A Speculation on Power and Sex in Greek Revival America.") Nonetheless, some relatively tame assertions on this subject may be in order here.

From the moment of its reassertion in the late 1820s, an architectural style that had been associated with a cult of masculine founders, reinvigorated by the pride of a nation recovering its expansionary nerve and becoming increasingly aggressive toward its neighbors, was, at its core, strangely anxious—and that anxiety was *not* discernibly feminine. Greek Revival interiors of the post-heroic age, or, one might say, of the age in which heroic energy went as much into commerce as into statecraft, became increasingly gluttonous of objects, like a nervous male or female at a cocktail party who cannot resist the hors d'oeuvre.

It may be merely a coincidence that, at the time, the "tastemakers," the writers of books from which the middle class drew its notions of architecture and interior design, ceased to address themselves to men and began, instead, to write primarily for women. Men catering to women's taste replaced men writing for other men working as carpenter-builders; this was the transition from the intended audience of Minard Lafever and Asher Benjamin to that of Andrew Jackson Downing, or, later, of Ward Macallister.

We have noted the abandonment of American national pride by the Gothic Revivalists among the literary Jacksonians. This process was completed by Downing and brought to fetid parody by Macallister. But that was long after the Greek Revival had died. In 1830, it was still livelier in America than anywhere else in the world, and had plenty of life to last for three decades.

THE PSYCHOLOGY OF THE INTERIOR:
AMERICAN AND EUROPEAN REVIVALISTS

Republican simplicity did not enjoy a long run in nineteenth-century Europe—only about as long as simplicity or republicanism taken singly. For a few years around 1800, some French architects made use of the stripped, straightforward Doric to score a point against the waning fashion for soft, sinuous, Rococo twinings. And in England from the 1750s onward, Greek card houses, teahouses, and orangeries—buildings serving as sumptuous garden furniture—were in fashion. Only in remote districts such as Devon, Northumberland, and Scotland were Greek structures created in earnest, and even that earnestness was aesthetic. In the United States it was political.

Perhaps the British use of Greek forms in their houses might have carried more intense symbolic content had it occurred before 1793. Until the decapitation of the king of France, even bankers might be overheard muttering republicanisms into their soup. But a great deal of money was made financing wars against revolution, and these bankers' underemployed offspring, aesthetes such as William Drummond and Thomas Hope, played it safe: their Hellenism may have been more expensive but it was still merely as decorative as the earlier fashion for Grecian gazebos. A Hampshire valley gained a stage prop of Arcadia—Drummond's Grange Park—and Hope became the sponsor and designer of some very pretty furniture. Americans did rediscover Greek architecture in the years before 1800, but they were Tories, slow to return to their own country after the Revolution, loath to be conspicuous thereafter, and in no position to initiate an expensive manifestation of hierarchy and, implicitly, of class differences. None of the Revolution's leaders in the United States had the leisure to visit Greece before the war, and they were fully occupied thereafter.

Among Americans, unlike Europeans, a second rediscovery of Greece and Greek architecture in Italy was required, this time by a generation of nationalistic young men such as William Short and Nicholas Biddle, successors and protégés of the founders. After 1800 Joseph Allen Smith and Biddle went to Greece and Thomas Jefferson's friend Short had himself painted in front of a Doric temple at Paestum. Slowly, thereafter, Americans took their own road into a Greek Revival, having rediscovered Greece again for themselves—so slowly that they never bothered much to carry into their own practices the exactitudes of archaeology. Instead, the ideological electricity in the air at the time resulted in Free Classicism, with wider consequences for their landscape than anything that occurred in Europe.

A variety of styles were available in this eclectic age, but the Greek suited more Americans than any other—for a time.

Architectural Hellenism in America was popular, not snobbish. It was polemical and political, not theoretical. The Scottish Greek Revival, on the other hand, was official, elite, and nonpolitical—but it was also theoretical, based in Enlightenment theories of an orderly universe (as the abortive French Greek Revival had been). Americans showed little more interest in such theories (as distinct from symbolic practice) than in archaeological exactitude. Literary reports of British, French, Danish, and German excavations arrived well cooled by time and distance, carrying neither the cachet of the latest fashion nor any implied invitation to make a jaunt to join in acquiring fresh archaeological evidence. Americans were therefore neither academic nor theoretical in the French sense. Americans did not engage in the tortuous intellectualizing Mordaunt Crook kindly calls "the programmatic, rationalist route . . . partly Italian in origin but largely French in fulfillment."[197]

It *has* become a ritual of art-history courses to expatiate on the influence upon Thomas Jefferson of the theories of Marc-Antoine Laugier, the Jesuit architectural critic and mythmaker of primitive huts. But there is no evidence that Jefferson or Latrobe, George Hadfield, Ithiel Town, or Nicholas Biddle paid any attention to Laugier; it is doubtful that Jefferson or Biddle ever heard of him.

The relatively modest British Greek Revival and the more expansive Scottish Greek Revival did attend to Laugierian theory, perhaps because it originated, as Crook says, in Italy, to which eighteenth-century

Englishmen gave the same obeisance some twentieth-century Americans accord England. Laugier's Hellenism was also consonant with the new classical wisdom of Germany or, more particularly, with that of Johann Joachim Winckelmann, a German aesthete living in Italy. The English were much impressed by the puissant erudition of "the founder of modern art history as well as scientific archaeology."[198]

Ganymede and the Doric Senex Much of the English and French Greek Revival is rather frail, when it is not heavy and academically dull; it is fair, I think, to attribute this dry yet frail quality to the influence of Winckelmann and the tradition he established as the greatest classical scholar of the eighteenth century. He took much of the sweaty vigor out of the accomplishments of the Greeks, removed their art from its commercial, and even its religious, setting, and almost deprived it of its universal symbolic charge. In England, John Addington Symonds and Walter Pater extended that kind of desiccating connoisseurship to the study of the Renaissance. Observant, meticulous, and stated in gorgeous, if somewhat overstarched, prose, this was sterile scholarship. By contrast, the American approach to the classical past felt free to experiment in the classical spirit. Carpenter-builders such as Minard Lafever, the creators of the ornamentation of such houses as Gaineswood, Milford, and Stanton Hall [152, 303] would have appalled Winckelmann by their impertinence in applying Greek ideas to their own ingenious, unprecedented ways.

Having enjoyed the patronage of Augustus the Strong of Saxony and acted as antiquary for an indulgent cardinal, Winckelmann died in Italy in 1768. By that time he had been more influential in shaping European ideas about Greece than any man since Plutarch. He had a post of influence, but his power was not bureaucratic. It was literary. He had a genius for the fresh observation of classic form, and he could make readers see.

Greece was Winckelmann's passion: his convincing version of antiquity, selected and tinctured by his preternaturally sensitive nature and conveyed through prose of great power, shaped the mindset of Western Europe. Indeed, art history is still conditioned by the coincidence that a librarian of Winckelmann's quality was available to comment as discoveries were made successively by others who were working in the sun, amid the ruins of the Roman towns of Pompeii and Herculaneum. Though available for centuries, a sudden rush of recognition brought visitors as well to the temples at Paestum and on Sicily. But the recognition of Winckelmann and his followers did not stimulate free adaptation.

Most northern Europeans who were contemporaries of Benjamin Franklin and Washington and were serious about Greece were serious about a Winckelmannian Greece. He himself never went there, but his way of looking—his spectacles, so to speak—*did*, in the saddlebags of every learned traveler after

1765. So powerful was his imagination that they saw what he wished them to see: "For Winckelmann, the ancient world was a repository of wise laws, good government, and above all of physical beauty. Greece was peopled by athletes seven feet tall, marble white, and generally adolescent. There were, of course, no Greek women."[199]

If one thinks of Winckelmann, Symonds, and Pater juxtaposed with George Washington and Andrew Jackson, one can see the differences in the dominant spirits of the English and American classical revivals. The contrast is parodistic, of course, but it helps to illustrate why even Scottish Hellenism, though livelier than the English, had no political ideology, only an aesthetic one. It did not crystallize about the archetype of a virile old hero. In England, one may say with just a little exaggeration, white columns carried only the delicate message of the archetype of Ganymede, the beautiful adolescent.

American connections to antiquity were neither dainty nor dilettantish. Winckelmann was the intermediary of Greece to Europe, but not to the United States. When the American Greek Revival arose, it was not an aesthete's special enthusiasm. It was associated with mature men, with heroic exertion and with wisdom, not with adolescents, whose chief virtue was that they were pretty. In Greece there may not have been any women, but in America there certainly were, and with important consequences to the development of its Free Classicism, especially, I think, to its exuberant interior design.

One of Andrew Jackson's most remarkable achievements was to capture the benefits of the gray phallicism of the Senex archetype and at the same time appear to be the embodiment of a new America. His presidential campaign was launched after Nicholas Biddle's aspirations to elective office had been frustrated. Jackson, not Biddle, was able to contend with Henry Clay and John C. Calhoun for a place of political eminence in the 1820s. The old man vied with much younger politicians in setting himself apart from the "feebleness" of his own contemporaries, though he contrived to do so while wearing George Washington's toga. Jackson was not an officer in the Revolutionary Army—only a casualty—and thus did not qualify for membership in the Order of the Cincinnati. He became in effect, however, Cincinnatus himself. Calhoun spoke for them all—even Jackson—in 1826, declaring that "the people of this country" required new leadership to pull them out of that "weakness . . . to which [they] . . . are peculiarly liable." Clay, at the time, was speaking of "supineness . . . which left him almost without hope."[200] The "withered arms and wrinkled brows of the illustrious founders" were still upon the scene, but what was needed was "a new race of heroes, proud of the American experiment."[201]

A new race of heroes—and an old set of masculine symbols (see Appendix A).

Symbolism in the Neoclassical Age   So much prudery has been interposed by the generations between us and the architects of the early Greek Revival that we tend to think that the phallic implications of columnar architecture could not have been understood by its architects, at least at the outset. But Latrobe and his contemporaries delighted in both symbolism and scatology. They knew what they were doing when they used phallic forms.

Claude-Nicolas Ledoux, that genius of architectural metaphor who brought to France in the revolutionary years a synthesis of architecture and the ideas of Enlightenment, left his statement of the phallicism of columnar classicism in his design for an Ionic house for sexual instruction, which he called, in Greek, an *Oikema*, the floor plan of which was to be a giant phallus.

Latrobe sometimes commented on such matters in scribbled notes to friends, as if in light conversation. While the U.S. Capitol was under construction, he wrote to his clerk-of-the-works, John Lenthall, that working on its interior columns brought to his mind the opportunity he was providing for that well-known rake, vice-president Aaron Burr, to "ogle" the ladies who were outside the "piers" of the Senate chamber. Both Latrobe and Lenthall were well aware that Washington gossips were saying that Burr's only competitor in venery among statesmen of small overall stature was Alexander Hamilton. The "piers" suggested to Latrobe that if, in some future life, the soul of Lenthall were to transmigrate to the service of a "Hindoo Rajah, provided the British leave any of them alive, you will see little Hamilton and little Burr standing in the temple of Lingam (the Hindoo priapus) like the Columns of Jachin and Boas in the temple of Solomon, in eternal and basaltic erection without fruition, for their sins."[†]

The lingering of eighteenth-century raciness into nineteenth-century architectural discourse gives incentive to turn to twentieth-century analytic psychology. After all, we, and the Greek Revivalists, are not very different as psychological organisms from the ancient Greeks. Human psychology was being formed for hundreds of millennia before history taught us to think a mere thousand years between one life span and another to be important. In this perspective, Pericles might be our grandfather, Latrobe our uncle, and each of us is on notice as to the power of symbols derived from the constants of anatomy.

Even if we were disposed to be shy about such matters, our forefathers called attention to them by the sudden and widespread construction of a great multitude of columns in the United States, explicitly derived from a culture that had associated the column and the phallus. The findings of feminist classicists and of recent historians of the Age of Jackson have forced us to take seriously such a phenomenon.

[†] (Latrobe to Lenthall, Jan. 7th, 1805, in Latrobe, *Papers,* vol. 2, p. 6; to Philip Mazzei, Dec. 28, 1806, ibid. pp. 331–32) Latrobe had more to say on the subject: referring to Hamilton as "an insatiable libertine" and Burr as a man who "indulged in amorous excesses without disguise." He noted: "It is singular that both Hamilton and Burr were *little* [his emphasis] of stature and both inordinately addicted to the same vice." (The footnotes to this correspondence in the recently published Latrobe Papers are models of caution. For other correspondence indicating that Hamilton was proud of his anatomical disproportions, see *Orders from France.*)

A Sudden Profusion of Columns   There was a moment, between independence and that nineteenth-century revival of public hypocrisy associated, as usual, with excessive vestment, when the clothing of fashionable males and females made it easy to tell which was which. As the Greek Revival gathered itself in private, women's bodices were gauzy, men's trousers were tight, and "Grecian" furniture had its patrons. This occurred inside the drawing room, where all sorts of experiments can be conducted. But the national mood was such that no one could be found to take a Greek Revival public.

The nation as a whole was not yet ready for an architectural Greek Revival. The Russians, the Hungarians, or the Scots, who at this time were creating Grecian public buildings by the score and even a few "private" palaces (though a palace is too big ever to be private in its effects). But Americans like William Bingham or John Jacob Astor, Robert Morris or David Parish, Thomas Gibbons or Christopher Gore, who had ample resources to build in the Greek, did not do so. We may legitimately wonder why. And as legitimately respond that their classically trained contemporaries would have thought them impudent in doing so. They were not heroes. No Arlington Houses for them.

So there were good reasons why heroic, masculine, columnar forms did not commend themselves in the first decades after the Revolution. Grecian furniture was purchased and revealing "Grecian" clothing worn by only a small group, and even they covered themselves more completely when they appeared in the streets. The old inhibitions of the Spartan founders remained strong. Then a reversal occurred: when the explicit revelation of sexual character in architecture could be seen in every hamlet in America thirty years later, both sexes were covering themselves over and males were assuming the colors of molting birds.

The profusion of phallic architecture that appeared after 1825 calls to mind the wise words of the cultural geographer Pierce F. Lewis. Lewis begins with a quotation from Louis Sullivan: "What people are within, the buildings express without; and inversely what the buildings are objectively is a sure index of what the people are subjectively." Lewis goes on to point out how very slowly do the traditions of "simple, unprepossessing 'folk' houses change . . . since culture is by its nature conservative, doggedly resisting fundamental change except under the most extreme duress."[202]

When the patterns used by tens of thousands of people suddenly and broadly alter, we are and should be astonished. "When the . . . architecture of a nation or a region changes in large and fundamental ways not merely in cosmetics, but in form as well [as it did in the United States during the onset of the Greek Revival], it is highly likely that the culture itself is undergoing a wrenching and enduring change. If a people changes its collective mind about its houses, there is a good chance that it has changed its mind about many other important things as well."[203]

Americans began changing their minds about themselves after 1815, and completed that change in the age of Jackson and Biddle. They changed their minds again between 1860 and 1865. Between these changes, the Greek Revival thrived.

Certain heroic—Jungians might say "constellating"—figures accelerated the progression toward Greek Revival America. Chief among them was Andrew Jackson. He was not by any means the only personification of antique, classic heroism in his time, nor was he alone responsible for the Greek Revival. Nicholas Biddle brought his own energies, for his own reasons, to its evolution, and the nation was ready for an architectural statement of its new feelings of confidence. But Jackson shrewdly caught up the enthusiasm that also animated the Greek Revival.

The Doric Senex

Photography was not quite ready to capture Andrew Jackson as he posed between the unadorned columns of Arlington House, each five feet thick at the base. James Fenimore Cooper made up for the absence of a "photo opportunity" by making the connection between a "Doric" Washington and a "Doric" Jackson, combining in a term (as Arlington House combined in a form) "grandeur," heroism, and the antique quality of "chaste simplicity" (no matter that interiors were becoming, if not unchaste, no longer simple). Marvin Meyers, after reflecting upon Jackson's image building, has concluded that Cooper's adjective captured "the virile qualities of decision, courage, and patriotism, joined to simple courtesy and stout independence, . . . [composing the] image of the Doric. . . . [To] an agrarian conservative of that age the last faint image of the Doric order could be found in the virile old patriot of the Democracy and in the cause of moral restoration."[204]

Since the earliest illustrated treatises, the Doric has been read to be masculine, even more so than the other two Greek orders. Vitruvius made much of the "strength" and "grace" of the virile body.[205]

In the Age of Jackson, the Greek Revival, Doric and otherwise, was associated, in its republican simplicity, with something called "manliness," a quality thought to be shared by Washington and Jackson. No longer were the founders present to poison the pleasures of the present with remorse for fallen virtue; they were almost out of the way, and one could feel heroic without being simple to the point of discomfort. The Greek Revival may have been austere in its forms, but it was opulent in its appointments.

Apparently many Americans wished to be included in this heroic company in the time when the old Jacobin Albert Gallatin rejoiced in Jackson's victories at New Orleans and in Florida. They "had renewed and reinstated the national feelings which the Revolution had given and which were daily lessened. . . . The people . . . are more American; they feel and act more like a nation."[206] American self-confidence rose again and, with it, a host of white columns.

That revival of confidence, long deferred and often disappointed, could now grow, despite setbacks, for a full forty years. Its prideful symbols were colonnades and porticos.

It had been nearly eight decades since the British and French first displayed Grecian *tempietti* in their gardens, nearly three since Thomas Jefferson first saw to it that the Virginia state capitol would take the form of a Greco-Roman temple. At last, Americans were ready to state themselves heroically, however ambiguous they might feel about such a statement. Paradoxically, they went on with their celebration, though they were anxious and dissatisfied with themselves. It was as if they knew how susceptible they were to disaster. Even while it lasted, that anxious celebration that gave rise to the Greek Revival always contained a strain of nostalgia for the sort of heroism that the founding fathers seemed to represent.

The Age of the Fathers—"when men were Men." One old man remained, however: Andrew Jackson, suggesting that men still might *be* men and, by implication, set above women.

The Doric column stood for this invidious increment; so did Andrew Jackson. Old Hickory–Cincinnatus was no classical scholar, but (by my informal count) his speeches contain more references to the *masculine* heroes of ancient history than did the combined public iterations of George Washington and William Henry Harrison, the two generals immediately preceding and following him in the presidency, Virginia gentlemen though they were. Washington, Harrison, and Jackson all satisfied a craving of their countrymen for heroes cast in a classic mold, described in classic phrases, and housed in classic architecture. Jackson's own need to be a stern father to a large number of people was perfectly attuned to a shrewd recognition of their yearning for a father writ large, for a visitation of the Senex.

The Senex, the wise, powerful, order-assuring old figure, was male. Very male. A good thing to be, Whig and Jacksonian men agreed. Indeed, they insisted upon the point architecturally. Though the Jacksonians tended toward columns of Roman dimensions and the Whigs to the Greek, columns in general celebrated masculinity and, as I suggest in Appendix B, they did so with increasing anxiety.

Without going too deeply into sexual politics, it is possible to agree that part of the anxiety arose from a desire to find, and thereafter to impose, a new order—one symbolized with masculine emblems.

This is not the sort of thing that people write into plans and specifications, but other literature of the time provides evidence to support this hypothesis. Contrary to the impression conveyed by their Whig opponents, there were custodians of order who were also Jacksonians, men such as Custis, Paulding, Irving, and Cooper. All along they had been natural conservatives. Indeed, if Cooper had not been so eager to become as Gothic as the British, he would have been the perfect pamphleteer of a Greek Revival: "The column of society," he wrote, "must have its capital as well as its base. It is only perfect while each part is entire and discharges its proper duty. On the supposition that this capital is broken, and hurled to the ground, of what material will be the capital that must be pushed into its place!"[207]

Cooper's Jackson was the successor to Washington, a man who would maintain "the usual balance of things." This Jackson, far from being a foe to social order, would occupy himself like Bonaparte, in "restoring balance and providing stability." He could become the central figure in a classic revival. Jackson played to spirits like Cooper's not so much by his renewal of the cult of republican simplicity as by restoring the virility of the presidency and invoking the potency of the Senex figure.

The radiance of that archetype had done well for the last fully credible hero among the founders, George Washington, and it worked even better for Jackson. The new Senex, the nation's second general-president, second father to his country, made much of confronting the "effete" East with the manly vigor of the frontiersman.[†]

To his protégé and successor, Martin Van Buren, Jackson was "that noble old man," exemplifying "the manly virtues [of] republican simplicity and economical habits . . . the . . . reward of our Revolutionary struggle" in opposition to a "sickly appetite for effeminate indulgence."[208]

Another Jacksonian, Richard B. Lee, foresaw an American empire, equal in extent to that of imperial Rome, renowned for the manly virtues of its citizens. The constant—almost obsessive—emphasis by Jacksonian pamphleteers upon their hero's manliness had a counterfoil: John Quincy Adams was charged with effeminacy and with having pimped for the czar of Russia during his service as ambassador to St. Petersburg where, it was said, he took to dancing "lascivious measures." Whig politicians were forced to defend their virility by a great show of musculature. Seward had his rowboat, and Webster began removing his coat, rolling up his sleeves, flexing a little, and saying, "The man who says that I am an aristocrat—is a LIAR!"[209]

In search, perhaps, of better biceps, Webster's fellow Whigs sought out a rail-splitter named Lincoln, in Illinois. He was still too young, however, so in Indiana they found for immediate presidential purposes an Indian fighter of their own. William Henry Harrison, living on the lands of his rich wife, permitted Webster to cut classical references from his speeches—Cincinnatus was already spoken for. After Harrison's managers substituted a log cabin for his Virginia tidewater birthplace and his pilastered villa in North Bend, Ohio, and talked of hard cider rather than his favored Madeira, they made him president, in 1840.

On the way they managed to transfer from Adams to Van Buren the stigma of effeminacy, charging that "the Democrats had turned dandies."[210] Jackson's chosen successor had grown corpulent and so unwary as to use very potent cologne. When Van Buren made the error of asking Congress for funds to stop the leaks in the White House roof, he was charged with "spending the people's money on FINGER CUPS, in which to wash his pretty, tapering, soft white lily-fingers, after dining on fricandeau de veau omelette soufflé."[211]

Nicholas Biddle's culinary tastes were no more frugal than Van Buren's, and he made no effort to pretend otherwise. Yet he too drew upon the potency of the Senex, placing the wise Hellenist banker at the center of a tableau. He offered not the muscularity of generals, but a new, nineteenth-century kind of hero—at once banker and savior of the people. Though such an idea may seen ludicrous to us, it did not seem so to him. He had a limited sense of humor and he was a man of his time, living without benefit of Freud.

If he had had a little prescience, he might have considered the possibility that his Greek Revival marked an advanced stage in the capitalist-commercial, masculine renaissance, as Palladio and Bronzino, with their columns and codpieces, had marked its beginning.

PART FIVE
THE DECLINE OF THE
GREEK REVIVAL

Every observer of Greek Revival America remarked upon its turbulence, its disorder, its discontinuities. While all seemed in flux, architecture expressed permanence. So fluid was the economy, especially, that historians love to debate when, how, and where America came into an industrial revolution, and seminars become very agitated in the discovery of the moment when it moved from a passive to an active role in the international finance-capitalism that combined industrial units into large corporations.

But there is general agreement that, even so early as 1800, these tendencies became ineluctable, thrusting aside Jefferson's attempted counterrevolution of that year. After capitalism engorged itself for thirty years more, stretched and grew more voracious, Jackson too set himself against it—with no greater success.

"Americans underwent a . . . further transformation in the organization of their economic lives between 1815 or 1820 and 1860." As a result of this transformation, "the conservative agrarian ideals of Jackson" were, in the North, consigned to Hollywood (such consignment took longer in the South). In their place was the modern world, the age of "bigness, specialization, administrative coordination, impersonality, and a wide-marketing orientation."[212]

The old order was passing—passing to the relief of some, such as Daniel Webster. Though everyone talked of tumult, beneath the surface was a steadily rising standard of living, and the role of the United States in the world became a source of pride—almost of truculence—to its people. Much transpired between the footrace-retreat of American troops through the streets of Washington following the disgrace at Bladensburg during the War of 1812 and the parade before the "halls of Montezuma" in 1847.

Below the level of seeming chaos, a new *order* was being established, and not so tumultuously as one might think from one visit to a White House party. Though the hoi polloi might be celebrating in Jackson's White House, the rising industrial and financial managers were too busy winning to celebrate. Webster's historic role was as attorney for the establishment, and he throve upon it. Lawyers such as Webster and bankers such as Biddle do not like disorder; it was remarkable how little they complained.

The bourgeoisie were creating the world they wanted, leaving sentimental Jacksonians to dream of some Arcadia to be shared with Horace, Hesiod, and Thomas Jefferson, as practical Jacksonians put new cotton lands under the plow. Jackson could not be beaten as a politician while he lived, but Old Hickory was becoming obsolete. He could "trash the Whigs," and deny their ambitions to men like Webster who were eager to get on with life—their kind of life, managed by their kind of people. But, in the end, they won, though Nicholas Biddle, personally, did not.

Biddle was the first American businessman to be a world figure. Though he was in no sense a symbol for the age—that symbol *was* Jackson, surely—he had a deeper effect upon its architecture and, probably as well, upon its economic history than did his great opponent. He thought of himself as a gentleman but never, in the British sense, as an aristocrat. He was a middle-class hero of a new variety. As an American aspiring to a protagonist's role in international finance, he was ahead of his time, not representative of it. Though he failed as a politician and went bankrupt striving to burst the bonds of traditional state banking, he was successful in one thing of great concern to him: he was the most important client for the revival, once again, of that Greek Revival initiated earlier in America by George Washington Parke Custis, Thomas Jefferson, George Hadfield, and Benjamin Henry Latrobe.

In one aspect of his life, the use of architectural symbolism, Biddle's timing was perfect. He understood, and found forms to express, the imperatives that were driving his country away from the world of Jefferson and Jackson toward big factories, big banks, and big cities.

The Greek Revival was in delicate and unstable balance—the consequence of change and the expression of an aspiration toward authority, hierarchy, and order, with new people in charge. They did not intend to be, again, revolutionary (few of the founding fathers intended to be very revolutionary, for that matter). Though they were proudly replacing discredited predecessors, they were careful not to say so and spoke nostalgically of the founders.

Beyond the horizon the clouds were gathering. Lightning flashed above the clouds. For a few decades, Americans thought themselves fit for temple residences, using architecture to contend against the chaos. But all the while, around and below them, lurking in the shadows behind their columns, mocking their pride, was the inevitable recompense for the institution of slavery.

False Faces   Houses with columns all around did not appear north of the Mason-Dixon line; the closest equivalents are Elias Carter's front-and-back-only versions in central Massachusetts [245]. The explanation does not lie in the climate—as we have noted, it gets very hot in the summer in Indiana and in Minnesota. Nor can we attribute this form merely to a blending of the creole cottage with a classical revival with a predilection for pillars. The creole cottage was to be seen in all French-speaking regions of North America from 1730 onward, including Canada as far north as a corner of Manitoba, and up the Atlantic coast as far as Maine. It acquired heavy, protective, classical columns and was called "Greek Revival" only in the South.

It seems to me that black slavery had something to do with this. The columned plantation house had a fixed smile of seeming confidence, but deep in its windows there was something else—fear. Slavery is civil discord, founded upon force, enforced by terror: it turns terror back upon those who employ it. Those who lived by fear lived in fear. It is small wonder that whites wanted to hide themselves and their women within screens of columns.

The brave face set by the South against slave revolt was the same face as that set, North and South, against something said to be disorder—*disorder* meaning somebody else's kind of order. The builders of the classic revival in Alabama and Mississippi were engaged in the dispossession of Native Americans. Upon the land they thus obtained, they then put to work people secured by force and brought from Africa as slaves. Everywhere the three races met, there was a threat either of slave insurrection or of Indian attack.[†]

Under these circumstances, a precinct of columned houses, in Natchez, Mississippi, for example, or in Washington, Arkansas, or Athens, Georgia, took on a special meaning. Southerners, building and inhabiting houses screened by portcullises of columns, created classically camouflaged stockades set against a special Southern chaos.

[†] John Marshall feared the "calamity" that the presence of slaves inevitably "portends." Jefferson thought freeing the slaves would mean that "all the whites south of the Potomac and Ohio must evacuate their States," and John Randolph opposed any suggestion that blacks were equal to whites as "advising them to cut their masters' throats." As Jefferson said, the South had "a wolf by the ears; and we can neither hold him, nor safely let him go." And his friend Madison quietly added: "Next to the black race within our bosom, that of the red in our borders is the problem most baffling to the policy of our country." (Marshall, Jefferson, and Randolph quoted in Miller, pp. 217–18)

As hundreds of thousands of Southerners swarmed across the Appalachians, some driving coffles of slaves before them, they began to construct a new "plantation," in the meaning of that term the English brought to Ireland. They denied thereby the consummation of Thomas Jefferson's dream of a republic of free and independent yeomen. Instead, the New South was the Old Tidewater South transported across the Piedmont. Prosperous beyond the visions of tidewater avarice, it was, however, removed from Tidewater traditions and Tidewater oversight, and it became, by common observation, more brutal.

Tobacco, rice, and indigo had bound the Tidewater to Europe. Now it was cotton and sugar, grown to be sold internationally. Every farmer, large or small, who produced those crops did so with the knowledge that their pricing and financing were out of his control. The same thing was true for the producers of other staple export crops in the North, but they did not have any illusions about independent kingdoms. They watched the prices in the pit and hoped to outwit and outwork the market. American agriculture briefly had loosed its bonds after independence and was the poorer for it. A lucrative neocolonialism returned to the South with the cotton gin.

The Roman Revival of the cotton South was a false face, a mask denying a demeaning truth beneath its pride: dependence upon the pricing and financing of Boston, Lowell, Manchester, Liverpool, and London. In its first upward phase, roughly from 1820 to 1837, it had many beneficiaries, of whom Andrew Jackson was the most prominent. The Romanizing of the Hermitage was made possible by British finance, as disseminated through the state banking system and the cotton factors of New Orleans. Without Manchester and London, it is unlikely that Andrew Jackson would have made his triumphant progress from Nashville to Washington.

America in the Age of Jackson and Biddle was, perhaps more than at any other period, a theater of ironies. It was nationalist and neocolonial. It was seething with reform yet becoming ever more committed to slavery, the most demoralizing and archaic means of organizing a labor force. Its leaders lived, as had Thomas Jefferson, lives of contradiction, believing in progress yet unable to break the hold of the past, dependent economically upon Europe and upon slavery yet talking constantly of independence and freedom. As they strove to sustain the founders' faith in improvement toward a perfected humanity, they required a reassuring architecture, and they found it. But it could not last.

The Seasons Change   There had been a springtime, hardly any summer, little warning of an autumn, and then winter. People trying to convey a sense of how Americans felt about the events of the midcentury often used images of the seasons—of blossoming and withering—drawn from rural life. The Civil War seemed to them a disruption in the natural order of things, as if the earth had been jolted out of orbit and the passage of the seasons had gone awry. The Greek Revival was, at its essence, a parable of order; it is natural that when modern critics have sought to explain how it came to an end, they too have made use of words drawn from the seasons and the countryside even though they were describing a catastrophe of human invention.

Talbot Hamlin tells us that, though the flowering of the Revival was brief, it burst out "lustily in hundreds of local centers . . . not yet centralized in the big cities." The culture "of which it was the perfect expression . . . [was] radical, libertarian, experimental, eagerly searching for American expression. A country rich, expanding, not yet densely populated; a country with its agriculture and its growing industry still in fundamental balance. A country with growing towns and cities, new-blossoming farms. . . ."[213]

This "quick leafing and efflorescence" between 1830 and 1860 seemed to Lewis Mumford "a few warm weeks." Then, the "Civil War shook down the blossoms and blasted the promise of spring. The colors of American civilization abruptly changed. By the time the war was over, browns had spread everywhere: mediocre drabs, dingy chocolate browns, sooty browns that merged into black. Autumn had come. . . . The nation not merely worked differently . . . the country *looked* differently—darker, sadder, soberer."[214] Autumn, in nature, is a time of slackening energy, of a turning inward. It is a healthy introversion. The Brown Decades, on the other hand, were exhausted, hopeless, cynical, deeply diseased.

Mumford was not writing about the Greek Revival, or of the Greeks themselves, but it is worth noting what the browns replaced: the Greek Revival, like the ancient Greeks, had a love of vehement color—intense, without compromise—applied to their entablatures without thinning the paint. These were the colors of American interiors in the Greek Revival period; neither the bleached exteriors of Grecian ruins nor the bleached interiors of American reconstructions give any sense of the originals or the revival. Brilliant and unashamed, the color applied to Lafeverish ornament swept any doubts before it—wild, exuberant, displayed as much as organized by a rectilinear grid.

Then came another "wintry season," like that fifty years earlier. It is well to recall that beginning, that "era of halting effort," of "withered laurels," as the founding fathers were growing old amid the rubble of their high hopes. Though Thomas Jefferson blamed "the unwise and unworthy passions of their sons," the debris was undeniably the product of the failures of the fathers themselves.[215]

Between 1790 and 1820, the times had seemed sadly out of joint. In those years, the United States was still felt to be the artifact of the founding fathers, and those fathers had themselves gone beyond the conventional limits of Oedipal resentment and rejection. In revolution, their act of symbolic patricide, they had cast off a king—reluctantly, they said—driven to it by "despair . . . and the exasperating effects of the war." But the guilt they felt remained in the memory of James Madison as late as 1828. The Revolution had been "a convulsive rupture," said Edward Everett, a rite of passage that George Fitzhugh likened to "a birth, a christening, a circumcision, the donning of the *'toga virilis.'*" But it had this difference from civilized rites: it was an act of violence—directed against the parent.[216]

Thereafter, Thomas Paine refused "to be a boy all his life"; John Adams spoke of independence as "manhood"; and Noah Webster told his own contemporaries that they had been "children long enough." Simon Bolívar extended the metaphor to Latin Americans kept "in a state of permanent childhood."[217]

The rebellious young had grown older and had become fathers themselves. Their sons needed them, and needed grandfathers too. It does not require Sophocles or Freud to tell us that rejection of fathers is alleviated in normal circumstances by the embrace of grandfathers. Lewis Mumford calls it "the commonest axiom of history that every generation revolts against its fathers and makes friends with its grandfathers."[218]

But the grandfathers must be embraceable. The prerevolutionary colonial grandfathers, a Tory hierarchy subverted and exiled as part of the nation's rite of passage, were beyond the grasp of succeeding generations. They were, like the lost king-grandfather, beyond a river of blood, and their descendants were, in truth, "bereft of ancestry."[219] Tocqueville was right—in this sense "the American" he came to know in the 1830s *was*, because he *had* to be, a "new man."

As sons had sons, each new generation sought grandfathers. To their own sons the founders may not have been heroes; later they were petrified into salt-white marble, no longer sires but statuary. Though no one could embrace Horatio Greenough's Washington, and though heroes of unrelenting virtue are too noble to serve as real grandfathers, at a distance of thirty or forty years they might encourage their progeny to think of themselves as fit offspring of a race of heroes.

Between the founders and their immediate successors no such intimacy had been possible. To the guilt of resentment of the father was added the unbearable responsibility of rejecting a perfect but unbearably proximate antiquity. "A nation is much to be pitied, that is weighed down by the past . . . by obstacles that grow out of its recollections," said one of the characters of James Fenimore Cooper.[220]

Later their lapidary burden lightened as the memory of their imperfections faded also. They had no faults—or so everyone said. A great show was made of "reverence for . . . the habits and opinions [of] the first founders." Schoolmasters such as Noah Webster required children to "praise . . . those illustrious heroes and statesmen." Orators like Rufus Choate insisted that adulation of the hallowed grandsires become "central to the emotional life of the child."[221]

As we have also seen, this sort of thing intrudes upon the fundamental necessity of children to make their own lives, to cut themselves free. Though filiopiety quieted the people of the Greek Revival period, its relentless requirements became a burden.

There was much to chafe against. Finally, in 1832, the last signer, Charles Carroll of Carrollton, departed. Then, suddenly, there was an outburst of patriotic poetry and even of the sort of monumental sculpture that had been conspicuous in its absence while the heroes were being statues themselves— James Monroe built a career upon enacting the closest American approximation to the Commandatore— the stone guest—of Mozart's *Don Giovanni*.

Ancestor worship was more assiduously propagated between 1826 and 1861 than at any other time in our history. Filial duty inspired poems and stories, statues and paintings, bric-a-brac, and the naming of children. "How pure they were, how few their faults and frailties" sang the *North American Review* in 1855. But, as Emerson said at the time, "Every hero becomes a bore at last."[222]

In the 1850s, "at last" came in a rush. Thoreau asserted that he had never had "the first syllable of valuable . . . advice from my seniors"; Emerson cried out against a "worship of the past," which had made Americans of his time "subservient to dead men." Hawthorne, anticipating Freud as he often did, warned that a sire who "would live forever" will drive his heir to "hate his own father, from the perception that he would never be out of his way."[223]

As time went on, the accomplishments of the sons and sons of sons—taming a continent, winning wars, enjoying a rising prosperity from a very low base—exceeded everything the founders had done, save for the Revolution itself. Their successors could never bring themselves to be set, explicitly, in competition with the "lingering" ones, as "one by one they totter and die,"[224] but the architecture of marble, which evoked their memory, became less and less appealing.

At its end, the Greek Revival was worse than a bore. After 1850 it seemed to some an ostentatious lie, unconvincingly asserted. It perpetuated the memory of a sinful system the fathers had established, which was especially noxious in the Grecian South, but which even the temples of the North seemed dedicated to maintain. The compact with human slavery, the sin of the founders, now forced itself to the surface. Despite all pious efforts to deny it, it was a sin to be expiated by their descendants at immense cost.

As the nation approached "irrepressible conflict," "a house divided, half slave and half free," many believed that the legacy of the founders was a corrupt order. The founders had knowingly built a continuance of the slave trade into the Constitution and had embedded into all the major institutions of government subtle means to protect slavery. Gouverneur Morris called their actions a "curse of heaven."[225]

When the Massachusetts legislature hesitated to repeal the Fugitive Slave Law of 1793 on the ground that "our fathers" might be distressed, Edwin Lawrence Godkin, founder of *The Nation*, scornfully dismissed that sort of "ancestor worship."[226] The most conspicuous of the sons, John Quincy Adams, was ready to acknowledge, in the privacy of his diary, that the fathers had been guilty of a "morally and politically vicious . . . bargain." By midcentury, William Lloyd Garrison was inveighing against it, and (by implication) them, as having struck a "covenant with death" and an "agreement in Hell."[227] And John Greenleaf Whittier set in verse:

> *Your world-wide honour stained with shame,*
> *Your freedom's self a hollow name!*[228]

People do not long sustain a filiopietistic architecture when that set of symbols reminds them that the fathers were sinners—and, even more poignantly, that they themselves are guilty of the same sins.

Midcentury middle-class America had made its own covenants, agreements, and bargains with evil. Though the conflict was becoming "irrepressible," though the house *was* "divided," Greek Revival–building, Whiggish opinion sought compromise to the end. The cost of a failure to compromise was hideous to contemplate.

But compromise with evil was equally hideous among people who took their public morality as seriously as did the abolitionists.

Irrepressible conflict cracked open the seamless façade of the Greek Revival. The temple-form house was divided, and a scarlet stain spread across it. It had been sustained by a social order that was, itself, a moral crime.

In the middle years of the 1850s, it was no longer possible to ignore that crime. The South demanded that slavery be accepted as beneficent and the "vicious bargain" as virtuous. The Kansas–Nebraska Bill of

1854 opened the territories to slavery, "stirring the ugliest forces in American life; deep hates and fears that the most careful statesmanship had coaxed into a fitful sleep . . . [were] now never . . . to rest until the nation had been torn apart and rebuilt by the sword."[229]

Though the Republican platform, drawn in the next year, could still summon enough filiopiety to insist that "our Republican fathers . . . ordained that no person be deprived of life, liberty, or property, without due process of law," anyone who knew the history of the Constitutional Convention knew, as well, that this was not the case. Any remaining illusions were ripped away by the Dred Scott decision in 1857, written by the chief justice of the United States, Roger B. Taney. What the founders had done, and what Taney proposed his contemporaries continue to do, was to define "persons" in order to exclude persons of color, thereby making a mockery of due process. The founders, said the chief justice and six other justices, regarded blacks "as beings of an inferior order and altogether unfit to associate with the white race, either in social or political relations."[230]

How long ago the 1830s seemed, when Andrew Jackson had supported the nomination and election to the vice-presidency of Richard M. Johnson of Kentucky, who made no effort to conceal his "association" with a black woman, whom he treated as his wife (which, in fact, she may have been). The Johnsons' daughters were brought up in full Southern style, well educated and endowed; they inherited his property at his death. (For the Johnsons' Ward Hall, see page 299.) This kind of behavior on the part of a serious Democratic candidate would have been inconceivable in the 1850s.

Order rooted in exploitation, enforced by the lash, and endorsed by the law, is tyranny. The Greek Revival was coming to seem a symbol of that sort of order. Hawthorne wished the marbles of the Parthenon "burnt into lime." And with them should go the American marbles: "Our capitols, state-houses, court-houses, city halls and churches . . . should crumble to ruin," to free each generation, "once in twenty years, or thereabouts, . . . to examine into and reform the institutions they symbolize."[231]

By 1855, temple-form houses and public buildings, though built after the fathers, had become symbols of the fathers' "living forever." Though it was not quite polite to say so, they were now symbols of shame, of a Jacksonian and Biddlean nationalism built upon a corrupt bargain of Northern merchants and Southern slave owners. The "curse of heaven" had been laid upon the moral core of the founding, of that proud nationalism, and upon the Union it purchased.

The Greek Revival, in its frozen ceremonial of order and serenity, was, in America, specifically the architecture of that Union. An architecture of national pride became a reproach as it lingered like the old founders, as architecture does, into the lives of later generations.

The failure of the statesmen of the 1850s was far costlier than any of the failures of the founders. The initial bargain with slavery had been iniquitous—that was now clear enough. But the tainted constitutional compact had for five decades seemed to purchase the Union. Lincoln desperately called that Union "perpetual" in an Inaugural Address delivered after South Carolina, Mississippi, Florida, Alabama, Georgia, Louisiana, and Texas had seceded—and after the mayor of New York, Fernando Wood, had reduced the myth of the Union to an ugly joke by proposing that the city secede as well, proclaiming its neutrality.

The chief work of statesmanship had been to keep intact the myth. Andrew Jackson had set it forth in his famous Jefferson Day toast: "Our Federal Union, it must be preserved."[232] It was not preserved. It came apart in 1861.

Four years earlier, when they read of Taney's decision, two aged lions of Jacksonian democracy, Martin Van Buren and Thomas Hart Benton, roused themselves to attack Taney in the final political papers written by each of them. Benton, having exhausted his energies, died in the arms of his black nurse. Van Buren, who headed the ticket upon which Johnson was nominated, wrote: "The end of slavery will come—amid terrible convulsions, I fear, but it will come."[233]

Two other old Jacksonian stalwarts, living in Tennessee-Greek mansions, governors Richard Keith Call of Florida and Sam Houston of Texas, having brought their states into the Union, were most unwilling that the hotheads of 1860 should take them out again. They fought and lost the battle against secession. A jubilant mob surrounded Call after Florida voted to secede, crying: "Governor, we have done it!" To which he replied: "And what have you done? You have opened the gates of Hell, from which shall flow the curses of the damned which shall sink you to perdition!"[234]

Houston faced another mob, from a balcony of the Tremont House in Galveston: "Some of you laugh to scorn the idea of bloodshed as the result of secession. But let me tell you what is coming. . . . Your fathers and husbands, your sons and brothers, will be herded at the point of the bayonet. . . . You may, after the sacrifice of countless millions of treasure and hundreds of thousands of lives, as a bare possibility, win Southern independence, but I doubt it. . . . The North is determined to preserve this Union . . . [and] they will overwhelm the South."[235]

After 1865 the ruins were regained, but the cost of reassembling a "Union" were so catastrophic that there could be no intelligent use of the term *restoration*. Something new was created by the war and Reconstruction, but it was not the federal Union of Daniel Webster, Clay, or Jackson. That Union was forever lost.

Northern statesmen, such as Lincoln, whose careers had been pledged to preserving it, had brought on the Civil War. Southerners such as Jefferson Davis had often spoken of the vindication of "the political rights . . . and State sovereignty which were the heritage purchased by the blood of our revolutionary sires." Davis and Lincoln both had seen, in Lincoln's words, the "last, best hope" of those "sires" collapse.[236]

Millwood

From Lincoln's Springfield, from Davis's rural Mississippi—where their houses, their offices, and the college Davis attended were all built in the ordered, rational, prideful spirit of the Greek Revival—the men of 1861 went forth to kill their own brothers. And then they saw the world devoured by a swarm of corrupt sutlers who had bought substitutes and sold rotten beef and defective powder. Carpetbaggers and scalawags took ownership of the South, and the North seemed to belong to profiteers and speculators.

Who would build a temple—a white temple—to memorialize such a world? The boldness to do such a thing had been possible only in the brief efflorescence of Mumford's springtime, between the first, disconsolate "wintry season" and the second winter, when the "leaves [again] are sere; the goldenrod [again] stands brown and threadbare in the fields, the branches of the maples [again] are stripped," when, once more, "only the red berries of the black alder, or the dull persistent greens of the buttonwoods and poplars, remind one of the summer that never came."[237]

As has been observed, some Americans of tepid nationalism, following the lead of Andrew Jackson Downing, James Fenimore Cooper, and Washington Irving, had already gone Gothic. In the 1850s more turned away from the contaminated Greek and asked their architects to give them English cottages, Swiss chalets, Italian villas, and French mansards. They might have done so much earlier, but as late as 1846 Downing saw the Greek Revival regimen everywhere, still retaining its fervor, even though the Greek Revival in England and Scotland had long been an architecture of pictures. Samuel Pepys Cockerell rejoiced that The Grange, a banker's temple set in a Hampshire valley, was "like the finest Poussin. It realizes the most fanciful representation of the painter's pencil."[238] When the American Greek Revival was drained of its symbolic content, it was reduced to this, a husk, or a flat. Thereafter, it was fit only to compete with other stage props in a contest of piquant triviality.

After 1865 picturesque architecture in America declined into *mere* picturesqueness and thus to a need for ever larger doses of cuteness. Then it became coarse, raucous from constant striving for effect. Architects trained in Europe who came to America before 1812, such as Latrobe, Hadfield, and Dr. Thornton, could still believe it to be the refuge of the Party of Hope; even the first German and Irish artists who appeared in the revolutionary 1830s might have thought so, Charles Reichardt and James Gallier among them. But by the time of Adolphus Heimann and Henry Howard, who practiced in the 1850s, the decline into mere virtuosity was obvious.

Bigger, wilder, more picturesque mansions, such as Belle Grove and Belmont, were at once the pride and the shame of the South. As the planters of Greater Tennessee and the Mississippi delta indulged themselves in the final paroxysm of extravagance of the slave system, the Greek Revival was reduced to a hollow chrysalis. To the literati, classicism seemed spent, waiting to be blown away by a few blasts from a competent critic.

Sculptor Horatio Greenough was on his way home from Italy, with his own reasons for being disillusioned. He had tried his best to turn American heroes into Olympians (the Smithsonian's George Washington as Jove is the most familiar of the consequences) and now rejoiced in calling himself a "Yankee stonecutter."

Greenough pronounced the potency of the Greek to be exhausted. Its symbolic charge had run out. Why bring such aesthetic embarrassments "into our streets"? Why try to make a "temple of Theseus work in our towns . . . like the captive king, stripped alike of arms and purple and drudging amid the Helots of a capital, the Greek temple, as seen among us, claims pity for its degraded majesty?"[239]

The temple, having lost its evocative power, became as sterile as Greenough's own statuary. Shrines to republican simplicity now seemed "symptoms of decline" from a heroic ideal. With all the invidious assurance of the converted, Greenough charged those still practicing classicism with "the adoption of admired forms and models for purposes not contemplated in their invention." As a result, the Greek courthouse (or house in which a mere merchant held court) stood "a stranger to us, and receives the respect akin to what we feel for a fellow citizen in the garb of Greece. It is a make-believe."[240]

Afterward   Only in Utah did Americans sustain a Greek Revival after the Civil War. Although two final monumental buildings were built elsewhere in the late 1860s and early 1870s, the circumstances were so peculiar that these edifices become interesting chiefly as curiosities.

In their remote, desert-girded domain, the Latter-Day Saints continued fervent in the convictions of the young Joseph Smith and Brigham Young. They built accordingly, as if they were still in the evangelical 1830s and 1840s, still in northern New York, where the architecture was Grecian and where, for a time, it had been possible to believe in a patristic ordering of landscape and of life.

Utah, the final colony of Greece, beyond the Pillars of Hercules and the Sea of Grass, was also the last Christian utopia. It had its own barbarities and its own intolerances, but its sheer isolation excepted it from the age of Grant, Blaine, and Conkling, of Gould, Fisk, and Daniel Drew. It could be entered from the north only through deadly lava fields; from the south only through flaming cliffs in shapes and of a scale so improbable that trespassers knew they were entering a realm secluded from ordinary America. In their oasis, surrounded by a wilderness more dangerous than Sinai, the Mormons held to a faith in the special redemptive mission of America.

The rest of the nation relapsed into a second period of cynicism, avarice, and self-disgust. Sometimes, however, even in the Brown Decades, some incantatory coalescence of peculiarities induced the welling up of the old spirit.

One such occasion produced a burst of nostalgia on the part of the supervising architects for a U.S. mint. It was safe to be *retardaire* in San Francisco, so in 1869 they reverted to the forms Robert Mills had given the national capital thirty years before.

The other grand-scale building built in the American Greek Revival style after 1865 had something in common with Arlington House, which had been commenced in 1804. It was a memorial to the founding fathers, built by one of their sons. Doctor Richard Rush of Philadelphia, son of a signer of the Declaration of Independence, had married a very rich woman, Phoebe Ann Ridgeway, and sustained a friendship with Addison Hutton, a Quaker architect who lived until 1916 but whose mind and style were formed in the 1840s and 1850s.

In his will Rush left a million-dollar trust to create tombs for himself, his wife, and for the books of the Library Company, of which his father had been a leading member during the great days of the Philadelphia Enlightenment.

So, from 1871 to 1877, a monumental anachronism was created at 901 South Broad Street, which has embarrassed Philadelphians ever since, though it should, instead, be taken as a memorial to the great days when their city could be thought of as an "Athens on the Schuylkill." Embarrassment had descended rapidly: in 1850, no one seems to have told George Carpenter that naming a series of temples after one's wife was presumptuous—the press did not call Phil-Ellena monstrous. People were still proud to lead tourists to the awesome classical compound built for Girard College in the 1830s. But, as early as 1875, guidebook writers sniggered at Rush for calling a library after Phoebe Ann and vied in derogation of the Agora along Broad Street and at the immense vacuities behind it.

That contest of derision, dedicated to disavowing the Greek Revival and treating its aspirations as inflations, continues to this day. The guide to Philadelphia published by the Foundation for Architecture in 1984 tells us that Hutton "abandoned . . . graceful elegance for a pompous and forbidding assemblage . . . tomblike . . . impossible to heat." *Philadelphia Preserved*, Richard J. Webster's 1981 edition of the Historic American Buildings Survey, rolls out "morbid . . . redundantly monumental . . . inappropriate . . . pomposity, . . . exaggerated . . . uncomely" and "cavernous." The point is made; grand-scale classicism is no longer in style.[241]

Rush waited too long to memorialize himself, his wife, and their fathers' generation in this way. Utica could get away with such a building for the insane a few years earlier, and scores of county courthouses strove to achieve this monumental quality in the 1850s, but now, suddenly, it was too late.

The staircase (*page 297*) and the parlor (*right*) of the Captain James P. White House (1840; Calvin A. Ryder, architect) in Belfast, Maine

The dining room of
Ward Hall (1855) in
Georgetown, Kentucky

Right: The Campbell-Whittlesey House dining room (1836), in Rochester, New York

Opposite: The parlor of the Elias Baker House in Altoona, Pennsylvania (1845; Robert Cary Long, Jr., architect)

Opposite: The parlor of New York City's Old Merchants House (1832), also known as the Seabury-Tredwell House

Left: Stanton Hall (1857), the work of Thomas Rose and Lewis Reynolds (?), in Natchez, Mississippi

Right: Samuel Russell House (1828–30), designed by Town and Davis, in Middletown, Connecticut

Opposite: George W. Polk's Rattle and Snap (1845) in Columbia, Tennessee

Right and opposite: Also by Francis Costigan and in Madison, Indiana, is the Shrewsbury-Windle House (1846–49), which is host to this staircase.

Right and opposite: Two of the lavish rooms at Gaineswood (1842–60), in Demopolis, Alabama

Right and opposite: The Croghan-Schenley Rooms (1830s), probably the work of John Chislett, are now part of the Cathedral of Learning at the University of Pittsburgh.

Right and opposite: Henry Howard created the designs for the lavish rooms at Nottoway (1857) in White Castle, Louisiana.

PART SIX
A HASTY HISTORY OF THE LATER
RENAISSANCE

What follows is a summary narrative of the careers of the chief architects of American Free Classicism, together with some of those who showed them the way, with birth and death dates, and some indication of their relationships one to another—a survey in brief compass, without claiming completeness. The emphasis is on chronology. (The Gazetteer, which follows, treats the subject geographically.)

When did the Greek Revival begin? Some have said that the Romans began it at Corinth 2,200 years ago by putting up structures in the Greek style amid the ruins they had themselves made of the "originals." There is some virtue in giving heed to such an event because it permits us to make occasional references to those aspects of American Free Classicism that are *especially* Greek—that the Romans might, in fact, have revived rather than invented. But that Free Classicism we have become accustomed to calling a "Greek" Revival was as Roman as Greek, as creole as Roman, and as Palladian as creole. It is just as well to take the broader view that the classical tradition was continuous and needed no reviving until the conditions which supported it sputtered out about 1,500 years ago. The classical period ended only when Rome fell to the Vandals, in A.D. 455, and the German chieftain Odoacer proclaimed himself king of Italy in A.D. 476, having deposed poor Romulus Augustulus, who had reigned as emperor of the West for one year.

If one uses the term *Greek Revival* to describe any building making use of columns proportioned roughly in the Greek or Roman fashion, one might say that the revival began as the first millennium arrived. Noting that the world did not come to an end in A.D. 1000, the people of Autun, in Burgundy, began to create a cathedral of neo-Roman pomp. Soon thereafter, the Florentines commenced construction of the marble-encrusted façade of San Miniato al Monte, pedimented gable, pilasters, Corinthian columns, and all. This may have been the beginning of the Greek Revival, indeed, of the Renaissance.

Though the pulse of classicism quickened several times between the fall of Rome and the fourteenth century, one cannot be permitted a Greek Revival until one has a Renaissance, and the onset of the true (not crypto- or proto-) Renaissance is seldom situated in survey courses earlier than that. The Byzantines were great builders until Byzantium followed Rome into alien hands 988 years later, in 1453. But they regarded Greek architecture as pagan and erected their own buildings in and around Greek remains with the freedom by which a cook may dispose of leftovers with a supply of reusable freezer bags.

After Byzantium fell to the Turks, only extraordinarily intrepid voyagers from the West made their way to the Aegean, now firmly in Muslim control. Renaissance architecture in Europe proceeded as if Greece were dead, despite the presence within Christian bounds, in Italy and Sicily, of readily accessible Greek buildings larger than anything in Athens.

Leon Battista Alberti (1404–72), the first universal genius of the Renaissance, was not overly inhibited by classical precedents but based his work entirely upon Roman, not Greek, proportions. That wonderful man Giuliano da Sangallo (c. 1443–1516) included in his sketchbooks an imaginary Renaissance version of the Parthenon, based upon the drawings made by Cyriaco d'Ancona, one of the brave ones who, on April 7, 1436, had recorded in his journal "*Athens veni.*"

A classical though not Greek revival of sorts commenced sometime between 1480 and 1500, when Sangallo affixed a more or less Roman portico upon the façade of the Medici villa at Poggio a Caiano. Only a few domestic porticular appendages like this appeared before Palladio invented an ideology for them. (Porticos had been used by the ancients only for temples and the habitations of emperors. They were not for private houses.)†

† Palladio freed everyone's hand by pretending to reconstruct a Roman house with a Corinthian portico from a plan shown by Vitruvius (who had not shown any such thing), smoothly explaining that he was merely returning the portico to domestic architecture—the ancients, he said, had taken the idea from private buildings anyway. This story has subsequently been richly embellished by French architectural theorists.

As we have noted, Western Europeans first took Greek temples seriously as models for domestic architecture in the early 1750s. The French and English led the way. One of the archaeologists who first visited the ruins of Greece and its colonies, Nicholas Revett (1720–1804), erected a templar garden pavilion at Brandeston, in Norfolk, in 1757. James Stuart (1713–88) created a Doric garden-temple at Hagley Park, Worcestershire, in 1757–58. Revett's chief contribution to the Greek Revival occurred thirteen years later, at West Wycombe Park, under the sponsorship of Sir Francis Dashwood, rake, chancellor of the exchequer, and friend of Benjamin Franklin.

It is not known how Sangallo and the Medici celebrated at Poggio a Caiano, but Dashwood annexed his Greek *tempietto* to his house to the accompaniment of "Bacchanals, Priests, Priestesses, Pan, Fauns, Satyrs, Silenus, &c., in proper habits and skins wreathed with vine leaves . . . paeans and libations . . . and discharges of cannon." (I like to think of Dashwood being joined in these celebrations by Franklin, who often stayed in the house, where, he said, he was "as much at ease as if it were my own." He and Dashwood worked out an abbreviation of the Book of Common Prayer intended to bring relief to those "whose age or infirmities will not suffer them to remain for hours in a cold church." It forms the basis for the current services of Episcopalians in the United States.)[242]

Five Traditions

America had many more Greek Revival buildings than England or France, but to relatively few of these can the term *Greek Revival* be applied strictly. By few, I mean that those truly Grecian in form appeared only in the hundreds rather than the thousands or tens of thousands of American buildings that took shape with the assistance of the intervening interludes of the Renaissance and emerged as composites. The "pure" few—rectilinear, symmetrical, gable-roofed, columned, and pedimented—came to America as the result of direct observation of Greek forms; the first of them, Arlington House, was not completed until 1817.

Before and after the "pure" Greek buildings appeared, American architecture was affected by four Renaissance traditions. (My categories, like all taxonomic distinctions in art, are somewhat artificial, but useful, I think, nonetheless.) All four made use of Greek details, including large details such as columns and pilasters, but all four were composites of Greek and Roman forms.

The first of these Renaissance composite traditions was Palladian. Its lineage extended from Alberti through Donato Bramante (1444–1514) to Andrea di Pietro della Gondola (1508–80), who called himself Palladio in a renaissance of the name of a Roman humanist. This second Palladio designed well, built well, and made good use of two recent inventions, the domestic portico and self-advertisement through the printed architectural book. His influence quickly spread from northern Italy to Britain through the mediation of Inigo Jones (1573–1652), Christopher Wren (1632–1723), James Gibbs (1682–1754), and a host of popularizers subsidized and encouraged by Richard Boyle, Lord Burlington (1695–1753), and his friend William Kent (c. 1685–1748), a man as hearty as Burlington was inhibited.

Kent and Burlington, like Palladio, Jones, and Wren, were deeply committed to the ideology of Freemasonry (Jones and Wren were Grand Masters), a fact of importance to American architecture, which learned much from builders' guides developed in accordance with that ideology. Thomas Jefferson made use of the guides of two Burlingtonian Morrises, Robert (c. 1700–c. 1750) and Roger (1695–1749).

A second composite Renaissance tradition might be called Serlian, descending from Bramante through his pupil Baldassare Peruzzi (1481–1536) to Sebastiano Serlio (1475–1554). Serlio was a pupil of Peruzzi in Rome and Palladio's chief competitor as a popularizer of classical ideas. Serlio was in France after 1541, while Palladio was hitting his stride in the Veneto. The Serlian tradition entered England as early as the middle of the sixteenth century, but its full impact was not felt until a century later when imported by the entourage of Charles II, returning from exile in Holland. In the Low Countries, architects such as Hugh May (1622–84) and Wren had discovered steep-roofed brick houses, derived not from Palladio but from Serlio, impressive though modest in scale.

From the models of May and Wren there emerged a vernacular that shaped many of those American mansions along the James, Piscataway, Schuylkill, and Severn rivers known as Queen Anne or Early Georgian, cube-and-a-half, rectangular boxes of brick, under high, hatlike roofs, such as Westover and Carter's Grove.[†] The Serlian tradition produced the grand-scale American houses of the late colonial period, red-brick and white-trim "Wrenaissance" boxes. There have been many lively variants thereafter, built by people who have had to content themselves with books, imagination, and observation. In the Greek Revival period, many of these variants were given porticos; in the South, especially along the Gulf Coast, they acquired columns all around, merging the creole to the Serlian.

† In the 1980s, their simplified progeny continue to appear labeled "colonial," ultimately derived from Serlian miniatures of symmetrical Italian palaces of the Renaissance, reduced in size to fit Dutch urban lots, and then reduced further to fit American resources.

A third composite Renaissance tradition, known in England as "artisan mannerism," flowed into American Free Classicism, a disorderly, heretical, but energetic use of classical motifs. Artisan mannerism appeared in England well before Palladio's ideas were discovered by noble Britons traveling in Italy. Its first distinguished practitioner was Hendrik van Paaschen (c. 1520–c. 1582), the architect of the Royal Exchange in London (completed in 1566). He was one of scores of craftsmen trained by the Renaissance in Italy or Flanders, quite independent of either the Palladian or Serlian traditions, who produced fine buildings in Northern Europe. Using the term *artisan mannerism* a little more freely than is customary, we can observe its reappearance in American variations as the Free Classicism of the nineteenth century.[243]

Batty Langley (1696–1751) was a carrier of some of this exuberance. Having integrated yet further ideas, he added enough vitality of his own to justify calling a fourth Renaissance tradition Langleyan or, perhaps, "Masonic Baroque." Though stemming from Italy, it reached America as a result of a competition between two circles of English Masons. One was that around Burlington; the other was sponsored and subsidized by the dukes of Richmond and Montagu. Finding Burlingtonian Palladianism rather bland and Burlington himself pretentious, the dukes and their following proclaimed the virtues of the vehement, muscular side of Wren's genius, which was sustained by his assistant, Nicholas Hawksmoor (1661–1736) and Hawksmoor's partner, the secret agent, courtier, and playwright, Sir John Vanbrugh (1664–1726). Hawksmoor and Vanbrugh produced stagecraft: immense in scale and military in feeling, the English Masonic Baroque.

American architects with a propensity for such grandiosity, such as Henry Howard, turned back to the Vanbrughian in their wildly asymmetrical Hellenistic work of the 1850s. But even earlier Montagu and

Richmond had bestowed upon American Free Classicism a great gift in their patronage of Langley, whose carpenters' guides were of great influence in the new nation. George Washington (another Mason) learned much from Langley.

These gentlemen were establishing a network of publishers and readers, as well as a basis for learning to build from books, through which a Greek Revival could later be disseminated. This was a precondition not only of means but also of program. The Freemasons were serious about the popularization of classical architecture. Palladio, Jones, Wren, Burlington, Kent, the Morrises, and Langley propagated ancient rules of architecture for practical use *and* as a means of redeeming society by the conscious deployment of very large, constructed symbols. Medieval architects had done so, and after the invention of printing, architecture and bookmaking joined as means to evangelize through architectural form.

In practice and through builders' guides, the Masonic popularizers also encouraged the use of architecture as a device to give common purpose to people of various stations in life, rich and poor, urban and rural. Their belief in a broad, redemptive role for good architecture in society led the way to Free Classicism first, then to the Arts and Crafts movement of the last quarter of the nineteenth century, and to the Prairie School evangelicals to follow. The American Greek Revival claims a place in the sequence of English eighteenth-century Masonic popularizers, the American writers of builders' and carpenters' guides, Langleyans and Burlingtonians, a sequence that culminated in the architecture and ideology of Louis Sullivan and William Gray Purcell.

Langley named his sons Vitruvius, Archimedes, Hiram, and Euclid, which reminds us that the most potent force for good architecture in New York, around 1800, were the Brethren of the Workshop of Vitruvius. It can also remind us of the veneration of Vitruvius, Archimedes, Hiram, and Euclid in Mormon Utah: the Masonic affiliations of the founders of the Church of Latter-Day Saints, Brigham Young and Joseph Smith, can be discerned in Mormon architecture from western New York through Ohio and Illinois all the way to Deseret.[244]

The Transition to the Greek

In the middle years of the eighteenth century, a few American buildings gained columns and pilasters, but the Greek Revival had yet to arrive. This was, instead, a Burlingtonian, neo-Palladian Renaissance. A "colossal portico" appeared in abstracted form as a pedimented set of pilasters set upon the Charles Pinckney House in bustling Charleston in 1747. In the following year, Peter Harrison, a gifted amateur in Newport, Rhode Island, gave the Redwood Library a full-scale portico, and at about the same time, the Spanish governor at St. Augustine, in Florida, saw to it that the gateway to his "palace," a modest enough creole house, was enriched by a set of monumental pilasters.[†]

Redwood Library, Newport, Rhode Island

† Harrison made use of a design by one of the English Palladians, Edward Hoppus, in London in the 1730s. Thus progressed a style—from a Roman Catholic church on an island in a Venetian lagoon to a library donated to the people of Newport by a Quaker slave dealer—by way of a picture to be found in a book published in London.

In 1753 another Burlingtonian prototype, this time by Colin Campbell, provided the first true temple-form building in America, Prince William's Church in Sheldon, South Carolina. Burned, rebuilt, and burned again by British raiding parties in two wars, it has lain ruined and largely ignored by historians, but it is still well worth inspecting.[245]

In 1793 Samuel Blodget, a China trader from Boston, prevailed upon one of two Irish draftsmen then in Philadelphia (there is dispute as to which) to provide him with a free adaptation of a porticoed building in Dublin to give dignity to the headquarters of the new Bank of the United States in Philadelphia. The portico was there, but not the temple; the bank looked nothing like the Parthenon. Neither did Latrobe's domed, porticoed, and infinitely more gracious Bank of Pennsylvania, which got under way five years later.[246]

The Wrenaissance required a cleansing—one might almost say bleaching—to become a Greek Revival. That did not occur until after 1800, when brick and wooden buildings were sheathed in neoclassical stucco to become "villas," with roofs flattened to become less conspicuous. (Many American houses of this period have been re-Georgianized by the removal of plaster and the reduction to a provincial, red-brick quality their builders sought to eschew. Two examples are Gore Place in Waltham, Massachusetts, and Oak Hill, the residence of James Monroe, in Loudoun County, Virginia.)

The Campbell sketch that produced Prince William's Church probably suggested to Thomas Jefferson, twenty years later, the concept of converting the Governor's Palace at Williamsburg into the first temple-form *residence* anywhere in the world. If George Washington had liked the idea, Jefferson's "elegant seat"

Prince William's Church, near
Sheldon, South Carolina

Competition drawings for the
United States Capitol by Philip
Hart (*top*), and Samuel
McIntire (*bottom*)

† "Light-Horse Harry" Lee had
Stratford, Nathaniel Greene and
"Mad Anthony" Wayne had
their Georgia plantations, and
Henry Knox seldom ventured far
from his vast speculations in
Maine. Nobody seems to have
thought Baron von Steuben
worthy of anything better than
the log house, amid the mus-
keg and heath, provided him by
a not-very-grateful legislature
of the state of New York (see
Orders from France).

might have been the American equivalent to the duke of Marlborough's
Blenheim Palace or the duke of Wellington's Stratford Saye—a nation's tribute
to a military hero.[247]

But Washington already had his Mount Vernon, and his generals were also
suitably provided.† So Jefferson's wartime scheme was never carried out, and
the ravaged Williamsburg capitol declined into weeds and rubble. When it
came time for its resurrection as a Rockefeller charity, it was not given its
proposed templar form but instead reconstructed into its first, truly "colonial"
condition. Thus it symbolized the government that lost the Revolutionary War,
rather than offering a glimpse into the imagination of the most architecturally
gifted of its winners.

In the 1780s, while he was in Paris, Jefferson *did* manage a prototypical,
amphiprostyle (two porticos, front and back) temple for America. Through the
mails he convinced the building committee of the Capitol Building to erect one
in Richmond as the new seat of Virginia's government. The most striking
aspect of that building for a visitor is not, however, its form but its scale. It is
enormous, with columns nearly forty feet in height. The classical age was
announced—but it was very slow in coming.

In the opening pages of his *Greek Revival*, Hamlin makes much of the
competition drawings for the Capitol in 1794 and 1795. They included a
handsome French submission in a conservative eighteenth-century style from
Etienne Hallet, which won but seemed too ambitious or, perhaps, too French.
On second thought, the winner became a British colonial design by Dr.
William Thornton, recently returned from his studies in Edinburgh to the
family plantations on Tortola. It was even more conservative; something very like it was soon to be built
as a hospital in Bombay.

There was also a series of homegrown drawings, only one of which—a very competent Adamesque
composition by Samuel McIntire—rose above the embarrassing. None of them presaged a Greek Revival
in any respect.

Aside from the Virginia capitol, very Roman and very solitary, no temple-form governmental buildings
were constructed for nearly fifty years after independence.[248]

The Regents

There was much competent building accomplished in the United States in the eighteenth and very early nineteenth centuries by such men as Peter Harrison (1716–75), Gabriel Manigault (1758–1809), Philip Hooker (1766–1836), and Samuel McIntire (1757–1811) and by scores of lesser-known craftsmen. Many of them worked in a style still sometimes called the Federal (or even Federalist, though that would be a political, not an aesthetic, description. The architecture was so derivative of British models as to render that term somewhat insulting to the founders). Popular in the 1780s, delicate, swaggy, and fanlit, it appeared at its sweet best in Charleston, South Carolina, in Halifax County, North Carolina, and in the work of McIntire in Massachusetts. It had a second vogue in the 1930s.

As noted earlier, the Federal style lacked energy; it was a bleached-out, exhausted, provincial version of the decorative ideas derived from Roman prototypes by Robert Adam and his contemporaries in the 1750s and 1760s. Americans did not experience antiquity directly until after 1800; their Adamesque Federal was learned in black-and-white from books; it did not make use of Adam's vigorous color. Latrobe and Ramée, who knew their antique services, did use Pompeiian decoration, but interior ornament in the United States did not fully embrace gorgeous Technicolor until the 1840s.[†]

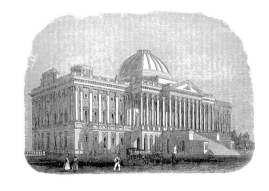

After 1790 revolutionary disorders in Europe sent many talented artists to the United States, where they became available to guide the early republic through its architectural "regency." These "regents" were refugees from individual disappointment as well as common disasters. In America they provided a kind of trusteeship over the Renaissance tradition until it was strong enough to be carried forward by the native-born talent they trained. (I use the term *regent* as it is used in law, not to refer to the roughly contemporary Regency in the management of the British monarchy, nor to the architectural style in England given the same name—a style similar to the Directoire in France, to the Gustavian in Sweden, and the Pauline or Early Alexandrine in Russia.)

The first regents to arrive, and the most numerous in the 1790s, were the French: Pierre-Charles L'Enfant (1745–1825), Pierre Pharoux (c. 1760–95), Joseph-Jacques Ramée (1764–1842), Joseph-François Mangin (c. 1760–c. 1820) and his brother Charles (older or younger, it is not known),

Competition drawings for the United States Capitol by Samuel Dobie (*top*) and Etienne Hallet (*center*). At bottom is a period engraving of the Capitol after construction.

† The restoration of the interiors of the Valentine Museum in Richmond, dating, probably, from the 1820s, shows that in a few places American designers such as Alexander Parris were following the colorful examples provided by Latrobe and Ramée.

Etienne-Sulpice Hallet (c. 1760–1825), Adrian Boucher (c. 1760–1804), and Bartholomy Lafon (c. 1765–1820). They were succeeded after 1796 by well-trained cosmopolitans with British passports, of whom the best known were Benjamin Henry Latrobe (1764–1820) and George Hadfield (1763–1826).[†]

† This array of bracketed life spans is offered to suggest how closely contemporary these lives were, as they initiated the Greek Revival.

The first to arrive during the Revolutionary War was L'Enfant, artist son of the "Painter Ordinary" to King Louis XVI. There is no evidence that L'Enfant was trained in either architecture or engineering; he came as an enthusiastic volunteer to the forces of American independence, a sort of proto-photojournalist, and he drew beautiful portraits of generals and useful depictions of fortresses.

He became a great favorite of George Washington, and though he returned with the French forces to Europe, after he returned to the United States in 1784, he was given a series of commissions for buildings, beginning with temporary pavilions and culminating in the 1788 remodeling of Federal Hall in New York, the first Capitol building of the new republic. As Richmond was being graced with Thomas Jefferson's capitol, L'Enfant gave New York the portico of Federal Hall, suggesting the possibility of an American style with its starry, massive entablature. L'Enfant was no master, but he had original ideas, and he kept his building clear and serene, anticipating the Greek Revival in an aversion to Rococo excess.

L'Enfant has been underrated as an architect. Among the amateurs who initiated the American style—including Thomas Jefferson and William Thornton—he came closest to the Greek Revival in its ultimate, American form, which, at its best, was sober, stripped, and economical. He, and the other French neoclassicists who followed him to New York, gave the city an aspect that remained predominantly French until the departure of Joseph-Jacques Ramée in 1816.

L'Enfant may have provided sketches, at least, for the presidential mansion and Capitol for Washington City. He was, after all, architect for that city as well as for Paterson, New Jersey, America's first company town and industrial park, and for a Parisian-style mansion for the nation's most famous financier, Robert Morris.[††]

†† The most beautiful structure remaining from this period is New York's City Hall, designed in 1804-1806, largely by Joseph Mangin. It was the culmination of the gallification of lower Manhattan; around it other French-designed buildings by Etienne Hallet, Pierre Pharoux, L'Enfant, the brothers Mangin, and Adrian Boucher were already clustered.

A new burst of French energy arrived with Joseph-Jacques Ramée in 1811–12, who created the finest garden and estate designs to be seen in the Western Hemisphere. Some of his work survives, but most is gone: a church, villas, icehouses, city mansions, and country houses. His Union College campus, begun in Schenectady, New York, in 1815, was the first to be laid out in pavilions around a rotunda. The University of Virginia, four years later, followed Ramée's pattern (a familiar one, it is important to note, having appeared in a half-dozen prize drawings for Paris's Ecole des Beaux-Arts in the 1780s and 1790s).

In Philadelphia and Washington after 1800, the master architects were English. (In New York, they were French until about 1810.) Chief among these were Latrobe, who had been trained in Germany and Italy and polished in the London atelier of Samuel Pepys Cockerell, and Hadfield, who deserves considerably more space than the simple statement that he introduced the Greek Revival to America. He also gave it an elegance and sophistication, at the very beginning, that set the standard for later practitioners such as Ithiel Town.

Under these French, English, Irish, and German instructors, Americans including Robert Mills (b. 1781), William Strickland (b. 1787), Elias Carter (b. 1783), and Ithiel Town (b. 1784) bridged the gap.

After the regents trained Mills and Strickland and the ingenious Ithiel Town grew to full maturity, the way was open for the virtuosos of the "native" Greek, Francis Costigan (b. 1810), James Dakin (b. 1808), Minard Lafever (b. 1798), Charles Bryant (b. 1803), Russell Warren (b. 1792), Alexander Jackson Davis (b. 1803), and the score or so of heretofore unsung local practitioners who will be sung about a little more in this section of this book.[†]

† Other contributors to America were born abroad, "regents" too, but arriving a little later. For example, there were the Prussians, Charles Reichardt and Augustus Heimann, who carried the revival into South Carolina and Tennessee, where their work was supplemented by the group I will call "The Somerset Four."

George Hadfield

Hadfield was born in Florence in 1763, a year before Latrobe. There do not seem to be any Hadfield Papers to attract funding by the National Endowment for the Humanities, but judging from what we can learn from the writings of others, his story is picaresque enough for fiction. He was swept early into fashionable circles by his ambitious mother. His sister, Maria Hadfield Cosway, became the inamorata of Thomas Jefferson and the prince regent, later King George IV, among others.

Washington City Hall

In his youth, he was thought to be a prodigy. As a student at the Royal Academy, he "received all the . . . prizes."[249] The academy sent him off for three years of further training in Italy and received him back with a major exhibition of his drawings. He was then taken into the atelier of James Wyatt. At the academy, one of his fellow students had been the American painter John Trumbull, who, while Hadfield was still with Wyatt, and for the best of motives, spoke to him about leaving England for America at a crucial moment. The young architect, living on the margin of the prince regent's circle and exposed to its vagaries, had been blackballed at the Architects Club during one skirmish in an extended power struggle between Wyatt and Sir John Soane.

† These were the two uncles of John Trumbull, the unwelcome son-in-law of Thomas Gibbons.

Trumbull had heard that the U.S. Capitol project needed rescuing from another set of squabblers, the commissioners of the Capitol. Acting through his brother, the governor of Connecticut,† Trumbull interceded in Hadfield's behalf with George Washington. Calling Hadfield "an acquaintance of ten years, a man of modesty and amiable qualities as well as talents," he overlooked the young man's lack of experience in supervising the actual work of construction, which was the job that needed doing.[250]

The result was an extended disaster for Hadfield, after which Trumbull regretted interposing his own American connections before those of Hadfield's own—those eminent persons "who had some influence with [the prince regent, who] might have procured for him the execution of those extensive and splendid works, which were committed to Mr. Nash."[251]

Hadfield was not the equal of John Nash in self-promotion or in breadth of vision, but he was a man of immense talent and, despite his morose disposition, came to have a commensurate influence in the United States. First, he gave the Capitol what coherence it had before Latrobe stepped in. It had been worked over by French, Irish, Scottish, Russian, and West Indian designers as well as local contractors and ambitious politicians.[†] Hadfield made sense of the beginnings of it. His executive office buildings, including the War Department Building for which he proposed America's first use of a canonical Greek "order" (in 1796–97), were sober, useful, and soundly planned in relationship to the White House. Arlington House set a new style, and his Washington City Hall (now the U.S. District Courts Building) was of great use to the development of the ideas of that great engineer and engine of architectural history, Ithiel Town.

[†] The Frenchmen were Etienne-Sulpice Hallet and Pierre-Charles L'Enfant, the West Indian was Dr. William Thornton, the Russian his associate DeMiroth—called by Trumbull "a Russian officer of engineers" (Trumbull, p. 176) —and the Irishman was James Hoban; all had a direct influence upon the design of the Capitol. The Scot was Colin Campbell, whose influence flowed through Thornton's use of his *Vitruvius Brittanicus*.

Latrobe, Hadfield, and the Greeks

† Crook quotes, with apparent approval, the strange statement of Sir John Summerson that Latrobe, "at the Bank of Philadelphia [oh, well, close enough] . . . married English Neo-Classicism to Jeffersonian Neo-Classicism [what can that be, in 1796? the Virginia capitol? the unexecuted Williamsburg palace?]. . . . From that moment the classical revival in America took on a national form." (Crook, p. 77) It was a glorious building, but neither unprecedented nor immediately influential. The bank was Latrobe's fifth essay in the Greek, the least Greek among them, and later than Hadfield's proposal for the War Department, but it was very beautiful. It had a scrupulous Roman dome, Venetian windows, vaulted spaces, and two porticos using the Ionic columns Hadfield had employed a year earlier. It was not as close to a Greek temple form as either St. Paul's Church, down the street and thirty-seven years older, or John Smibert's 1741 design for the Holden Chapel at Harvard (though these steepleless, domeless buildings had pilasters only, no columns). William Pierson (p. 350) is certainly correct in putting aside quibbling about Greeks and Romans and pointing out that while the bank was neoclassical, it was an original work of art, not a classical replica. Unlike the Virginia capitol, it was not a rectilinear block with a portico, but a sculptured form, whose curves invited the visitor to explore fluid, surprising spaces inside, anticipating the profound psychological uses of space to be found in Latrobe's Baltimore Cathedral.

†† A few houses on a grand scale also did this, such as the governor's mansion in Milledgeville, Georgia, and Waverley, near Columbus, Mississippi, which is mostly tribune and very little house. But this amalgamated classic style *(continued)*

Despite much talk that it should be built to achieve Athenian duration, none of the architects who labored on the Capitol until Latrobe had suggested that any part of it might actually *look* Athenian. Latrobe took such matters seriously and proposed to add to it one of his little Greek porticos as a strange, almost subterranean, entrance beneath their Roman domes and pilasters. He had used such one-story temple fronts upon the wings of Hammerwood, a country house south of London and his first large commission in England; the idea remained a staple of his residential work after he arrived in America.

Soon thereafter, in March 1796, he gave a portico to Captain William Pennock for his mansion in Norfolk and, a little later, suggested a much bigger Corinthian colonnade for another Virginia project, a house to be called Mill Hill, which was never built. Two years later, his version of a primitive Doric *tempietto* appeared in Richmond as the entry portico of a mansion for Colonel John Harvie.[252]

Latrobe combined his Greek ideas with Roman and Renaissance precedents in the amalgam often asserted to have marked the "birth . . . of the Greek Revival," the Bank of Pennsylvania.†

More important than any finicking about what was Greek and what was Roman in the parentage of Latrobe's bank, or the degree to which it was, itself, precedented, is the delay—and then the fecundity—of its precedential potency. For, after a sterile two decades, it had a host of progeny. The designers of most American "Greek" *public* buildings followed Latrobe's lead in combining a Greek portico with a Roman dome (or the suggestion of such a dome in a large, airy space at the center—sometimes circular, in the form of a drum or "tribune"—surmounted by a cupola).††

The best candidate for distinction as the first-born among Greek Revival houses in America is George Hadfield's Arlington House. Unlike the bank, its central temple form was of uncompromising Greek character, without a hint of a dome or a Venetian window. Construction commenced before 1804 and the portico was complete by 1818; it was built upon a site that no one who came to the nation's capital could miss.[253]

As Arlington House was becoming the nation's most conspicuous private residence, brooding in Doric splendor over the federal city, Hadfield's largest commission (next to the Capitol itself) got under way: it was Washington's city hall, begun in 1820. It was constructed at the same time as the Second Bank of the United States in Philadelphia, which was designed in Doric in 1818 by Latrobe's prodigious student William Strickland and completed after the Washington City Hall, in 1824.

did not commend itself for domestic use to the same degree as the domeless sequence established by Hadfield and followed by Ithiel Town.

Ithiel Town, shrewd, generous, ingenious man that he was, knew quality when he saw it, and despite Hadfield's reserve, the two became known to each other through Trumbull and William Parker Elliott, who was the son of Town's closest friend in Washington and who studied for five years with Hadfield and later worked as a draftsman for Town and Davis.[254] Town wrote his daughter from Washington on February 7, 1826, the day after George Hadfield's funeral: "I attended the funeral of one of my acquaintances yesterday in this City. . . . He was an Architect of respectable standing sent to this country at the instance of George Washington some twenty years ago. He was born in Florence, Italy, and some years supported at Rome by the Royal Institute as a pension student in Architecture."[255]

The old bachelor was lucky in his acquaintance, at the end of his life, with a man such as Town, who provided him with artistic descendants. He had labored, largely unrecognized and alone, except, it seems, for the help of young Elliott on the Washington City Hall project. Perhaps history offers some means of compensation; for thirty years Trumbull rued having impelled Hadfield, his old friend of student days, to leave England at the start of what might have been a great career, by introducing him to George Washington.

Even before Hadfield and Custis did so, Ithiel Town had made the connection between Washington and Greece in a schoolboy poem. Writing a few months after Washington's death in 1799, Town said more than he intended, perhaps, about the pervasiveness of the Greek influences that gave powerful impetus to his later career:

The Architect's Dream, by Thomas Cole (detail)

> *The friend of Man, Columbia's Son*
> *The first in War and Peace*
> *The conqueror of Proud Albion*
> *Never matched by Ambient Greece*[256]

Hadfield was not an "instructor" to Town in the same direct way that Latrobe instructed Robert Mills and William Strickland (and, through Strickland, Thomas Walter and Gideon Shryock of Kentucky). But if intensity of learning is a measure of instruction, and if magnitude of consequence be a measure of the importance of the things learned, Hadfield was an ample mentor.

The Washington City Hall had two features that Town used repeatedly thereafter, to the greater glory of the Greek Revival. Its huge, six-columned Ionic portico at the center was the first American expression of the east front of the Erechtheum, in Athens. On its hilltop location overlooking the Capitol grounds, it was more impressive than Latrobe's Bank of Pennsylvania could be on a crowded street on flat terrain. And Hadfield's design for the wings of the city hall brought another new concept to America: two giant columns, in a recessed niche, on a raised platform.[257]

Bowers House, Northampton, Massachusetts

Variations on Themes by George Hadfield The Washington City Hall portico quickly reappeared in Town's design for the Bowers House in Northampton, Massachusetts (1826–28), at the center of a temple-with-wings format like that of Arlington House. (The Bowers House has been lost, but one can get some sense of its grandeur by observing the two much-reduced versions that were built within a year or two in nearby Haydenville, Massachusetts.)

Town's draftsman was a young man named Alexander Jackson Davis, who decided to become an architect during the years 1819 to 1822, when he was living in Alexandria, Virginia. Arlington House, on the horizon, was being completed and so was Washington's city hall.

Davis's diary began to be filled with his own studies of the Erechtheum. After he went to work for Town in 1829, the two together broadened the reach of Town's brilliant "Bowers synthesis" of the city hall and Arlington House. It reappeared in Buffalo, Batavia, Canandaigua, Geneseo, Auburn, Oswego, Skaneateles, and Utica—just to list the temple-and-wing formats they built in the region of New York where Davis had spent his youth.[†]

† It may be that Rose Hill and Roosevelt Hall belong on this list, though no proof in correspondence or plans has so far been found.

After Hadfield's death in 1826, Davis recorded the firm's debt to him by securing, perhaps from Town, Hadfield's drawings of the city hall and by making his own elegant transcriptions of the variations on the dome Hadfield had contemplated. (Like Mozart's reworking of Handel, these drawings were respectful but fresh.) And he went off to Arlington House to sketch the view of Washington Hadfield had framed, looking out from between the immense columns of the portico.

Another associate of Town's, James Dakin, launched his own sequence of derivations from this form with the four-columned Ionic Perry House in Brooklyn, New York (1832), from which stemmed, in turn, two subvariants: a more cubical, massive form, with only one row of pillars, that retained Dakin's peculiar heavy entablature. This was the idea Thomas U. Walter picked up for Matthew Newkirk, in Philadelphia (1835); it was probably Dakin himself who used it five years later for the Commercial Bank of Natchez—he was working nearby at the time.[†]

† Walter's Newkirk House (Ionic) seems to me to bear a closer relationship to Dakin's Perry House (Ionic) than to the four-columned Powelton (Doric), executed by Walter's mentor, William Strickland.

Other householders of ample but not profuse means, beginning with Elias Brown in Mystic, Connecticut (1835), settled for four-columned porticos with wings. They did not require signed and authorized Town, Davis, Dakin, Reichardt, Gallier, or Lafever plans; they could borrow ideas from the pattern books that Lafever and Gallier began producing at the end of the 1820s and early 1830s.

Another graduate of the Town circle, John Francis Rague (1799–1877), set up shop in Springfield, Illinois, selling "plans and elevations . . . in any of the orders of architecture. . . . Rough casting in imitation of granite or any other stone . . . composition egg and dart moldings . . . for less than half the cost of carving." Through men like Rague, Minard Lafever's designs for ornament reached customers from Natchez and New Orleans to Belfast, Maine. Builders' guides made for Lafever clients who never met him and, in fact, may never have heard his name. Rich ornament, some of it manufactured in New York by his brother, appeared in a dozen states, often attributed to mythical Italian, French, Hessian, or "convict" carvers. Like New Orleans's ironwork balconies, fine plasterwork was largely a manufactured product, sold by the yard.[258]

Rague was quite capable of independent architectural work in the Town and Davis style; his, and Abraham Lincoln's, Springfield became a Greek Revival village. (Lincoln's own house and the office building where he and William Herndon served their railroad clients were respectably Periclean.) Rague's chief works were the Illinois state capitol of 1837 [ii, 357, 358], and the Iowa state capitol (1842) in Iowa City (where his name is pronounced "Rag-oo"), which is now a part of the University of Iowa.

Study for a Greek Revival interior by Alexander Jackson Davis

Meanwhile, Town and Davis, the principal partners in the firm, were building the capitols of North Carolina, Ohio [46], and Indiana. Town had already executed the state house for Connecticut in New Haven. Robert Cary Long, Jr., of Baltimore, who spent his own time of apprenticeship in New York, went on to a celebrated career in Maryland and, ultimately, back in New York again. Long extended himself to Altoona, Pennsylvania, to build yet another huge Erechtheum portico, this time largely of iron, in 1844–48, for the metals master Elias Baker. It is still there, as is Long's Church of St. Peter the Apostle in Baltimore (1843–44), which owes much to Arlington House.

In the early 1830s, Charles Reichardt introduced German neoclassicism to New York, New Jersey, and South Carolina with his own theme of a central block without a pediment and with wings tucked discreetly at the back, reached by a **T** hallway with a very long head. This was the format of Milford and The Forest.

The Reichardt colonnade, though without a **T** plan, was taken up again by James and Charles Dakin when they reached Louisiana. (James Dakin left New York for the South in 1835, Reichardt in 1836.) Its next appearance was in New Orleans, in 1844, for Mrs. Abigail Loyal Armitage Slark. Dakin's student Henry Howard (1818–84) turned it Ionic at Woodlawn for the mighty Pughs of Assumption Parish in 1849. He had already brought the Erechtheum–Arlington House–Washington City Hall–Bowers House–Perry House scheme into play for another set of Pughs in his first great commission, Madewood [158], in 1846: Howard learned nearly as much from Dakin as Town had from Hadfield.[259]

The tradition set by the wings of Hadfield's Washington City Hall was equally fertile. It produced Town's Sachem's Wood (1828) in New Haven and extended to a small masterpiece by James Goldsmith, an emigrant from New Haven, the Bank of Geauga in Painesville, Ohio (1837, destroyed by fire in 1925). The best of its descendants is Dakin's wonderful Bank of Louisville [372], which was built in 1834, but is now a theater.[260]

One man's masterpiece may not reach the routine level of a genius. Goldsmith was a good journeyman, Dakin a good architect; Davis *was* a genius. Variations by Town and Davis of Hadfield's city hall wings and of Sachem's Wood appeared at Highwood (1835) for Henry Whitney, also in New Haven, and culminated in Stevens' Palace, on Murray Street in New York, in 1843, much amplified and provided with a domed tribune.

By that time, the Greek Revival epoch was well under way, propelled by the second wave of English talent who came to serve as regents after the deaths of Latrobe in 1820 and Hadfield in 1826.

Somerset Four

Four sons of Somersetshire, somewhat younger than Latrobe and Hadfield, were trained for their profession amid the gray-stone crescents of Bath, the playground of fashionable England. These men, who took vigorous part in the American "regency," and followed it into a Greek Revival, were John Chislett (who worked in the 1830s and 1840s), William Jay (1793–1837), William Nichols (1777–1853), and John Haviland (1792–1852).

Haviland found his clients in Pennsylvania, Jay in Savannah and Charleston, Chislett in Pittsburgh, and Nichols worked his way across the upland South, creating college campuses, state capitols, and scores of residences. Sad to say, nearly all his work has been lost. Hayes Plantation in North Carolina and those portions of the Mississippi governor's mansion left undesecrated by a recent occupant without sufficient respect for history are about all that remain to remind us of him.

But Nichols was using Greek elements in his North Carolina work as early as 1815, and it is likely that it was he who invented the classic "Tara" version of the classicized creole cottage a decade or so later. He arrived in North Carolina around 1800 and moved on to Alabama in the late 1820s. There, within a year or so, a new form appeared in American architecture. Near Florence, James Jackson built Forks of Cypress, probably to designs by Nichols. This was the first house in America to be completely surrounded by columns in classical proportions (as distinguished from the spindly posts that supported the roofs of creole cottages); it lasted until it burned in 1966.[†]

The Caribbean house-within-a-house now gained an elegance refined around another island-studded sea, the Aegean. Though Forks of Cypress was the first and only house of its sort to be built in Alabama, hundreds more appeared in each of two clusters, the first centered in Piedmont Georgia (there was one house just over the South Carolina–Georgia border, and another just over the Mississippi–Georgia border), and the other in the Mississippi delta. There, the creole cottage had been maturing since the 1730s; now, in Louisiana, Arkansas, and especially in the area of Mississippi around Natchez, there was a rage for classical cottages. To this day it is very difficult to distinguish those built new in the 1830s, 1840s, and 1850s from remodelings that thickened the columns and added rectilinear doorways and windows, and a little Grecian ornament, to older buildings.

Because one of the earliest of these remodelings was to be seen at Houmas House, the headquarters of the holdings of the South Carolina Hamptons in the delta, one is led to the thought that they, and other investors in the delta from Georgia and South Carolina, carried back with them a new acquaintance with

† It is foolish to spend much time wondering who "invented" what, when so many good ideas were in the air, to be brought to earth by one or another of the gifted men who were at work at the time. But here are two sequences:

The four-columned Ionic portico of the temple on the Ilissus was recaptured by Nichols for his governor's palace and New Chapel in Raleigh, North Carolina, in 1824–26. James Dakin used it to modify Ithiel Town's Bowers House prototype when he designed the J. W. Perry House in Brooklyn in 1832, as did Thomas U. Walter for his Matthew Newkirk House in Philadelphia in 1835. Charles B. Cluskey and John Pell used it for the governor's mansion in Milledgeville, Georgia, in 1838, and my guess is that it was James Dakin who went back to it for the Commercial Bank in Natchez in 1837–39.

It is also my guess that Nichols added one more building to his Hillsborough, North Carolina, work in 1818–20: the otherwise inexplicably elegantly Palladian Hazel-Nash House, with its three pediments facing forward, presaging Henry Howard's Madewood in Louisiana (1846–48), which fuses the Hadfield-Town-Dakin tradition (Dakin was Howard's mentor) with the kind of Palladian compositions used by Nichols. There is even a remote possibility that the tri-pedimented Turner-Saunders-Good-Hall House, Alabama's most Palladian, near Town Creek, might have been affected by Nichols's presence as it was being built from 1830 to 1835.

the creole cottage form in the early 1830s, admixed it with Greek Revival ideas, and created this new and very convenient format at both ends of their investment transactions.

Nichols left a widely diffused legacy in the South. William Jay, charming, profligate, and immensely gifted, did not. His American career lasted less than a decade, and the marks of his capacity to treat architecture as a branch of sculpture were limited to the coastlands from Savannah to Charleston. He showed later Georgian builders how to play with "Greek-key" ornament, stunted Doric columns, and the hollowing out of two-story Doric atria. His house for William Scarbrough, built in 1819, is one of a handful of buildings in America to re-create the actual format of a Greek house of antiquity—rather blank on the exterior but open to a columned court on the inside. (Belsay Castle, in Northumberland, is the most conspicuous British example; John Holden Greene achieved a smaller version, now lost, in Providence, Rhode Island.)

Jay returned to England in the early 1820s, leaving the other three sons of Somerset, Nichols, Chislett, and Haviland, to blow the dust off their Grecian handbooks, while Latrobe's students Robert Mills and William Strickland—followed, in turn, by Strickland's students Gideon Shryock and Thomas U. Walter—and the graduates and affiliates of Town's office were in midcareer in the New Hellenism. Contemporary to our Somerset Four were the great Scottish Hellenists, led by William Henry Playfair (1789–1857).

† Nichols's governor's mansion for Mississippi, designed in 1836–39 and built from 1839 to 1842, shares a rounded portico with Chislett's Schoenberger Villa, Thornton's Tudor Place, and Jay's Bulloch House, but it does not complete the French (De Wailly) theme by scooping out the rest of the circle from the façade of the house.

Nichols was still at work in the 1850s. Chislett produced neoclassical architecture of a high order: photographs show a temple-bank; a regency town house for the Schoenberger family as well as their country villa (which shared the motif of an impaled circular *tempietto* with Jay's Bulloch House); and a domed-and-porticoed Allegheny County courthouse (1842), which lasted only forty years in turbulent Pittsburgh. Only his Burke's Building (1836), recovered from the wreckers at the last moment, remains in the city.†

The Great Tradition

John Haviland, a diffident master, built only a few Grecian buildings, but two are still to be seen in Philadelphia, the Franklin Institute (1825–27), now the Atwater Kent Museum, and St. Andrew's Episcopal Church (1822–24), now St. George's Greek Orthodox Church, nearby.

Though Haviland was not adept at self-promotion, he greatly influenced the American constructed landscape, beginning at the explosive moment when Nicholas Biddle was promoting the cause of Grecian architecture in Philadelphia. The Second Bank of the United States competition got under way in 1817–18. Biddle had published the essays of George Tucker and Latrobe's Anniversary Oration, but these theoretical discussions were of little practical use to a carpenter or a client who wished to know how to go about building in the ways these essays enthusiastically urged.

Enter John Haviland, with the first American publication to show how a Greek Revival might be achieved, in simple, practical, well-illustrated terms. *The Builder's Assistant* of 1818 went into direct competition with the builders' guides of Asher Benjamin, who spoke for "many ingenious builders who have for a long time rigidly adhered to the Roman system." A decade later, Benjamin came around, finally willing to "confess myself an admirer of Grecian architecture," having been "witness . . . [to with] what rapid progress the Grecian system has . . . advanced beyond the Roman."[261]

Haviland's adaptation of Stuart and Revett's drawing of the choragic monument of Thrasyllus, a façade laid across the opening of a cave below the Acropolis intended to serve as a celebration of a festival award won by an Athenian boys' choir, appeared in his Franklin Institute Building of 1825–27. James and Charles Dakin saw that building in Philadelphia, coupled it with their own fresh reading of Stuart and Revett, and husbanded the possibilities of square, unadorned columns under a severe horizontal entablature until they went to practice architecture along the lower Mississippi.

Soon, beside houses owing a debt to Nichols's Forks of Cypress, there appeared colonnades owing a debt to Thrasyllus, Stuart, Revett, and Haviland. The Dakins tried out the idea for the state arsenal in New Orleans (1839); it was probably they who developed it at Bocage and Belle Helene (or Ashland [159]), both about 1840, and at Belle Alliance (Lafourche) in 1846.[262]

Haviland, unlike Benjamin, was a professional architect. Accordingly, he led other writers of builders' guides to accept a premise of which Latrobe had attempted to convince them: builders who ordered their activity according to classical rules might, thereby, gain the right to think of themselves as practicing a learned profession, not merely a craft.

There was, therefore, a connection between the development of architecture as a profession and the spread of the Greek Revival. The ideas of Scottish Enlightenment theory had been helpful; Nicholas Biddle, Joseph Dennie, George Tucker, Latrobe, and Jefferson had earlier used them to connect American nationalism to professionalism and to classical forms. But until the men with the hammers and saws gained an interest in the matter, the impulse to build Hellenically depended upon the whims of the rich. Though important, "fashion" is not enough to create a full-scale change in the vernacular.

As one examines the intellectual development shown in American builders' guides and carpenters' guides or, specifically, in the careers of carpenter-contractor-builder-architects such as Russell Warren or Haviland's "student" Minard Lafever, it appears that the professionalizing of architecture in the United States was accelerated by the Greek Revival.

This process goes back to the beginning of that revival, with Stuart and Revett, and continues through James Elmes, Haviland, and Lafever. It reached countless country builders who drew upon the books of Elmes, Haviland, Lafever, and even the late convert Benjamin for the shaping of their buildings and of their ideas.

"Athenian" Stuart (1713–88) was indolent and inefficient, but the industrious Elmes (1782–1862) admired him enormously for introducing the Greek Revival to Britain: "No event that ever occurred in the history of architecture in England, and thence throughout all Europe, produced so sudden, decided, and beneficial effect as did the works of James Stuart."[263] Haviland was "bound" as an indentured student to Elmes from 1811 through 1814, while Elmes was developing the popular arguments for the primacy of Greek over Roman taste. Haviland went off to America; Elmes published his views shortly before Haviland put Minard Lafever to work upon the construction of the Arcade on Maiden Lane in New York (1826–27). Stuart and the British pan-Hellenists, especially in Edinburgh, had found a spokesman who could be heard on both sides of the Atlantic.

Minard Lafever's elevation for "A Country Residence"

Haviland's textbook, the first provided for an American Greek Revival, extended Elmes's ideas toward the production of many more American builders' guides. Lafever followed in the 1830s; his *Beauties of Modern Architecture* contained a long extract from Elmes's "dictionary" of 1823. Lafever's reasons for doing so would have been balm to the spirit of Latrobe: he wished to give the American builder "a more magnified and pleasing idea of his profession . . . more than a mere mechanical art . . . [one that] requires an exclusive and thorough study." The Brethren of the Workshop of Vitruvius would have concurred. This group of masons in New York City, like that around Burlington and Kent in England earlier, included both gentry with an interest in architecture, and carpenter-builders.[264]

One of its members, Levi Weeks (1776–1819), formerly of Deerfield, Massachusetts, set in motion the Anglo-Palladianizing of Greater Tennessee. In 1800 he had rallied the Brethren and the artisans of New York around a nonarchitectural cause: Weeks, then a popular carpenter-builder, had been indicted for the murder of his mistress and for then dumping her body in a public well. He was successfully defended by an august biparty assemblage of legal counsel, headed by Alexander Hamilton, Aaron Burr, and Brockholst Livingston. I once wrote that they took the case for political reasons, but I have recently stumbled upon the fact that these were all fellow Masons, and that Weeks was a member of the Brethren.[265]

When Weeks was in New York, most carpenter-builders, such as Hamilton's protégé John McComb (another of the Brethren), were still reluctant to arrogate to themselves the title "architect." Weeks was not; proudly, and uniquely in New York, he gave that alone as his profession. He continued to do so after he followed his friend Burr to Natchez, Mississippi. Once there, he was no more diffident; proud of Yankee origins and his Vitruvian profession, he wrote a friend "with pleasure . . . that the owner of [his first commission for a completely new house, Auburn] . . . is a Yankey . . . Lyman Harding . . . I love to think and speak of my own countrymen who will not let the saucy Virginian and supercilious Carolinian ride them down." In 1812 Weeks gave Harding, who had been attorney for Burr, "Ionic columns with the Corinthian entablature . . . the first house in the territory on which was ever attempted any of the orders of architecture."[266]

Not quite the first. Winthrop Sargeant, a Massachusetts Federalist who sheltered Weeks after Burr passed from the scene, had commissioned him four years earlier to add a Roman portico to Gloucester, which became his executive mansion when he arrived in Natchez from Boston to become Mississippi's first territorial governor. And Weeks had given the city other classical remodelings: among them Cherokee, a year earlier than Auburn, which was not quite Vitruvian, but quite classical. Thereafter, he found his pace designing and building a bank and a church.

Auburn [52], the product of Weeks and Harding, two Yankees, is an immensely important prototype in American architecture. Its grand, Palladian portico was taken, along with much else in the house, from drawings by Abraham Swan, one of the Burlingtonians.[267] It was thought to be "the handsomest house about Natchez," amazing Southern planters who came to that sophisticated city from raw, central Tennessee (among them Andrew Jackson). And its lesson was reinforced by the anthology of similar lessons assembled by Jefferson and his advisers, Thornton and Latrobe, around the green at Charlottesville.

"Diffusion patterns" are merely dated dots set across a map, to be penciled together into risky hypotheses. But with Auburn at one end of their world and the University of Virginia at the other—two symbols of order and continuity—the Jacksonians of Greater Tennessee had every reason to give themselves an Anglo-Palladian style, since it had been given absolution from truckling to British fashion by American carpenter-builders, by Jefferson, and finally, at the Hermitage, by Old Hickory himself. From the Bluegrass region around Nashville it spread where they spread, to Richard Keith Call's Tallahassee and Sam Houston's Austin.

Call had built as his old leader, General Jackson, had built in Tennessee. Houston was not able to produce anything so grand for his own house, The Wigwam, in Huntsville, Texas, but as governor of the state he too lived in a Tennessee-porticoed mansion [242]. It had been designed by Abner Cook (1814–84), who learned his architecture in Nashville, where the governor of Florida and the governor of Texas had learned their politics.

Farther Afield

The American Greek Revival did not limit itself to Grecian precedents. Following the lead of the regents, it made frequent use of arcade-implying pilasters as well, a Renaissance idea much favored in France and first transferred to New York by Joseph Mangin to give dignity to its city hall. The descendants of that city hall were the Albany Academy of 1826 by Philip Hooker, and Lorenzo in Cazenovia, New York, designed by Hooker's brother, John, for the agent of a Franco-Dutch real estate syndicate led by the Cazenoves of Geneva.[268]

Pilaster-gridded houses spread westward and northward from Albany and Cazenovia, forming a subspecies often cross-pollinating with the columned temple forms that entered the same region from the Arlington House–Perry House–Bowers House tradition. The arched arcades of earlier "regency" buildings and the rectilinear grids of the Mangin–Hooker tradition were often employed to suggest a columned portico on a gable front presented to the street. Then, in the 1850s, the Renaissance refreshed itself yet again from Italy. American arcades developed two "new" Italianate forms, the cubical palazzo style of Florence and the irregular villa-with-campanile beloved by seventeenth-century painters (and supposedly by the ancient Romans themselves). Haviland became very adept at both, especially after he was joined in Philadelphia by an English interior decorator, Hugh Bridport, who had been employed by Latrobe, and the Scotsman John Notman. Thereafter, a new stream of Caledonian-Italianate invention and a renewal of Scottish Enlightenment ideas, now with a somewhat more radical tinge, began to emerge from that city.

As the steamboat began to tame the Mississippi, New Orleans could gratify its propensity to draw upon Philadelphia for financial and artistic support. The arrival of the Latrobes—father, Philadelphian wife, and son—was part of this process. Henry Latrobe died young, but only after he had given the city its first Greek Revival building, in 1814. (It still exists, tucked away at 721 Governor Nichols Street.) His father, Benjamin Henry, did not have opportunities to follow up and work in the Grecian idiom during his two hectic years in New Orleans before his death there in 1821.

The Greek Revival picked up steam when a new group of Northern and Eastern architects arrived a decade later. James Gallier and the brothers Charles and James Dakin came to the delta and gave further training to Henry Howard. Howard was more Hellenistic than Hellenic in his taste; his clients of the 1840s and 1850s erected buildings aspiring to the gaudy grandeur of the Seleucids. The Garden District contains some of them, though his famous Belle Grove, the most extravagant of all the plantations of the South, has fallen to the great river. New Orleans spread its influence to converge with that of

Philadelphia at Natchez, where Stanton Hall, now a museum, shows how Minard Lafever's ornament could be deployed on an enormous scale. Howard's friend and competitor, the Masonic theoretician Lewis Reynolds (1816–79), may have had a hand in Stanton Hall; he certainly built a mansion in New Orleans for Henry S. Buckner, Henry Stanton's partner. At this writing, the Buckner House on Jackson Avenue, long a school, was still resisting demolition. New Orleans has stretches of Greek Revival town houses much like those that once graced New York, Philadelphia, and Baltimore, not on the icy stone scale of Edinburgh or Leningrad but impressive nonetheless.

Belle Grove, near White Castle, Louisiana

Baltimore and New Orleans are contemporaries—their growth began after the Revolutionary War. Architecturally, Baltimore was a slightly older brother to Cincinnati, which grew with the Greek Revival to become by far the largest city in the West. (Cleveland had less than one thousand people in 1830, and Chicago was a huddle of huts on a sand spit.) Not much has been left of Hellenic Cincinnati; even its great Cathedral of St. Peter in Chains, by Henry Walter (1840–45) has been remodeled. Walter was one of the dominant forces in shaping the extraordinary Ohio state capitol in Columbus [46]. In the design competition, he won the "first premium" and was the first supervising architect, but the building actually owes as much to the medicinal changes suggested by Town and Davis, and to the exuberant submission of the Hudson River painter Thomas Cole, as to Walter's own first thoughts.

Another unchronicled Ohio architect was Howard Daniels, a major talent, judging by the Montgomery County courthouse [45] in Dayton, one of the best buildings created in the Western Hemisphere in the first half of the nineteenth century.

No other architectural work of Walter and Daniels is known. In fact, the obituary of Daniels (appearing in *The Horticulturist*) does not mention his work as an architect. He was born in 1815, began working as a landscape gardener on the grounds of the Cincinnati Cemetery, and gained sponsorship from someone to study in Europe. He returned to Cincinnati to practice horticulture but, after winning the competition for the Dayton courthouse in the summer of 1844, he announced that he had "permanently located himself in Dayton . . . prepared to make designs for Public Buildings, Villas, Cottages, Country Seats, Farm Houses, Ornamental Gardens, etc. Also Drawing for the Patent Office, Machinery etc. at the shortest notice and reasonable terms."[269]

Permanency, as Latrobe had discovered long before, was not an easy achievement in those days; by March in the following year, Daniels was back in Cincinnati, where he settled into the superintendency of the Spring Grove Cemetery. In 1853, when he designed Woodland Cemetery in Cleveland, he was described as "an architect of New York City"; it seems that he moved there, hoping to inherit the practice of Andrew Jackson Downing after Downing was drowned in a steamboat disaster. Downing's successor turned out to be Frederick Law Olmsted, but Daniels did run a strong second to the formidable competition of Olmsted and Calvert Vaux in the Central Park design competition. There are wisps of information that Daniels had a hand in the design of Llewellyn Park in New Jersey and the campus of Vassar College. His death occurred in Baltimore, where he was designing Druid Hill Park.[270]

Baltimore, which had already had the benefits of the presence of Latrobe, Mills, Godefroy, Ramee, and the Robert Cary Longs, Senior and Junior, was as fertile an incubator of architectural talent as Bath and Somersetshire had been a half-century earlier. Francis Costigan (1810–65) began his career in Baltimore, though his best work on a residential scale is to be found in Madison, Indiana. Centering upon Costigan's mansions for Francis Lanier [154, 307] and Charles Shrewsbury [308–309], his tiny puzzle-solving residence for himself, his double, speculative houses, and the memory of his grand hotel, Madison is the most diverse assembly of high-quality Grecian work to be found anywhere in America. Costigan also built on a large scale, though his institutions for the deaf and blind in Kentucky and Indiana were destroyed long ago.[271]

Interregional cross references manifest the peripatetics of the architects of the time. Not only did Latrobe, Gallier, and the Dakins migrate from New York and Philadelphia to New Orleans, and Costigan from Baltimore to Madison, Indiana, but the remarkable pirate-architect Bartholomy Lafon was the first of a succession of talents to find their way to Galveston, Texas; Charles Bryant of Maine was there at about the same time as both Henry Howard of Cork and Lewis Reynolds of Norwich, New York.[272] Boston-based Isaiah Rogers (1800–69) produced hotels from Maine to Louisiana, and Ammi B. Young (1798–1874) was the architect of custom houses from Boston [366] to San Francisco.

Reynolds, Howard, and Bryant shared a common affinity for a sort of Regency (in the English usage) Hellenism. Howard demonstrated it in New Orleans in his Garden District residence for Robert Grinnan, which is laid out like one of the villas in Regent's Park. The influence of those villas can also be easily observed in Lafever's and Haviland's designs, in Bryant's work in Maine, and as we noted in our second case study, in Alabama.

Gallier drew up a much simplified version of the Greenhough villa when he was working as an assistant, at the same time Lafever was preparing his *Modern Builders' Guide* of 1833. That sketch became the model for hundreds, perhaps thousands, of American house builders. Others, who knew no more of Greenhough than they did of the Bowerses of Northampton, continued to rely upon patterns set by Ithiel Town. They provided six columns to their clients instead of Greenhough's and Lafever's four.

Greenough Residence (Grove House), in Regent's Park, London

Cosmopolitans such as Nathan Bryan Whitfield, though they lived in remote places, did not limit themselves to the British branch of international neoclassicism. As we have noted, Gaineswood owes a debt to the villas of Potsdam as well as those of London, possibly because Charles Reichardt moved from our first case study to our second, or possibly, as we suggested in the latter, because another German classicist followed him to the United States. Adolphus Heimann (1809–62) arrived in Nashville in the 1830s. His father had been a construction superintendent for Schinkel, a fact of some interest in Nashville, which shared some of the Prussophilia of New York and Charleston. Heimann produced buildings in a wide diversity of styles, including Belmont [318–19] for Adelicia Cheatham.[273]

Sophisticated buildings like Gaineswood did not require the presence of architects or even of architectural books; true, its lush interior ornament is derived from plates in the guides of Lafever, but composition ornament was shipped throughout the South from Northern manufactories, and so, too, was much of that ornamental ironwork that today is identified more with its purchasers in New Orleans and Natchez than with its manufacturers in Cincinnati and Philadelphia.

Architectural historians are, by their nature, playful. Games of all sorts are composed of slides projected upon screens to the delight or despair of students, depending upon whether or not recognition earns credit. How does one parse out a house like Gaineswood? How does one solve other puzzles?

How did Abner Cook get to Austin, Texas, with such an advanced training in Greek Revival style? Who was the architect or builder who made such a unified, consistent composition in Old Washington, Arkansas? Was he the person who produced Myrtle Hill, in the same fashion, but on a much grander scale (eighteen-foot ceilings on the piano nobile), near Gloster, Louisiana, south of Shreveport? Where did Leverett Osborne of West Andover, Ohio, learn of Thomas Jefferson's abandoned plans for Monticello I, or did he compose his house [217] as Jefferson had, with a British Palladian builders' guide in hand?

The architectural history of the Greek Revival raises more interesting questions than these. As in all human affairs, affinities and antipathies are more important in their real unfolding than taxonomy, influence, and precedents. Therefore it would be good to know whether or not, soon before his death,

George Hadfield reached an understanding with his old enemy, Dr. Thornton. Is that why the former felt free to engage William Elliott, though the latter remained the sponsor and employer of Elliott's father? Did Hadfield get the commission for Washington's city hall over Thornton because he had run for office as a Federalist, and the Federalists were (briefly) back in power under new banners? Thornton could rouse himself only to whisper the Federalist sentiments he shared with John Trumbull, the Elliotts, and George Washington Parke Custis. Why else did Jefferson tell Maria Cosway, after Latrobe's death, that Hadfield was America's preeminent architect, yet fail to consult him, along with Latrobe and Thornton, for the University of Virginia?

Friendships and party loyalties are important in such matters, and so, sometimes, are other scruples. Did Latrobe cut his old friend Bartholomy Lafon on the street in New Orleans because it had become too obvious that Lafon had supplemented his income from architecture by piracy? Or was it that Latrobe was himself embarrassed that he had sunk to using an *admitted* pirate, Lafon, and a far less admirable knave, General James Wilkinson, to secure his own commissions? Such things are beyond our reach in this book, though we have tried to extend somewhat the range of matters relevant to understanding the American Greek Revival.[274]

We shall stop here. The real feast for readers of this work will not be the puzzles or the games historians play, but the buildings themselves, as they appear in photographs. This text is intended to provide a framework within which to place those images and as an inducement to go forth and experience the architecture itself.

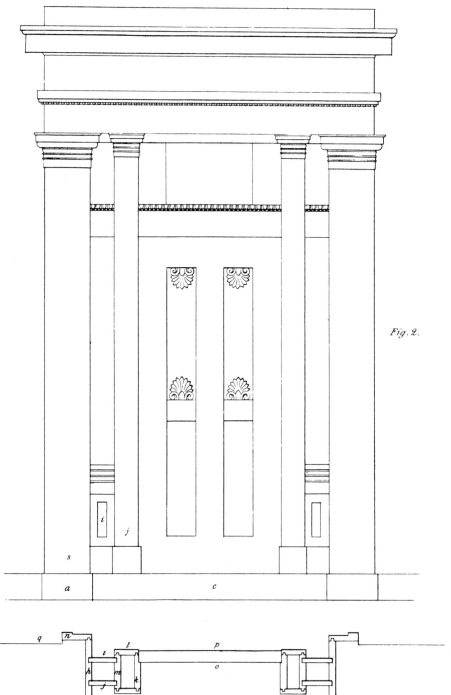

Fig. 2.

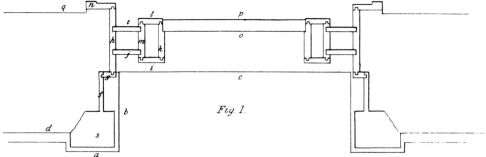

Fig. 1.

Minard Lafever design for a
doorway

Page 353: The state capitol of Tennessee (1845–59), in Nashville, was designed by William Strickland.

Opposite and left: North Carolina's state capitol in Raleigh (1833–40) designed by William Nichols, David Paton, and the firm of Town and Davis

Page 356: The state house in Vandalia, Illinois, was begun in 1836 to designs by John Taylor and William Hodge.

Page 357: Also in Illinois is the Old State Capitol, in Springfield, which was built to designs by John Francis Rague in 1837.

Right: Interior views of the Vandalia state house (*top, left and right*), and the Old State Capitol in Springfield, Illinois *(bottom)*

Opposite: Thomas Jefferson and Jacques-Louis Clerisseau collaborated to design the state capitol in Richmond, Virginia, in 1792.

Opposite and left: The interior spaces and details of Mississippi's Old State Capitol, in Jackson. The portions shown were designed by William Nichols in 1839.

Five courthouses: The Fluvanna County courthouse (*opposite*), in Palmyra, Virginia, was designed in 1831 by John Hartwell Cocke. Norwich, New York's Chenango County courthouse (*left, top*) was built in 1839, as was the Berrian Springs courthouse in Berrian Springs, Michigan (*left, bottom*). The Knox County Courthouse is found in Mount Vernon, Ohio (*right, bottom*), and Rising Sun, Indiana, is home to the Ohio County courthouse (*right, top*).

Page 366: Ammi B. Young's design for Boston's Custom House (1837–47) did not include the tower seen today.

Page 367: The Old Norfolk Academy Building (1840), in Norfolk, Virginia, was designed by Thomas U. Walter and today is that city's Chamber of Commerce building.

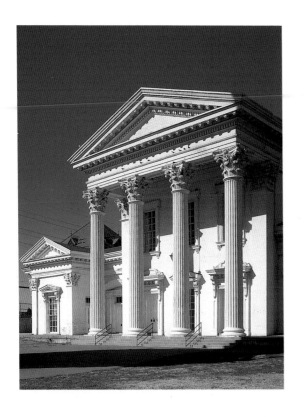

Opposite and left: The Louisville Waterworks complex was designed in 1860 by Theodore R. Scowden; it now houses the Water Tower Art Association.

Pages 370–71: Thomas Jefferson worked with William Thornton and Benjamin Henry Latrobe to create his famous University of Virginia campus (1817–26) in Charlottesville. Shown here are the colonnade (page 370) and the rotunda (page 371).

A collection of five buildings all of which were created for institutional purposes: James H. Dakin was the architect for the Bank of Louisville in 1837 (*left, top*), which today is that city's Actor's Theater; the Naval Hospital (1832) in Portsmouth, Virginia, is the work of John Haviland (*right, top*). Educational institutions include: Charleston College in Charleston, South Carolina (*right, bottom*), the main building of which was designed by William Strickland in 1828–29 and its portico was added in 1850 to designs of Edward B. White; the McKim Free School (*left, bottom*), which was built in Baltimore in 1822; and Washington and Lee University (*opposite*), in Lexington, Virginia, which is the work of John Jordan and Samuel Darst.

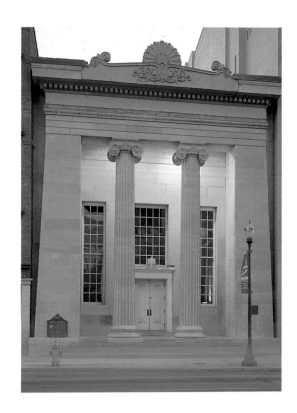

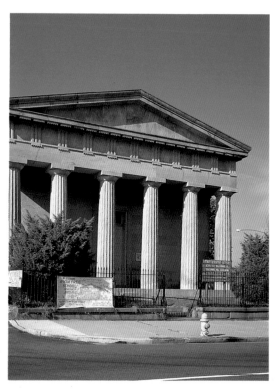

Right: Charles B. Cluskey's Medical College (1834–36), in Augusta, Georgia

Opposite: Basing his work on designs by Asher Benjamin, Benjamin S. Deane created the Baptist church in Sedgewick, Maine, in 1837.

Two Southern Greek Revival churches: Petersburg, Virginia's Tabb Street Presbyterian Church (*right, top, and opposite*) is the work of Thomas U. Walter, who designed it in 1842; the Government Street Presbyterian Church (*right, bottom*) was designed in 1836–37 by James Gallier and Charles and James Dakin.

Pages 378–79: Robert Mills was the architect for the Monumental Church (1814) in Richmond, Virginia.

Opposite: The Beth Elohim Synagogue (1840) in Charleston, South Carolina, was the work of Charles F. Reichardt and Charles B. Tappan, who may have been assisted by James Curtis and George W. Noble.

Left: First Presbyterian Church, in Sag Harbor, New York—also known as Old Whalers Church—was designed in 1844 by Minard Lafever.

A five-stop tour of Greek Revival churches includes: the Congregational church in Ellsworth, Maine (*left, top*), built by Thomas Lord in 1846; the 1845 Presbyterian church in Lexington, Virginia, designed by Thomas U. Walter (*right, top*); Montgomery, Ohio's Universalist church from the 1840s (*right, bottom*); the Racine, Wisconsin, Presbyterian church (*left, bottom*), which was designed by Lucas Bradley in 1851; and Jonesboro, Tennessee's Presbyterian church (1850) is the work of W. H. Clyce (*opposite*).

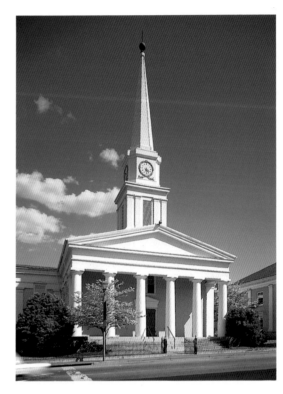

APPENDICES

Appendix A:
A Speculation on Power and Sex
in Greek Revival America

The story is told that some years after David Selznick made a motion picture of her novel, *Gone with the Wind*, Margaret Mitchell was traveling incognito in central Georgia. A series of guides showed her a sequence of classicized creole cottages and one Victorian gem of the 1880s, and told her that each was "the original Tara. . . . Firmly letting in the clutch, Miss Mitchell fled the country of the Taras."[1]

It was too late. Though none of them was her "rambling, antebellum, whitewashed brick structure," an image of a house of the Mississippi delta, not of Piedmont Georgia, had been added by Selznick to our national stock of visual clichés. Thereafter, tour guides and guidebook writers have taken things one step farther and identified Selznick's Tara—which is peripherally columned under a hipped roof, with double galleries—as a paradigm of "the purest Greek Revival."[2]

That it is not. What Selznick gave us back was an American invention, reviving nothing, but telling us much about ourselves in the antebellum period.

The "real" Tara, Mitchell's accurate depiction of the kind of place Scarlett O'Hara might have inhabited, was an up-country product of the New South, as was Scarlett. The plantation headquarters, ruled by women though nominally owned by men, was a machine for dominance, devised to take its place just up the hill from the cotton gin. Mitchell did not invent that sort of

heroine; there were real-life heroines who were lustier and more resilient than she, such as Adelicia Hayes Franklin Acklen Cheatham of Belmont in Nashville. And many ancestresses of Scarlett—voracious, victorious victim-vixens—played roles in novels between 1830 and 1860, contemporarily with the events they described.[3]

In Roman Tennessee, and even more so in Georgia and in the Natchez of immense, colonnaded classical cottages, the houses may seem to the casual visitor to be statements of a rampant phallocracy, a showing off. Yet, as we come to know the inhabitants, we learn that the master of the house had ceased to be master at home (if he ever had been) long before Ashley Wilkes went off to war.[4]

Casual observation is always risky. Close acquaintance is required to avoid accepting appearances too quickly. Here are the words of Ibn Khaldūn (1332–1406): "At the end of a dynasty there often appears some show of power that gives the impression that the senility of the dynasty has been made to disappear. It lights up brilliantly just before it is extinguished, like a burning wick the flame leaps up . . . a moment before it goes out, giving the impression it is just beginning to burn, when in fact it is going out."[5]

In most parts of the United States, the dynasty of founding fathers, as extended by the Age of Jackson, came to an end as a new kind of plantation literature was becoming popular among women readers, composed by Northerners and Southerners alike. *Gone*

[1]Richard Harwell, *Gone with the Wind as Book and Film*. Columbia, SC: University of South Carolina Press, 1983. pp. 52–53.

[2]Ibid.

[3]For Adelicia Cheatham and her ilk, see *Architecture, Men, Women and Money*, pp. 313–18.

[4]While the picture I have presented of the female in charge of the space behind the columns is, I think, a respectable generalization, there were plenty of exploited, impotent, dragooned plantation mistresses. I am grateful to Michael Zuckerman for bringing to my attention the work of Catherine Clinton and Anne Firor Scott, who might sharply disagree with me.

[5]Khaldūn quoted in Michael Wood, *In Search of the Trojan War*. London: British Broadcasting Corporation, 1985. p. 247.

with the Wind, though written a century later, borrows most of its stereotypes from this body of literature. Margaret Mitchell reinvented the dreary planter Ashley Wilkes, the swaggering merchant Rhett Butler, and the man-eating Scarlett O'Hara.

While novels are not history, a concurrence of similar characters in many contemporary novels is a crowd of witnesses testifying to the fact that something is happening, perhaps something noiseless or unaccountable, but something important nonetheless. Along with the reaffirmation of national pride, and the growth of a continental, aggressive masculine culture, the first half of the nineteenth century marked the beginning of a new division of work between the sexes in middle-class America, and, as a consequence, of the feminization of the home. Men may have come to rule the workplace, but that dominion was gotten in trade for the loss of full functioning in aesthetic and domestic life.

The Greek Revival could be seen as a phallic protest at the door in the guise of a statement that there was nothing to protest against, that the home was still a *man's* castle. A little too emphatically it denied the enshrining of the new woman-goddess in a space that, in the Parthenon, was occupied by the gilded figure of Athena.

The temple-house marked out its precinct of calm, of changelessness, of sanctuary. Yet inside it was, in paradoxical America, the most conspicuous arena of change. Males and females were moving apart, tearing *themselves* apart as they did so. There came to be a widening division of roles and specialization of labor on the assembly line of life. Only in our own time are we beginning to heal this breach between the sexes and to learn to share both the workplace and the home.

[6] *Architecture, Men, Women and Money*, p. 320.

[7] Balcombe in Taylor, p. 174.

A Show of Power

John C. Calhoun could be counted on to aver with emphasis the opposite of any truth inconvenient to his myth of the patriarchal South. His boldness was breathtaking; he promulgated a myth in the face of economic fact and psychological fact. Despite the perpetual fear of slave revolt throughout the South, he could write of Southern life as "perfectly harmonized. Hence the harmony, the union, the stability of that section."[6] His classical studies in rhetoric had taught him the value of repetition for emphasis.

Calhoun presented the "little community" of the plantation as independent, "with its master at its head." This image was false on two counts. The true masters of the Southern plantation were the mill owners of Manchester and Lowell, for the plantation depended on an international cotton market. And if one restricted one's vision to the domestic scene, it did not have a master; it was coming under the rulership of its women.

Southern males, like Northern males, wished to feel themselves in charge and proclaimed themselves to be so. They wished to believe their rule to be unchallenged, so they asserted in their architecture what Beverly Tucker's hero said in *George Balcombe*: "I am well pleased with the established order of the universe. I see gradations in everything. I see subordination everywhere."[7]

Did he really? Or is that what he wanted to see? Was the "established order" of the plantation headquarters secure, as its architecture implied?

Among the most anxious and turbulent of peoples, undergoing radical changes in sexual relationships and, simultaneously, an economic revolution, a columnar architecture was both what it said it was and what it betrayed. The screens of columns could not forever exclude the world, nor could they imprison the Southern female. A defensive grid had been set up to preserve the sanctuary of the isolated white family and to mask the murmurs of the slave quarters. But inside the screen was a new kind of woman who was taking charge and, in all probability, a man who wished that the Greek Revival genuinely represented the truth.

By the middle 1850s, new pictures of Southern life were presented in fiction; some novels were sympathetic to the planter class while others were written with abolitionist hostility. Whether or not the author agreed that slavery had "destroyed the planter's initiative and made him passive and indolent," there seemed little dispute that something had "made the woman stronger and increased her status and dignity." Furthermore, "the real focus of fictional plantation life was not the planter but his wife. . . . Alongside the Southern matriarch, the gentleman planter becomes a shadowy figure, hovering in the background, or . . . he disappears altogether and leaves the woman to preside over the family unobstructed."[8]

Daniel Hundley, one of those novelists, gave a picture of the Southern woman as she presided in her columned house: "She it is who rules the destinies of the world, not man." That house may suggest a huge, white-painted version of a Japanese cricket cage, but it was a spider's roost for Hundley. Thomas Nelson Page agreed. The plantation mistress was "the most important personage about the home, . . . the center of all . . . the queen of that realm . . . mistress, manager, doctor, nurse, counsellor."[9]

These instances could be repeated by the score. A change was being observed; a brief equilibrium— marked by an equilibrious architecture—was being upset.

A Postscript on Millwood and The Forest

Two aspects of the life of Wade Hampton II, of Millwood, were stressed in the eulogies delivered at his funeral in Columbia, South Carolina, in 1858. The first was that after the death of his wife he had become Calhoun's ideal patriarch—the nurturer—and how remarkable was this quality among his peers. Employing euphemisms of the time, the *Southern Christian Advocate* spoke of him as he performed "the duties of life [including] that most difficult [one] . . . to his servants, [in which] he most excelled. . . . His humane and considerate treatment of his dependents" offered copious refutation to those who would criticize a "much maligned institution of our Southern states," which the *Advocate* stopped short of calling slavery.[10]

The nurturing male was rare enough. But Hampton, at the end, offered an example of the repentant male, and of one so willing to concede the direction of his life to his women that he would abandon an activity which was his chief joy and his principal distinction. Governor Alfred Huger said of him that he gave up his love of horse racing to please "the wishes of his children, especially 'those pious daughters'. . . . They have taken refuge in the church, and Hampton himself left the turf as an offering to their feelings—*this I know*" [emphasis Huger's].[11]

At the end, Millwood was occupied by those three "pious daughters," deprived of husbands, so the local rumor said, by their having been defiled by their rapacious uncle, the unspeakable John Henry Hammond.

Another spinster lady was the last Gibbons to be a resident of The Forest, William Gibbons's daughter Caroline. This brought things full circle, for it was her mother (according to family lore) who selected the location in the first place, and who determined the

[8]Ibid. pp. 174, 162.

[9]Hundley and Page quoted ibid., pp. 162–63.

[10]*Southern Christian Advocate* quoted in Meynard, p. 191.

[11]Huger quoted ibid.

style of its luxurious interior fittings in anticipation of balls and house parties. After her death, William Gibbons left it in the hands of his overseers, staying at his hotel (Delmonico's) in New York and Savannah.

Only once, in fact, did The Forest serve its original purpose, five years after Caroline's death. Ward McAllister, her brother-in-law—who was living upon his wife's money and providing a lifetime of devotion to Mrs. Astor—realized a dream in 1862. Thirty years later he told of engaging "an army of scrubbing women" to shine up the place. Then he assured that "fish, vegitables [sic] and flowers . . . [would] be sent up by train daily from New York [along with] ices, bon-bons, and cakes. [I] . . . sent up my wines, but no Madeira, as I knew there was enough . . . in the wine cellars of that old house to float a frigate. . . . The conservatories were full of orange and lemon trees." Old Thomas Gibbons, "my wife's grandfather," was scrubbed up too, to be presented as "a distinguished lawyer" and, in the presence of the ghost of the old Tory who was the source of all the Madeira, McAllister "lived for ten days as thoroughly an English life as one could have lived at a country house in England."[12]

Northern Domesticity

Ward McAllister's dream was incompatible with the American Greek Revival of either Andrew Jackson or Nicholas Biddle, however.

The Forest had been the residence of William Gibbons. In his crabbed and, at the end, irritable way, Ward McAllister's father-in-law was one of those most responsible for the creation of an American economy of continental sweep. He was a Southerner who came north; The Forest was not the headquarters of a planta-

tion but of an agribusiness with industrial and financial subsidiaries. Thus it was no longer Southern, but American.

Gibbons was not a farmer but a professional manager; though he inherited a substantial position, he augmented it, and thereby encouraged others, largely in the North, who were forming a new middle class of industrial managers. (There was industry in the South, and an industrial middle-class life. There were also portions of the North, especially in the Hudson Valley, where agricultural life was very much like that of the slave system in the South. But the means of economic organization, of generating wealth and showing power, were evolving quite differently in the two sections.) Males were offered new power at work—and outside the home. Each rising manager might hope that, if *he* worked hard, *he* might come to own and manage a company of his own, with a work force to boss and, at home, an obedient female. One primer stated the reward system: "Be attentive to your work, be sober and religious, and you will find a devoted and submissive wife; you will have a more comfortable home than many of the higher classes of Europe. . . . Work."[13]

They did work at it, and they consumed the poisoned fruit. They had wrested from women power outside the home, even before the onset of Jacksonian democracy. Universal *manhood* suffrage replaced property qualifications; all *white* citizens could vote. That left out blacks (some of whom might once have voted if they held enough property) and women. The mass of men were elevated while the mass of women were kept in their place.

Males who chose not to be managers gathered themselves into professional associations, one of the purposes of which was to eliminate the competition of

[12]Quoted in Cunningham, p. 54.

[13]Remini, *Revolutionary Age*, p. 7.

women. In the eighteenth century, women had been renowned as practitioners of the healing arts, including midwifery. In the nineteenth century, doctoring became a profession, and doctors were men. But midwifery continued, and the children midwifery helped bring into the world were thereupon raised by women.

In the eighteenth century, women had kept stores with their husbands or worked as artisans in the home with full knowledge of "the business." The stereotypical middle-class woman now remained at home, while men went to work, where the books were kept by male accountants. (It is true that in some places the work force was overwhelmingly female and that in such places, despite long hours and ugly conditions, going to work sometimes brought women opportunities they never had at home.)

The middle-class American woman might be treated as so fragile as to be useless outside the home. She might be told that her children were the property of the husband and could be taken from her at his direction; but she was beginning to fight back. Women were appearing in public, from Seneca Falls to Savannah, to contend that they "lived in a kind of legal bondage to their husbands." When one recalls the endemic alcoholism of the Southern planters, one can imagine what this meant: as Mary Chesnut said, "for no crime a person may be condemned to live with one [a drunk] for thirty years."[14]

In the South and in the North, women found allies among each other, among the clergy, the artists—and the children. The "home," as the preserve of gentility, was an invention of the Greek Revival period, as Robert Remini has noted: "It was in the Jacksonian era that exaggerated, if not distorted, views of women as to their gentleness, frailty, piety, morality, and

purity developed. During this period, the pronounced male affection for his mother—'Momism'—is first observed. The higher woman rose on her pedestal, the more she lost ground in attempting to gain equality with males."[15]

Momism, the cult of the passionless proprietress of the immaculate "home," often to be called "Mother" rather than "Wife" (a familiar though gruff term of the preceding age), did not exist earlier. Even that sheltered emotional workshop known as "adolescence" may have begun to be devised as early as this.

American women did not desecrate herms (see Appendix B), nor (so far as I have been able to learn) did they saw down columns. In the industrial, specialized areas developing in the North, a few women of extraordinary courage and energy commenced the long campaign for suffrage and equality in the public world. Others, probably the great majority of middle-class women, simply concentrated on assuming dominance in the realm of feeling and of the arts. In the South, men like Ashley Wilkes withdrew into the "private pursuit of sensibility."[16] In the North, many sought, instead, the solace of the saloon and the consoling arbitrariness of power over the office or the plant. Having "removed the father from the home, . . . mothers played a greater role in raising their children. . . . The child-rearing literature substituted maternal love for paternal discipline. Separated from work and worldly intrigue, the home became in Jacksonian America an isolated repository of virtue; mother was its symbol."[17]

The words *separated* and *isolated* resonated through the literature of the North, while *caged* echoed through the South. Catharine Beecher told her sister in 1842 that "in no country has such constant care

[14]Listing of women's disadvantages is by Taylor (p. 166), from which also comes the quotation on living with a drunk (p. 169).

[15](Remini, *Revolutionary Age*, p. 8) I am informed by Michael Zuckerman that Nancy Cott, Linda Kerber, Jan Lewis, Ruth Bloch, and many other fine scholars have set the arrival of Momism, female frailty and purity, and the cult of the home at an earlier period than the Age of Jackson, say 1800 to 1830. They may be right, and neither Remini nor I profess to be a family or gender historian. But I have also been admonished that these changes did not become important until after the Civil War.
Let us assume that Remini is wrong, and that the change of gender valences in the space behind the columns occurred earlier. What then? The *phalloi* become pathetic notes, pinned by males to the door, rather than the final expressions of an anxious sense that something was going on that made them uncomfortable at the midriff.

[16]Zuckerman quoted from a letter to the author of December 15, 1988.

[17]Rogin, p. 49.

been taken, as in America, to trace two distinct lines of action for the two sexes . . . in two pathways which are always different." She did not seem to lament her observation that "the women of the United States are confined within the narrow circle of domestic life. [She was not thinking of the women in the mills.] . . . In civil and political affairs, American women take no interest or concern. . . . [But] in matters pertaining to the education of their children . . . and in all questions relating to morals or manners, they have superior influence."[18]

[18]Beecher quoted in Davis, pp. 14–17.

The education of the children, including the male children, was becoming a sphere within which the woman had "superior influence," in large part because many men had less and less of value to impart to their sons. In the Northern factory towns, the diminished male, even if the title deeds were his, departed his house at dawn and became a visitor at dusk. Dim and dull, he was an inadequate example to any son. Even the great industrial managers of the end of the century could no longer gain the respect commanded by the earlier entrepreneurs. A conspiracy of respectables, including, perhaps, his own wife, would find his cigar-chewing vulgarity embarrassing and instruct his own sons to look to more-elegant models.

In their autobiographies, male children reared in these "homes" recalled reciprocal hostility with their fathers and the unconditional love of their mothers. Where farming and ranching remained the primary occupations of the family, fathers and sons might still hunt or fish together or jointly tend the crops and animals. Transmittable skills still passed from father to son. Some people, such as the Amish, refused to permit external forces to pull the traditional family apart. Their autobiographies were different. In these areas the Greek Revival did not take hold, perhaps because it was expensive or, perhaps—for the more complex reasons suggested here—it was not needed.

Proclamation and Presentation

In the 1830s the feminization of the home had only begun. Men were fighting to retain their integrity—their entirety—and so, from the other side, were women. The forces pulling them apart were very strong, but there are poignant instances in letters of the time in which males protested that they were *not* ready to be turned into engines of gain, nor did they wish to abandon their homes and children emotionally.

The Greek Revival came to an end well before phallocracy degenerated into second childhood. Infantilism was the offspring of Momism, the ultimate, ironic conclusion of a sequence of dislocations that began with Jane Crow and proceeded into the stylomania that implied, among many other things, illusory male dominance of the doorstep; it could not survive long in an era in which both sexes were impoverished and declined into torpid, middle-class gentility. By 1860, Victoria began to reign—even in America. The Civil War ruptured all continuities. Building stopped. When it resumed, the symbols of phallocracy were not to be seen (exceptions noted elsewhere notwithstanding). Architecture molted; it adopted the elements of women's costume—layers of dark-hued materials—in the last half of the nineteenth century.

As the rupture of personality and the division of the sexes proceeded, the "conspiracy" of middle-class women to own the children and the *temenos* was joined by some of the clergy and by artists who would have had ART capitalized, and sterilized as well. Unpolluted by bourgeois corruption—though their art was, of course, for sale—artists might keep themselves a little apart and somewhat patronizing. This artist–consumer distinction had occurred in the Revolutionary period, but it was deepened by this bifurcation of male society preceding that between the sexes of the middle class. The Protestant clergy drew upon a tradition that reached back to colonial days when family worship was the central liturgy, and the religious revival of the nineteenth century built upon that tradition. (Always, in this discussion, are omitted those families that did not make such a division because they were too poor to survive without the hard labor of the women, or too rich to wish to do so—for that would have made the men entirely idle.)[19]

So long as middle-class males were willing to grind out their lives answering the "pressing needs of business" (as *Godey's Lady's Book* sweetly put it) and ignored the fact that the home was the workplace of women, middle-class women, consorting with clergy and artists, had no obligation to offer the men much voice in what was done there. Who wants to contend with phallocracy out in the soot and sweat? Sarah C. Edgerton permitted herself to aver that a woman's "operations are in private . . . [not in] a more open and blustering sphere of duty. . . . She wants . . . not a character, power and independence which erects 'liberty poles,' and shouts 'freedom.'"[20]

As the feminization of the home proceeded, there came to be considerable irony in the presence of "poles" set up according to the classical orders, in front of that "center and sanctuary of our social sympathies—HOME."[21]

By the 1870s, women were told by their magazines and instruction books to treat men as "only children of a larger growth, to be loved and cared for . . . in the same way as their real children." Eliza Duffey wrote that it "is the motherly element which is . . . to be the salvation of the world. The higher a woman rises in moral and intellectual culture . . . the more pure and perfect and predominating becomes her motherhood. The real woman regards all men, be they older or younger than herself, not as possible lovers, but as a sort of step-sons towards whom her heart goes out in motherly tenderness."[22]

So much for Mom and her infantalized mate; what of the home? The unfolding of a long process, begun in the 1820s or even earlier, was described by Mrs. A. J. Graves later in the nineteenth century and immortalized by James Thurber in a cartoon after the process had little farther to go: Woman and Home had become a composite animal like the Sphinx: "To woman it belongs . . . to elevate the intellectual character of her household. . . . The men of our country . . . find little time for the cultivation of science and general literature."[23]

She mentions neither art nor architecture, but one must assume the men were to have little time for them as well, for their "absorbing passion for gain, and the pressing demands of business [engrossed] their whole attention."[24]

Mrs. Graves, dancing upon the grave of the Renaissance Man, was willing on occasion to pause, wipe her dewy brow, and reach out to "draw her husband away from his constricted sphere of thought." Together perhaps, they might then stroll to her parlor, where the clergyman or the architect awaited, and the husband might be permitted "to enter with her upon a more extended field of observation and reflection."[25]

Who would rule the home? Who would preside over the new, domestic *temenos*, standing "apart, neither subject to overlooking or overhearing" the masculine turmoil of commerce? "The house should be within an enclosure sacred to it."[26] And within? The figure of Athena—or perhaps Hestia.

[19]McDannell, in one of a series of striking distinctions between Roman Catholic and Protestant versions of the Christian home in this period, points out that the Irish Catholic tradition "separated the sacred space of the church from that of the home. . . . Whereas Protestant writers had to cope with men moving away from the home, Catholic authors had to create a home to drive men toward." (McDannell, p. 124) I have found no major Greek Revival houses built by Roman Catholics in the United States except those of the Croghans of Pittsburgh, although there may be some others. And it is also interesting to observe how few Catholic churches were built in the Greek Revival style. The reasons for this, in part ethnic, in part symbolic, include the following: the Church still had apprehensions about the pagan Greeks, and about the "heretical" Eastern Orthodox Greeks. The Irish Catholics had no Greek Revival tradition; literate Irish Catholics were aware that Rome never conquered Ireland, and German Catholics rejoiced in lively neo-Baroque and Gothic revivals. Wealth—or lack thereof—was not a factor: no one any longer believes the canard that there were no rich Catholics in the Greek Revival period.

[20]*Godey's Lady's Book* and Edgerton quoted, ibid., pp. 75–7.

[21]For the house as sanctuary, see authors quoted and cited ibid., p. 25.

[22]Duffey, writing in 1876, quoted by Harvey Green, *The Light of the Home: An Intimate View of the Lives of Women in Victorian America* (New York: Pantheon Books, 1983), p. 57.

[23]Mrs. Graves quoted in Davis, pp. 19–20.

[24]Ibid.

[25]Ibid.

[26]Ware quoted in McDannell, p. 46.

Grandmothers

Lewis Mumford's "commonest axiom" was that "every generation revolts against its fathers and makes friends with its grandfathers." Though the survivors of the Civil War could not make friends with their symbolic grandfathers, the inaccessible founding fathers, they found it easy to make friends with their grandmothers, the feminine spirits of the colonial past.

The thought of such an alliance was abroad at midcentury and, increasingly, beyond. One of Longfellow's characters in *Hyperion* spoke of "falling in love with one's own grandmother,"[27] and Henry James presented the same syndrome when, in *The Sense of the Past*, Ralph Pendrel becomes so infatuated with the family portraits in his London house that he falls in love with a female ancestor, the spirit of grandmotherhood.

That spirit was very powerful in the Gothic Revival movement and in the later rediscovery of the shingled, rambling Queen Anne colonial style in the 1870s and 1880s. Perhaps that is why it was associated with a queen. The full career of this feminine architecture lies beyond the boundaries of this book, but we have already observed its essential preconditions as they moved beneath the surface of the Greek Revival period.

Though the Greek Revival spread across America through pattern books written by males largely for males, and though it placed phallic pagan symbolism at the threshold, many a "Christian Home" developed behind these screens of columns. Middle-class women formed alliances with males (not their husbands) who were specialized in religious observance, aesthetic activity, and moral instruction. Mothers became the strongest forces determining life during childhood, along with parsons (and as the century wore on, priests or rabbis), schoolmasters or schoolmistresses and, among the upper middle class, instructors in the arts. Fathers faded.[28]

As a result, if a son were to differentiate himself from anybody, he had to differentiate himself from his mother—a new requirement in American psychological history—and from the mother's male accomplices. He would have to turn as willingly as did his sisters to the grandmothers to escape his omnipresent mother. (This would be especially true among middle-class families; in working-class families, the mother was often at work out of the home, leaving the grandmother to tend the children.)

And who were the grandmothers? They were the ancient ones, who lived in Houses of Seven Gables, houses dun colored and consolingly full of the smells of canning and old leather, irregular and crannied, where one could play and hide, eat pickles and cookies, and be indulged.

In the 1860s and early 1870s, a time as fraught with emulative anxieties as the 1920s, nothing could compete with fashions brought from elsewhere to fill the void of sorrow and shame, even the fashions of the meretricious Paris of Napoleon III. Mansard roofs were everywhere. But thereafter, in the countryside, the small towns, and the suburbs—even the resorts— an acceptable American past was slowly rediscovered. The Queen Anne led the way to a shingled informality that could hardly be said to be patriotic—what is patriotic about colonialism? But the country had had enough patriotism. It wanted something at once undemanding and vaguely respectful of a shared past. The Shingle Style offered just what an exhausted nation required.

And the country might forget its recent past. The Greek Revival seemed to have been dead a long time.

[27] Longfellow quoted in Lowenthal, pp. 116–7.

[28] For the alliance of parsons and artists to middle-class Protestant women, see Ann Douglas, *The Feminization of American Culture* (New York: Knopf, 1977).

APPENDIX B:
SOME QUESTIONS ABOUT COLUMNS

In Greece, and later in America, there were many, many columns, and many phalluses. The phallus is a symbol of male potency, taking the form of an oversize, permanently erect member. It is not a penis; the distinction between the two could readily be made, for both were conspicuous in Athens, if one accepts the testimony of Eva C. Keuls, one of the handful of female classicists in the world: "As foreigners were astonished to see, Athenian men habitually displayed their genitals and their city was studded with statues of gods with phalluses happily erect."[1]

These herms, or shrines to Hermes, were everywhere, at crossroads and downtown intersections. A herm at the doorstep was the first work of sculpture one encountered upon visiting the home of a friend: a four-sided column with an old man's head, no arms or legs but (according to some, but not all, surviving examples, and some, but not all, classical scholars) testicles and an erect, enlarged penis. (This is, in fact, still the first object one finds when visiting a friend among unwesternized peoples on Timor, the Celebes, Borneo, and Nias.)[2]

In the Athens of Socrates and Plato, so many of these votive objects were concentrated in one area near the Agora that it was called "the Herms." The worship of male libido was not only on static display; it received required ritual performance at regular times and, for this reason, Tragedy and Comedy were born. They came as a liturgy at the height of the festivals of a Dionysiac religion that arose from the worship of that libido. The cults of Hephaestus and Asclepius had their own phallic processions and choreography, during the reign of what Keuls calls "the phallocracy."[3]

When a distinguished architectural historian such as Peter Kidson states that it required several centuries for the Athenians to develop temple forms with columns all around to express their complex of religious ideas and psychological needs, one is free to wonder why. Perhaps it was because those ideas became, over that span, increasingly male centered. When Kidson comments that "the most conspicuous effect of these developments was to call into special prominence the column as a unit of decoration," following Keuls's line of sight one can juxtapose the column and the herm, which was probably becoming obtrusive at about the same time.[4]

Athenian architecture is available to us only in a ruined state and, so to speak, are the fragments of ancient architectural criticism. But from surviving scraps we can be sure that much classical architecture was seen in its own time as bluntly phallic. If our architects who revive the use of those forms have done so with their Lucian or Vitruvius before them, they may be enjoying a quiet joke all along. Allan Greenberg, for example, remodeled the study of the United States secretary of state in 1984–85 in so meticulous a Hellenic style that the classicist George Hersey concluded that, "like Ithiel Town before him, Greenberg unconsciously preserved the meaning of the forms simply by copying precedent."[5]

[1] Keuls, p. 2. One cannot safely accept her account on all counts.

[2] I have not visited the remoter portions of Indonesia, but the Danish anthropologist Thorkil Vanggaard commented upon the similarities of the wooden doorstep statues there and the herms of Doric Greece in his *Phallos: A Symbol and Its History in the Male World* (London: Cape, 1972), p. 59.

[3] Keuls, pp. 1–2.

[4] Kidson's essay appears in Finley, p. 382.

[5] Hersey, pp. 30–31.

It is consequently delightful to imagine a classically trained secretary of state, say George Shultz, in the midst of Greenberg's animal sacrifices and phallic symbolism, meditating upon the devices necessary to guard the republic. With his Lucian or Vitruvius before him, Shultz, a learned man, might find the passage in which Lucian called the columns of the Temple of the Dea Syria at Hieropolis *phalloi*, or the frequent instances in which Vitruvius likened columns to naked men. It is not whimsical to suggest that temples surrounded by columns were, essentially, very long pauses—stationary expressions—in a phallic parade of "human-scale phalloi carried in processions," or clusters of those "colossal ones . . . erected throughout the Greek-speaking world."[6] These were not pillars of salt, subject to dissolution in rain or flood, but pillars of stone.

Hersey's research cut through a millennium of usage to the etymology of the original Greek. All three of the chief Greek orders, though especially the Doric, carried implications of the celebration of masculine supremacy over the female, as well as the conquest of other tribes. He examines the first Dorian shrines, and finds that they were erected to celebrate occasions in which the victors killed their enemies "by the spear, accompanied by sexual menace." He sees those at Paestum as intentionally evoking the memory of "files of gigantic warriors marching ashore, armed and menacing, bearing aloft their weapons and supplies." Though the Ionic is sometimes thought to be feminine, Ion was a male, and as Hersey points out, the associations of the Ionic "are as bloody as those of the Doric, if not more so." Nor was there anything sweet or seemly about the origins of the Corinthian. Once again, sexual violence was present; "to Corinthize, so to speak, means to have sex with a prostitute"—not with just any prostitute, but with a woman forced into temple prostitution.[7]

Suddenly, after 1825, Americans erected tens of thousands of columns. It is doubtful that all but a handful of those who built them knew the full symbolic significance of what they were doing, not even Ithiel Town. But, as Hersey says of Town, one cannot traffic in potent symbols without contamination.

It is worth noting that an architecture presenting columns on the exterior was not a revival of Greek domestic practice. Except for the presence of herms at the doorstep, ancient Greek houses could be described as modest. Unlike Greek Revival houses, they demurely hid their columns inside, within a courtyard; the herm had made its statement at the door.

Athenian domestic architecture did not have porticos or colonnades on the exterior façades. It was diffident in public display of large-scale reproductions of phallic images, reserving them for public buildings. The Romans scrupulously reserved the use of porticos for temples, the habitations of the gods; even in its degeneracy the senate begrudged the assumption of such potent symbolism to ornament the palaces of godemperors.

When one thinks of externalizing phallic architecture by putting porticos on the outside of buildings, one thinks of Palladio (1508–80). Likewise, when one thinks of portraits of eminent men wearing ornamental codpieces stating the same theme, one thinks of Palladio's contemporary, Bronzino (1503–72), and of England's King Henry VIII, who reigned from 1509 to 1547. This phallic dawn of the Renaissance passed quickly; Shakespeare attributed such display only to fools and madmen.

What is one to think about Palladio's inversion of the Greek (and Roman) villa form, disrobing it to place the columns on the exterior? Is this strutting a sign of

[6] Ibid. p. 52.

[7] Ibid. pp. 53, 58, 63, pp. 64 ff.

humanist Renaissance pride? Does it merely manifest a diminished sensibility for the balance struck by earlier peoples between the male sort of human pride and a reverence for other powers in the universe? Or does it represent a dulling of a symbolic sense?

And what does all this suggest about the rise and fall of the American Greek Revival? A book like this one, which cannot seek to answer inquiries that admit of no dispositive responses, may at least pose such questions for rumination on long airplane and automobile journeys.

Appendix C: A Gazetteer of Important Greek Revival Buildings in the United States Today

(Note: This Gazetteer is arranged alphabetically by state, then by municipality. Those buildings that have been included in the photograph sections of this volume have the appropriate page numbers in square brackets.

I have devised a system to indicate those buildings that deserve special efforts—or detours—to see:

    *   of special interest

    **   worth a detour

    ***   worth a journey

    ****   worth a long journey

And, finally, unless otherwise indicated, all houses included here are private. Some may be available to visitors through local, advance arrangements.)

ALABAMA

Athens:

Founders Hall, Athens State College (1843–45) Hiram H. Higgins   east side of Beaty Street

Robert Beaty House (1826, remodeled to Greek 1845) Hiram H. Higgins   211 South Beaty Street

Autaugaville:

Ivy Creek Methodist Church (1854) 8½ miles west of town on Alabama route 14
Unusually intact, with slave gallery

Camden:

Franklin Beck House (c. 1845) 312 Clifton Street

Youpon (1847–48) south of Canton Bend on County Road 19

Cherokee:

Barton Hall, or Cunningham Plantation * (1847–49) south side of old Memphis Road, east of Buzzard Roost Creek (Private)
Extraordinary central stair hall; a counterpart in England is Kingstone Lisle in Oxfordshire

Decatur:

State Bank Building (1834–36) southwest corner of Bank Street and Wilson Avenue

Demopolis:

Dayton Methodist Church (1849–50) Alabama route 25, 8 miles south of US 80

Gaineswood **** (1842–60) General Nathan Bryan Whitfield (?)   805 South Cedar Street [pages 149 and 312–13]. Open to the public
The most interesting fusion of Prussian, English Regency, and American neoclassical ideas in American architecture—beautifully restored and maintained

Eufaula:

Lewis Lewellen Cato House (1859) 823 West Barbour Street
One-story frame house, five-bay front, set-back wings (forms a T-plan), balustraded porch

Eutaw:

Catlin-Wilson-Herndon-Dunlap House (1844–45) 237 Wilson Avenue

First Presbyterian Church (1851) David R. Anthony northwest corner of Wilson and Main streets

Kirkwood, or *Dr. H. A. Kirksey House* (1850s) northeast intersection of Mesopotamia Street and Kirkwood Drive [page 241]

Florence:

George Washington Foster House, or *Courtview* (1855) John Ballinger or Adolphus Heimann (?)   north end of Court Street, on University of Alabama campus

Forkland:

Rosemount ** (c. 1835–40) William Nichols (?)   between County Road 19 and US 43, 0.2 mile north of County Road 19, midway between Eutaw and Demopolis
Immense, ballroom-size cupola, like that of Nichols's Hayes Plantation in North Carolina
Thornhill (c. 1835–40, though possibly remodeled in 1850s) William Nichols (?)   0.1 mile north of County Road 19, approx. 4.2 miles northwest of Forkland

Gainesville:

Austin Hall (1844) ranch-style Greek Revival
The Magnolia (c. 1845) another ornament for a lovely village

Greensboro:

Magnolia Grove, or Hobson Memorial (1835) Colonel Isaac Croom   1002 Hobson Street

Huntsville and vicinity:

Bibb-Bradley-Bierne House (c. 1835) 303 Williams Street
Northern Bank of Alabama, now First Alabama Bank of Huntsville (1835–40, often remodeled) George W. Steele   northwest corner of Jefferson Street and Fountain Row
Belle Mina, or Thomas Bibb House (c. 1826) between Mooresville and Belle Mina
Oak Place (1840–44) George W. Steele's own house   808 Maysville Road

Sober exterior hides split-level plan
Oak Lawn (c. 1845) George W. Steele (?)   Meridianville Pike

Mobile:

Barton Academy, now Public Schools Office (1835–37) James Gallier, Charles and James H. Dakin   504 Government Street [page 51]
Carolina Hall (c. 1845, remodeled 1880s and c. 1917) George B. Rogers   76 South McGregor Avenue (Spring Hill)
Government Street Presbyterian Church ** (1836–37) James Gallier, Charles and James H. Dakin   300 Government Street [page 376]
Candidate for title of America's most beautiful Greek Revival church
Christ Episcopal Church (1838–40) Charles and James Dakin (?) and Cary Butt   Government Street [page 54]
Marshall-Esleva House (1853) 152 Tuthill Lane
Hellenized creole cottage with recessed wings
Oakleigh, or *Dennison House* (1833–38) James W. Roper   350 Oakleigh Place, at Savannah Street [page 229]
Old City Hospital, now Mobile County Department of Pensions and Securities (1833–36) William George   850 Saint Anthony Street
Fourteen Tuscan columns across front, Roman Doric columns at basement level
Stewartfield (c. 1850) 4307 Old Shell Road
Semicircular ballroom at rear
Washington Fire Engine Company No. 8 (c. 1851) 7 North Lawrence

Montgomery:

Alabama State Capitol (1851) east end of Dexter Avenue
Figh-Gilnmer House (1844–47) 235 South Court Street
William Knox House * (c. 1848) Stephen Decatur Button   South Perry Street
Grand-scale portico and interior trim from Minard Lafever

John H. Murphy House (1851) 22 Bibbs Street
Owens-Teague House, now Chamber of Commerce offices (1848) Bery Owens   468 South Perry Street
Interior with fluted freestanding Corinthian columns

Pittsview vicinity:
Glennville Plantation, or *Americus Mitchell House* * (1842–44; octagonal dependency added 1850s, refurbished 1920 and 1937)   west side of US 431, about 5.1 miles south of Hatchechubbee Creek Bridge

Selma:
Stoutenborough Hall (c. 1850) Alabama Route 41, 20 miles south of town
Sturdivant Hall * (1853–55) Thomas Helm Lee   713 Mabry Street
Mabry-Jones House (1849–50) 629 Tremont Street

Talladega:
Masonic Female Institute, now Manning Hall (1850) Hiram H. Higgins   205 East South Street (see also Higgins's work in Athens, AL)

Talladega County:
Orangevale (1851) near Winterboro
Six slender, marble-based, fluted columns with bell-like capitals; somewhat similar to Mount Ida (burned 1956)

Tuscaloosa:
Alexander Dearing House (1838) 2111 14th Street
James H. Dearing House (c. 1834, remodeled in 1922 and 1957) William Nichols (?)   421 Queen City Avenue
University of Alabama: Once an assemblage of splendid buildings by William Nichols; all have been destroyed (Civil War) or sadly remodeled, but some sense of his mastery can be gleaned from:
Gorgas House (1828–29, remodeled often)
President's House (1839–41, remodeled often) Michael Barry

Tuskegee:
Varner-Alexander House, now President's House for Tuskegee Institute (1854–57, altered in 1920s and 1950s) [page 156]
U-shaped colonnade

Uniontown:
Pitts Folly (1851–52)   south side of Alabama 21

ARKANSAS

Little Rock:
Old State House, now the Arkansas History Museum (1833–36) Gideon Shryock   300 West Markham Street [pages 362–63]
Elegantly detailed Doric temple with wings; appearance now considerably simplified by removal of statuary (mob action occasioned by classic undress)

Washington:
A simple Greek Revival village of the 1840s and 1850s. Some of its best buildings are: *Grandison Royston House*, *Augustus Garland House*, *Methodist Church*, and *Johnson House*

CALIFORNIA

Benicia:
First California State Capitol (1853)

Mariposa:
County Courthouse (1854–66) being rehabilitated in 1988

Monterey:
Merritt House and *Larkin House*: With their barely perceptible touches of the Greek, these houses might have been built in Brazil in the 1680s. Open to the public

San Francisco:

Old United States Mint, now Monetary Museum (1870) Alfred B. Mullet   Mission and 5th streets
Stone building, pedimented portico supported by Tuscan Doric columns, very late yet very effective

Wilmington:

Phineas Banning House (1864) Lakme Avenue and M Street. Open to the public
Double portico of squared pillars with observatory atop

CONNECTICUT

Chester:

Three Greek houses dating from the 1820s, possibly designed by Ithiel Town: *John Gilbert House, Clark Smith House*, and *Hamilton Bates House*

Middletown:

Samuel Russell House, now part of Wesleyan University * (1828–30) Town and Davis   Wesleyan University campus [pages 153 and 304]. Open to the public
Splendid small mansion, without the standard Town and Davis wings; Corinthian columns, open plan

Mystic:

Elias Brown House * (1835)
One of the finest of the Bowers House descendants

DISTRICT OF COLUMBIA

National Portrait Gallery, originally U.S. Patent Office *** (1840) Robert Mills, William D. Elliot, and Ithiel Town   between 7th, 9th, and G streets
Accretions to a masterful core; wonderful interior spaces by Mills
Treasury Building (1842) Robert Mills   1500 Pennsylvania Avenue, NW

Including accretions and amendments
U.S. District Court Building, formerly *Washington City Hall* *** (1817–25) George Hadfield   Indiana Avenue between 4th and 5th streets [page vi]
One of America's first and finest Greek Revival buildings

FLORIDA

Apalachicola:

Trinity Episcopal Church (1838) prefabricated in New York

Bradenton:

Gamble Mansion (c. 1840)
Proto-Doric colonnade around tabby core; house-within-a-house

Tallahassee:

The Grove (1829 ?–36) Adams and First avenues
Four-columned portico of the Tennessee type; residence of Richard K. Call, the Jacksonian–Unionist governor of Florida—Florida's Sam Houston
The Columns, or *William Williams House*, or *Bank of Florida*; now the Chamber of Commerce (1831) 100 North Duval Street. Open to the public
Combination residence and bank (see also Erie, PA, and Natchez, MS)

GEORGIA

Athens:

Chapel (1831–33) Charles B. Cluskey   on the University of Georgia campus
A. P. Dearing House (1850–56) 338 South Milledge [page 244]
Phi Kappa Hall (1836) University of Georgia campus
President's Home (1855) 570 Prince Avenue
Joseph H. Lumpkin House (1843) 248 Prince Avenue

Taylor-Grady House (1845) 634 Prince Avenue
Dr. Marcus Franklin House (1847) 1022 Prince Avenue

Augusta:
Medical College ⋆ (1834–36) Charles B. Cluskey 642 Telfair Street [page 374]
Robert Reid House, or Montrose (1849) 2249 Walton Way

Columbus:
Robert Alexander House (1845) 1543 Second Avenue
John Woolfolk House (1840s) 1615 12th Street
Swift-Kyle House (1840s) 303 12th Street
Wynn-Butler House (1812) 40 Wynnton Road

Eatonton:
Mosley-Adams House (1837) 200 Church Street
Reid-Green House ⋆ (1855) 208 Church Street
Reid-Lawrence House (c. 1840) Wayne Street
Panola Hall (c. 1850) 400 North Madison
Slade-Harris House ⋆ (1836) 206 Madison

La Grange:
James F. Culberson House (1840s) 207 Broad Street
Philip Hunter Greene House (1843) Vernon Street
Benjamin Hill House, or *Bellevue* ⋆ (1855) 204 Bellevue Street
Splendidly restored, with complete surround of columns rare in the Southeast

Macon:
City Hall (1836–60) 700 Poplar Street
Holt-Peeler-Snow House (c. 1840) Elam Alexander 1129 Georgia Avenue
Hugenin-Proudfit House (1843–44) Elias Carter (?) 1261 Jefferson Terrace
Napier House ⋆ (c. 1847) Elias Carter (?) 156 Rogers Avenue
Napier-Smith House (c. 1846) 2215 Napier Avenue
E. A. Nisbet House (1844) 988 Bond Street

Overlook, or *Cowles-Bond House* ⋆ (1836–50) 988 Bond Street

Milledgeville:
Executive Mansion ⋆⋆ (1838) Charles B. Cluskey 120 South Clark Street
Very grand, with central rotunda
Lockerly, or *Tucker-Hatcher House* (c. 1839) Irwinton Road

Roswell:
The local Hellenizer was Willis Ball, whose chief surviving houses are:
Barrington Hall (1840) 60 Marietta Street
Bulloch Hall (1840) Bulloch Avenue
Mimosa Hall (1842, rebuilt 1847)

Savannah:
William Scarbrough House ⋆⋆ (1819) William Jay 41 West Broad Street. Open to the public
Qualifies as Greek Revival only on basis of Doric portico, stables, and atrium two stories high; lit (un-Hellenically) by a wide fanlight. Otherwise the house represents Jay's Regency style.
Telfair House ⋆⋆ (1820) William Jay 121 Barnard Street. Open to the public
Corinthian portico but, in truth, Regency
Aaron Champion House ⋆ (1844, third story added 1896) Charles B. Cluskey Orleans Square
Rotunda plan with circular opening in the middle of the hall, which is divided into three equal spaces by square columns
John Hunter House (1822, enlarged with Ionic porticos 1854) 101–105 East Oglethorpe Avenue
U.S. Custom House ⋆ (1846–52) John S. Norris 1–3 East Bay Street
Interior stairway in the New York City Hall–Kentucky State Capitol tradition

Sparta:
Bird-Campbell House (c. 1834) 204 West Broad Street

Washington:

William H. Pope House, or Tupper-Barnett House (1832 and 1860) 101 West Robert Toombs Avenue
Campbell-Cleveland Jordan House (1808 and 1841–46) 208 Liberty Street
Robert Toombs House (1797, portico added 1837) 216 East Robert Toombs Avenue

HAWAII

Honolulu:

John O. Dominis House, or *Governor's Mansion*, or *Washington Palace* (1840s)
This house would be at home in the Mississippi Valley or the Gulf Coast, but it is not what might be expected of a Yankee sea captain. Recently restored to its original form.

IDAHO

Franklin:

Lorenzo Hatch House (1874) 127 East Main Street
Idaho's best example of Mormon Hellenism (see also Utah)

ILLINOIS

Galena:

Hoge House (1845) Henry I. Stouffer 512 Park Avenue
Doric portico introduces a handsome cottage
Dowling House (1847) 120 North Bench Street

Knoxville:

Old Knox County Courthouse, now Knox County Museum ★ (1837–40) John Mandeville

Marengo:

Rogers House (1849) US Route 20 south of Marengo
Beautiful cottage

Metamora:

Old Woodford County Courthouse (1844–46)

Mount Vernon:

Appellate Court Building ★ (1854–74) 14th and West Main Street
Double, curved cast-iron stairway leading to the front

Old Shawneetown:

Old State Bank, or Bank of Illinois ★ (1836) Main and Cross
Greek Doric columns, set upon Roman pedestal; very handsome survivor of Ohio River town

Oquawka:

Henderson County Courthouse (1842) Fourth and Warren streets
Similar to Knoxville's Old Knox County Courthouse, but with a cupola

Ottawa:

Hossack House (1854–55) Sylvanus Grow   210 West Prospect Avenue
Double-decked creole cottage in an unexpected setting

Springfield:

Old State Capitol ★★ (1837, restored in 1966) John Francis Rague   Adams Street between 5th and 6th streets [pages 357 and 358]
Roman dome with Greek Doric portico

Vandalia:

State House (1836, 1858–59, 1899, 1933–39) John Taylor and William Hodge   315 West Gallatin Street [pages 356 and 358]

Waukegan:
Swartout House, now Chamber of Commerce (1847)
414 Sheridan Road [page 226]
Temple-front cottage, Doric columns

INDIANA

Attica:
McDonald-Scribner House (1855) Main and Jackson streets

Bristol:
Wheeler-Gould-Mosier House (1834) Charles Street
Central temple unit (one-and-a-half stories high) and
lower lateral wings; Palladian plan

Connersville:
Canal House (1842) 111 East Fourth Street
Fluted columns without bases, but otherwise the
proportions are Roman

Dupont:
Butler-Lewis House (1847) off State Road 7

Evansville:
Carpenter House, now offices of WNIN radio and
television station (1848–49) 405 Carpenter Street

Southeast of Glenwood:
Gray-Thompson House ** (1846) intersection of routes
650W and 300S [page 220]
Wonderful brick cottage, interior intact

Goshen:
Rowell-Champion House (1847) 101 North Third
Street

Laconia:
Kitner-Withers House, or *Cedar Farm* (1837)

Elevation facing the riverfront has four large Doric
columns—a rare survival of the Ohio Valley
plantation.

Madison:
Jefferson County Courthouse (1854–56) David Du-
bach (?)
Second Presbyterian Church, now John T. Windle
Memorial Auditorium (1845?) Edwin J. Peck (?)
101 East 3rd Street
James F. D. Lanier House, Lanier Historical Site ***
(1840–44) Francis Costigan 511 West 1st Street
[pages 154 and 307]. Open to the public
Costigan's masterpiece
Shrewsbury-Windle House ** (1846–49) Francis
Costigan 301 West 1st Street [pages 308–309].
Open to the public
Costigan Double House (c. 1840) Francis
Costigan 415–417 Vine Street
Costigan House *** (1846–49) Francis
Costigan 408 West 3rd Street
A prime candidate for the finest surviving Greek Re-
vival town house in America; miracles of space plan-
ning on a tiny lot

New Albany:
Indiana State Bank (1837) Hugh Pugh 203 East
Main Street

New Castle:
Murphy-Bailey House (1847) 321 South Main Street

Paoli:
Orange County Courthouse (1847–50) intersection of
state routes 37 and 156

Rising Sun:
Ohio County Courthouse Main Street [page 365]

Terre Haute:

GAR Memorial Hall, formerly Second State Bank of Indiana (1834) Edwin J. Peck

Vevay:

Schenck House (1844–46) George H. Kyle   209 West Market Street

Grizard House (1848) George H. Kyle (?)   East Main Street

Vincennes:

State Bank of Indiana (1838) Edwin J. Peck   112 North Second Street

IOWA

Iowa City:

Old State Capitol (1842) John Francis Rague   Iowa Avenue and Clinton Street

KENTUCKY

Bardstown:

Carothers House (1830) 402 North 3rd Street

Danville:

McClure House (1852) Robert Russell   304 4th Street

Frankfort:

Old Capitol ** (1830) Gideon Shryock   Clair Street and Broadway [page 47]

Marble temple with rotunda in the Wardour Castle–Savannah (GA) City Hall–New York City Hall tradition

Scotland (1840–45) 4 miles south on Versailles Pike

Georgetown:

Ward Hall *** (1855) [page 299]. Open to the public

Kentucky's largest and most complete Greek Revival mansion; splendid ornamented interior

Harrodsburg:

Diamond Point (1840)

Beaumont Inn, Daughter's College (c. 1845). Open to the public

Aspen Hall (1840) 558 Aspen Hall Drive

Hopkinsville:

Robert Dillard House (1845 ?)

Direct product of carpenters' guide by Minard Lafever

Lexington:

"Old Morrison," Transylvania College * (1834) Gideon Shryock   3rd Street

John McCauley House (1850s) John McMurtry 319 Lexington Avenue

Whitehall (1832) 312 North Limestone

Waveland (1847) Washington Allen (?)   approximately 20 miles south of Lexington via US 25

Tightly paired columns and pleasant Lafever doorway

Betty Bryon House (1838) south on US 68

McCann House (1847) 6 miles southeast on Richmond Pike   Smaller version of Waveland

Buenna Hill (c. 1848) John McMurtry   9 miles on Russel Cave Road

Pettit House (c. 1857) Nicholasville Pike, north of Stone Road

Fairlawn, or *Greentree* (1850s) 6 miles on the Paris Pike

Hartland (1840s) 5 miles south on Armstrong Mill Road

At the center of a group of Greek Doric houses of the succeeding decade, including: *Delta*, *Belair*, *Highland Hall*

Cedar Hall (1857) Bowmans Mill Road near Harrodsburg Pike

Lemon Hill * (1840s) Cleveland Road, 2 miles north of Winchester Pike

Remarkable Jeffersonian-Palladian House, related to Peter Harrison's Redwood Library of 1757 in Newport, RI

Mansfield (1845) Thomas Lewinski   Richmond Pike
As enlarged, it became a five-part, neo-Georgian design of a conventional Maryland type, but it was once the best of the compact Greek cottages west of the Appalachians.

Louisville:

Bank of Louisville, now Actors Theater ** (1837) James H. Dakin   320 West Main Street [page 372]
Model demonstration of adaptive reuse; often misattributed to Gideon Shryock

Waterworks, now Water Tower Art Association ** (1860) Theodore R. Scowden   3005 Upper River Road [pages 368–69]
America's most exuberant testimonial to Hellenistic decadence; could have been built by any of the satraps of Alexander the Great had they possessed the technology of steam.

Jefferson County Courthouse (1838–59) Gideon Shryock

Versailles:

Adam Childers House (1840) 131 Maple Street

LOUISIANA

Baton Rouge:

The Pentagon (1819–29) 3rd Street, west of the capitol
Four (!) pink-painted, brick, army-barracks buildings arranged as a pentagon, with the river side open; balconies on second level, behind Doric columns. If the traditional date is correct, this is one of the earliest Greek Revival buildings in the West.

Burnside:

Houmas House–Burnside (1800 (?), remodeled in 1840 with Greek details) via Old River Road or LA 942 (west of New Orleans) [page 151]

Clinton:

Lawyers' Row   Five small office-buildings opposite the courthouse form an assemblage somewhat like old Washington, AR, and Taylors Falls, MN—villages where the Greek Revival style predominates. The *East Filiciana Parish Courthouse*, a square building under a vainglorious cupola, shows how the Hellenized creole cottage, brought to immense size, can become a civic structure.

Convent:

Jefferson College, now Manresa Retreat House (1831 with later additions) 26 miles west of New Orleans [page 55]

Geismar:

Bocage, or *Shady Retreat* * (1801, remodeled 1840) probably by Charles Dakin   Old River Road or LA 942 (west bank of Mississippi River)

Gloster:

Myrtle Hill Plantation (1852)
Bears the stamp of the unknown architect-builder of nearby Washington, AR

Napoleonville:

Belle Alliance (1846) Highway 1 to Belle Rose Bridge, across Bayou Lafourche to Highway 308, northwest 0.5 mile   Grand-scale, Hellenized creole cottage
Belle Helene, or *Ashland* (1840–41) James Gallier, Sr.   Old River Road or LA 942, above Sunshine Bridge [page 159]
Twenty-eight tall, square columns form a colonnade around an immense creole cottage

Madewood ** (1846–48) Henry Howard on LA 308, 2 miles south of Napoleonville on Bayou Lafourche [page 158]. Open to the public

Howard's first major commission, also his most Palladian; disciplined and Irish (Abraham Hargrave worked in this métier in Howard's native Cork—he may have been Howard's mentor).

New Orleans:

Carrollton Courthouse, now the Benjamin Franklin School (1854–55) Henry Howard 719 Carrollton Avenue

Old City Hall, now Gallier Hall ** (1845–50) James Gallier, Sr. 545 Saint Charles Avenue

Sculpted figures, including Justice and Liberty, in the pediment; it manifests Gallier's progression toward Henry Howard's Hellenistic scale.

Bank of Louisiana, now Tourist Commission (1826 and 1840) 334 Royal Street

Town houses: New Orleans has many fine Greek Revival row houses—probably more than any other city in America. Examples are:

620 Saint Peter Street (1838), opposite James Gallier's brutalist-Grecian *Arsenal* (1839);

numbers 621–639;

1206–1234 Decatur Street (1845) J. N. B. De Pouilly's five two-story speculative houses;

721 Governor Nichols Street (1814) H. S. B. Latrobe and A. L. Latour, and perhaps Bartholemy Lafon; restored in 1940 by Richard Koch

1717–1731 Corondelet Street (1850)

Garden District, "Lower Garden District," Carrollton, and "Uptown": There are thousands of galleried creole cottages, and Greek-, Roman-, or Renaissance-influenced houses in these areas, with tens of thousands of Free-Classical variations of plaster, wood, and ironwork details. Some buildings are more Greek than others; see, for example, *1638 Arabella Street*, of the 1840s ("Uptown"), or Henry Howard's *Carrollton Courthouse* (1854–55).

St. Francisville:

Greenwood * (c. 1835, reconstructed after 1960 fire)

Rosedown (1835) Doric double veranda, balanced wings, fine garden

Vacherie:

Oak Alley, or Bon Sejour (1839) Joseph Pilie River Road (west bank of Mississippi River)

Wallace:

Evergreen (1830) River Road or LA 18, 5 miles west of Edgard

The double, circling, freestanding staircase in front is a Caribbean feature added later to a big creole cottage.

White Castle:

Nottoway (1857) Henry Howard River Road or LA 405, 1.5 miles north of White Castle [pages 316–17]. Open to the public

Very large, very elaborate, late Henry Howard mansion for the Louisiana branch of the Randolph family. Interiors are spacious and splendid, handsomely restored.

MAINE

Bangor:

Bangor House Hotel (1833–34) Isaiah Rogers Main and Union streets

Jonas Cutting–Edward Kent House *** (1833) Charles G. Bryant 48–50 Penobscot Street [page 34]

The most interesting double houses in the Greek Revival style in the nation

Nathaniel Hatch House (1832, wing added in 1846) Charles G. Bryant 123 Court Street

Portico at both ends; early, large-scale temple-form essay by Bryant

Bath:

Swedenborgian Church (1843) [page 33]
Splendid small temple-form church

Belfast:

James P. White House * (1840) Calvin A. Ryder
1 Church Street [pages 240 and 297–98]
Derived from villa in Regent's Park, London, by way
of Minard Lafever. Recently well restored.
Joseph Williamson House (1842) Calvin A. Ryder

Ellsworth:

Ellsworth Congregational Church (1846) Thomas
Lord   State Street [page 382]

Richmond:

David Stearns House (1851–55) 3 Gardiner Street
[page 231]
America's only Romanesque Revival Greek column
capitals
Pleasant Street has five carpenter-Greek temples.

Sedgewick:

Baptist Church (1837) Benjamin S. Deane [page 375]
Based on designs by Asher Benjamin

MARYLAND

Baltimore:

Evergreen (1850) 4545 North Charles Street
The house retains Maryland's grandest Corinthian
portico. Frequently extended and remodeled; later
(early twentieth-century) interiors are even more
interesting.
McKim Free School (1822) Baltimore and Asquith
streets [page 372]
George C. Morton House West Monument Street
Tiffany-Fisher House, now Mount Vernon Club (1840)
8 West Monument at Vernon Place

Represents the large town houses that once graced
Philadelphia, Baltimore, Washington, DC, and
Cincinnati

MASSACHUSETTS

Barre:

This is a Greek Revival town, with a number of
houses, probably by Elias Carter, including the
Charles Lee House (1835), with six columns, the *Samuel Lee Cottage* (1836), and the *Barre Historical Society Building* (possibly by Carter).

Boston:

Custom House (1837–47) Ammi B. Young   India and
State streets [page 366]
32 fluted Doric columns of Quincy granite
59 Mount Vernon Street (1837) Edward Shaw (?)
Boston's only distinctly Greek Revival town house
(there are some Greek Revival villas in poor repair in
Roxbury and Jamaica Plain), and the only house
likely to be the personal work of Shaw, the carpenters'-guide maker.
St. Paul's Cathedral (1819; remodeled) Alexander
Parris   138 Tremont Street
Walls of Quincy granite; Ionic columns and pediment
of Virginia sandstone

Haydenville:

Joel Hayden House (1828)   The immediate successor to Ithiel Town's nearby Bowers House (now
destroyed)
Josiah Hayden House (1839)

New Bedford:

Unfortunately, little remains of the work of Russell
Warren, but there is some, including:
Double Bank Building (1831) Russell Warren   Water
Street

Joseph Grinnell House (1831) Russell Warren   379 County Street

Rodman House, now Swain School (1833)   388 County Street

Perhaps a prototype for The Forest, the Gibbonses' house now part of Drew University (see Madison, NJ)

Town Hall, now Free Public Library (1838–39; remodeled and extended) Pleasant Street

Sturbridge:

Levi Lincoln House (1835) Elias Carter   (formerly in Worcester). Open to the public

Worcester:

Stephen Salisbury House (1836–38?, 1842?) Elias Carter   61 Harvard Street

Dowley-Taylor House (1842) Elias Carter   768 Main Street

MICHIGAN

Ann Arbor:

William Anderson House (1831) 2301 Packard Avenue [page 222]

Henry DeWitt Bennett House * (1853) Arden Ballard (?)   312 South Division Street [page 221]

Fine cottage of a pattern for which Ballard was responsible elsewhere

Judge Robert S. Wilson House (1843) 126 North Division Street [page 235]

Dexter:

Samuel Dexter House (1841) Island Lake Road

Stone temple-form house with wooden portico

Grand Rapids:

Caulkins Law Office (1840s) [page 218]

Grass Lake:

Sidney Smith House (1840) Michigan Avenue west of Maute Road

"Village Farm" (1840) 971 East Michigan Avenue

Marshall:

Fitch-Gorham-Brooks House (c. 1840) Kalamazoo Avenue and Prospect Street [page 48]

Hays House (1838) Kalamazoo Avenue and Prospect Street

Pontiac:

Governor Moses Wisner House (1845) 405 Oakland Avenue

Tecumseh:

Elijah Anderson House * (1832) 401 West Chicago Boulevard

First-rate Free-Classical cottage with bold, square cupola

James McAllaster House * (1839) 501 West Chicago Boulevard   Splendidly restored Palladian-Greek cottage

Ypsilanti:

Ladies Literary Club (1842) Arden Ballard (?)   218 North Washington Street

Story-and-a-half, temple-form building; Doric columns with square modifications

MINNESOTA

LeSueur:

George D. Snow House (c. 1865) 129 2nd Street

Dignified stuccoed villa with portico

Minneapolis:

Ard Godfrey House (1848) University and Central. Open to the public   Simple cottage

John H. Stevens House (1849) Minnehaha Park at 50th Street, East. Open to the public

Taylors Falls:
Winslow-Scott House (1853) near southwest corner of Government Road and Basil Street

MISSISSIPPI

Aberdeen:
Sunset Hill (1847) Commerce and Jett
Magnified creole cottage with unusually Greek proportions
Old Homestead (1852) Commerce at Long Avenue
Greek with Gothic implications, like those of Errolton, Shadowlawn, and Themerlaine in Columbus

Columbus:
Wonderful town, full of interesting buildings including combinations of Greek, creole, and Gothic forms unique to this area of Mississippi
Errolton (1848) 216 3rd Avenue, South
Shadowlawn (1860) 1024 Second Avenue, South
Themerlaine (1844) 510 Seventh Avenue, North
Riverview * (1850) 514 2nd Street, South
Elaborate plasterwork and one of the enlarged cupolas characteristic of this region
Camellia Place (1847) James L. Lull 416 Seventh Street, North
Waverly *** (1852) on Route 50 on the way to Aberdeen [pages 150 and 310–11]. Open to the public
Mostly interior "tribune" around which revolve the rooms; splendidly restored (see also Longwood—not Greek Revival—in Natchez, and Barton Hall in Cherokee, AL)

Jackson:
Old State Capitol ** (1839) William Nichols State Street [pages 360–61]

Much remodeling has resulted in the loss of Nichols's best ornament. Still, a grand building and the neologisms are not bad.

Natchez:
Auburn * (1812 and subsequent remodelings) Levi Weeks 400 Duncan Avenue [page 52]
The first house in Mississippi to "use the orders"
Stanton Hall ** (1857) Thomas Rose and Lewis Reynolds (?) 401 High Street [pages 152 and 303]. Open to the public
Magnificent mansion with fine interior plasterwork
D'Evereux ** (1836) James Hardie D'Evereux Drive
Magnified and slightly Hellenized creole cottage
Dunleith ** (1856) Homochitto Street [page 157]
Magnified and slightly Hellenized creole cottage
Richmond * (c. 1832) Tripartite house of which only one part is Greek, but that third is *very* good
Commercial Bank, now First Church of Christ, Scientist (1838) [page 117], connected to a small *banker's house* [page 116] 206 Main Street
Britton and Koontz First National Bank, originally Agriculture Bank (1833) 422 Main Street

Port Gibson:
Bethel Presbyterian Church * (c. 1826) Highway 522 north of Alcorn   Very striking and very early
Windsor (1859) ruins [page 160]

Vicksburg:
Old Court House (1861) Cherry Street between Grove and Jackson

MISSOURI

Fulton:
Westminster College, Main Building (c. 1852)

St. Louis:

Basilica of St. Louis, King of France, or *Old Cathedral* (1834) Joseph C. Laveille and George Morton Walnut Street and Memorial Drive
Oldest cathedral west of the Mississippi River
Grand Avenue Water Tower (1870) George I. Barnett East Grand Avenue and 20th Street
Just a column—could be Greek, could be Roman, could be Palmyran

NEW HAMPSHIRE

Alstead:

Around the center of town, on Route 123, are a group of three pilastered Grecian houses (c. 1840), and north of the river is the *Church of the Good Shepherd–Universalist* (1844) by Ansel Glover, and the smaller *Third Congregational Church*, or United Church of Christ (c. 1843).

Clermont:

Dutton, Ide, and Russell houses (1833–36) Aaron Howland (?)
Three in a row on Central Street (see also Walpole)

Walpole:

Walpole Academy (1831) Aaron Howland (?) Main Street

Winchester:

Winchester National Bank, now Cheshire National Bank (1847, remodeled and with later additions) Route 10

NEW JERSEY

Flemington:

Doric House * (1846) Mahlon Fisher   14 Main Street

Four large square pillars with Free-Classical details
Reading-Large House * (c. 1847) Mahlon Fisher 119 Main Street
Six Ionic pillars, with two pilasters; elaborate carving without too much archaeological deference, though the builder knew his Stuart and Revett
Richard Kuhl House (c. 1845) Mahlon Fisher   21 Mine Street
Samuel Southard Law Office, now Alexander Wurts Law Office (1811, remodeled by Mahlon Fisher in 1840)   Main Street [page 219]
Small, flat-roofed cottage with Fisher's square columns

Madison:

The Forest, now Mead Hall, Drew University ★★★ (1832–36) Charles F. Reichardt and Russell Warren (?) [pages 147–48]

Princeton:

Whig and Philosophic halls (1837–38; moved and rebuilt in 1890s) on Princeton University campus

NEW YORK

(Note: New York State has many fine examples of Greek Revival architecture. Therefore, those listed below have been arranged alphabetically by town or region; within regions they are arranged in a roughly geographical manner to facilitate visitors in their explorations.)

Auburn:

Theodore Willard Case House (1836) 203 Genessee Street

Binghamton:

John Hilton Jones House (1840) 8 Riverside Drive

Canandaigua:

Sibley House (1845) Russell Warren   134 North Main Street

Cazenovia:

Cazenovia Public Library (1840s) and *John Williams House, Brabant* (1835) 9 Albany Street
Another combination bank and residence (see also Natchez, MS, Tallahassee, FL, and Erie, PA)
Sage Hill (1830s?) 107 Lincklaen Street
Roswell Beckwith Cobblestone House * 2 miles north on Route 92

Cooperstown:

Woodside Hall (1829; remodeled) Main and Estli streets
Otsego County Bank, now Leatherstocking Corporation Building (1831) 19 Main Street
Doctor's office (1840s?) now at Farmer's Museum [page 218]

Chautauqua County:

There is a wealth of Greek Revival buildings in this county—and most in towns so small that street addresses are not required. It seems easiest to place them in a block, arranged counterclockwise as the traveler might enter the county from Buffalo.

Silver Creek:

Holman Vail House (1835) Holman Vail

Gerry:

Hip-roofed cottage (c. 1860)

Sinclairville:

Brick house * (c. 1860 ?) 2 miles north
Pilastered and paneled, story-and-a-half, hip-roofed, slightly Italianate (brackets); fine, free ornament and ironwork

Fredonia:

Joel J. Parker Cottage (c. 1855)   Free-Classical brick house, with little colonnades on the sides
William Risley House * (c. 1837) John Jones Risley Street [pages 238–39]
Elijah Risley House (c. 1840) John Jones Risley Street
Anna Jones House (1835; remodeling of 1806 house) John Jones   403 East Main Street

Westfield:

A long, seven-bay, one-story white wooden cottage with a recessed distyle *in antis* doorway, said to be as early as 1820 (doubtful)
Tennant House * (c.1830) in the Hadfield-Town-Bowers House Ionic tradition, four-columned pavilion with balanced wings

Along the Panama-Asheville road are a series of fine temple-form houses, several designed and built for Sardius Steward by John Capple.
Smith-Bly-Baxter House *** (1835) just north of the crossroads of Asheville [page 243]
One of America's finest Free-Classical houses, with a profusion of vigorous, idiosyncratic ornament upon a grid of pilasters; recently restored and rescued from the underbrush

Jamestown:

William Hall House much amended, the central colonnaded pavilion built in 1846

Busti:

The Root House (c. 1835) another pilastered pavilion

Fentonville:

Fenton House (1840s?) shows the pilastered pavilion form adapted to a hip-roof form, with good, fresh, ornament.

The Catskill Region
Rensselaerville:
Renowned for its earlier architecture, this village does have a fine one-story Greek farmhouse (c. 1845).

Meridale:
Farmhouse (c. 1835) Route 28 [page 227]

Roxbury:
Farmhouse (c. 1845)

Worcester:
Asymmetrical farmhouse (1857)

South Worcester:
Doctor's office (c. 1830) [page 218]

Delhi:
Presbyterian Church (1831)

North Blenheim:
Presbyterian Church (1853)

Breakabeen:
Store * (1840s) [page 218]
One of the best of the commercial cottage-temples

Laurens:
Maplehurst (1840s ?) Main Street

Gilbertsville:
Post office (1840s ?)

Geneva:
Rose Hill *** 1835   In impeccable condition; on a superb site on the east shore of the lake. Open to the public
Also see, on *Washington Street*, numbers 128, 218, 226, 273; on *Pulteney Street*, numbers 92 and 96; on *Delancey Street*, number 46; and on *Genessee Street*, numbers 140 and 152.

Hudson:
Cyrus Curtiss House * (1834–37) 32 Warren Street

Central New York
There is at least one notable Minard Lafever–derived temple-and-wings house in each of these villages: **Candor, Eaton, Poolville** [page 230], **Randolph** (where there is a local tradition of generous ornament), and **Willseyville**.

Norwich:
Chenango County Courthouse (1839) North Broad and West Main [page 365]
136 North Broad Street (1838)
27 North Chenango (1838)

Ovid:
The Three Bears * (Baby Bear 1845, Papa Bear 1845, and Mama Bear 1860)
Three municipal offices in declining sizes; red brick with columns

Trumansburg:
Camp House ** (c. 1845) Camp Street
Wonderful brick mansion with unpedimented portico; on a huge scale (see also The Forest in Madison, NJ)

Morrisville:
Community Church (c. 1830)

Spencertown (Columbia County):
Lawrence House (1845–50) South Street

Jerusalem:
Henry Rose House (c. 1840)

Syracuse and Onondaga County
Syracuse:
Hamilton White House (1842) 307 South Townsend Street   Splendid cube with small portico

Canal Museum ** (1849) Montgomery Street and Erie Boulevard
Unique use of an arcade over a canal switching-station

Camillus:
Calvin D. Bingham House (1819?; possibly remodeled)

Lysander:
Whig Hill * (1833) Very grand

Skaneateles:
Roosevelt Hall * (1839) 83 West Lake Street
Interior much remodeled, but site and exterior are impressive
Two examples of the regional "Skaneateles columns" are at *62 West Genessee Street* and *19 Leitch Avenue*

Fabius:
Benson House (1852) 1799 Ridge Road
Asymmetrical prototype for innumerable Midwestern buildings

Lafayette:
Many cobblestone-Greek buildings, of which the most exciting is the *Bailey House* at Webster Road and Route 11A

Baldwinsville:
One of the great Greek Revival villages in America; see especially:
Wilson House (1847) 69 Oswego Street
Downer House (c. 1845) 19 Downer Street
Browning Nichols House (1840s?) 93 Downer Street
Van Allen House (c. 1864) 21 Downer Street
41 Tappan Street * (1850s?) Deconstructionist temple

Manlius:
Flint House (1830; remodeled 1850?) 7134 Genessee Street
Kirkville Road House (c. 1840)

Fayetteville:
Gage House (1854) 210 East Genessee Street
Seymour June House (1840) South Manlius Street and Salt Springs Road

Marcellus:
Curtis Moses House (c. 1838) 36 South Street
Dr. Tefft House * (c. 1830) 18 North Street
Early Palladian-Greek

Liverpool:
Hicks House (c. 1854) Vince and Aspen streets

Tully:
A town with a peculiarly foursquare Hellenism; see:
13 State Street (after 1820)
Tully Baptist Church (1849) 24 State Street

Morris:
The Grove (1840s?)

New York City
Manhattan:
Many of the houses on *Bank Street* have Greek Revival elements, especially number 37.
Federal Hall National Memorial, formerly Subtreasury Building *** (1842) Town and Davis   26 Wall Street [page 41]
Suave, elegant interior in temple-form casing
Henry Street Settlement (1827–34) 263–267 Henry Street
Lafayette Terrace, or *LaGrange Terrace* (early 1830s) Charles F. Reichardt (?), Town and Davis (?) Lafayette Street, opposite the Public Theater (off Astor Place) [page i]
Badly mauled and truncated
First National Bank (1842) Isaiah Rogers   55 Wall Street
With an imaginary removal of all stories above the "Altes Museum" colonnade, Rogers's initial accomplishment emerges.

Old Merchants House, or *Seabury-Tredwell House* *
(1832) 29 East 4th Street [page 302]. Open to the
public
A time capsule—complete, and lovingly maintained;
it has no peer as an illustration of comfortable,
middle-class taste of the 1830s.
The "Row" ** (1831) Martin Thompson or Town and
Davis [pages 246–47]
A strip of Greek Revival houses—1–3 and 21–26—at
Washington Square North. If their interiors were intact, they would get another star. A wonderful
ensemble.

Some Greek Revival churches and temple-forms in
Manhattan:
Baptist Meeting House, or *Mariners Temple* * (1842)
Minard Lafever   12 Oliver Street
St. James Church (1837) Minard Lafever (?)   22 Bar-
clay Street
St. Peter's Church (1840) John R. Haggerty and
Thomas Thomas   33 James Street
Village Presbyterian Church (1846) Samuel Thomp-
son (?)   143 West 13th Street

Queens:

25–37 and *25–29 14th Street* (between Hoyt and 26th
avenues)

Brooklyn:

20–26, 43–49, 57, and *70 Willow Street*
Middle-class survivors of the 1840s

Richmond (Staten Island):

Captain Biddle House (1840) 70 Saterlee Street
Columbia Hall (1835) 404 Richmond Terrace
Sailors Snug Harbor (1831; remodeled often, but still
a fine ensemble in 1883) Martin E. Thompson [page
42]
Richmond Terrace between Tysen Street and Kissell
Avenue South

Ward-Nixon House (1835) 141 Nixon Avenue
Ornate cornice, monumental Ionic portico

Rochester:

Campbell-Whittlesey House * (1836) 123 South
Fitzhugh [page 300]. Open to the public
Fine interiors, restored with daring fidelity to the
original colors

Sag Harbor:

Old Whalers, or *First Presbyterian Church* ** (1844)
Minard Lafever   Madison between Main and Union
streets [page 381]
Even without its tower, it shares with Government
Street Presbyterian in Mobile and First Presbyterian
in Nashville the honor of reuniting the Greek and
Egyptian more effectively than any set of buildings
since Knossos burned.
Suffolk County Whaling Museum, or Benjamin Hunt-
ing House * (1845) Minard Lafever (?)   Main and
Garden streets   Exuberant whaler's mansion

Troy:

Russell-Sage College Building, formerly Presbyterian
Church * (1834) James Dakin   Congress and First
streets

Utica:

Psychiatric Center * (1843) Whitesboro Street
Huge, heartless complex; it could as well be found in
St. Petersburg.

North Carolina

Chapel Hill:

Playmaker's Theater, formerly the Library of the
University of North Carolina (1850) Captain John
Berry (?); Town and Davis (?)   University of North
Carolina campus
Gerrard Hall (1820–37) William Nichols

Charlotte:

U.S. Mint, now Mint Museum (1840) William Strickland 501 Hempstead Place

Edenton:

Hayes Plantation * (1814–17) William Nichols
Nichols's first major work, the huge cupola anticipating those he built later in Alabama and Mississippi
Matthew Pope House (1840s) West King Street

Raleigh:

North Carolina Capitol *** (1833–40) William Nichols, Town and Davis, and David Paton   Capitol Square [pages 354–55]
Nichols's finest surviving building; actually improved by Town, Davis, and Paton. Wonderful interior

Salisbury:

Rowan County Courthouse (1855) 200 North Main Street
Columns are almost twice as high as classic proportions.

Washington:

Bank of Washington (1854) 216 West Main Street
Pedimented windows and doors

Wilmington:

Dr. John Bellamy Mansion (1859) James F. Post/Rufus H. Bunnell (?)   503 Market Street
Orton Plantation (1725; rebuilt 1840 and remodeled since)

Winston-Salem:

Edward Belo House * (1848–58) 45 South Main Street
[page 53]   A mansion jammed against a village street

Ohio

Cincinnati:

Cathedral of St. Peter in Chains * (1845) Henry U. Walter   8th and Plum streets
Walter was a genius, but the architect of the recent desecrating "renewal" was not.

Claridon:

Charles B. Smith House, or *Colonel Hathaway House* (1828) Charles B. Smith [page 224]

Columbus:

Reeves-Woodrow-Butler House (c. 1845) 62 South Paint Street
McLandburgh-Fullerton House (c. 1840) 64 South Paint Street
Atwood-Wilson House (1845) 122 South Paint Street
Bartlett-Cunningham-Gerber House (1848) 134 South Paint Street
State Capitol *** (1839–61) Henry U. Walter, Thomas Cole, Nathan B. Kelly, Isaiah Rogers, Town & Davis   between Broad, State, 3rd, and High streets [page 46]
An instance where a committee salvaged the best ideas of several architects, especially Cole, who is better known as a painter

Dayton:

Old Courthouse *** (1850) Howard Daniels   3rd and Main streets [page 45]
A masterpiece, and the only known architectural work of Daniels, a landscape designer of great sophistication

Granville:

Avery-Downer House ** (1842) 221 East Broadway [page 232]. Open to the public
Faithfully and effectively based on Minard Lafever designs, handsomely maintained

Milan:

Mitchell-Turner House *** (1828) [page 233]
Brick house with white-painted Lafeverish ornament

Mount Vernon:

East Gambier Street has a series of village Greek houses, specifically between numbers 110 and 519, and a fine town hall.

Norwalk:

Sturgis-Kennan-Fulstow House (1834) William Gale Meade
Wooster-Boalt House (1848)

West Andover:

Edmiston House (1845) Leverett Osborn [page 217]

OREGON

Oregon City:

Dr. John McLaughlin House (1846) approximately 15 miles southeast of Portland

PENNSYLVANIA

Altoona:

Elias Baker House ** (1845) Robert Cary Long, Jr.   3500 Baker Boulevard [pages 236–37 and 301]. Open to the public

Erie:

U.S. Bank of Erie, now Erie Art Museum *** (1839) William Kelly   409 State Street
With its Greek Revival cashier's house next door, this Roman temple set high on its base is the finest remaining example of Biddlean Hellenism outside Philadelphia (now that John Chislett's Bank of Pittsburgh is gone).

Charles M. Reed Mansion, now Erie Club (1849) Edward B. Smith

Meadville:

Independent Congregational Church (1830) attributed to G. W. Cullum

Philadelphia:

St. Andrew's Church * (1822–23) John Haviland   8th Street above Spruce
Asylum for the Deaf and Dumb, now Philadelphia Museum School of Art ** (1824–25) John Haviland   southwest corner of Broad and Pine streets
Haviland at his masterly, neoclassical best—free and dignified at the same time
Franklin Institute, now Atwater Kent Museum (1825–27) John Haviland being brutalist   15 South 7th Street
St. Luke and Epiphany Church (1839–40) Thomas S. Stewart   330 South 13th Street
Hatfield House (c. 1760, remodeled c. 1835) 33rd and Girard, in Fairmount Park
The remodeling added a five-columned portico.
The Fatlands, once known as *Vaux Hall* * (1775; with 1845 Hellenic remodeling or rebuilding) in Audubon, on the edge of Valley Forge Park
Strangely little is known about this extraordinary house in the Hadfield–Town, six-columned Ionic tradition, with one four-columned wing. Was another wing planned to give it the balance of Phil-Ellena (now gone), not far away in Germantown and built a year earlier? Did Robert Cary Long, Jr., have a hand in them both? (The portico looks somewhat like that for his contemporary Elias Baker House in Altoona.)
Andalusia **** (1798; remodeled 1836) Thomas U. Walter and Nicholas Biddle   13 miles northeast on the banks of the Delaware River [pages 109–111]
On historical grounds it deserves all those stars though, as a remodeling of a remodeling, it lacks unity of conception.

Fairmont Waterworks * (1812–22) Frederick C. Graff   near Fairmont Avenue [pages 118–19] (see also Louisville, KY)

Founders Hall, Girard College **** (1833–47) Thomas U. Walter   Girard and Corinthian avenues [page 120]

America's finest complex of Greek Revival buildings

Merchants Exchange, or *Philadelphia Exchange* ** (1835) William Strickland   143 South 3rd Street [page 44]

Strickland's semicircular portico with Corinthian colonnade is not an original idea and its interior is gone, but it is part of an unexcelled group, including the Second Bank of the United States (see below) and the First Bank of Pennsylvania.

Ridgeway Library * (1873–78) Addison Hutton   901 South Broad Street

Second Bank of the United States *** (1824) William Strickland   420 Chestnut Street [pages 114–15] Strickland's masterpiece

U.S. Naval Asylum Home (1833) William Strickland   Gray's Ferry Road and Bainbridge Street Cast-iron columns on balconies; ornamental ironwork has naval symbols (dolphins, etc.)

Two rows of Greek Revival houses are left in Philadelphia, though many better—by Mills and Latrobe—are gone:

Girard Row (1831–33) William Struthers 326–334 Spruce Street

Portico Row (1831–32) Thomas U. Walter 900–930 Spruce Street

Pittsburgh:

Croghan-Schenley Rooms, now in the University of Pittsburgh's Cathedral of Learning * (1830s) John Chislett (?) [pages 314–15]

The glorious ballroom and anteroom have been rescued.

RHODE ISLAND

Bristol:

Russell Warren (?) House (1808–10) Russell Warren   86 State Street

Very early, very idiosyncratic, by a master who later became modest

Newport:

Levi H. Gale House (1833–38) Russell Warren 89 Touro Street

Providence:

Arcade * (1828) Russell Warren and James Bucklin   Weybosset through Westminster streets [pages 38–39]

The Weybosset façade is a portico topped by a paneled parapet, while the Westminster façade is a portico resting on Ionic columns; America's best Greek Revival commercial building.

Athenaeum (1838) William Strickland   251 North Benefit Street

Manning Chapel ** (1834) Russell Warren (?) Prospect Street, between University Hall and Hope College   Wonderful overscaling

SOUTH CAROLINA

Camden:

Bethesda Presbyterian Church (1822) Robert Mills   502 DeKalb Street (30 miles northeast of Columbia)

Charleston:

Beth Elohim Synagogue ** (1840) Charles Reichardt, James Curtis (?), Charles B. Tappan, and George W. Noble (?)   90 Hassell Street [page 380]

Centenary Methodist Church (1842) Edward B. White   60 Wentworth Street

College of Charleston (1828–29 and 1850) William Strickland designed the main building, Edward B. White the portico [page 372]

Fireproof Building, or Public Records Office (1826) Robert Mills   100 Meeting Street
More Palladian than Greek Revival

First Baptist Church (1819–22) Robert Mills
61 Church Street
A low Greek pediment but Roman Doric columns

Hibernian Hall (1840) Thomas U. Walter
105 Meeting Street

Charles Kerrison House (1842) 138 Wentworth Street
Lafeverish doorway; idiosyncratic attenuated columns

Market Hall * (1841) Edward B. White   188 Meeting Street

Mikell House (1853) 94 Rutledge Avenue
Ram's-head column capitals

Robinson-Aiken House (1833–36, with remodeling) 48 Elizabeth Street
Extraordinary Doric entrance hall added to older house

Spring Street Methodist Church (1858) 68 Spring Street

Alexander Hext Chisholm House (1836) Charles Reichardt (?)   172 Tradd Street
Charleston Hotel columns used residentially

Trinity Methodist Church, formerly Westminster Presbyterian (1850) Edward C. Jones   275 Meeting Street

U.S. Custom House (1853–79) Ammi B. Young   200 East Bay

Columbia:

Ainsley Hall House, or *Robert Mills Historic House* (1825) Robert Mills   616 Blanding Road

Pinewood (near Sumter):

Milford **** (1838–41) Charles Reichardt and Russell Warren (probably) [pages 145–46]
The most magnificent Greek Revival mansion east of the Appalachians; remarkably intact

TENNESSEE

Clarksville:

Tip Top (1859)

Columbia:

Rattle and Snap ** (1845) George W. Polk
7 miles southwest of Columbia via US 43 [pages 155 and 305]

Clifton Place (1832) [page 50]

Pillow-Bethel House (1840)

Pillow-Haliday House (1845)

Donelson:

The Hermitage (1819, 1831, and 1836) David Morrison and Robert Mills (?)   12 miles east of Nashville on Lebanon Road [pages 112–13]. Open to the public

Tulip Grove (1836) Joseph Reiff (?)   Lebanon Road

Belair (1832, remodeled 1838) Lebanon Road

Jonesboro:

Presbyterian Church (1850) W. H. Clyce [page 383]

Nashville:

Belle Meade * (1854) Adolphus Heimann (?)
5025 Harding Road. Open to the public
(See Milford in Pinewood, SC, for possible prototype)

Belmont ** (1850–60) Adolphus Heimann   1900 Belmont Road [pages 318–19]. Open to the public
Adelicia Cheatham's grand gesture; elaborate interior

Cleveland Hall (1839–41) 4041 Old Hickory Boulevard

State Capitol ** (1845–59) William Strickland [page 353]

Spring Hill:

Chears Place (1850) One of a group of local houses with Tower-of-the-Winds capitals

TEXAS

Austin:
Governor's Mansion (1855) Abner Cook   Colorado and 11th streets [page 242]
Washington L. Hill House, also called *Neill Cochran House* (1855) Abner Cook   2310 San Gabriel Street
John M. Swisher House, also called *Scott House*, or *Sweetrush* (1853) Abner Cook   moved in 1925–26 to 2408 Sweetrush Drive
Woodlawn, or *James B. Shaw House* (1853) Abner Cook   6 Niles Road
Westhill, also called *Mrs. Reuben Runner House* ★ (1855) Abner Cook   1703 West Avenue
Cook's other Austin houses listed above are grand, in the Greater-Tennessee style he learned in Nashville, but this split-level house is his most ingenious.
Beriah Graham Cottage (1861) Abner Cook   2605 Salado

UTAH

Simple structures with Greek details:

Box Elder County:
Willard, *George Mason House* (c. 1865)

Davis County:
Bountiful, *Latter Day Saints Tabernacle* (1857–63)

Millard County:
Fillmore, *school* (c. 1865)

Sanpete County:
Ephraim, *Niels Ole Anderson House* (1868); *Latter Day Saints United Order Cooperative Store* (1872)

Utah County:
Springville, *Jacob Houtz House* (1865)

Washington County:
Virgin, *Latter Day Saints Meetinghouse* (1870); St. George, *Washington County Courthouse* (1866–76); Washington, *Washington Cotton Factory* (1865–70)

VERMONT

Arlington:
Arlington Inn (1848) Martin Deming   off Route 7
Four square, pithy American Free Classicism

Burlington:
Follett House (1840) Ammi B. Young
on Lake Champlain
First Congregational Church (1842) Henry Searle
38 South Winooski Avenue
Very fine temple-form church with choragic monument atop (see also Tennessee State Capitol)

Castleton:
Rehlen House (1848) Thomas Dake (?)
Probably the last major work of Thomas Dake; well preserved

Danby:
LaBatt House (1860s)
Unusually literal temple-form; started as a bank, then a church, now a residence

Danville:
Old Bliss Davis Place (1845) US Route 2 and TH 14
Idiosyncratic wraparound in Greek proportions

Manchester:
Equinox House ★ (1853) One of the last surviving Greek Revival hotels, now being restored (see also Sweet Springs, WV)

Montpelier:

Vermont State Capitol * (1833–38 and 1857–59)
Ammi B. Young, rebuilt and substantially remodeled
by Thomas Silloway   State Street
Vestiges of an early work of Young (see also Charleston, SC and San Francisco, CA)

Orwell:

Wilcox-Cutts House, or *Brookside* (1790s and 1843)
James Lamb and Thomas Dake   2 miles south of
Orwell on State Highway 22A [page 35]

St. Johnsbury:

Kitchell House (1840s?) northwest of US Route 2 on
town highway 14

VIRGINIA

Accomac:

St. James Episcopal Church (1838) Trompe l'oeil
interior

Alexandria:

Lyceum, formerly McGuire House (1840) 212 South
Washington Street

Arlington:

Arlington House, or Custis-Lee Mansion **** (1802–
18) George Hadfield [pages 105–108]
Interior is confused, but on historic grounds—as the
great prototype—this most conspicuous of American
houses (except for the White House) is worth a
journey.

Charlottesville:

University of Virginia **** (1817–26) Thomas Jefferson, William Thornton, Benjamin H. Latrobe [pages
370–71]
Not "Greek" Revival in any narrow archaeological

sense. Assembled by a master with masterful help,
ten templelike pavilions are arranged in two parallel
rows forming colonnades, and exemplify the French
and English neo-Palladian prototypes for what came
later in the South.

Halifax County:

Berry Hill *** (1842–44) John E. Johnson
The South's greatest temple-form mansion, even in its
present state of disrepair

Leesburg:

Morven Park (1840s; since remodeled and de-
remodeled) E. G. Lind. Open to the public
Large but incomplete statement of an eclectic conception—now minus towers—surrounding a house of the
1780s

Lexington:

Lexington Presbyterian Church (1845) Thomas U.
Walter [page 382]
Washington and Lee University * (1824, 1831, 1843)
John Jordan and Samuel Darst [page 373]

Luray:

Aventine Hall (1852) 143 South Court Street
Unexpected Northern style with Tower-of-the-Winds
capitals

Lynchburg:

Old Courthouse (1855) William S. Ellison

Norfolk:

Old Norfolk Academy Building, now Chamber of
Commerce (1840) Thomas U. Walter   420 Bank
Street [page 367]

Palmyra:

Fluvanna County Courthouse * (1831) John Hartwell
Cocke [page 364]

Petersburg:

Merchants Exchange (1839–41) Calvin Pollard
East Bank Street
Petersburg Courthouse (1838–40) Calvin Pollard
Tabb Street Presbyterian Church (1842) Thomas U.
Walter   21 West Tabb Street [pages 376 and 377]

Portsmouth:

Old Naval Hospital (1832) John Haviland
Effingham Street near the river [page 372]
Ten-columned portico, ninety-two feet long

Powhatan:

Powhatan County Courthouse ** (1849) Alexander
Jackson Davis

Richmond:

Linden Row * (1847–50) Otis Manson (builder)
East Franklin Street
The South's rival to Washington Square North in New
York City; being renovated as an inn
Monumental Church ** (1814) Robert Mills
1224 East Broad Street [pages 378 and 379]
Early, uncharacteristic, manneristic, and Soanian; no
longer in use as a church
Old First Baptist Church (1840) Thomas U.
Walter   Broad and 12th streets
St. Paul's Episcopal Church (1845) Thomas S. Stew-
art   815 East Grace Street
State Capitol * (1792) Thomas Jefferson and Jacques-
Louis Clerisseau, with several remodelings and exten-
sions [page 359]
Derived from a Roman temple (the Maison Carrée in
Nîmes); with the destruction of Prince William's
Chapel in Sheldon, SC, became the nation's oldest
surviving temple-form building (the Redwood Library
in Newport, RI, had wings).

Staunton:

Virginia School for the Deaf and Blind ** (1828–47)
William Small and Robert Cary Long, Jr.
Splendid complex

WASHINGTON

Port Gamble:

There are a number of Greekish houses in the historic
district of this old sawmill town (25 miles northwest of
Seattle via State Route 3).

Port Townsend:

George Starrett House (1855) 744 Clay Street

WEST VIRGINIA

Sweetsprings:

A. W. Rowan Home for the Aged, formerly
Sweetsprings Hotel ** (1833)

WISCONSIN

Dodgeville:

Iowa County Courthouse (1859) Alexander Carl Guth

Green Bay:

Henry S. Baird Law Office (1835)
Cotton House (1840)

Hudson:

Frederick L. Darling House (1858)

Milwaukee:

Benjamin Church House, or Kilbourntown House
(1844) in Estabrook Park

Racine:

Eli Cooley House (1851–53) Lucas Bradley (?)
1135 South Main Street
First Presbyterian Church (1851) Lucas Bradley [page
382]

ENDNOTES

Introduction

1. For assistance in thinking through the foregoing summary paragraphs, I wish to thank Robert Wiebe.

2. McPherson, p. 31.

3. Hamilton and Adams quoted in Miles, p. 263; Livingston in Meyers, p. 247; Everett in *U.S. Magazine and Democratic Review* 6 (November 1839), p. 427.

4. Jones quoted from his *O Strange New World*, p. 228; Miles, pp. 270ff.

5. Ibid.

6. Jefferson to Joseph Priestley, quoted in Wright, p. 224.

7. Ibid., p. 225.

8. Miles, p. 263; Tallmadge, pp. 92–93.

9. Jefferson quoted in Padover, pp. 470–71.

10. Parrington, pp. 79–81.

11. For Osterweiss's and Eaton's ideas, see Kennedy, *Architecture, Men, Women and Money*, pp. 339ff.; Miles and Jones quoted in Miles, pp. 270ff.

Part One
The Political Economy of the Greek Revival

12. This entire paragraph is, essentially, a precis of Robert Alexander's wonderful article entitled "The Grand Federal Edifice," published in *Documentary Editing* 9, no. 2 (June 1987), pp. 13ff. I am much indebted to him for these references.

13. Adams, *Jefferson Administration*, p. 107.

14. Moore quoted in Jones, p. 305.

15. Wordsworth quoted in Adams, *Jefferson Administration*, p. 116.

16. Moore in 1807, quoted in Adams, *Jefferson Administration*, p. 113.

17. Jameson, p. 19.

18. Ibid.

19. Ibid., p. 16.

20. Ibid., p. 19.

21. Jarratt quoted in Jameson, p. 20

22. Wood, p. 477.

23. Thurman and Constable appear at length in my *Orders from France.*

24. Jameson, p. 94.

25. Ahlstrom, p. 365.

26. Rorabaugh, pp. 181–82.

27. Ibid.

28. Wood, p. 123.

29. Ibid., pp. 476 and 498. For much more on this fascinating subject, see Michael Zuckerman's "Thermidor in America," in *Prospects* 8 (1983), edited by Jack Salzman, Cambridge, Eng.: Cambridge University Press.

30. Paine quoted in Zuckerman, supra, p. 350.

31. "New England," published by the Boston Chamber of Commerce in 1911, quoted in Turner, p. 48. By 1850, Turner estimates, nearly half of all New England natives lived elsewhere.

32. Brooks, p. 61.

33. Horace Bushnell quoted in Adams, *Jefferson Administration*, p. 1121.

34. Turner, pp. 52–53.

35. Ibid.

36. Adams, *Jefferson Administration*, p. 1058.

37. Adams, *Jefferson Administration*, pp. 95–96, and 21. While Henry Adams was thoroughly jaundiced, his perceptions of conditions in New England and in Virginia are supported by most later scholars.

38. Ibid., pp. 1121–25.

39. Ibid., p. 117.

40. Kammen, *Season*, pp. 42–43.

41. Ibid.

42. Shi, p. 58.

43. Adams quoted ibid., pp. 78–91.

44. Warren and Adams quoted ibid., pp. 74–75. With bedollared and bewildered in place, if "bewitched" had been reintroduced to the lexicon, Joel Barlow might have saved Cole Porter some trouble.

45. Abigail Adams quoted in Alberts, p. 378.

46. *New Economic Review* quoted ibid., p. 45.

47. Shi, pp. 56–57. As late as 1830, George Washington Parke Custis was holding celebrations of homespun-weaving behind the portico at Arlington House.

48. Adams, *Jefferson Administration*, pp. 749–50.

49. Ibid., p. 1233.

50. John B. McMaster quoted in North, p. 55.

51. Adams, *Jefferson Administration*, pp. 1118–19.

52. Cochran, pp. 13, 31, and 42.

53. Latrobe to Dolley Madison, April 21, 1809, quoted in Latrobe *Papers*, vol. 2, pp. 754–55.

54. Remini, *Jackson*, vol. 2, p. 15.

55. Hadfield's qualities from George S. Hunsberger, "The Architectural Career of George Hadfield," in *Records of the Columbia Historical Society*, 1951–52, p. 65.

56. The quotation and the term *post-heroic*, together with much else in this analysis, are from George B. Forgie's remarkable book *Patricide in the House Divided*. See especially p. 2.

57. Ward, p. 3. This is a short and elegant book analyzing the uses to which his age put Jackson, to which I am very much indebted. My only quibble with Ward is that he presents the War of 1812 as if it came as a "blow" that "threatened to destroy the young nation's pride." Henry Adams might have responded that, by that time, there was very little pride left.

The three architects known by me to have assisted in Jackson's victory—there may well have been others—were Benjamin Henry Latrobe, son of Henry, Bartholemy Lafon, and Arsene Latour.

58. Ingersoll and Clay quoted in Ward, pp. 4–6.

59. Ibid. But Ward and I differ as to the timing of the circumstances that needed purging and restoring; they began to accumulate as early as 1783, increasing in the profligate 1790s, and cluttering the American psyche throughout the administrations of Jefferson and Madison.

60. Ibid.

61. Washington McCartney's eulogy to Jackson quoted ibid., p. 1.

62. Kammen, *Season*, p. 43.

63. Kendall quoted in Kennedy, *Architecture, Men, Women and Money*, p. 277.

64. Cooper quoted in Ward, pp. 59 and 73.

65. Quoted in Somkin, p. 135.

66. Custis quoted ibid., p. 139.

67. Ibid., pp. 151–53.

68. Adams quoted ibid.

69. The association of Jackson's luxurious personal preferences and his persona, together with the Cincinnatus meetings, comes from Ward's generally approving picture, p. 43. Rantoul's role is examined in Meyers, p. 228.

70. This dating of the stages of the Hermitage is in Patrick, pp. 119ff.

71. Jackson quoted in Patrick, p. 237, n. 14.

72. Troup quoted in Ward, pp. 7–8; for Custis and Jackson, see Kennedy, *Architecture, Men, Women and Money*.

73. *Putnam's Monthly* 3 (1854), p. 495, quoted in Forgie, p. 10.

74. Van Buren quoted ibid., p. 7.

75. There is a hot scholarly dispute as to the rates of growth in the American economy between 1790 and 1860. I have tried to sort out the arguments as best I can: a summary of the contending views can be found in Lee and Passell, pp. 52ff.

It is bad form to use the Rostovian term *takeoff*, as I have done, but even if Claudia Goldin, at the University of Pennsylvania, and Ted Weiss, at the University of Kansas, find that Douglass North, Paul David, and Stanley Lebergott were wrong as to the pace and date of the recovery after 1820, and if there was a plateau, not a decline, in per capita living standards before that date, I believe my general statements are true. I am grateful to Goldin and Michael Zuckerman for sending me back to the primary sources.

76. Per capita income, 1800–30, cited in North. These numbers will certainly be revised, but their direction still seems good.

77. For the depression of the 1830s thesis, see Bray Hammond, Milton Friedman, and Douglass North: Friedman and Schwarz in Temin, p. 229; North and Hammond quoted ibid., p. 155. The standard text is Robertson and Walton, ibid., p. 148.

78. Temin, pp. 189–203.

79. None of the lovely statistics we have been using take any more account than is conventional in the textbooks of economic history of the welfare, felt or economic, of either the Native Americans or the slaves.

80. Temin, pp. 157, 164, and 176.

Part Two
A Case Study: The Forest and Milford

81. Hampton, his son, and his sons-in-law are treated at greater length in *Architecture, Men, Women and Money*.

82. Thomas Gibbons's biography is given in short in the *Dictionary of American Biography*, at better length and more accurately by the WPA writers compiled in Granger, and in several unpublished papers by Arthur Jones, in the Drew University Library. Jones is the expert on the subject and has assisted a number of graduate students with their own dissertations on the subject, also at Drew; see especially James Briscoe (1980). See also, at Drew, Arthur P. Whitney (1933) on William Gibbons.

83. Lane, *Georgia*, p. 74.

84. *Savannah Gazette* 9 (August 1798).

85. Ibid.; also, Granger, p. 307, apparently drawing on other sources.

86. William Gibbons to his father, quoting his father, in Lane, *Georgia*, p. 79.

87. Gibbons's will can still be found in Savannah records.

88. For Reichardt and Schinkel, see *Charleston Mercury*, December 26, 1836; January 12, 1837; and *Courier*, December 18, 1837.

89. For more on Reichardt, see the chapter on the Hamptons in *Architecture, Men, Women and Money*, the sources cited there, and Landy, p. 19. He was listed in the city directories of New York at 8 Wall

Street in 1835–36 and at 45 William Street for 1837. This is a puzzle, since he was certainly in Charleston by Christmas 1836. He must have been in New York long enough to gain recognition by March 1835, for the penitentiary competition.

90. Irving, p. 148. I am grateful to Mrs. Virginia Meynard of Columbia, South Carolina, for this reference and many other leads; see her *The Venturers*.

91. Morison, p. 179. For an extended discussion of this trade, see Kennedy, *Orders from France*.

92. Ticknor quoted in Taylor, pp. 38–39.

93. The Drew University library has some Gibbons documents, for which I am grateful, including William Gibbons's letterbook and an archaeological study of the area. But they offer nothing on the architect of The Forest or of Gibbons's town house on Greenwich Street in New York.

94. Meynard, p. 161.

95. Cunningham, p. 51; Meynard, p. 157. The expert on the associations of Johnson, architecture, and horses is Henry W. Lewis, of Chapel Hill, whose *More Taste than Prudence* traces the connections between the Bruces of Halifax County, Virginia, the horse-breeding Colonel William Johnson of Chesterfield County, his architect-son John (who worked in New York in the penumbra of Ithiel Town in 1837), and the colonel's cross-breeder, Nicholas Biddle. From his study of equine bloodlines, Lewis assures me that Gibbons horses "knew" Biddle horses and Hampton horses.

96. Mackay-Smith letter to author of September 16, 1987, citing his *The Race Horses of America 1832–1872: Portraits and Other Paintings by Edward Troye*

(Saratoga Springs, New York: National Museum of Racing, 1981), and John Hervey, *Racing in America 1665–1865* (New York: Privately published for the Jockey Club, 1944).

97. Bruce quoted in H. W. Lewis, p. 65.

98. See H. W. Lewis, pp. 65ff. Lewis has discovered many a horse and house connection and has shared them with me.

99. Kenneth Severens comments that Reichardt's "immediate work on two important city buildings suggests that he had been invited to Charleston." Severens appears in David Moltke-Hansen's *Art in the Lives of South Carolinians* (Charleston: Carolina Art Association, 1979), wherein can be found the newspaper reports of Reichardt's arrival and his claim to have studied with Schinkel.

100. For Reichardt in Charleston, see Ravenel, pp. 177ff. For the racecourse, see Irving, pp. 148ff.: "The present Grand Stand . . . erected in 1837, from designs by Reichardt, an architect from Germany, a pupil of the great Shinkle [sic]."

101. For Warren in Charleston, see Robert L. Alexander, "The Architecture of Russell Warren" (master's thesis, New York University, 1952), n.p.; Waddell and Liscombe, p. 35.

102. The German-born architect was cited in a paper by James M. Stubbs, delivered to the Sumter County Historical Society, October 17, 1966. For the German furniture, see Sally Baxter Hampton to Lucy Wainwright Baxter, January 18, 1861, quoted in Hampton, p. 101.

103. The contract documents for Milford were reprinted in the *Newsletter of the Victorian Society in*

America 5, no. 7 (Winter 1973–74), from the Williams-Chestnut-Manning Collection of the South Caroliniana Library. This reprint, however, omits two payments in Governor Manning's account books to Warren, one on November 3, 1839, for "drawing," and the other on November 17, 1840, for "plans out building." I am indebted to Gene Waddell for pointing these out. It is apparent that Warren supplemented plans and elevations prepared earlier for the main building, probably by Reichardt, and then supplied some compatible plans for outbuildings, after Reichardt had left South Carolina earlier in 1840.

104. John B. Irving, *Charleston Courier*, September 27, 1844. This is the same Irving who stated in his Jockey Club book that Reichardt was its designer. In the *Courier* he says Milford was "completed from designs by Potter," thereby giving rise to a series of misconceptions. Neither of the brick-contracting Potters ever designed a building.

105. There may or may not have been a two-story addition to the house's bedrooms. See John Califf III, "Millwood, Its Architecture and Ambiences" (1982), manuscript available from Mr. Califf, Columbia, South Carolina. Since only the columns of the portico are two stories high, the rest being one story, the house is not a direct descendant of the Forks of Cypress–Houmas House line.

Part Three
Reviving Greece

106. For the birth of the Greek Revival, see McCarthy's essay in *Paestum*, p. 48. North quoted in Winston S. Churchill, *History of the English-Speaking Peoples: The Age of Revolution* (New York: Dodd, Mead, 1957), p. 212.

107. Jefferson quoted in Wright, p. 230.

108. Tsigakou, p. 25.

109. Biddle quoted in Govan, p. 17; Smith was in correspondence with Lusieri well into 1806, and may have provided his name to Biddle.

110. William Nickerson Bates published portions of Biddle's Greek journal in the *Proceedings of the Numismatic and Antiquarian Society of Philadelphia* 28 (1916–18), pp. 167ff. His commentary is full of small errors; for example, he fails to pick up Biddle's explicit recognition of Joseph Allen Smith's previous visit. Thanks to Pamela Scott's exertions, a complete typescript has been made of the text, and I have found Smith so irresistible a character that he led me to the relationship of Tory Americans to ancient monuments noted in these pages. Biddle speaks of himself as "the second of my countrymen who has been here" (Corinth) on page 35 of the typescript (the original pages are obscurely numbered when numbered at all), and of "my countryman Smith of Carolina" and his discovery of Ulysses' well on pages 70 and 71. (Scott's typescript may be obtained from the Pennsylvania Historical Society.)

Mordaunt Crook puckishly suggests that George Sandys (1578–1644) was "the first American to visit Greece" (p. 2). Sandys, it seems, chanced to be born in the West Indies. I do not think he counts. In any case, I use "American" narrowly, to mean a citizen of the United States.

111. How was he able to make his patriotic correction? This part of the story has remained a mystery until we correlated a manuscript copy of Biddle's journal, in the form of letters to his brother, and a group of documents from the correspondence of Smith, cited below.

112. See *Orders from France*.

113. Biddle manuscript.

114. Ibid.

115. Ibid.

116. Ibid.

117. Monroe quoted in Govan, p. 20.

118. For more about Biddle and Craig, see both *Architecture, Men, Women and Money* and *Orders from France*. I have learned to be more skeptical since writing the first of the two; I believed Philadelphia myths about Girard being an orphan and having sailed for the first time to the West Indies as a common seaman. Both tales are corrected, at some length, in the second account. But I note with some embarrassment having described Craig's house as a "pleasant Georgian building"; pleasant it was, but after Latrobe's remodeling it was no longer Georgian, but neoclassical.

119. Tucker's "Thoughts As a Hermit," in *The Port Folio* 5, pp. 459ff.

120. Monroe Doctrine quoted in Dangerfield, *Era*, pp. 298–308.

121. Adams quoted ibid., pp. 271–72.

122. I am indebted to S. Frederick Starr for the information that the Russian historian Bolkhovitinov has dug out of the Seward collection of documents splendid new information (1988) about the apprehensions of Americans concerning imperial Russia, embodied in the Monroe Doctrine. Here was America, on the brink of a Greek Revival, fearful of Roman-imperial Russia.

123. Clay quoted in Carl Schurz, *Life of Henry Clay* (New York: Houghton Mifflin, 1915), vol. 1, pp. 208ff.; Biddle, in the Biddle manuscript.

124. Harrison quoted in Crook, p. 41.

125. Miranda's plan appears in Jaffe, p. 294, and the reference to Trumbull's handwriting is on the preceding page.

126. Trumbull quoted ibid., p. 183.

127. For Miranda, see Peggy K. Liss, *Atlantic Empires: The Network of Trade and Revolution, 1713–1826* (Baltimore: Johns Hopkins University Press, 1983), p. 166; Liss gives a fine recent study of relations between the United States and revolutions in Latin America. For Jefferson and Toussaint, see *Orders from France*.

128. Morgenthau on Adams and Monroe quoted in Burns, p. 254; Adams, and Old Republicanism, Dangerfield, *Era*, p. 298; Monroe Doctrine quoted ibid., p. 302.

129. Major, p. 45.

130. Gilpin quoted in Rogin, p. 296; Fisk and Wright quoted in Schlesinger, p. 321.

131. Tsigakou, pp. 47–48.

132. Ibid.

133. Ibid.

134. Adams, *Jefferson Administration*, p. 107.

135. Jameson, p. 20.

136. Jackson quoted in Meyers, p. 22.

137. Harris, ibid., pp. 41–42.

138. Webster quoted in Peter Harvey, *Reminiscences and Anecdotes of Daniel Webster* (Boston: Little, Brown, 1901), p. 582.

139. Gilchrest, p. 23ff.

140. For Jefferson and Scottish "Common Sense" philosophy, see Wills and his hostile reviewers. Some of those critics were themselves criticized in advance by Wills (see p. 200) for failing to give sufficient weight to the influence of the Scots upon Jefferson.

141. Tucker's articles can be found in *The Port folio*, 3rd series, 1814–15.

142. Latrobe's Anniversary Oration was bound to the end of *The Port folio* of June 1811. It is reprinted in the Latrobe *Papers*, vol. 3, pp. 67–91.

143. Ibid.

144. Ibid.

145. *The Port folio*, 3rd series, vol. 78 (1812), p. 196.

146. Latrobe, *Papers*, vol. 3, pp. 67–91.

147. Tracing Latrobe's sources is not easy, but it is clear from his two drawings, made to illustrate the poems of "the Homer of the North," James Macpherson, and from his tendency to follow the arguments of Hume, that he was thoroughly acquainted with the work of the Edinburgh School. For Latrobe and Macpherson, see Latrobe, *Latrobe's View of America, 1795–1820* (published for the Maryland Historical Society; New Haven: Yale University Press, 1985), p. 35.

148. Ibid. Hume had put it this way: "Rome . . . received all its refinements from Greece . . . [where] the arts and sciences came to perfection." (Quoted in Sterling M. Boyd, "The Adam Style in America: 1770–1820," Ph.D. dissertation, Princeton University, 1966.)

149. Latrobe, *Papers*, vol. 3, pp. 67–91.

150. Ibid. Latrobe's indignation is to be found in the Latrobe microfiche, 195/F9, Library of Congress. W(83–18) Prints and Photographs.

151. Mills quoted in the autobiography printed as Appendix 3 in Gallagher, pp. 159ff. Mills apparently intended to comment somewhat further upon the distinctions between his Greek and Jefferson's Roman, but he broke off after referring to Jefferson's library, where he found "several works, all of Roman character, principally Palladio."

152. Walter quoted in Hamlin, *Greek Revival*, p. 62.

153. *The Port folio*, 3rd series, vol. 7 (1812), p. 196.

154. Somkin, pp. 57 and 61.

155. Jefferson quoted in Paul F. Norton, "Thomas Jefferson and the Planning of the National Capital," in William Howard Adams, et al., *The Eye of Thomas Jefferson* (Washington, DC: National Gallery of Art, 1976), p. 227.

156. Thoreau quoted in Somkin, p. 59.

157. Ibid., p. 159.

158. Whitman quoted ibid., p. 73.

159. Biddle and the committee quoted in Gilchrest, p. 23.

160. Paulding quoted in Schlesinger, p. 42.

161. Pierson, p. 185. For the Ecclesiologists in association with Gothicism, see my *American Churches* (New York: Stewart, Tabori & Chang, 1982).

162. Downing quoted in Andrews, pp. 38, 40, and 41.

163. Ward, pp. 229–30.

164. Ibid.

165. Scott, pp. 37ff.

166. Kennedy, *Minnesota Houses*, p. 122.

167. Aristotle, *The Art of Rhetoric*, book I, chapter 2, paragraph 1.

168. Martineau quoted in Meyers, p. 122.

169. Corbusier quoted in Tzonis and Lefaivre, p. 287.

170. The reference to *temenos* and the quotation from Friedrich Hölderlin are taken from the opening pages of Tzonis and Lefaivre.

171. Tsigakou, p. 152.

172. Biddle manuscript, p. 68.

173. Ibid., p. 29; Biddle also quoted in Remini, *Revolutionary Age*, p. 5.

174. Staughton Lynd, *Class, Conflict, Slavery and the United States Constitution*. 1968 reprint (Westport, CT: Greenwood Press, 1980), p. 139.

175. For more on Marshall, and Bruce, see *Architecture, Men, Women and Money*.

176. Remini, *Jackson*, vol. 3, p. 452.

177. Jackson quoted in Ward, p. 147.

178. Marsh and Sumner quoted in Miles, pp. 271–72; description of Sumner from Allan Nevins, *The Emergence of Lincoln* (New York: Scribner, 1950), vol. 1, p. 26.

179. Benton and the Whigs quoted in Remini, *Revolutionary Age*, p. 172.

180. *Rose Hill* (Geneva, New York: Geneva Historical Society, 1984), pp. 23–24. Strong ran for the U.S. Senate on the Whig ticket in 1842.

181. Seward quoted in Miles, p. 285.

182. Ibid.

183. Seward, pp. 47ff.

184. Ibid.

185. Ibid.

Part Four
The Interior

186. Quotation on the Tombigbee from Walter S. Patton, in association with J. Glenn Little and Luther Hill, "General Nathan Bryan Whitfield and Gaineswood" (1972), unpublished (but available from the Alabama State Historical Commission), p. 6. I am grateful to Robert S. Gamble for making this paper available.

187. Whitfield's reports and summaries from Patton, supra, pp. 3, 5, 187, and 188.

188. Stanley quoted in Harry S. Ashmore, *Arkansas: A Bicentennial History* (New York: Norton, 1978), p. 60.

189. Chief Eufaula quoted in Peatross, p. 16.

190. Whitfield quoted in Kenneth Severens, *Southern Architecture* (New York: Dutton, 1981), p. 119. Severens cites Patton's unpublished study of 1972 (see note 186).

191. In his *White Pillars* (New York: Brainhall House, 1941), p. 93, Joseph Frazer Smith refers to Colonel Young's diary, which has subsequently been lost, and to "family records," which have also disappeared and are therefore beyond critical scrutiny. They "show that Waverly was designed by an Italian architect by the name of Pond (which does not sound Latin). However, there was an architect in St. Louis at this time named Charles I. Pond, who possibly was the man." I share the skepticism (implied by his parentheses) for this tale.

192. Whitfield's library, Ralph Hammond, *Antebellum Mansions of Alabama* (New York: Bonanza Books, 1951), p. 116.

193. Meynard, p. 411.

194. John Julius Norwich, *The Buildings of Southern England* (London: Macmillan, 1985), p. 498.

195. Gerry quoted in R. L. Raley, "Interior Designs by Benjamin Henry Latrobe," *Antiques* 75, no. 6 (June 1959), p. 571.

196. Mrs. Trollope quoted in Russell Lynes, *The Tastemakers* (New York: Universal Library, 1954), p. 10.

197. Crook, pp. 41 and 80.

198. Rykwert, p. 269.

199. Anita Brookner on Winckelmann in the *Times Literary Supplement*, October 18, 1980; see also L. D. Ettlinger, "Winckelmann, or Marble Boys are Better," in *Art, the Ape of Nature: Studies in Honor of H. W. Janson*, edited by Moshe Barasch and Lucy Freeman (New York: Abrams, 1981), pp. 505ff.

200. Calhoun and Clay quoted in Adams, *Madison Administration*, pp. 1256–67.

201. Clay quoted ibid., p. 134.

202. Pierce F. Lewis, "Common Houses, Cultural Spores," in *Landscape* 19, no. 2 (January 1975), pp. 1–22. I have considerably simplified Lewis's careful and extensive argument and in the process may have distorted what he meant to say. I regard the Greek Revival as so widespread, extending so deeply into the practice of people of all classes, and continuing so long (nearly seven decades from beginning to end) that it qualifies as vernacular. Lewis and others may not, as I have been cautioned by Michael Zuckerman. Lewis spoke of "simple, unprepossessing 'folk'

houses" changing; of "patterns" altering "among the 'folk'"; and of "the vernacular." I think my essential argument is correct even if the Greek Revival does not quite attain vernacular status, because it was so nearly ubiquitous, so very popular, dominant, and lasting.

203. Ibid, p. 3.

204. Meyers, pp. 71, 73, and 98n.

205. For Vitruvius, and much, much more, see Tzonis and Lefaivre, p. 42. I am especially grateful for Michael Tomlin's comments upon this section, and for pointing out the antiquity of the association of the Doric to the masculine. Tzonis and Lefaivre explore the "erotic" and "suggestive" names and forms of a column—a "shallowly grooved cylinder—[its] gently curved ovolo and apophyge, swollen as if by smooth caressing. . . . Indeed, if one leans against a column on a summer afternoon, it really can make the heart quiver, the skin tighten, the cheeks flush, breathing quicken."

206. Gallatin quoted in Dangerfield, *Nationalism*, pp. 3–4.

207. Cooper, pp. viii–ix.

208. Van Buren quoted in Meyers, pp. 147 and 161.

209. Webster quoted in Schlesinger, p. 293.

210. Ibid., p. 297.

211. Ibid., p. 293.

Part Five
The Decline of the Greek Revival

212. Meyers, pp. 115–117.

213. Hamlin, *Greek Revival*, p. 329.

214. Mumford, *Brown Decades*, p. 2.

215. Jefferson quoted in Miller, p. 245; other phrases at the pages in this text previously cited.

216. Michael Kammen has identified the Revolution as a rite of passage; my quotations are from his *Season of Youth*, though they are not used in the same way. For Madison see p. 47; for Fitzhugh and Everett, pp. 208–209.

217. Paine, Adams, Webster, and Bolívar quoted in Lowenthal, p. 107.

218. Mumford, *Brown Decades*, p. 1.

219. R. W. B. Lewis, pp. 1–7, 49–50, 127–29.

220. Cooper's Natty Bumppo quoted in Lowenthal, p. 110.

221. Quotations are from Forgie, pp. 18n., 19–20, 64–65.

222. The *North American Review* and Emerson quoted in Kammen, *Season*, pp. 51 and 104.

223. Thoreau, Emerson, and Hawthorne quoted in Lowenthal, pp. 115–19.

224. The *North American Review* (1855) quoted in Kammen, *Season*, p. 51.

225. Morris quoted in Finkelman, p. 212.

226. Godkin quoted in Lowenthal, pp. 115–19.

227. Adams quoted in *Memoirs of John Quincy Adams*, ed. by Charles Francis Adams. 1874–77 reprint (Freeport, NY: Books for Libraries, 1969), vol. 5, p. 11. Garrison quoted in Finkelman, p. 188.

228. Whittier quoted in Kammen, *Season*, p. 123.

229. Agar, p. 363.

230. Dred Scott opinion quoted in Agar, p. 385.

231. Hawthorne quoted in Lowenthal, pp. 111 and 115. I have made use of many of Lowenthal's quotations but, I suspect, not in ways of which he would wholly approve. We read George Forgie and Edwin Miles quite differently, but Lowenthal is so compelling that I have had difficulty in not sliding either into his own elegant language or his point of view, which is not quite mine.

No writer of genius is ever merely "representative" of his or her generation, but Emerson, Hawthorne, Whittier, and Thoreau (born in 1803, 1804, 1807, and 1817, respectively) spoke for many of their contemporaries.

232. Jackson's toast quoted in Agar, p. 279.

233. Van Buren quoted in Schlesinger, p. 487.

234. Call quoted in Herbert J. Doherty, Jr., *Richard Keith Call* (Gainesville: University of Florida Press, 1961), p. 158.

235. Houston quoted in Marquis James, *The Raven: A Biography of Sam Houston* (Covington, GA: Mockingbird Books, 1977), p. 336.

236. Davis and Lincoln quoted in McPherson, p. vii.

237. Mumford, *Brown Decades*, pp. 1–2.

238. Cockerell quoted in Robin Middleton and David Watkin, *Neoclassical and Nineteenth Century Architecture* (New York: Abrams, 1980), p. 48.

239. Greenough quoted in Mumford, *Roots*, pp. 32ff.

240. Greenough quoted ibid.

Part Six

A Hasty History of the Later Renaissance

241. *Philadelphia Architecture: A Guide to the City* (Cambridge, MA: MIT Press, 1984), p. 66; Richard Webster, et al., *Philadelphia Preserved: Catalog of the American Buildings Survey* (Philadelphia: Philadelphia Historical Commission, Temple University Press, 1981), pp. 162–63.

242. Dedicating the temple of Bacchus, from Gervaise Jackson-Stops, *National Trust Guide to West Wycombe Park*, 1972, p. 10. Franklin is quoted at p. 5.

243. We know of van Paaschen and other practitioners of "artisan mannerism" largely through the sleuthing of John Fitzhugh Millar, who promises a book to be entitled *Colonial Architecture: British, Danish, Dutch, French, German and Russian High-Style in America*. Unsatisfied with the usual Palladio-Inigo Jones-Christopher Wren sequence as a full explanation of high-style architecture in America (even as amended to include Gibbs), Millar has filed an interim report of his researches in *Classical Architecture in Renaissance Europe, 1419–1585* (Williamsburg, VA: Thirteen Colonies Press, 1987).

244. For Masonic traditions, see Dora Weibenson's provocative essay in *Paestum*, pp. 176ff.; Harold F. Pfister, "Robert Morris, Isaac Ware, and John Gwynn: Studies in English Architectural Theory, 1715–1759" (master's thesis, University of Delaware, 1974); Clay Lancaster, "Jefferson's Architectural Indebtedness to Robert Morris," in *Journal of the Society of Architectural Historians* 34 (December 1945), p. 257; Alan Gowans, "Freemasonry and the Neoclassic Style in America," in *Antiques* (February 1960), pp. 172ff.; and Haddon, pp. 287ff.

For Palladio as Mason, see Douglas Lewis, "Freemasonic Imagery in a Venetian Fresco Cycle of 1716," in *Hermeticism and the Renaissance*, edited by Ingrid Merkel and Allen G. Debus (London: Associated University Presses; Washington, DC: Folger Shakespeare Library, 1988).

For Langley, Richmond, and Montagu, see Eileen Harris, "Batty Langley, A Tutor to Freemasons (1696–1751)," in *The Burlington Magazine* (May 1977), pp. 327ff.

245. Campbell's "Design For a Church in the Vitruvian Style," in *Vitruvius Brittanicus*, vol. 2 (1731 ed.). A less fully developed temple form, also probably derived from Campbell, was St. James Church at McClellanville, South Carolina (1768).

246. Which Irish draftsperson? Beatrice Garvan, not a person with whom one contends lightly, says it was "probably" Christopher Myers, citing Robert Raley's contribution to a catalog for *The University of Pennsylvania Hospital Antiques Show* (Philadelphia: University of Pennsylvania Hospital, 1984), pp. 70–74. Garvan's statement is in her catalog to *Federal Philadelphia: The Athens of the Western World* (Philadelphia: Philadelphia Museum of Art, 1987), p. 38.

Matthew Baigell suggests James Hoban in "James Hoban and the First Bank of the United States," *Journal of the Society of Architectural Historians* 28, no. 2 (May 1969), pp. 135–36.

The source is the Royal Exchange, in Dublin, in any case.

247. Jefferson quoted in Marcus Whiffen, *The Public Buildings of Williamsburg, Colonial Capital of Virginia: An Architectural History* (Williamsburg: Colonial Williamsburg, 1958), pp. 179–80.

248. With regard to the solitariness of the Virginia capitol, I am baffled by some assurances by admirable scholars that Jefferson intended a temple complex, which might be imagined to resemble those at Berry Hill, Girard College, or even the "Three Bears" at

Ovid, New York. William Seale speaks of "a cluster of temple-type buildings crowning a hilltop" (in "James Hoban; the Man and His Taste," from a Symposium Report on the Baum-Taft House in Cincinnati), and Marie Kimball speaks of "Jefferson's governmental village" (in her *Jefferson: The Scene of Europe, 1784 to 1789.* New York: Coward-McCann, 1950. p. 70). Though she earlier quotes a bill he drafted in 1776 for a Capitol and another building, the "Halls of Justice," requiring them to have "walls of brick or stone and porticos where the same may be convenient or ornamental, with pillars and pavements of stone" (p. 69), two buildings do not make a village or even a cluster. Furthermore, by 1780, when he had apparently thought out what was "convenient or ornamental" for the halls of justice, a sketch (which all hands seem to agree he made in that year) shows a plain building with no portico. Let us concede that the floor plan for a rotunda building he apparently also sketched in that year "was doubtless intended for the Governor's Mansion" (though I have doubts). It may have columns, but, judging from its clear relationship to a sketch produced by Robert Mills in 1803 under Jefferson's direction, they were for little porticos like the second Monticello, *not* for a temple-form building like the Maison Carrée. The Pantheon, it is true, was a temple, but not of the same kind.

From this, the picture emerges of a Maison Carrée–temple of 1784, a plain brick or stone hall of justice of 1780, and a highly ambiguous description of 1776, which might as well describe a Williamsburg-brick set of structures (like the second governor's palace) as any contemplated Acropolis.

Jefferson, in short, was ahead of his time, but we should be chary of moving his taste all the way to the 1830s or 1840s.

249. Trumbull, p. 177.

250. Ibid.

251. Ibid.

252. For more about Jefferson and Latrobe and their disagreements over what is Greek and what is not, and about their differences in symbolic intention, see *Orders from France.*

253. The story of Arlington House is told in an unpublished thesis by Murray Nelligan (obtainable from the U.S. Park Service) and in his "The Building of Arlington House," *Journal of the Society of Architectural Historians* 10, no. 2 (May 1951), pp. 11–15. There are no plans or specifications or, for that matter, correspondence tying the house to Hadfield, though his obituary in a newspaper friendly to George Washington Parke Custis gives him that credit while Custis was in his prime and most attentive to his own reputation (see *Architecture, Men, Women and Money*), and was repeated in print several times in the next few years.

Nelligan, who did most of the archaeology of the house, is emphatic that the portico was planned from the outset, basing this opinion on the position of the floors, among other things, and concludes from bills that it was completed in 1817.

254. For William Parker Elliott, see Jane B. Davies, "A. J. Davis' Projects for a Patent Office Building, 1832–34," *Journal of the Society of Architectural Historians* 24, no. 3 (October 1965), p. 229.

255. Town's letter appears in Newton, p. 50. Newton goes on to wonder: "Who can he be—Stephen Hallet?"

On another point: Hadfield *was* born in Florence, despite the statement in most biographies that he was born in Leghorn.

256. Town quoted in Newton, p. 23.

257. For the Washington City Hall, see H. F. Cunningham, "The Old City Hall, Washington D.C.," *Architectural Record* 37, no. 3 (1915), pp. 268ff. The columns *in antis* of Jefferson's Christ Church in Charlottesville, Virginia, were not built until 1824.

258. For Rague in Lafever's office and his announcement, see Betty I. Madden, *Art, Crafts, and Architecture in Early Illinois* (Urbana: University of Illinois Press, 1974), pp. 144–45.

259. For Slark and its evidence, see Scully, pp. 117–18.

260. Scully rescued this date and attribution from 1828 and Gideon Shryock. Ibid., pp. 29ff.

261. Benjamin quoted from Dell Upton's remarkable summary of this material in his essay "Pattern Books and Professionalism: Aspects of the Transformation of Domestic Architecture in America, 1800–1860," *Winterthur Portfolio* 19, no. 2/3 (Summer/Autumn 1984).

Upton links the Scottish Enlightenment to ideas of architectural professionalism, stressing a somewhat later period than that to which I have addressed myself, but saying much about the Greek Revival period, by implication.

262. Bocage and Ashland are often attributed to the Dakins' sometime partner, James Gallier, Sr., but without evidence. Arthur Scully, Jr., has made the case for the Dakins convincingly, p. 99.

263. Elmes quoted in Watkin, p. 14.

264. Lafever, in his *Beauties of Modern Architecture*, published in 1835, republished in 1839, 1849, and 1855.

265. My political suggestion was in *Architecture, Men, Women and Money*. For the Brethren, see Haddon, pp. 287–88.

266. Weeks to Ep Hoyt, September 27, 1812, Weeks Papers, Mississippi Department of Archives and History.

267. Swan may or may not have been intimately associated with the inner circle of Burlingtonians. See Rudolph Wittkower, *Palladio and English Palladianism* (London: Thames and Hudson, 1983), p. 105.

268. For more about Cazenovia, the Cazenoves, and XYZ, see *Orders from France*.

269. For Daniels, see *The Horticulturist* 19 (February 1864), p. 71; Neville H. Clouten, "The Old Montgomery County Courthouse, Dayton, Ohio," *Journal of the Society of Architectural Historians* 26, no. 4 (December 1967), pp. 294ff. Daniels's advertisement appears in Clouten, p. 299.

270. For Daniels at Vassar, see Roselie Thorne McKenna, "A Study of the Architecture of the Main Building and the Landscaping of Vassar College, 1860–70" (thesis, Vassar College, 1949). He appeared in the Cincinnati city directories for 1846 and 1849, the New York city directory for 1857, and the Baltimore directory for 1864. A letter from Gary B. Schuman to Phoebe B. Stanton dated December 2, 1971, in the files of the Montgomery County Historical Society, suggests that Daniels's estimate of $44,000 to build the courthouse was so far below the actual cost of more than $100,000 that it "led to the ruining of his career." Schuman also suggests that Daniels "may have started with Gideon Shryock in Kentucky." Writing of "Idealism and the Origin of the First American Suburb: Llewellyn Park, New Jersey," in *The Ameri-*

can *Art Journal*, October 1979, pp. 79ff., Richard Guy Wilson speaks of Daniels as a "minor" figure in its formation; he "probably contributed some physical details."

271. There is no reliable monograph on Francis Costigan. I have done my brief best for him in *Architecture, Men, Women and Money*.

272. The best source of information on both Reynolds and Howard is Starr. For Bryant, see Earle G. Shettleworth, Jr., and James H. Mundy, *The Flight of the Grand Eagle: Charles G. Bryant, Maine Architect and Adventurer* (Augusta, ME: Maine Historic Preservation Commission, 1977). For Lafon, see *Orders from France*.

273. There is no monograph on Heimann; the best one can do is consult James Patrick of Dallas or James Hoobler of Nashville. Patrick's *Architecture in Tennessee* (Knoxville: University of Tennessee Press, 1981) contains a number of provocative references.

274. The Lafon-Lafitte-Latrobe puzzle is considered at some length in *Orders from France*.

BIBLIOGRAPHY

Esteem for the founding fathers, for their initial successes and for their courage and dignity during their subsequent defeats, has made it difficult for us to give due credit to the accomplishments of those who immediately followed them. It is true that a hardy crew of scholars has in recent years striven to remind us of the vernacular achievements of the seventeenth and eighteenth centuries but, by and large, strange, paradoxical creatures that we are, we persist in using the term *colonial* as though colonial status were a mark of pride. We spend vast sums rebuilding communities that chiefly demonstrate provincial expressions of European hegemony, political and cultural. We look for satisfaction in that frail, tentative, and derivative "high Federal" style that was all that could be achieved in the first decade and a half after political independence. And, if we are to judge from space allocated in our museums and lines in our budgets for preservation, we have apparently found it difficult to take delight in the Greek Revival, which, though it meant many things to many nations, was for early nineteenth-century America the expression of cultural independence.

It is a mark of our strange lack of cultural self-assertion that there have appeared only two books about that American Popular Classicism that produced tens of thousands of idiosyncratic, uninhibited, and beautiful buildings from the St. Croix River of Maine to the St. Croix River of Minnesota, from the realm of the moose to that of the alligator. Suddenly, sweepingly, the Greek Revival accorded with the emotional requirements of the nation and, as suddenly, it was gone. Thereafter for nearly a century, the Greek Revival went uncelebrated and nearly uncontested until it was rediscovered by Howard Major and Talbot Hamlin.

Their two books are not of the same quality. Hamlin's *Greek Revival Architecture in America* was published nearly half a century ago. He had good reason to replace Major's *The Domestic Architecture of the Early American Republic*, which was written in 1924–25, during a time when America was suffering one of its recurrent periods of overassessment of its economic assets and underassessment of its art. At the time, Americans apparently felt themselves to be at a great distance from some imaginary center of things, doubting any artistic achievements accomplished independently of Europe in general or Great Britain in particular.

The glories of the Greek Revival had been almost forgotten, together with the Furness-Richardson-Sullivan-Root Renaissance of the 1880s. It was fashionable to disdain even the consummate work of the immediately preceding generation in the mid- and far West. Frank Lloyd Wright was thought by many to be an embarrassment, Louis Sullivan a crank, and the masterpieces of the brothers Greene subjects of parody. Suburbs were being afflicted by local versions of the "Georgian," the "Tudor," and, in extreme cases, a bouldery-turrety "Norman" that had nothing to recommend it except that it was not American.

In 1926, Major, with considerable boldness, began a counterattack upon this sort of pusillanimity by offering some words of appreciation for the American Greek Revival.

Things were not much better in the 1940s, when Hamlin's book found a publisher, except for the presence of Hamlin himself, a great natural force. Hamlin did not have access to color photography, and the format of his book (published in the midst of the war of 1941–45) was so reduced that even its black-and-white illustrations were barely larger than postage stamps or advertisements in a farm-foreclosure catalog. Hamlin's stylistic analysis, especially his wonderful parsing of buildings to show their reliance upon pattern books, does not require much restatement here, though the appendix just preceding this bibliography comprises an updated gazetteer intended to make it easier to seek out the noteworthy structures that have survived to our own time.

Admirers of Hamlin's book will also find here some recognition of the annotating, supplementing, and correcting that has occupied monographists since he wrote. The chronology—and therefore the psychological and economic setting—of the Greek Revival presented here differs from that offered by Hamlin and his contemporaries; it was then conventional to depict it as blossoming continuously from the Peace of Paris, in 1783, until the Civil War, in 1861.

Two other magisterial works have been essential to the preparation of this work. They are Henry Adams's multivolume histories of the administrations of Thomas Jefferson and James Madison, now conveniently republished in two of the Library of America series, listed below. None of Adams's critics has dislodged him from his position as the most perspicacious historian to have written about the first two decades of the nineteenth century. His prejudices are worn on his sleeve, as are those of Arthur Schlesinger, Jr., our best guide to the next two decades. The vitality bestowed on the work of both these great writers by their fervent convictions gives greater potency to their marvelously pungent prose and their awesome range of research.

Schlesinger will probably have to await posthumous recognition in the Library of America for *The Age of Jackson*, but no one who has tried to write history with grace and precision can fail to admire his achievement, which towers over the works of most contemporaries. Schlesinger is a great writer; we are fortunate that we can supplement his eloquence with the more comprehensive works of Robert Remini, surely the most painstaking and thorough chronicler of the Age of Jackson. There are also many other fine works on the period, of which I have found especially provocative John William Ward's *Andrew Jackson: Symbol for an Age*, a short and piquant book analyzing the uses to which his age put Jackson. My only quibble with Ward is that he presents the War of 1812 as if it came as a "blow" that "threatened to destroy the young nation's pride." Henry Adams might have responded that by that time there was very little pride left.

Thanks to paperback reprints, we have in recent years recovered ready access to other primary works demonstrating how differently the Age of Jackson and Biddle appears to people who come to it from different ideological directions. Samuel Eliot Morison thought Andrew Jackson vulgar though entertaining (see his *Oxford History of the American People*, vol. 2, reprinted in a Mentor edition in 1972). James Parton's approving biography of Jackson, as edited and condensed into *The Presidency of Andrew Jackson*, appeared as a Harper paperback in 1967. George

Bancroft was a firm partisan of Jackson's and wrote with immense verve and conviction; his *History of the United States of America from the Discovery of the Continent*, as edited by Russel B. Nye, was reissued in a University of Chicago paperback in 1966. Nye himself contributed a pioneering inquiry into the arts of the time, though he did not include much architecture, with *Society and Culture in America* (New York: Harper, 1974).

I discovered Fred Somkin's remarkable *Unquiet Eagle* with immense delight as this book was in its final editing. Without any apparent interest in architecture, Somkin has been able to work out a thesis about the yearning for order among the Jacksonians that seems to me quite compatible with what I have tried to say in this work. Somkin's is a most remarkable work, focusing upon the theme of the betrayal of the cult of republican simplicity by the pecuniary instincts of the American people in the first half of the nineteenth century, and their resultant feeling of guilt.

Somkin listed admiringly some masterworks by our contemporaries. These are the necessary under-pinnings of this study as well as his, although their influence is so pervasive that I have cited them in few individual instances. They are *there*, thank goodness: Henry Nash Smith's *Virgin Land: The American West as Symbol and Myth* (Cambridge, MA: Harvard University Press, 1950); Richard W. B. Lewis's *The American Adam: Innocence, Tragedy, and Tradition in the Nineteenth Century* (Chicago: University of Chicago Press, 1955); and Leo Marx's *The Machine in the Garden: Technology and the Pastoral Ideal in America* (New York: Oxford University Press, 1964). I would add Rowland T. Berthoff's *An Unsettled People: Social Order and Disorder in American History* (New York: Harper and Row, 1971), and of course the works of Michael Kammen, to which frequent reference is made in the text. Kammen's books are full of useful ideas about the ebb and flow of poetic, literary, and artistic expressions of veneration for the founders. I owe a major debt to him.

Of the writers of the previous generation, I have especially enjoyed the work of Howard Mumford Jones and Van Wyck Brooks, though I differ from them in many particulars of interpretation, and am puzzled by their lack of interest in the evidence of architecture. Brooks, for example, was as eager as Jones to find an instant Greek Revival in the early years of the republic, and marred an otherwise splendid book, *The World of Washington Irving*, with the then-conventional insistence upon the prepotency of Jefferson's Richmond capitol. Brooks says that Benjamin Henry Latrobe's remodeling of Kalorama, the Washington, D.C., residence of the epic poet Joel Barlow, produced a building like the Virginia capitol. This is simply not true; Kalorama was nothing of the sort. It was a pleasant, cubical, Regency villa, bearing no relationship to a pedimented rectangle with porticos and columns.

Aside from notes and notations, luncheon admonitions and corridor commentary from many of the people listed in the acknowledgments, I have benefited from monograph-length letters from the wise and unrelenting Michael Zuckerman. I wish also to make grateful acknowledgment of the help from others required to sort out the intricacies of relationship among the architects in the circle of Ithiel Town in New York, and to dispose of misinformation contained either in Talbot Hamlin's work or in the dreadful volume on Town and Davis by Roger Hale Newton. I have relied upon Robert Alexander, the expert on Russell Warren; Jane B. Davies, the Town and Davis authority; on Arthur Scully, the expert on the brothers Dakin; and on Denys Peter Myers and Jacob Landy for Minard

Lafever. Conversations have supplemented Scully's *James Dakin, Architect*, Landy's *The Architecture of Minard Lafever*, Myers's introduction to the 1968 Da Capo Press reprint of Lafever's *Beauties of Modern Architecture*, Davies's articles on Davis—and Town and Davis—in the *Macmillan Encyclopedia of Architects* (vols. 1 and 4), and Alexander's "The Architecture of Russell Warren" (New York University, 1961). Like some of the best work in American architectural history, this meticulous, well-written, and well-illustrated work remains unpublished. One of the purposes of books like the one before you is to bring to the attention of academic publishers the richness of material lying about. In England, worse architects have received much more generous attention.

For the genealogy of horses, there is no one better informed than Alexander Mackay-Smith, and for the genealogy of Hamptons the expert is Mrs. Virginia Meynard. I thank them both here for their contributions to bibliography and for subsequent letters of further explication. Mrs. Meynard provided both the reconstruction drawing of Millwood that appeared in her *The Venturers* and in my *Architecture, Men, Women and Money*, and also a lead to the research reported by John Califf III in his "Millwood, Its Architecture and Ambiences" (1982; manuscript available from Mr. Califf, Columbia, South Carolina).

Listed below are works to which reference is made more than once. If a work is referred to but once, it is listed only in its pendant footnote or endnote. The objective here is to facilitate pursuit and further exploration. Therefore many books, articles, newspapers, memoirs, theses, and monographs essential to the study of this period are found only in the footnotes or endnotes because they relate only to the single point asserted in the text at that point.

One small procedural note: I have listed a work under its editor when that editor dominates the proceedings (e.g. David Brion Davis and Mary Granger), and under its subject when that subject is the specific person or place of whom or which we tend to think first when seeking information (e.g. Latrobe).

Adams, Henry. *History of the United States of America during the Administrations of James Madison*. New York: Library of America, 1986.

———. *History of the United States of America during the Administrations of Thomas Jefferson*. New York: Library of America, 1986.

Agar, Herbert. *The Price of Union*. Boston: Houghton Mifflin, 1950.

Ahlstrom, Sydney E. *A Religious History of the American People*. New Haven: Yale University Press, 1972.

Alberts, Robert C. *The Golden Voyage: The Life and Times of William Bingham, 1752–1804*. Boston: Houghton Mifflin, 1969.

Andrews, Wayne. *The American Gothic: Its Origins, Its Trials, Its Triumphs*. New York: Random House, 1975.

Brooks, Van Wyck. *The World of Washington Irving*. New York: Dutton, 1950.

Burns, James MacGregor. *The Vineyard of Liberty: The American Experiment*. New York: Knopf, 1982.

Cochran, Thomas C. *Frontiers of Change: Early Industrialism in America*. New York: Oxford University Press, 1981.

Cooper, James F. *The Chainbearer: The Littlepage Manuscript*. Boston: Houghton Mifflin (no date).

Crook, J. Mordaunt. *The Greek Revival*. London: Murray, 1972.

Cunningham, John T. *University in the Forest*. New York: Afton, 1972.

Dangerfield, George. *The Awakening of American Nationalism, 1815–1828*. New York: Harper and Row, 1965.

——. *The Era of Good Feelings*. New York: Harcourt, Brace and World, 1952.

Davis, David Brion, ed. *Antebellum American Culture: An Interpretive Anthology*. Lexington, MA: Heath, 1979.

Finkelman, Paul. "Slavery and the Constitutional Convention," in *Beyond Confederation: Origins of the Constitution and American National Identity*. Edited by Richard R. Beeman. Published for the Institute of Early American History and Culture, Williamsburg, Virginia. Chapel Hill: University of North Carolina Press, 1987.

Finley, M. I., ed. *The Legacy of Greece: A New Appraisal*. Oxford: Oxford University Press, 1984.

Forgie, George B. *Patricide in the House Divided: A Psychological Interpretation of Lincoln and His Age*. New York: Norton, 1979.

Gallagher, H. M. Pierce. *Robert Mills: The Architect of the Washington Monument, 1781–1855*. New York: Columbia University Press, 1935.

Gilchrest, Agnes A. "Girard College: An Example of the Layman's Influence on Architecture," in *Journal of the Society of Architectural Historians*, vol. 16, no. 2 (May 1957).

Govan, Thomas Payne. *Nicholas Biddle, Nationalist and Public Banker, 1786–1844*. Chicago: University of Chicago Press, 1959.

Granger, Mary, ed. *Savannah River Plantations: The Savannah Writers Project*. Savannah: Georgia Historical Society, 1947.

Haddon, Rawson W. "The First Architectural Society in America," in *Architectural Record*, vol. 38, no. 2 (August 1915).

Hamlin, Talbot. *Benjamin Henry Latrobe*. New York: Oxford University Press, 1955.

——. *Greek Revival Architecture in America: Being an Account of Important Trends in American Architecture Prior to the War Between the States*. New York: Oxford University Press, 1944.

Hampton, Sally Baxter. *A Divided Heart: Letters of Sally Baxter Hampton, 1853–1869*. Edited by Ann Tripp Hampton. Spartanburg, SC: Reprint Co., 1980.

Harris, Neil. *The Artist in American Society: The Formative Years, 1790–1860*. New York: Braziller, 1966.

Hersey, George L. *The Lost Meaning of Classical Architecture*. Cambridge, MA: MIT Press, 1988.

Irving, John Beaufrain. *The South Carolina Jockey Club*. 1857. Spartanburg, SC: Reprint Co., 1975.

Isaac, Rhys. *The Transformation of Virginia, 1740–1790*. Published for the Institute of Early American History and Culture, Williamsburg, Virginia. Chapel Hill: University of North Carolina Press, 1982.

Jaffe, Irma B. *John Trumbull: Patriot-Artist of the American Revolution*. Boston: New York Graphic Society, 1975.

James, Marquis. *Andrew Jackson: Portrait of a President*. New York: Grosset and Dunlap, 1961.

Jameson, J. Franklin. *The American Revolution Considered as a Social Movement*. 1926 reprint. Princeton: Princeton University Press, 1973.

Jones, Howard Mumford. *O Strange New World: American Culture, The Formative Years*. New York: Viking, 1964.

Kammen, Michael. *People of Paradox*. New York: Knopf, 1973.

——. *A Season of Youth: The American Revolution and the Historical Imagination*. New York: Knopf, 1978.

Kennedy, Roger G. *Architecture, Men, Women and Money in America, 1600–1860*. New York: Random House, 1985.

——. *Minnesota Houses: An Architectural and Historical View*. Minneapolis: Dillon Press, 1967.

——. *Orders From France*. New York: Knopf, 1989.

Keuls, Eva C. *The Reign of Phallus: Sexual Politics in Ancient Athens*. New York: Harper and Row, 1985.

Lafever, Minard. *Beauties of Modern Architecture*. 1835 reprint. New York: Da Capo Press, 1968.

Landy, Jacob. *The Architecture of Minard Lafever*. New York: Columbia University Press, 1970.

Lane, Mills. *Georgia: Architecture of the Old South*. Savannah, GA: Beehive Press, 1986.

——. *South Carolina: Architecture of the Old South*. Savannah, GA: Beehive Press, 1984.

Latrobe, Benjamin Henry. *Correspondence and Miscellaneous Papers*. Edited by John C. Van Horne, et al. (3 vols.) Published for the Maryland Historical Society. New Haven: Yale University Press, 1984–88.

Lee, Susan Previant and Peter Passell. *A New Economic View of American History*. New York: Norton, 1979.

Lewis, Henry Williams. *More Taste Than Prudence: A Study of John Evans Johnson (1815–1870), an Amateur with Patrons*. Chapel Hill, NC: Borderer Press, 1983.

Long, Orie William. *Thomas Jefferson and George Ticknor: A Chapter in American Scholarship*. Williamstown, MA: McClelland Press, 1933.

Lowenthal, David. *The Past is a Foreign Country*. Cambridge, Eng.: Cambridge University Press, 1985.

McDannell, Colleen. *The Christian Home in Victorian America, 1840–1900*. Bloomington: Indiana University Press, 1986.

McLean, Robert Colin. *George Tucker: Moral Philosopher and Man of Letters*. Chapel Hill, NC: University of North Carolina Press, 1961.

Macmillan Encyclopedia of Architects. Edited by Adolph K. Placzek. New York: Free Press, 1982.

McPherson, James M. *Battle Cry of Freedom: The Era of the Civil War.* New York: Oxford University Press, 1988.

Major, Howard. *The Domestic Architecture of the Early American Republic: the Greek Revival.* Philadelphia: Lippincott, 1926.

Meyers, Marvin. *The Jacksonian Persuasion: Politics and Beliefs.* Stanford, CA: Stanford University Press, 1957.

Meynard, Virginia. *The Venturers: The Hampton, Harrison and Earle Families of Virginia, South Carolina and Texas.* Easley, SC: Southern History Press, 1981.

Miles, Edwin A. "The Young American Nation and the Classical World," in *Journal of the History of Ideas,* vol. 35, no. 1 (January–March 1974).

Miller, John C. *The Wolf by the Ears: Thomas Jefferson and Slavery.* New York: Free Press, 1977.

Morison, Samuel Eliot. *Maritime History of Massachusetts, 1783–1860.* 1921 reprint. Boston: Northeastern University Press, 1979.

Mumford, Lewis. *The Brown Decades: A Study of the Arts in America 1865–1895.* New York: Dover, 1971.

———. *Roots of Contemporary American Architecture.* New York: Dover, 1972.

Newton, Roger Hale. *Town and Davis: Architects, Pioneers in American Revivalist Architecture, 1812–1870; including a glimpse of their times and contemporaries.* New York: Columbia University Press, 1942.

Nichols, Frederick Doveton. *Early Architecture of Georgia: With a Pictorial Survey by Frances Benjamin Johnston.* Chapel Hill: University of North Carolina Press, 1957.

North, Douglass C. *The Economic Growth of the United States, 1780–1860.* 1961 reprint. New York: Norton, 1966.

Padover, Saul K. *Jefferson.* New York: New American Library, 1952.

Paestum and the Doric Revival, 1750–1830: Essential Outlines of an Approach. Edited by Joselito R. Serra. New York: National Academy of Design, 1986.

Parrington, Vernon Louis. *Main Currents in American Thought: An Interpretation of American Literature from the Beginnings to 1920.* New York: Harcourt, Brace and World, 1958.

Patrick, James. *Architecture in Tennessee 1768–1897.* Knoxville: University of Tennessee Press, 1981.

Peatross, C. Ford. *William Nichols.* Exhibition Catalogue. Tuscaloosa: University of Alabama Art Gallery, 1979.

Pierson, William. *American Buildings and Their Architects: Technology and the Picturesque, the Corporate, and the Early Gothic Style.* Garden City, NY: Anchor Press, 1980.

Ravenel, Beatrice St. Julien. *Architects of Charleston.* 2nd revised edition. Charleston, SC: Carolina Art Association, 1964.

Remini, Robert Vincent. *Andrew Jackson and the Bank War: A Study in the Growth of Presidential Power.* New York: Norton, 1967.

——. *Andrew Jackson and the Course of American Freedom, 1822–1832.* (vol. 2) New York: Harper and Row, 1981.

——. *Andrew Jackson and the Course of American Democracy, 1833–1845.* (vol. 3) New York: Harper and Row, 1984.

——. *The Revolutionary Age of Andrew Jackson.* New York: Harper and Row, 1976.

Rogin, Michael Paul. *Fathers and Children: Andrew Jackson and the Subjugation of the American Indian.* New York: Vintage Books, 1976.

Rorabaugh, W. J. *The Alcoholic Republic: An American Tradition.* New York: Oxford University Press, 1981.

Rykwert, Joseph. *The First Moderns: The Architects of the Eighteenth Century.* Cambridge, MA: MIT Press, 1980.

Schlesinger, Arthur M., Jr. *The Age of Jackson.* Boston: Little, Brown, 1953.

Scott, Geoffrey. *The Architecture of Humanism: A Study in the History of Taste.* London: Constable, 1914.

Scully, Arthur. *James Dakin, Architect: His Career in New York and the South.* Baton Rouge: Louisiana State University Press, 1973.

Seward, Frederick W. *Seward at Washington as Senator and Secretary of State.* (2 vols.) New York: Derby and Miller, 1891.

Shepard, Barnett. "Sailors' Snug Harbor Reattributed to Minard Lafever," in *Journal for the Society of Architectural Historians*, vol. 35, no. 2 (May 1976).

Shi, David. *The Simple Life. Plain Living and High Thinking in American Culture.* New York: Oxford University Press, 1985.

Somkin, Fred. *Unquiet Eagle: Memory and Desire in the Idea of American Freedom, 1815–1860.* Ithaca, NY: Cornell University Press, 1967.

Starr, S. Frederick. *Southern Comfort: The Garden District of New Orleans, 1800–1900.* Cambridge, MA: MIT Press, 1989.

Stuart, Reginald. *The Half-Way Pacifist.* Toronto: University of Toronto Press, 1978.

Tallmadge, Thomas Eddy. *The Story of Architecture in America.* NewYork: Norton, 1936.

Taylor, William R. *Cavalier and Yankee: The Old South and the American National Character.* 1961 reprint. Cambridge, MA: Harvard University Press, 1979.

Temin, Peter. *The Jacksonian Economy.* New York: Norton, 1969.

Trumbull, John. *The Autobiography of Colonel John Trumbull: Patriot-Artist, 1756–1843.* Edited by Theodor Sizer. New Haven: Yale University Press, 1953.

Tsigakou, Fani Maria. *The Rediscovery of Greece: Travellers and Painters of the Romantic Era.* New Rochelle, NY: Caratzas Brothers, 1981.

Turner, Frederick Jackson. *The United States, 1830–1850.* 1950 reprint. New York: Norton, 1965.

Tzonis, Alexander and Liane Lefaivre. *Classical Architecture: The Poetics of Order.* Cambridge, MA: MIT Press, 1986.

Waddell, Gene, and Rhodri Windsor Liscombe. *Robert Mills' Courthouses and Jails.* Easley, SC: Southern History Press, 1981.

Ward, John William. *Andrew Jackson, Symbol for an Age.* New York: Oxford University Press, 1955.

Watkin, David. *Athenian Stuart: Pioneer of the Greek Revival.* London: Allen and Unwin, 1982.

Wiebe, Robert H. *The Opening of American Society: From the Adoption of the Constitution to the Eve of Disunion.* NY: Knopf, 1984.

Wills, Gary. *Inventing America: Jefferson's Declaration of Independence.* Garden City, NY: Doubleday, 1978.

Wood, Gordon S. *The Creation of the American Republic, 1776–1787.* New York: Norton, 1972.

Wright, Louis. "Thomas Jefferson and the Classics." Paper read before the American Philosophical Society, midwinter and autumn meetings, Philadelphia, 1942–43.

INDEX

Florida, 17–18, 22, 97, 329
Tallahassee, 346; bank in, 207; governor's mansion, 18
Footner, William: Bonsecours Market, 3n
Forest, The, 12n, 13, 124, 131, 132n, 135–36, **142, 147, 148,** 212n, 340, 389–90; Reichardt as architect of, 132, 134, 135; similarity to Milford, 132, 136, 142–43; Warren as architect of, 132, 136
founding fathers: ambiguous public feelings about, 94, 99; classical architectural metaphors used by, 59–60; political failure of, 61, 72, 73, 76–77, 85; preference for Greek by, 60; promotion of austerity by, 6, 80–81, 85; public rejection of, 72, 73, 76–77, 183, 288, 289–90; rejection of ancient traditions by, 25–31, 59n; as reproaches to extravagance, 86, 87, 98; symbolic patricide by, 64–65, 288; veneration of, 288–89
Fox, Samuel M., 188, 191
France: American rejection of Roman tradition in, 60, 169; assistance to Greece by, 181, 182; furniture design from, 265; Greek Revival in, 5, 269, 270, 271; naval war against, 74; "regents" (architectural) from, 79, 331–32
Franklin, Benjamin, 28, 325
Freemasonry, 9, 326, 328, 345
furnishings, 265–66

Gaineswood, 10, **149,** 252, **312, 313,** 350; floor plan of, **259;** influence of British Regency style on, 259–60; influence of Reichardt on, 259, 350; ornament of, 258, 264, 272
Gallatin, Albert, 83, 123, 138n, 175, 178, 276
Gallier, James, 8, 133n, 260, 261n, 294, 347, 349; Barton Academy, **51;** Belle Helene, 141n, **159,** 343; builders' guides of, 258, 260, 261n, 339, 349–50; Christ Episcopal Church (Mobile), 8, **54;** Government Street Presbyterian Church, 8, **376**
Garrison, William Lloyd, 290
Georgia, 10, 20, 21, 204, 387
Athens: A. P. Dearing House, **244;** University of

Georgia, 256–57
Augusta: Old Medical College, 257, **374**
Milledgeville: Executive Mansion, 257, 336n, 341n
Savannah: custom house, 263; Gibbons's town house, 128–29, 130; Jay's Greek Revival bank, 207
Germany: affinity of Americans to, 134–35; and American Greek Revival, 10, 133, 135, 332n; Greek Revival in, 5
Gerry, Elbridge, 265
Gibbons, Thomas, 67, 124, 125, 126, **127,** 128–29, 130–31, 136, 274
Gibbons, William, 126, 129, 130, 132, 135, 136, 137–39, 390
Gibbs, James, 9, 326
Girard, Stephen, 175
Glover, Williamson Allen, 258n, 264
Goldsmith, James: Bank of Geauga, 340
Gothic Revival, 196–98, 200, 209n, 214–15, 293
Gould, Jay, 136n, 196
Graff, Frederick C: Fairmont Waterworks, **118, 119,** 190, **191**
Granger, Gideon, 128
Great Britain: American rejection of Roman architecture in, 60, 169, 189, 193, 209; assistance to Greece by, 181, 182; dependence of American commerce on, 74, 180, 213, 286, 388; embargoes on trade with, 75–76, 83–84; Gothicists' enthusiasm for architecture of, 197, 198; Greek Revival in, 5, 269–70, 271, 272, 324–25; Jefferson's policy toward, 74–76; Regency style in, and U.S. architecture, 259–60, 261n, 331, 349; "regents" (architectural) from, 332, 333, 341; Renaissance architecture in, 326–27; and War of 1812, 76, 83, 89, 90
Greece: American public support for, 178, 181; American travelers in, 78, 169–71, 192, 270; ancient, 163, 395, 396; conquests of, 164; failure of U.S. government to support, 177–78, 179–80; fight for independence by, 168, 177, 178, 181–82; ignorance of, by Palladians, 9, 164, 324;

rejection of ancient traditions of, by founding fathers, 25–31; Russian incursion into, 164–65, 168
Greek Revival: ambiguity of, 6, 7, 87, 277; in ancient Rome, 191–92, 323; and banking, 188, 190, 206–8, 210; as celebration, 3, 6, 61, 87, 102, 176–77; cultural upheaval symbolized by, 274–75, 284–85, 286; delayed arrival of, 7, 27n, 29–30, 60, 65, 78–80, 86, 101, 330, 336; early American forerunners of, 18, 329; emotional appeal of, 199–200; in Europe, 5–6, 12, 167, 190, 269–72, 324–25; Federalists' rejection of, 171; founding fathers' rejection of, 26, 28, 65; heroism expressed by, 274; historical beginnings of, 9, 23n, 323–24; hope expressed by, 71, 215, 286; Jacksonian values symbolized by, 183, 272, 275, 276–78; Latrobe's framework for, 188–89; made obsolete by Civil War, 287, 293; masculine connotations of, 206–7, 266–67, 274, 277, 279, 388, 394; as Northern tradition, 7n, 23–24, 73, 204, 215; order expressed by, 183, 185, 200, 277–78, 284–85, 286; Palladian tradition of, 19–20, 326, 329; phallic symbolism of, 273–74, 387, 392, 395–97; popular feeling expressed by, 12, 177, 185, 270; post–Civil War, 294–96; power expressed by, 22; pride expressed by, 177, 276; as rejection of European values, 183, 185, 192–93, 202; Roman elements in, 19, 23, 326, 329, 336; Serlian tradition of, 326–27; and slavery, 285, 289, 290, 291; Southern differences in, 23–24, 31, 73, 203–5, 209–10, 285; as timeless architecture, 191–92, 199, 200; uncanonical nature of, 9, 16, 19, 190, 270, 271, 326
Greenberg, Allan, 395
Greenough, Horace, 294

Hadfield, George, 23, 24, 79, 168, 194, 262, 270, 284,

294, 332, 333, 334–35, 351; Arlington House, 13, 19, 20, 22, 25, **30,** 31, 78, 86, **105, 106, 107, 108,** 204, 211, 276, 326, 335, 336, 339; and Ithiel Town, 211n, 337, 338; U.S. Capitol, 334–35; War Department Building, 29, 335, 336n; Washington City Hall, **vi,** 132n, 211, 263, **335,** 337, 338, 340, 351; work studied by A. J. Davis, 133, 338
Hallet, Etienne-Sulpice, 79, 330, 331, 332n, 335n; Capitol design, **331**
Hamilton, Alexander, 26, 72, 175, 179, 273, 345
Hamilton, Gavin, 170, 187
Hamlin, Talbot, 59n, 287, 330
Hampton, Wade I, 67, 124, **125,** 126, 127–28, 252
Hampton, Wade II, 126–27, **126,** 137–39, 140–41, 253
Hampton family, 21, 252; western interests of, 253
Harrison, Peter, 168, 331; Redwood Library, 18, 168, **329**
Harrison, William Henry, 93, 178, 185, 277, 278
Hart, Philip, **330**
Haviland, John, 133n, 194, 206, 341, 342, 344, 349; builders' guides of, 343, 344; Franklin Institute, 343; Italianate style of, 347; Portsmouth Naval Hospital, **372;** St. George's Greek Orthodox Church, 343
Hawaii, 15
Hawksmoor, Nicholas, 327
Hawthorne, Nathaniel, 289, 291
Heimann, Adolphus, 10, 259n, 294, 350; Belle Mead, 141n; Belmont, 87, 260, 294, **318, 319,** 350; Nashville Masonic Hall, 260
Henry, Patrick, 73, 77
herms, 395
Hill, Chester, 261
Hoban, James: Oak Hill, 8, 329; U.S. Capitol, 335n
Hodge, William: Illinois state house, **356, 358**
Hooker, John: Lorenzo, 347
Hooker, Philip, 331; Albany Academy, 347
Hope, Thomas, **265,** 266, 269–70
horses, 137–39, 208
Houston, Sam, 18, 292, 346
Howard, Henry, 8, 261n, 294, 327, 340, 347, 349; Belle Grove, 87, 261n, 294, 347, **349;** Grinnan Residence, 349;

Madewood, **158,** 340, 341n; Nottoway, 261n, **316, 317;** Woodlawn, 340
Hume, David, 187, 189
Hutton, Addison: Ridgeway Library, 18, 295–96

Illinois, 15
Chicago, 348; Clarke House, **306**
Galena, 15, 16
Princeton: Clark House, **225**
Shawneetown, 15
Springfield, 339; Old State Capitol, **ii,** 339, **357, 358**
Vandalia: state house, **356, 358**
Waukegan: Swartout House, **226**
Indiana, 15; state capitol, 339
Glenwood: Gray-Thompson House, **220**
Madison: 11, 13, 15, 16; Lanier Mansion, **154, 307,** 349; Shrewsbury-Windle House, **308, 309,** 349
Rising Sun: Ohio County courthouse, **365**
Vevay, 15, 16
interior space, 257, 258, 262–64, **340**
Iowa
Iowa City: old state capitol, 339
Irving, Washington, 93, 197, 277, 293
Italy, 5, 270–71
Izard family, 78, 171n, 167

Jackson, Andrew, 91n, **92,** 103, 213, 252, 278n, 291, 292, 346; and Adams (John Quincy), 77, 91n, 97, 278; agrarian values of, 283, 284; American Gothicists' admiration of, 196–97, 276; as American Senex, 93, 97–98, 272, 277–78; austere patriotism symbolized by, 183–84; and bank war with Biddle, 92, 137–38, 184, 212–13; and Battle of New Orleans, 90, 91; conservative politics of, 92–93, 283; Greek Revival symbolizing, 183, 185, 272, 275; Hermitage, 92, 95–97, **112, 113,** 265, 286, 346; as heroic figure, 93, 94, 183, 275, 276, 277; Lafayette as model for, 93, 94, 192; as restorer of American pride, 77, 90, 91, 276; as Roman symbol, 23, 91, 92, 94, 95, 186, 209–10, 272; Southern Roman Revival associated with, 207, 209–10; success and

Acknowledgements

The Gazetteer alone for this work has required the willing complicity of scores of people, including the Historic Preservation officers of many states as well as historians of the period. Travel writers contributing to *The Smithsonian Guide to Historic America*, which was being edited while this book was in the final stages of drafting, caught several prize fish that had eluded other weirs and grids. I have listed below only those from whom there is correspondence in our files; there is no way to acknowledge the innumerable telephone calls in which valuable suggestions were made.

Equally generous have been members of the staff of the National Museum of American History—in corridor conversation, readings of endnotes and paragraphs in special fields, and, in some cases, whole chunks of manuscript. Rather than unwittingly omit some who have reason to know their ideas are presented here, it has seemed wisest to omit all, offering instead thanks for their help in yet another common enterprise. However, I do want to express my gratitude to those who have labored with me on the whole book: Naomi Glass, Joyce Ramey, and Elsie Mosqueda.

There have also been readings of bits and pieces of this text by scholars over many years, only some of whom have seen it all, and none of whom are responsible for what I have done after we talked or corresponded. I especially wish to thank Michael Zuckerman of the University of Pennsylvania; S. Frederick Starr of Oberlin; Leonard Eaton of Michigan; Robert Gamble of Alabama; the Knight of Clyn; J. Mordaunt Crook of London; Daniel Bluestone of Columbia University; Michael Tomlan of Cornell; Arthur Scully, Jr., of New Orleans; Clay Lancaster of Kentucky; Henry Lewis of North Carolina; Richard Guy Wilson of the University of Virginia; Malcolm Bell, Jr., of Georgia; Marcus Cunliffe of George Washington University; Mills Lane; William Jordy of Brown University; James Hoobler of Tennessee; Governor John Waihee and Senator Spark Matsunaga of Hawaii, and Sherry Matano of Senator Matsunaga's staff; Douglas Lewis of the National Gallery of Art; Walter C. Kidney of Pittsburgh; Abbott Lowell Cummings, now of Yale; Dell Upton of Berkeley; Douglas Bucher of Albany, NY; Marion Clough of Martinsville, NJ; Ronald Miller of Natchez; Joyce K. Bibber of the University of Southern Maine; Samuel Wilson, Jr., of New Orleans; William M. Shepherd of Arkansas; Jane K. Davies of New York; Robert Alexander of Iowa City, Iowa; Pamela Scott of Washington, DC; C. Ford Peatross of the Library of Congress; Robert Remini; Alexander Mackey-Smith; and Denys Peter Myers of the HABS.

State historic preservation officers, historical commissions, resource commissions, and tourist commissions have been very helpful. I wish to thank, especially, Calder Loth of Virginia; Robert Gamble and Gwyn Turner of Alabama; Kenneth Story and Tonia Jones of Arkansas; Barbara Mattick, William Thurston, and Elizabeth Kirby of Florida; Jeff Cohen and Greg Ramsey of Pennsylvania; Michael Devine of Illinois; D. Martin Perry of Kentucky; Terry Karschner of New Jersey; Earle Shettleworth of Maine; Ray Luce, Stephen C. George, and Richard V. Francaviglia of Ohio; David Kroll of Indiana; William Fleischli and Ann Swallow of Illinois; Leonard T. Gargield of Washington; and Russell Nagata (comptroller of the State of Hawaii).

In the ordinary course of business, this book could not have been produced—it would have been too expensive and complex. The ordinary course was miraculously altered by three extraordinary willingnesses: first, that of Sam Yanes, who caused Polaroid to underwrite the entire cost of the photographs. Second, that of the photographers, who disrupted their other work to travel to many not easily accessible places.

And third, that of an editorial team at Stewart, Tabori and Chang, headed by Brian Hotchkiss, who went far beyond any ordinary level of publisher's care and editorial attention.

I thank you all.

PICTURE CREDITS

Principal Photography

(Note: Nearly all of the color photographs commissioned for GREEK REVIVAL AMERICA were created using Polaroid Polachrome film, and were shot in the 4 × 5 format. Those made with other film and formats are indicated by an asterisk (*) following the page number.)

John M. Hall: front jacket, i, iii, v, 35, 36, 38*, 39*, 40, 41, 42, 52, 53, 55, 116, 117, 145, 146, 149, 151, 152, 153, 156, 157, 158, 159, 160, 241, 243 (bottom), 244, 245, 246, 247 (top, left), 247 (top, right; bottom, left and right)*, 293, 302, 303, 304, 312, 313, 316, 317, 354, 355, 372 (bottom, right), 374, 380, 381, back jacket

Jack Kotz: ii, 48, 49, 50, 51, 54, 105*, 106, 107, 108, 112, 113, 155, 218 (bottom, right), 221, 222, 223, 225, 226, 228, 229, 235, 242, 305, 306, 308, 309, 318, 319, 353, 356, 357, 358, 359, 360, 361, 362, 363, 365 (bottom, left), 376 (bottom), 382 (bottom, left), 383

Robert Lautman: vi, 33, 34, 43, 44, 45, 46, 47, 56, 109, 110, 111, 114, 115, 118, 120, 154, 217, 220, 224, 231, 232, 233, 234, 236, 237, 238, 239, 240, 243 (top), 297, 298, 299, 300, 301, 307, 314, 315, 320, 364, 365 (top, right; bottom, right), 366, 367, 368, 369, 370, 371, 372 (top, left and right; bottom, left), 373, 375, 376 (top), 377, 378, 379, 382 (top, left and right; bottom, right), 384

Mark Zeek: 218 (top, left and right; bottom, left), 227, 230, 365 (top, left)

Other Pictures

© **Peter Aaron/ESTO:** 37*, 147, 148, 219

© **Wayne Andrews/ESTO:** 134

Courtesy of The Charleston Museum, Charleston, South Carolina: 125

© **David Dunlap:** 119*

Gibbes Museum of Art, Carolina Art Association, Charleston, SC: 340

Courtesy Historic Beaufort Foundation; photograph by Robert W. Jenkins: 330

Courtesy of the Historic Columbia Foundation, Columbia, SC: 126

© **1981, The Historic New Orleans Collection— Photographer: Clarence John Laughlin, #1981.247.1.878:** 348

Historic Houses of the South, *Rebus Publications*, NY; photographs by Paul Rocheleau: 150*, 310*, 311*

Courtesy of The Library Company of Philadelphia: 12, 15

(Reproduction) from the Collections of the Library of Congress: 169

Maryland Historical Society, Baltimore: 29, 330, 331

Courtesy of The New York Historical Society, New York City: 339

© **Michael Orscheln:** 142 (top and center); © **Michael Orscheln, derived from John Califf:** 142 (bottom)

The Toledo Art Museum, Gift of Florence Scott Libbey: 337, 456

Victoria and Albert Museum, London: 350

Virginia State Library: 23

© **Alex Zaras, derived from HABS:** 257, 259

The Architect's Dream, by
Thomas Cole (detail)

Greek Revival America

was designed by John Kane, Sametz Blackstone Associates, Boston,
Massachusetts. Photographs commissioned for the book were shot
on Polaroid 4x5 Polachrome film. The text was set in Bodoni
Book, Copperplate Gothic 31 and Trade Gothic Condensed by Graphic Arts Composition, Philadelphia, Pennsylvania. The book was
printed and bound by Toppan
Printing Company Ltd.,
Tokyo, Japan.